CANON LAW SOCIETY OF AMERICA

PROCEEDINGS
OF THE SEVENTY-THIRD
ANNUAL CONVENTION

Jacksonville, Florida
October 10-13, 2011

Canon Law Society of America

© Copyright 2011 by the Canon Law Society of America

ISBN 1-932208-31-3
ISSN 1543-4230
SAN 237-6296

The Canon Law Society of America's programs and publications are designed solely to help canonists maintain their professional competence. In dealing with specific canonical matters, the canonist using Canon Law Society of America (CLSA) publications or orally conveyed information should also research original sources of authority.

The views and opinions expressed in this publication are those of the individual authors and do not represent the views of the CLSA, its Board of Governors, staff or members. The CLSA does not endorse the views or opinions expressed by the individual authors. The publisher and authors specifically disclaim any liability, loss or risk, personal or otherwise, which is incurred as consequence, directly or indirectly, of the use, reliance, or application of any of the contents of this publication.

Unless otherwise noted, all canons quoted are from the *Code of Canon Law, Latin-English Edition* (Washington, DC: Canon Law Society of America, 1999) and the *Code of Canons of the Eastern Churches, Latin-English Edition* (Washington, DC: Canon Law Society of America, 2002).

Printed in the United States of America.

Canon Law Society of America
Office of the Executive Coordinator
3025 Fourth Street, NE
The Hecker Center, Suite 111
Washington, DC 20017-1102

TABLE OF CONTENTS

Foreword vii

Keynote Address
The CLSA and the Protection of Rights: Legacy and Vision
    Reverend James A. Coriden 1

Major Addresses
Rights in the Church: Great Expectations, Meager Results
    Reverend John P. Beal 33

Parish Reconfiguration: Protection of Rights of Bishops and
    Parishes
    Very Reverend Lawrence A. DiNardo 54

Seminars
Obligation of the Tribunal to Report Child Abuse
    Doctor Diane L. Barr 67

Tips for Building Better Law Sections
    Reverend John J.M. Foster 75

Bishops and Religious: Right Relationships for Ecclesial Mission
    Sister Sharon L. Holland, IHM 108

Restoring and Reintegrating a Priest Falsely Accused of Sexual
    Abuse of a Minor
    Reverend Monsignor Daniel F. Hoye 118

Tribunal, Seminary, Clergy and Personnel Files: Is There a Right to
    Privacy? A Civil and Canon Law Perspective
    Rita F. Joyce 130

Simulation: New Lyrics to an Old Tune
    Very Reverend Anthony L. Kerin 149

The Holy See and the Protection of US Clergy Rights: A Historical
    Perspective
    Reverend Kevin E. McKenna 162

Drafting the Definitive Sentence: Law and Craft
    Reverend Monsignor Mark A. Plewka...177

Home-Schooled Children and the Right to the Sacraments in the
Code of Canon Law
    Margaret Romano-Hogan 197

The Sexual Abuse Crisis: Care for the Canonists
    Brother Loughlan Sofield, ST 223

Issues for Latin Tribunals by the Presence of Eastern Catholic
Cases
    Reverend Monsignor Michael A. Souckar...232

Officers' Reports
President
    Reverend Michael P. Joyce, CM...251

Treasurer
    Reverend Gregory T. Bittner..255
    Independent Auditor Report
        Linton Shafer Warfield & Garret, P.A...258
    Fiscal Year 2011-2012 Budget 271

Executive Coordinator
    Sister Sharon A. Euart, RSM 282

Committee Reports
Constitutional Committees
    Nominations 290
    Resolutions...291
    Resource and Asset Management...292
    Professional Responsibility..295

Standing Committees
    Church Governance..296
    Clergy...297
    Convention Planning..298
        General Convention Chairperson 300
        Convention Liturgies..302
    Institutes of Consecrated and Apostolic Life 303
    Laity 304
    Publications Advisory Board..305

Research and Development 312
Sacramental Law 313

Varia
Business Meeting Minutes
   Siobhan M. Verbeek 319

Convention Mass Homily
   Reverend Michael P. Joyce, CM 327

Role of Law Award Citation
   Reverend Michael P. Joyce, CM 329

Role of Law Award Response
   Chorbishop John D. Faris 331

Tribunal Statistics 2010 336

Contributors 345

2011 Convention List of Participants 347

Foreword

The Canon Law Society of America (CLSA) is pleased to present the Proceedings of the seventy-third annual convention held in Jacksonville, Florida, October 10-13, 2011. The CLSA annually publishes for its members, and others in the canonical community, the major addresses, seminars and reports presented at the annual meeting.

We are grateful to the presenters who provided their final texts in a timely fashion. Texts have been edited for consistency in conformity with the CLSA Style Sheet and Publication Guidelines including capitalization, use of footnotes, gender-inclusive language, and citation of canons. Included in this edition of *CLSA Proceedings* are the Tribunal Statistics collected from participating (arch) dioceses and (arch)eparchies along with a listing of the participants who attended the convention in Jacksonville.

The CLSA, established on November 12, 1939 as a professional association dedicated to the promotion of both the study and the application of canon law in the Catholic Church today, numbers over 1,400 members who reside in the United States and 37 other counties. *CLSA Proceedings 73* (2011) should take its place among previous volumes as a professional resource. Additional copies of this volume may be purchased from the CLSA website: www.clsa.org.

For information on how to become a member of the CLSA, please visit the CLSA website (www.clsa.org) or contact the Office of the Executive Coordinator.

Sr. Sharon A. Euart, RSM
Executive Coordinator
Canon Law Society of America
3025 Fourth Street, NE
The Hecker Center, Suite 111
Washington, DC 20017-1102

KEYNOTE ADDRESS

THE CLSA AND THE PROTECTION OF RIGHTS:
LEGACY AND VISION
Reverend James A. Coriden

A) Two Historical Antecedents:
These two very diverse historical vignettes throw light on the involvement of canon law with the origins and rise of the human rights movement.

1) *Origins of Personal Rights in Twelfth Century Canon Law*
Where did "rights talk" come from? What was the origin of the notion of innate human rights in the sense of "We hold these truths to be self-evident, that all men (and women) are created equal, that they are endowed by their Creator with certain inalienable Rights, that among these are Life, Liberty, and the pursuit of Happiness?"[1] Quite commonly, a series of seventeenth century theorists are given as the sources and developers of the idea: Francisco Suarez (1548-1617), Hugo Grotius (1583-1645), Thomas Hobbes (1588-1679), and John Locke (1632-1704).

For those, historically-minded, who look beyond those eminent philosophers to deeper roots the most widely accepted account of the origin of natural rights (in the sense of individual subjective rights) theory is that it was a revolutionary innovation inspired by the nominalist and voluntarist philosophy of the English Franciscan William of Ockham (1285-1347) in the first half of the fourteenth century.[2] This narrative was developed and defended over many years by the French historian Michel Villay.

Brian Tierney, the distinguished medievalist and historian of canon law challenges this view. "Villay was correct to see the Franciscan Order as a 'cradle' of rights doctrines even though he exaggerated the importance of Ockham as an innovator."[3] Indeed, before Ockham, the spiritual Franciscan Peter Olivi (1248-1298), in the late thirteenth century discussed subjective rights as powers or fac-

---

[1] *Declaration of Independence* (1776). The same meaning of natural human rights is used in the *United Nations Universal Declaration of Human Rights* (1948).

[2] Brian Tierney, *The Idea of Natural Rights: Studies on Natural Rights, Natural Law and Church Law 1150-1625* (Atlanta, GA: Scholars Press, 1997) 8. Villay's extensive writings are cited in Tierney's first chapter, "Villay, Ockham, and the Origin of Individual Rights," 13-42, and listed on 365-366.

[3] Ibid., 35.

ulties inhering in the human person.[4] But Tierney's thesis points beyond these Franciscan theologians to the Decretists, the late twelfth century commentators on Gratian's *Decretum* (*Concordantia discordantium canonum*, 1140) as the originators of innate human rights. These were authors like Rufinus, Ricardus Anglicus, Huguccio, and Alanus, whose canonical writings influenced later theorists including William of Ockham.[5]

These canonists were dealing with controversies that pitted popes against emperors, cathedral canons against bishops, peasants against feudal lords. "In a world where rights were constantly being asserted and demanded, the language of the jurists reflected the realities of their age."[6] "For the canonists *ius naturale* itself could be defined as a subjective force or faculty or power or ability inherent in human persons."[7] For Huguccio, the greatest of the Decretists, *ius naturale* in its primary sense was always an attribute of individual persons, not an abstract norm or legal system.

In sum, for the twelfth century canonists "the subjective idea of natural right was not derived specifically from Christian revelation or from some all-embracing natural-law theory of cosmic harmony but from an understanding of human nature itself as rational, self-aware, and morally responsible."[8] However, this idea of natural rights grew up in a religious culture that supplemented rational argumentation about human nature with a faith in which humans were seen as children of a caring God.[9] It was the early canonists of the classical period who originated the notion of innate human rights, according to Brian Tierney.

2) *Role of John XXIII in the Canonical Turn to Rights*

The rights of the Christian faithful were thrust onto the agenda of canonists with the promulgation of the 1983 code with its prominent "bill of rights" (cc. 208-223). But the topic caught the attention of those following the code revision process well before that, for the 1967 "principles for revision" mentioned rights in three of its ten principles, with numbers six and seven squarely focused on the issues of acknowledging and safeguarding rights.[10]

---

4   Ibid., 39.
5   Ibid., 54.
6   Ibid., 58.
7   Ibid., 65.
8   Ibid., 76.
9   Ibid., 343.
10 Principle 1, "The Juridical Nature of the Code," closes with these words:
    The pre-eminent and essential object of Canon Law is to determine and safeguard the rights and obligations of each individual person with respect to others and to society, to the extent that this can be done within the Church as it pertains to the worship of God and the salvation of souls.

Where did this sudden, strong emphasis on canonical rights come from? It was hardly a major focus of canonical reflection in the years before the revision.[11] The term (*droit* = right) is not even among the entries in the massive *Dictionnaire de Droit Canonique*, the last volume of which was published in 1965.[12] I reviewed the canonical literature listed in *Canon Law Abstracts* and *Ephemerides Theologicae Louvaniensis* from 1964 through 1967, the time during which the principles for revision of the code were formulated, and found no major emphasis on rights in the Church, much less any call for a catalogue or bill of rights.[13] If rights were not a major theme in the canonical literature, what was the cause of the notable attention given to rights in the principles for revision and then articulated prominently in the first draft of the *Lex Ecclesiae Fundamentalis* just two years later?[14]

I am convinced that the emphasis on rights in the code revision process and then in the 1983 code itself emerged, not from the canonists, but from Pope John

---

Principle 6, "Safeguarding the Rights of Persons," says in part:

> The rights of each and every one of the Christian faithful must be acknowledged and safeguarded, both the rights which are contained in natural or divine positive law, as well as those duly derived from the social condition which they acquire and possess in the Church.
>
> And because not everyone has the same function in the Church, the same status is not suitable for everyone, it is rightly proposed that in the future Code, because of the radical equality which ought to exist among all of the Christian faithful on account of their human dignity and the baptism they have received, a common *juridic status* be established for everyone, before the rights and duties which pertain to the diverse ecclesiastical functions are enumerated. (Emphasis in the original.)

Principle 7, "Ordering Procedures for Protecting Subjective Rights," is a lengthy statement of the values of judicial and administrative procedures and the due process to be observed within them.

Pontificia Commissio Codici Iuris Canonici Recognoscendo, *Communicationes* 1:2 (1969) 78-83. Translation is the author's.

11   The rights of the laity were scarcely mentioned in the 1917 code, though canon 682 did assert their right to receive spiritual goods from the clergy.

12   Edited by R. Naz, seven volumes (Paris: Letouzey et Ané, 1935-1965). The subtitle of the series states that it contains "all the terms of canon law."

13   Two decades earlier there was a debate among canonists about the very existence of personal rights in canon law, with some prominent authors (like Pio Fedele) claiming that subjective rights had no place in the Church whose public order was directed to the salvation of souls. This discussion was simply swept aside by the developments in social teaching under John XXIII. See James Provost, "Rights of Persons in the Church," *Catholicism and Liberalism: Contributions to American Public Philosophy*, ed. R. Bruce Douglass and David Hollenbach (Cambridge: Cambridge University Press, 1994) 299-300.

14   Pontificia Commissio Codici Iuris Canonici Recognoscendo, *Schema Legis Ecclesiae Fundamentalis cum Relatione* (1969) canons 10-24. This "bill of rights" is virtually identical with that in the 1983 code.

XXIII and the major development of Catholic social teaching during and immediately after his pontificate. (He was elected in 1958 and died in 1963). Specifically, Pope John was responsible for the recognition of the human rights tradition in his two major social encyclicals, *Mater et magistra* (*Christianity and Social Progress*, 1961) and *Pacem in terris* (*Peace on Earth*, 1963, during the council), and then in the documents of the Second Vatican Council, especially *Gaudium et spes* and *Dignitatis humanae* (1965).

These powerful treatises changed the direction of the Church's social teaching on the matter of human rights, from a position of staunch opposition to the enlightenment's revolutionary proclamation of rights and freedoms to an activist engagement in the global struggle for human rights. They made the Church into one of the world's most vigorous advocates of human rights and the equality of persons.[15]

So the modern *canonical* focus on rights in the Church was much more a reflection of the church's contemporary social teaching than a development of its own "rights tradition." Having stated that broad conclusion, permit me to add two points of refinement to it, one historical, the other personal.

a) Historical Convergence

John XXIII came to office on October 28, 1958. A major part of his agenda was the issue of social justice with its ultimate aim (*ad extra ecclesiae*) nothing less than the unity and peace of all humankind.[16] On May 15, 1961, he issued the encyclical *Mater et magistra*, to mark the seventieth anniversary of Leo XIII's *Rerum novarum* (1891) and the thirtieth anniversary of Pius XI's *Quadragesimo anno* (1931). But *Mater et magistra* differed from preceding encyclicals in tone, content, and methodology. He spoke directly to the troubling concerns of the modern world by proposing a new way of engagement. It would be dialogical, cooperative, and "from the ground up."

Pacem in terris followed *Mater et magistra* in less than two years (April 11,

---

15   David Hollenbach, "Commentary on *Gaudium et spes*," in *Modern Catholic Social Teaching: Commentaries and Interpretations*, ed. Kenneth Himes (Washington, DC: Georgetown University Press, 2005) 282-283. Hollenbach's excellent study, *Claims in Conflict: Retrieving and Renewing the Catholic Human Rights Tradition* (New York: Paulist Press, 1979) puts the development of the Church's rights tradition into historical perspective.

16   Canonists frequently quote the astonishing announcement of his program that Pope John made at St. Paul's Outside the Walls on Sunday, January 25, 1959: a synod for the Diocese of Rome, an ecumenical council, and an updating of the Code of Canon Law (see Allocution, "Questa festiva Ricorrenza," in *The Pope Speaks* 5 [1958-1959] 398). That was only half of his agenda, the internal Church renewal part, *ad intra ecclesiae*, that also included the ecumenical thrust for unity among Christians.

1963). The context for *Pacem in terris* was the height of the Cold War, at the time of an impending threat of nuclear war. In the United States the apprehension was so great that many administration officials in Washington were sending their wives and children away from Washington out of fear of a nuclear attack. President John Kennedy proposed sending his own wife and children to Camp David, a place of greater safety, but Jacqueline Kennedy insisted that she would stay at the White House with the President:

> Please don't send me away to Camp David ... Please don't send me anywhere. If anything happens we're all going to stay right here with you ... even if there's not room in the bomb shelter in the White House ... I just want to be here with you and I want to die with you.[17]

The fear and alarm were real and widespread, not confined to Washington and Moscow.

The Second Vatican Council opened in October 1962, at the very moment of the Cuban Missile Crisis. Vatican officials considered suspending the council to permit the bishops to return home, the threat of nuclear war was so grave.

An appeal was made to Pope John to intervene between the Americans and Soviets. Soviet ships carrying nuclear missiles were on the high seas on their way to Cuba. On October 25 Vatican Radio reported the pope's message:

> We remind those who bear the responsibility of power of their grave duties ... may you listen to the anguished cry from all points ... that rises toward heaven: peace! peace! ... We beseech all the rulers not to remain deaf to this cry of humanity. May they do all that is in them to safeguard the peace ... and keep the horrors of war from the world—a war whose consequences no one can foresee.[18]

Within hours the Soviet ships turned around and headed for home. The Cuban Missile Crisis had been averted. Krushchev later acknowledged the pope's role in the event.

The pope's success on this critical occasion, plus his awareness of his own serious illness (his doctors told him on November 16, 1962 that he had cancer) compelled him to address the international situation and search for peace soon, at greater length, and with the solemnity of an encyclical. A key feature of his

---

17   Arthur Schlesinger, *Jacqueline Kennedy: Historic Conversations on Life with John F. Kennedy* (New York: Hyperion, 2011) 263.

18   Quoted in Drew Christiansen, "Commentary on *Pacem in terris* (Peace on Earth)," *Modern Catholic Social Teaching*, ed. Kenneth Himes (Washington, DC: Georgetown University Press, 2005) 221.

approach was insistence on human rights:

> *Pacem in terris* provides a distinctively Catholic approach to peacemaking, focused on the realization of human rights as the substance of a peaceful world order. The encyclical advances the view that peace consists in the promotion, safeguarding, and defense of human rights at every level of social life, whether interpersonal, social, political, international, or global. Peace consists in the realization of the common good conceived of as the realization of rights.[19]

The encyclical promoted a Catholic theory of rights that is communitarian rather than individualistic, and features 1) the correlation of rights and duties, 2) an attitude of cooperation, collaboration, and adjustment, and 3) the assimilation of rights into the common good.[20]

Pacem in terris presented the most complete and systematic list of human rights in the modern Catholic tradition.[21] The encyclical was published during the council and led the Catholic Church to a dramatic change of direction on the matter of human rights.

> *Pacem in terris* moved the leadership of the Church from a position of staunch opposition to modern rights and freedoms to activist engagement in the global struggle for human rights. This shift was one of the most dramatic reversals in the long history of the Catholic tradition.[22]

On March 28, 1963, just three weeks before he issued *Pacem in terris*, Pope John appointed the Pontifical Commission for the *Recognitio* of the Code of Canon Law. The close convergence of these two events was not lost on those appointed to the Commission for Revision.[23] Human rights had been placed high on the canonical agenda. After months of suffering, Pope John died on June 3, 1963.

---

19   Christiansen, 223.

20   Ibid., 226.

21   *PT* 11-17; summarized in Hollenbach, *Claims in Conflict*, 66-67.

22   Hollenbach, "Commentary on *Gaudium et spes*," 280.

23   A similar coincidence, with similar "cross pollination" of ideas took place when Pope Paul VI told the Commission for Revision to begin its work "promptly and resolutely" on November 20, 1965, little more than two weeks before the promulgation on December 7, 1965, of the council's pastoral constitution *Gaudium et spes* and its declaration *Dignitatis humanae*, both of which emphasize human rights. The Commission members and their consultors had to be well aware of that message. It was in that allocution on November 20 that Paul VI suggested the project of a fundamental or constitutional law for the Church (*CLD* 6:141-145).

Gaudium et spes, although approved by the council (on December 6, 1965) after the death of John XXIII, was an integral part of his conciliar vision and set the Church fully within the world. Perhaps the document's greatest achievement related to human rights was "to combine the traditional view of human rights as rooted in human nature with modern historical consciousness."[24]

> There are domains of human existence which cannot be suppressed without oppressing human beings. These include respect for the bodily, interpersonal, socio-political, economic, and cultural dimensions of human existence. Because of the increasing interdependence of persons the means to this respect must be more and more through the organized action of communities and of society as a whole. Thus from the perspective of the Council, social, economic, and cultural rights, defined in relation to historical conditions, assume a new place of importance in the Catholic human rights tradition.[25]

Pope John XXIII and the historical convergence he created between the *recognitio* of the code and his encyclical *Pacem in terris* directed canonical attention on human rights in a whole new way.

b) A Personal Collaborator

John XXIII put together a team of trusted personal advisors in the first years of his pontificate to whom he also gave positions on the Council Preparatory Commissions.[26] One of them, Pietro Pavan, professor of social ethics at the Lateran University, was the pope's chief consultant on *Mater et magistra* and the author of the first draft of *Pacem in terris*.[27] He also played a major role in the composition of two council documents, *Gaudium et spes* and *Dignitatis humanae*.[28]

Pavan, like Angelo Roncalli, was a diocesan priest from northern Italy. He was born in 1903, ordained in 1928, took doctorates in philosophy, theology, and the social sciences in Rome and Padua, and taught moral theology in the semi-

---

24 Hollenbach, *Claims in Conflict*, 75.

25 Hollenbach, *Claims in Conflict*, 75. A key text on human rights within *Gaudium et spes* is n. 26.

26 Paul Johnson, *Pope John XXIII* (Boston: Little, Brown and Company, 1974) names them, 141-142.

27 Marvin Mich, "Commentary on *Mater et magistra*," in *Modern Catholic Social Teaching*, 205, and Drew Christiansen, op. cit., 221-222.

28 Donald Pelotte, *John Courtney Murray: Theologian in Conflict* (New York: Paulist Press, 1975) 94, and Hollenbach, "Commentary on *Gaudium et spes*," 270. Pavan wrote the commentary on the "Declaration of Religious Freedom (*Dignitatis humanae*)," in Vorgrimler's *Commentary on the Documents of Vatican II* (New York: Herder & Herder, 1969) 4:49-86.

nary in Treviso. He became deeply involved with the Italian Catholic Institute for Social Activity (ICAS) and in various facets of the lay apostolate. Pavan met Roncalli while the latter was nuncio to Paris (1944-1953).

Pavan began to teach social economy at the Lateran University in 1948. His long tenure on the faculty of the Lateran ended with his term as Rector of the University, 1969-1974. In 1975 he retired to live in a religious house in a Roman suburb. John Paul II made Pavan a member of the College of Cardinals in 1985. Pavan died in 1994.[29]

This jolly, rotund, priest-academic, relatively unheralded, together with his equally optimistic and equally rotund papal patron, influenced the development of Catholic social teaching more than any other one person in the twentieth century, except possibly his collaborator, John XXIII.

B) Focus on Rights: Meanings and Sources

Some quick clarifications here might help with what follows. What do we mean when we speak of rights, and what do we think are the sources of those rights?

Rights are viewed as either freedoms or claims. That is, rights are expressed either as protected zones of activity, immunities, areas of free choice (like freedom of religion or the right to choose one's state in life), or, on the other hand, as entitlements, empowerments, positive claims to participate actively in the life of the community that enable specific actions (like the right of the baptized to the sacraments or the right of members of religious chapters to vote).

The rights of Catholics are exercised in the context of the Church, "in communion," with all of the privileges and limitations that this context implies.

Canonical rights are commonly categorized as human, ecclesial, ecclesiastical, or communal. *Human* rights are those based on the dignity of the human person (like the right of association, or the right to marry). *Ecclesial* rights are those which flow from a person's incorporation into Christ and the Church through baptism (like the right to participate in the Eucharist, or the right to Christian burial). *Ecclesiastical* rights are those that accrue to a person based on his or her position of an office in the Church, in accord with the Church's traditions and rules (like the bishop's right to preside or the pastor's right to stability). *Communal* rights attach to those who are members of the community, association, or institute, in keeping with the statutes of the community (like the right to stand for

---

29 Franco Biffi, *Prophet of Our Times: The Social Thought of Cardinal Pietro Pavan* (New Rochelle, NY: New City Press, 1992, translation by Rosemarie Goldie of Biffi, *Il Cantico dell'uomo* (Rome: Città Nuova, 1990) 1-6, 128; *Religious Freedom: 1965 and 1975; A Symposium on a Historic Document*, ed. Walter Burghardt, Woodstock Studies 1 (New York: Paulist Press, 1977) 73.

election in a religious order or the right to partake of the spiritual benefits of an association of the faithful).

The theology of the Church as the new people of God forms the theological basis for rights. The radical equality among all those belonging to that people is a basic ecclesiological conviction.[30] The principles adopted to guide the revision of the code explicitly linked personal rights to the fundamental equality of all members of the Christian faithful.[31] Commentators have stressed this radical equality among all the baptized, *a common juridical status*, as the root of the canonical rights attributed to the Christian faithful.[32] This common and equal canonical status of all who are incorporated into Christ (cc. 204 §1, 208) is comparable to the notion of citizenship in sovereign states.

In this presentation we are referring to the various rights found in the code, not only those attributed to all the Christian faithful (cc. 208-223), but also those of lay persons (cc. 224-231), those of sacred ministers (cc. 273-289), those of members of religious institutes (cc. 662-672), those of parents (in several places), of office holders (like bishops and pastors), of those engaged in judicial procedures (in Book VII), and of members of consultative bodies (like presbyteral and finance councils).

C) CLSA Legacy on Rights: Attempts and Achievements—Milestones

What follows is a series of milestones, major markers, along the forty-five year journey of encounter between the Canon Law Society of America and rights. They are of unequal importance, and some were not very successful, but they illustrate our collective attention to rights over several decades. They are roughly in chronological order.

1) *An Early Statement*

In October 1965, before Paul VI instructed the Commission for Revision to begin its work, and even before the final session of the Second Vatican Council (wherein *Gaudium et spes* and *Dignitatis humanae* were approved) concluded, the CLSA unanimously approved a statement at its twenty-seventh annual convention in Chicago, "The Renewal of Canon Law." It included these recommendations (from a longer list) "as expressing norms considered necessary by the

---

30   *Lumen gentium*, chap. 2, and n. 32.

31   "On account of the fundamental equality of all members of the Christian faithful and the diversity of offices and functions rooted in the hierarchical structure of the Church, it is expedient that the rights of persons be appropriately defined and safeguarded." Principle no. 6, as quoted in the Preface of the code.

32   For example, James Provost, *The Code of Canon Law: A Text and Commentary* (Mahwah, NJ: Paulist Press, 1985) 140; Sharon Holland, "Equality, Dignity and the Rights of the Laity," *The Jurist* 47:1 (1987) 103-128; Jesu Pudumai Doss, "Freedom of Inquiry and Expression of *Christifideles*? Some Juridical Considerations Starting from Canon 218," *Studia canonica* 44:1 (2010) 55-58.

members of this Society":

> That the safeguarding of the rights of persons be on a par with the safeguarding of the dignity of sacraments.
>
> That the rights and interests of priests and religious, other than pastors and superiors, be defined and safeguarded.
>
> That the rights and interests of the laity be clearly defined and safeguarded.[33]

The members of the Society had heard the message about rights in the Church and fully supported it.

2) *A Symposium on Rights*

In October 1968, the Society co-sponsored (with the Catholic University of America's School of Canon Law) a symposium entitled "Rights in the Church, A Symposium on a Declaration of Christian Freedoms." It was an interdisciplinary gathering of about twenty men (no women), scholars from several fields—biblical studies, history, theology, sociology, civil law, as well as canon law—that took place on the campus of the Catholic University of America. The proceedings were published in *The Case for Freedom: Human Rights in the Church*.[34]

Eight papers were prepared and circulated in advance, and a position paper, "Toward a Declaration of Christian Rights," was composed during the meeting. The papers were of exceptional quality, and bear reexamination today. The position paper concluded with a list of twelve "Christian Rights," a few of which cover the same ground as those in the 1983 code's "bill of rights," especially in the areas of due process.[35]

3) *On Due Process*

In response to an invitation from the National Conference of Catholic Bishops in 1968, a distinguished CLSA *ad hoc* Committee on Due Process,[36] chaired by Robert Kennedy, composed a report to the CLSA dated October 21, 1969.[37] The report was then submitted to the National Conference of Catholic Bishops. It was presented at the November 1969, meeting of the NCCB by Bishop Ernest

---

33   *The Jurist* 26:2 (1966) 165-166.

34   Ed. James Coriden (Washington, DC: Corpus Books, 1969).

35   Ibid., 12-14.

36   The members of the Committee were: William Ball, William Bassett, Avery Dulles, Raymond Goedert, Bertram Griffin, John Mansfield, John Noonan, Anthony Padovano, Marion Reinhardt, and George Tavard.

37   "Report of the Ad Hoc Committee on Due Process to the Canon Law Society of America," *CLSA Proceedings* 31 (1969) 19-51. The report was unanimously accepted at that convention and became the report of the entire Canon Law Society of America.

Primeau, chair of the Canon Law Committee, and Robert Kennedy, who gave an extensive and persuasive explanation of the document to the bishops.

The general membership of the Conference approved a resolution recommending the report's procedures for conciliation, arbitration, and structuring administrative discretion, for experimental use and "prompt implementation on diocesan, provincial and regional levels." The document was forwarded to the Holy See in relation to the work of the Code Revision Commission's *coetus* on administrative tribunals. With a few changes, the Holy See offered a *nihil obstat* on October 23, 1971. The document was published by the NCCB in 1972, entitled simply *On Due Process*, and widely distributed.[38]

The preamble of *On Due Process*, little noticed in comparison with the procedural center of the document, articulates a strong, clear, and solidly resourced "bill of rights" expressed as a conviction of the members of the Society. This powerful declaration of rights was included in both NCCB publications (1972 and 2002) of *On Due Process*.[39]

---

38 NCCB, *On Due Process* (Washington, DC: NCCB [no date]) 48 pages. This version was reprinted verbatim (including Robert Kennedy's 1969 address) in 2002, on the request of Bishop A. James Quinn, chair of the Canonical Affairs Committee, along with the Conference's procedures for its Committee on Conciliation and Arbitration (adopted in 1979) under the title *Procedures for Resolving Conflict* (Washington, DC: USCCB, 2002) 91 pages.

39 "In accordance with the authentic teaching of the Catholic Church, the members of this Society express their conviction that all persons in the Church are fundamentally equal in regard to their common rights and freedoms, among which are:

The right and freedom to hear the Word of God and to participate in the sacramental and liturgical life of the Church;

The right and freedom to exercise the apostolate and share in the mission of the Church;

The right and freedom to speak and be heard and to receive objective information regarding the pastoral needs and affairs of the Church;

The right to education, to freedom of inquiry and to freedom of expression in the sacred sciences;

The right to free assembly and association in the Church;

and such inviolable and universal rights of the human person as the right to the protection of one's reputation, to respect of one's person, to activity in accord with the upright norm of one's conscience, to protection of privacy.

The dignity of the human person, the principles of fundamental fairness, and the universally applicable presumption of freedom require that no member of the Church arbitrarily be deprived of the exercise of any right or office" ("Report of the Ad Hoc Committee," 19; *On Due Process*, 4-5). Each of the rights is supported by extensive references to the encyclical *Pacem in terris* and the documents of the Second Vatican Council ("Report of the Ad Hoc Committee," 45-49, *On Due Process*, 34-37).

4) *Critiques of the Lex Ecclesiae Fundamentalis*

The Society followed the code revision process with close attention, and the first document to emerge, the 1969 draft of the *Lex Ecclesiae Fundamentalis*, contained the "bill of rights." The CLSA committee appointed to study the *Lex* stated in its report to the membership that "The articulation of the fundamental rights of all in the Church is a most welcome addition to canon law."[40] However, the critique followed: "Although it is most heartening to see that the schema has included a presentation of the rights of all the faithful, it must be noted that nearly every declaration of a right in these canons is accompanied by a statement of qualifications and limitations of the right."[41] Legal norms are not absolutes, but their limitations should not be stated as forcefully as the rights themselves; this tends to dim and weaken the rights.

The committee's seventeen-page report focused on the larger issues of the timeliness of the entire project of a constitution for the Church, the theological adequacy of the draft, and the methodology of consultation employed, and its final judgment was that the 1969 draft was unacceptable.

The Commission for Revision of the code followed with a second draft of the *Lex* in 1971. The CLSA committee on the *Lex* found that this draft, too, was unacceptable. Among the reasons given was that "The *Lex*'s treatment of the basic rights and prerogatives of the Church people is ... inadequate."[42] Again the committee found the very restricted and qualified statement of the rights unwarranted. In addition, adequate remedies were not available in the event of violation of the rights. The CLSA committee was clearly hoping that its critique would contribute to improvements in the eventual text on rights.

The chair of the CLSA committee, William LaDue, later wrote, "This statement of the rights of all represents a considerable step forward and should be recognized and applauded as such, in spite of the substantial defects under which it labors."[43] He went on to expand upon the same reservations that the committee had raised.[44]

A later theological evaluation, presented to the CLSA in 1980 by Joseph Komonchak, was slightly more positive on the *Lex*'s treatment of rights.[45]

---

40   *CLSA Proceedings* 32 (1970) 36.

41   Ibid., 39.

42   *CLSA Proceedings* 33 (1971) 70.

43   William LaDue, "A Written Constitution for the Church?" *The Jurist* 32:1 (1972) 6.

44   Ibid., 10-11.

45   "A genuine and generally successful effort has been made to fulfill the mandate to compose a "common juridical statute" before speaking of the different states in the Church. In these canons, the Church commits itself, with respect to its own members, to the same acknowledgment and respect for the dignity and basic rights of Christians that it

5) *Equality for Women in Church Law*

At its 1973 convention the Society approved a resolution to constitute "a committee ... to address itself to the achievement of an equality for women in the Church's law."[46] This vigorous committee continued in existence until 1990. In 1975 it produced a study entitled "The Status of Women in the Church."[47] In October 1976, at the committee's prompting, the Society sponsored a symposium on "Women and Church Law," co-sponsored by Rosemont College and held on its campus. The papers prepared for the symposium and the consensus statement elaborated there were published in a book, *Sexism and Church Law: Equal Rights and Affirmative Action*.[48] The recommendations of the symposium's twenty-four participants (fourteen women, ten men) to the CLSA, which were extensive and detailed, were approved by the Society's membership at the 1976 convention.[49]

In 1983, just after the new code was issued, the Committee on Women in the Church presented a stimulating and interactive convention seminar, "The Canonist: Obstructionist or Enabler for Women in the Church," accompanied by a twenty-page learning handout.[50] The following year the committee's report included an "Educational Package: Women in the Revised Code."[51]

It is well worth noting that in 1979 the Society's members in convention at Albuquerque, NM, voted to endorse the Equal Rights Amendment to the United States Constitution.[52]

6) *"Cooperation between Theologians and the Ecclesiastical Magisterium"*

This 1982 joint report of the CLSA and the Catholic Theological Society of America led to the NCCB document, *Doctrinal Responsibilities*, issued in 1989.

The president of the CTSA, William Hill, took the initiative in 1980. He appointed a committee to search "for more cooperative and constructive relations between theologians and the Church's teaching authority."[53] The CTSA committee proposed a joint project with the CLSA to develop a "set of norms to guide

---

makes ... with respect to all persons." Joseph Komonchak, "A New Law for the People of God: A Theological Evaluation," *CLSA Proceedings* 42 (1980) 24

46   *CLSA Proceedings* 35 (1973) 160-161.

47   *CLSA Proceedings* 37 (1975) 185-192.

48   Ed. James Coriden (New York, NY: Paulist Press, 1977).

49   Ibid., 155-158.

50   *CLSA Proceedings* 45 (1983) 126-153.

51   *CLSA Proceedings* 46 (1984) 254-263; the package included a list of names of volunteers for a speakers bureau.

52   *CLSA Proceedings* 41 (1979) 155-156.

53   "CTSA Committee Report on Cooperation between Theologians and the Church's Teaching Authority," *CTSA Proceedings* 35 (1980) 325.

the resolution of difficulties which may arise in the relationship between theologians and the magisterium in North America."[54]

This collaborative effort of the CTSA and the CLSA took the form of a joint committee, chaired by Leo O'Donovan, and consisting of three other theologians and three canonists, appointed in September 1980. The members authored six background papers on the rights and responsibilities of bishops and theologians, and evaluations of the procedures available to settle misunderstandings or conflicts between them. The committee added a consensus statement, "In Service to the Gospel," that included a section on the rights and responsibilities of both bishops and theologians.

This "Report of the Joint Committee," entitled *Cooperation between Theologians and the Ecclesiastical Magisterium* was published by the CLSA in 1982.[55] The committee continued its work, entering into further collaboration with bishops, theologians, and canonists, and formulated the procedural document, *Doctrinal Responsibilities*. This work product was presented to and approved unanimously by the national meetings of both societies in 1983.[56] It was then submitted to the NCCB Committee on Doctrine, where it was revised and amended. It was subject to a consultation at the Holy See,[57] and then approved by a vote of 214 to 9 by the body of American bishops (NCCB) in June 1989, under the title, *Doctrinal Responsibilities*.[58]

Doctrinal Responsibilities is divided into three sections. The first, "The Context of Ecclesial Responsibilities," sketches the active participation that all members of the Body of Christ have in the proclamation of the gospel, and then the particular rights and responsibilities of bishops and of theologians. The second section, "Promoting Cooperation and Informal Dialogue," recommends various ways in which bishops and theologians can enhance cooperation in their common service to the gospel. The third section is entitled, "A Possibility for Formal Doctrinal Dialogue." It sets out in detail a suggested procedure to deal with

---

54   Ibid., 331.

55   Ed. Leo O'Donovan, it was issued as a 189 page booklet.

56   The document as presented to the two societies is found on pages 261-284 of the *CLSA Proceedings* 45 (1983). The CLSA minutes report the unanimous votes of both societies on pp. 328-329.

57   The concerns of the CDF are reflected in a communication from Archbishop Bovone, the secretary of the congregation, "Development of Text Regarding Relationship between Bishops and Theologians" (Nov. 11, 1988) *Canon Law Digest* 12:476-478; also in *Origins* 18 (1988) 389-391.

58   The full title of the document is *Doctrinal Responsibilities: Approaches to Promoting Cooperation and Resolving Misunderstandings between Bishops and Theologians*. It was published by the NCCB in 1989 as a 29 page booklet. Final report of the Joint Committee on "Doctrinal Responsibilities," *CLSA Proceedings* 51 (1989) 226-227.

doctrinal disputes between bishops and theologians in dioceses. It is intended to be flexible and adaptable to local situations and needs. The document makes clear that its suggested procedures are not church law, but guidelines that may be followed when needed. The process set forth in *Doctrinal Responsibilities* was recommended for use more recently in the NCCB "Guidelines Concerning the Academic *Mandatum* in Catholic Universities (Canon 812)."[59]

Doctrinal Responsibilities has not been replaced, remanded, or revoked. The document's official endorsement by the bishop's conference, that is, by the body of bishops and not simply by a committee of the conference, gives it enhanced status and should engender both respect and more frequent use.

7) *Permanent Seminar on Protection of Rights*

This seminar event was the first step of an investigation of optional procedures for the protection of the rights of persons in the Church.[60] This project was triggered by a resolution passed at the 1983 CLSA convention.[61] A set of research papers were commissioned, prepared, and circulated in advance of the seminar which met in two sessions, first on March 22-26, 1985, in Arlington, VA, and then, after the authors revised and exchanged their papers, on November 1-3, 1985, at the University of San Francisco. After further revisions, the ten research papers were then published as the entire contents of a 344-page issue of *The Jurist* in 1986.[62] With one exception, the authors of the papers were all canonists. Their sound and serious studies covered a range of issues, and are still well worth consulting.

This first phase of the investigation of "possible options for diocesan, regional, and national procedures for the protection of rights of persons in the Church" was designed to serve as its theoretical foundation. It was then followed by a survey of the actual experiences in dioceses.

---

59   *Origins* 31:7 (June 15, 2001) 128-131.

60   The plan to carry out the investigation was outlined in a report of the permanent seminar in 1984: *CLSA Proceedings* 46 (1984) 244-245. (The permanent seminars began in 1975 as a process for continuing research on foundational issues related to canon law. The label "permanent" signified that it was ongoing project.)

61   *CLSA Proceedings* 45 (1983) 329-330.

62   *The Jurist* 46:1 (1986) 1-344. This was the fourth such "permanent seminar" sponsored by the CLSA and published as an issue of *The Jurist*. John Folmer's introductory article, "Promoting and Protecting Rights in the Church: An Introduction," (pages 1-13) outlines the project and the papers, and puts it all in historical perspective. James Provost's concluding article, "Promoting and Protecting the Rights of Christians: Some Implications for Church Structures," (289-342) draws out some of the implications of the studies for the Church.

8) *Survey of Diocesan Experience with Due Process*

The second step of the investigation mentioned just above, was a task force survey of the actual experience of due process procedures in American dioceses from 1970 to 1985.[63] This was intended to ascertain the actual use of the *On Due Process* program recommended by the NCCB in 1972. The survey of 185 dioceses and eparchies was conducted by mail and telephone; 153 were heard from.

The results of the survey were mixed but revealing. Over half of the dioceses had some experience with due process, either in developing materials or in actually processing a case. Over one-third of the total responded that they had some experience in dealing with actual due process cases; more than 900 cases had been submitted, and decisions reached in nearly 500 of them.

But 8% of those dioceses with some case experience accounted for over two-thirds of the cases reported; only twenty-one dioceses reported having more than five cases within the fifteen year period, and only five dioceses (St. Paul and Minneapolis, Cleveland, Detroit, Rockville Centre, Milwaukee) had substantial experience (from 46 to 245 cases). The cases involved mostly employment, school, and pastoral issues. Eighty-five percent of cases were handled by conciliation, ten percent by arbitration. Most cases were submitted by lay persons, the respondents were mostly administrators.[64]

After the collection of data the task force met with sixteen consultants from "active" dioceses in March 1987, and formulated a summary of the report's findings as well as a set of recommendations for the future. The task force concluded that the experiences of dioceses validated the worth of due process services, and it recommended that they be retained, expanded, and integrated with other approaches to resolving conflicts and grievances.[65]

9) *"Protection of the Rights of Persons in the Church"*

The task force to survey diocesan experience of due process referred to above recommended a revision of the Society's 1969 Report on Due Process (which formed the basis for the NCCB *On Due Process* document finally approved in 1972).[66] As a third step toward the original goal of the 1983 resolution, a Committee on Procedures for the Protection of Rights of Persons in the Church un-

---

63   The task force began its work in 1985 and in 1987 published: CLSA Task Force to Survey Due Process Experience, *Due Process in the Dioceses of the United States, 1970-1985.* Draft Report on A Due Process Survey (Washington: CLSA, 1987) dated March 20, 1987, in the form of a multilithed typescript of 251 pages.

64   Ibid., these results are found on pages 23-29.

65   "Task Force to Survey Due Process Experience," *CLSA Proceedings* 49 (1987) 291-296.

66   The specific recommendations are found of pages 295-296 of the 1987 Task Force Report.

dertook to rewrite and streamline the procedures for conciliation and arbitration. They also added a set of models for administrative tribunals at the diocesan and regional levels (since the hoped-for administrative tribunals failed to materialize in the 1983 code). This revised report, with an eloquent background statement by John Beal and a reprint of Robert Kennedy's 1969 address to the NCCB, was issued in 1991. It remains as the Society's "last word" on recommended procedures for the protection of rights of persons in the Church.[67]

10) *Sponsored Pilot Projects on Due Process*

As a follow-up to the 1991 revised report, the Society in 1993 constituted a Committee on the Experiment in Due Process in the Church to "test drive" the new models of conciliation/mediation/arbitration and of administrative tribunals. The committee was to select sites for "pilot projects," encourage and support them (even with some money from the Society), monitor their progress over a three-year period, and evaluate their effectiveness at the end of that time.

The committee chose two dioceses for the "alternative dispute resolution"[68] part of the experiment, Dallas, TX, and Portland, ME, and two for the administrative tribunal projects, Milwaukee, WI, and St. Paul and Minneapolis, MN. The committee contacted the diocesan bishops and local canonists, helped with training personnel, and encouraged the "pilots" along the way. The committee's 1999 Final Report reveals mixed results, general satisfaction with the modest outcomes, and valuable lessons learned.[69] One notable result was that the very existence of the administrative tribunal served as an incentive to settle at earlier levels of dispute resolution.[70]

11) *Committee on the Protection of Rights in the Church*

As another attempt to foster and implement the procedures for the protection of rights, in 1992 the Board of Governors of the Society established a committee to study current issues related to the protection of the rights of persons in the Church.[71] A hearing was held at the 1992 convention in Cambridge, MA, on the protection of rights. It surfaced proposals for the future, and its report was ac-

---

67 *Protection of Rights of Persons in the Church: Revised Report of the Canon Law Society of America on the Subject of Due Process* (Washington: DC: CLSA, 1991) 54 pages.

68 Alternative dispute resolution or ADR is a commonly used civil-law label for the triad of conciliation/mediation/arbitration, employed as alternatives to judicial trials.

69 "The Final Report of the Committee on the Experiment in Due Process in the Church" *CLSA Proceedings* 61 (1999) 137-159. Thomas Brundage, "Canonical Issues in Due Process," *CLSA Proceedings* 63 (2001) 37-48 should be read in conjunction with the Final Report.

70 "The Final Report," 157.

71 *CLSA Proceedings* 54 (1992) 209.

companied by a series of helpful outlines, sources, and case studies.[72] The initial broad scope of this committee's interest was soon narrowed to focus on canonical issues related to allegations of clerical sexual abuse, and the need of canonists for specialized training to participate effectively in related penal procedures. The committee successfully organized and conducted workshops to meet this need.[73]

In 1995 the committee, with entirely new membership, shifted its focus to workshops on canonical advocacy. It also proposed to edit a volume of studies on rights in the Church.[74] The last report of the committee listed a set of topics for "a broader foundational study of rights in the Church."[75] The committee went out of existence, with no explanation, after its 1997 report.

12) *Millennium Seminar on Rights in Canon Law*

This was an event, an extended seminar within the 1999 CLSA Minneapolis convention, consisting of two presentations, by James Provost of the Catholic University of America, and Rik Torfs of the canon law faculty at the Catholic University of Leuven, both entitled "Rights in Canon Law: Real, Ideal, or Fluff?" The canonical presentations were followed by small group discussions of six case studies involving conflicts of rights.

The seminar explored the following dimensions of the reality of canonical rights:

1. The relationships between rights, duties, and the common good;
2. The applicability of the Church's social teaching on human rights within the Church itself;
3. The extent of the fundamental equality of the Christian faithful within a hierarchical Church;
4. The rights of communities of the faithful;
5. What protection and vindication of rights exist in the Church?
6. Do rights have a "fundamental" or superior status within canon law?

These six issues framed the serious and substantial content of the two papers, and, not unexpectedly, the authors took quite diverse approaches to them.[76]

---

72   Edward Pfnausch, "Protection of Rights of Persons in the Church," *CLSA Proceedings* 54 (1992) 195-207.

73   Committee reports, *CLSA Proceedings* 55 (1993) 266; *CLSA Proceedings* 56 (1994) 230-231; *CLSA Proceedings* 57 (1995) 455-456.

74   Committee report, *CLSA Proceedings* 58 (1996) 416-417.

75   Committee report, *CLSA Proceedings* 59 (1997) 370-371.

76   James Provost, "Rights in Canon Law: Real, Ideal, or Fluff?" *CLSA Proceedings* 61 (1999) 317-342; Rick Torfs, "Rights in Canon Law: Real, Ideal, or Fluff?" *CLSA Proceedings* 61 (1999) 343-384.

Those are a dozen "milestones" or markers along the Society's forty-five year engagement with the rights of Catholics in the Church. More initiatives could be mentioned, but these may serve to convey the range and success (or lack of same) of our efforts over the years.

D) A Judgment about the Present State of Things

Have we succeeded? It depends on what you call success. Are we more conscious of the rights of the faithful than we were before the 1983 code? Do we begin our analysis of a conflict or grievance with an assessment of the rights of a person or group or with the rule that was broken? In other words, do we give a priority to rights, or are they usually an afterthought? Are rights in the forefront of our canonical minds? How would you answer that question?

However, our topic is not rights-consciousness, but the safeguarding, the actual protection of rights of the Christian faithful. Have we succeeded in this task? I haven't found any of our writers who think so. All the evaluations I've found indicate that it is a goal not yet achieved, an ideal not yet realized.[77]

Two surveys of American dioceses' experiences with due process have been made. The survey published in 1987 was reported above (at milestone number 8). It showed a small percentage of dioceses with truly active and effective programs measured by number of cases submitted.[78] In April 2011, the Office of the Executive Coordinator carried out a mini-survey on due process by email. It was sent to the chancellors of 174 dioceses, responses were received from 39 (23%). Of that number 25 (60%) reported that their diocese had a due process program, and 21 (55%) described it as active. Thirty-eight of the 39 (92%) dioceses responded that there is a person or persons in the diocese "who deals fairly and effectively with grievances." The question that hangs over this recent quickie survey is: what is the situation in the 135 dioceses (77%) that were not heard from? Why was there no response from them?

---

[77] See James Provost, "Promoting and Protecting the Rights of Christians: Some Implications for Church Structure," *The Jurist* 46:1 (1986) 313, 341; Idem., "Rights of Persons in the Church," *Catholicism and Liberalism: Contributions to American Public Philosophy*, ed. R. Bruce Douglass and David Hollenbach (Cambridge: Cambridge University Press, 1994) 313-314; Idem., "Rights in Canon Law: Real, Ideal, or Fluff?" *CLSA Proceedings* 61 (1999) 341-342; John Beal, "Protecting the Rights of Lay Catholics," *The Jurist* 47:1 (1987) 129-164; Idem., "Administrative Tribunals in the Church: An Idea Whose Time Has Come or An Idea Whose Time Has Gone," *CLSA Proceedings* 55 (1993) 39-71; James Coriden, "What Became of the Bill of Rights," *CLSA Proceedings* 52 (1990) 47-60; Idem., *The Rights of Catholics in the Church* (New York: Paulist Press, 2007) 125-127.

[78] Five dioceses processed more than 45 cases in the 15-year time frame covered by the survey (1970-1985), and 16 dioceses processed between 6 and 22 cases. *Due Process in the Dioceses of the United States*, 93.

Many reasons have been offered for the relatively low rate of functioning diocesan due process programs, from the lack of awareness on the part of the people or resistance on the part of the clergy (for example, respondents who refuse to participate) to the effective functioning of diocesan human resources offices and departments of education.

Bottom line: important strides have been made: theoretical studies, designs and models of procedures, experiments, and evaluations. A great deal of good work has been done. But we still have a long way to go. I cannot judge, from my study, that the protection of rights is a success story for our Society.[79]

Is it worth trying to do better on the protection of rights? Listen to what James Provost wrote on that subject in 1999:

> Each generation must engage in the deeply human and Christian struggle to actualize rights in the Church as a means of living the Christian life. The rights of Christians are not an attempt to elude the gospel, but to live it afresh. They are not an attempt to escape the responsibilities of Catholics, but to empower them in a more effective evangelization. They are not a means to isolate Christians, but to build communion.
>
> Is this project worth the effort? The only answer to that question is another question: is the economy of salvation, and the credibility of the Church to evangelize, worth the effort?[80]

E) CLSA Vision for the Future: Needs and Projects Related to the Protection of Rights

These are things that our Church needs, and that are within both the purview and abilities of our Society to accomplish. They are practical matters that would, in my judgment, promote the protection of rights and enhance the credibility of the Church.

---

79   An example of a CLSA failure on a rights issue: the Task Force on Issues Related to Marriage and Undocumented Persons, was empowered in 2001 (*CLSA Proceedings* 63 [2001] 359); reported in *CLSA Proceedings* 64 (2002) 363; 65 (2003) 357-358. In 2004 the Task Force projected a 100-page, seven-chapter report (*CLSA Proceedings* 66 [2004] 332-333). In 2005 it reported the titles and authors of seven chapters; drafts were due by July 25, 2005 (*CLSA Proceedings* 67 [2005] 323-324). The Task Force did not report in 2006 or 2007 (*CLSA Proceedings* 68 [2006] 276-277; 69 [2007] 329). In 2008 the Task force reported that an eight-chapter, bilingual book was near completion (*CLSA Proceedings* 70 [2008] 467). There was no report in 2009, but the Publications Advisory Board chair stated that the Task Force "has put together several articles that can be of use in this area;" he suggested that they might be more successfully distributed through the CLSA website (*CLSA Proceedings* 71 [2009] 348). They have not yet appeared.

80   James Provost, "Rights in Canon Law: Real, Ideal, or Fluff?" *CLSA Proceedings* 61 (1999) 342.

1) *Facilitate the establishment of due process in dioceses and parishes.*

The theoretical studies have been done, the models are in place,[81] and successful experiences are on record.[82] These procedures have been proven to work, to enhance the Church's credibility, even to save money and avoid civil suits. They are explicitly encouraged in the code (c. 1733). They have been recommended by some of our leading canonical colleagues. It is time for action. It is time to put them in place and to make use of them.[83] The Society should find a way to stimulate and monitor progress on due process.

A simple and flexible format seems preferable to a large and elaborate structure.

An "intake officer" or "gatekeeper" or "conciliation clerk" is the first point of contact. He or she sorts out the petitions and recommends a way forward, an appropriate procedure, usually to an ombudsman (or woman) who can also serve as a conciliator or mediator.[84] Other further steps can be utilized: fact-finding, settlement conference, binding arbitration, and finally, a diocesan court of equity (like an administrative tribunal). But keep the procedures clear, straightforward, with relatively short time frames.

Basic grievance procedures should be encouraged at the parish level. That is where most disputes arise, and that is where a first attempt should be made to resolve them. Such early and local intervention is not only a prudent exercise of the principle of subsidiarity, but it helps to prevent grievances from festering and growing into public and hardened divisions.

Thomas Brundage's "concluding thoughts" on due process offer wisdom for reflection:

> a) Take every case seriously, and always provide a path for appeal within the Church.
>
> b) Provide a level playing field for disputants; try to establish a repu-

---

81 See the documents cited in footnotes 37 and 66 above as well as the clear and succinct outlines provided as appendices to Edward Pfnausch's hearing at the 1992 convention, footnote 71.

82 For example: in St. Paul and Minneapolis, Cleveland, Detroit, Rockville Centre, Milwaukee, Seattle, Cincinnati, and Harrisburg.

83 Francis Morrisey strongly endorsed this view in his "Enduring Justice for All," address to the Pacific Northwest Canon Law Society (Yakima, WA: April 12-14, 2010), a modified form of his "The Rights and Duties of the Faithful," *Studies in Church Law* 1 (2005) 25-48. (Specific remarks on pages 2 and 25 of the 2010 address.)

84 John Alesandro, "Response to Bishop Malone's Address," *CLSA Proceedings* 50 (1988) 35; Thomas Brundage, "Canonical Issues in Due Process," *CLSA Proceedings* 63 (2001) 39-40; Diocese of Harrisburg (booklet, no date), *Office of Mediation Services*.

tation for objectivity and fairness for the due process structures.

c) Never forget that we are a Church; by its nature the Church fosters peace and reconciliation.[85]

2) *Administrative tribunals have a place in the process.*

Controversies arising from acts of administrative power can be brought only before the superior or an administrative tribunal (c. 1400 §2). Administrative tribunals were explicitly recommended in the 1967 principles to guide the revision of the code, and were included in drafts of the revised code, but dropped from the 1983 code as promulgated. Because these tribunals were so highly valued in the code revision process, because of the precedent set by Paul VI in establishing the second section of the Apostolic Signatura in 1967,[86] and because of the desire to have another avenue of recourse besides that to the superior, canonical interest in administrative tribunals remained high even after 1983. As a result we have valuable studies on administrative tribunals,[87] and even an experiment (see milestone number 10 above).[88]

From the research studies and the pilot study experiment, I conclude that such administrative tribunals can be established by the authority of the diocesan bishop (but they are not to be *called* administrative tribunals), and that they can serve a valuable role as a part of an integrated diocesan due process structure. Such is the case in Milwaukee and Harrisburg, for example, where the tribunals are termed "Courts of Equity."

It should be acknowledged that the main function of such tribunals is, by their very existence, to put pressure on claimants to reach settlements at earlier stages of the dispute resolution process, i.e., conciliation, mediation, or arbitration. In other words, the fact that an authoritative resolution to their conflict or grievance can be reached, even should they chose not to participate in it, serves as a "stimulation to seriousness" in the earlier attempts at settlement. Cases should reach the court of equity very rarely. It seems to me that larger dioceses should

---

85 Thomas Brundage, "Canonical Issues in Due Process," *CLSA Proceedings* 63 (2001) 46-48. Brundage was Judicial Vicar in the Archdiocese of Milwaukee at the time of their "experiment with due process."

86 Paul VI, apostolic constitution *Regimini Ecclesiae universae*, Aug. 15, 1967: *AAS* 59 (1967) 885; *CLD* 6:324 at 351. (Continued in John Paul II, apostolic constitution *Pastor bonus*, Nov. 20, 1982, art. 123.)

87 Kevin Matthews, "The Development and Future of the Administrative Tribunal," *Studia canonica* 18:1 (1984) 4-223; Michael Moodie, "Defense of Rights: Developing New Procedural Norms," *The Jurist* 47:2 (1987) 423-448; John Beal, "Administrative Tribunals in the Church: An Idea Whose Time Has Come or An Idea Whose Time Has Gone," *CLSA Proceedings* 55 (1993) 39-71.

88 "The Final Report of the Committee on the Experiment in Due Process in the Church" *CLSA Proceedings* 61 (1999) 147-157.

at least consider making an administrative tribunal (aka court of equity) a part of their due process panoply, to be constituted whenever a persistent dispute resists the lower levels of dispute resolution.

3) *Attend to the rights of communities.*

The rights of Catholics in the Church are *communal* in three senses: first, ecclesial communion is the context for our rights and obligations, they are defined and exercised within the community of faith; second, rights are communal in that they accrue to communities, because our communities have juridical personality, they are juridic persons, "subjects in canon law of obligations and rights which correspond to their nature" (c. 113 §2); third, some rights attach to individual persons by reason of their belonging to specific communities within the Church, like religious communities or associations of the faithful.

The second of these three communal meanings is what is of interest here. The second meaning refers to the rights and duties of the communities themselves. Parishes are the leading example. These rights and obligations are not as thoroughly articulated as are those of individual Catholics and are in need of greater attention. In fact, while the code was in the process of revision, Cardinal Joseph Ratzinger called for the recognition of the rights of local churches:

> Each time that the Church exists as a community it is a subject of rights in the larger Church. It isn't only the office-holders on the one hand, and the individual believers on the other, who have rights in the Church. The Church as such, as it exists in each community, is a holder of rights. These churches are, properly speaking, the subjects of rights, in fact they connect all the other subjects of rights in the Church.[89]

The rights and obligations of parishes were not spelled out in the 1983 code. Some of us have tried to articulate them, mainly by extrapolating from the stated rights and duties of the Christian faithful (cc. 208–223).[90] Are these statements of the basic rights and duties of parishes accurate, are they adequate? More importantly, are they taken seriously when it comes to the staffing of parish ministry or when there is a question of the possible closing or merger of parishes? Who has the right and duty to defend the prerogatives of a parish besides the pastor, e.g., when the pastor either neglects to do so (as was the case at St. Brigid Parish, San Francisco, 1993) or chooses not to (in the case of St. Rocco Parish, Chicago

---

89   Joseph Ratzinger, "Demokratisierung der Kirche?" *Demokratie in der Kirche* (Limburg: Lahn, 1970) 38-39.

90   For example, James Coriden, "The Rights of Parishes," *Studia canonica* 28 (1994) 293-309; Idem, "Do Parishes Have Rights? *New Theology Review* 7:3 (August 1994) 23-34; Idem, *The Parish in Catholic Tradition: History, Theology, and Canon Law* (New York: Paulist Press, 1997) 71-81.

Heights, IL, 1991)? Who in the diocesan curia has such a duty? The Society should explore this issue and find answers to these questions.

4) *Revive "Doctrinal Responsibilities."*

Recent events[91] have shone a spotlight on a twenty-two year old document of our bishops' conference called *Doctrinal Responsibilities* (see milestone number 6 above). The procedures recommended in the document apparently were not used in any of these recent instances despite the fact of their overwhelming approval by the full body of bishops in 1989. The board of directors of the Catholic Theological Society of America criticized the Doctrinal Committee's failure to use its own approved procedures in its action in regard to Elizabeth Johnson's book,[92] and the CTSA membership in convention more recently adopted a resolution that "regretted deeply that the provisions established by the American bishops" were ignored in passing judgment on Johnson's book.[93] The resolution went on to recommend that the American bishops evaluate the procedures of the Committee on Doctrine that led to their statement on her book.

These events and the procedures used in dealing with theological issues are of more than personal concern; more than the reputation of authors and the security of their teaching positions are on the line. They are of far larger concern to the teaching authority of the Church and how it is shared between theologians and bishops (cc. 218, 386, 753, 756 §2, 823). They are of highest interest to those concerned about freedom and good order within the Church. What we as a Society did more than thirty years ago we need to do again today, that is, collaborate with the bishops and the theologians to assure fairness, balance, and the protection of rights in the exercise of this form of the teaching office. We need to assist in the revival of *Doctrinal Responsibilities*.

5) *Promote the active participation of the faithful.*

---

91   For example, USCCB Committee on Doctrine, "Statement on *Quest for the Living God: Mapping Frontiers in the Theology of God* by Sister Elizabeth A. Johnson," March 24, 2011; Idem, "Inadequacies in the Theological Methodology and Conclusions of *The Sexual Person: Toward a Renewed Catholic Anthropology* by Todd A. Salzman and Michael G. Lawler," Sept. 15, 2010; Idem, "Clarifications Required by the Book *Being Religious Interreligiously: Asian Perspectives on Interfaith Dialogue* by Reverend Peter C. Phan," Dec. 17, 2007; Idem, "A Statement Concerning Two Pamphlets Published by Professor Daniel Maguire, 'The Modern Roman Catholic Position on Contraception and Abortion,' and 'A Catholic Defense of Same-Sex Marriage,'" March 21, 2007.

92   Statement issued April 8, 2011. All are aware of the fact, made clear in Archbishop Dolan's response (letter of July 7, 2011) to the CTSA resolution, that the procedures of *Doctrinal Responsibilities* were proposed for resolving misunderstanding between theologians and individual bishops, not directly to the Committee on Doctrine of the bishops' conference. The Committee on Doctrine now has a protocol (in the form of a draft, dated August 19, 2011) to guide its responses to requests for assistance and proposals for action.

93   Resolution passed on June 10, 2011, in San Jose, CA.

All of the faithful have the right and duty to participate fully in the life of the Church. This basic right of participation is sounded clearly in canon 204 of the code.[94] The mode of active engagement that is stated explicitly in regard to liturgical celebrations, "knowingly, actively, and fruitfully,"[95] is also true of other forms of sharing in the mission of the local church. Good pastors try very hard and persistently to help their people to participate fully in eucharistic celebrations. We must try just as hard to stimulate our people to take part in other forms of activity, both the routine (pastoral and finance councils, parish and diocesan) and exceptional (parish programs and events, diocesan synods). The Society's special focus is on the area of governance.

Our role is to design, facilitate, and promote forms of active participation that work, that attract and engage our members—for their sake and for the benefit of the Church at every level. The reason for doing so is not simply to enliven the parish or diocese, to "keep the numbers up," or even because it is the people's right to "have a place at the table," but because the people "possess the Spirit of Christ,"[96] and we desperately need to listen to them and learn the guidance of the Holy Spirit.

As one example, I have long had the impression that diocesan pastoral councils are not working very well as consultative organs in many dioceses.[97] If that is true, we should be able to find out why, and be creative enough to adapt them, perhaps using newer technologies or reconfiguring them, so that they function more effectively. What about the vitality and usefulness of other consultative organs like presbyteral councils or diocesan synods? Can they be employed more effectively? What are the keys to their success or "best practices"? Or, thinking more broadly, what are new and better ways of listening to the people, of structuring policy decisions?

6) *Articulate the rights and responsibilities of lay ecclesial ministers.*
Everyone is aware of the post-conciliar phenomenon often described as the "explosion of lay ecclesial ministry," a movement of the Holy Spirit, in response to the needs of contemporary parishioners, initiated and encouraged by wise and willing pastors, and made possible by the generous response of thousands of the

---

94   "The Christian faithful ... incorporated in Christ through baptism, have been constituted as the people of God ... made sharers in their own way in Christ's priestly, prophetic, and royal function ... are called to exercise the mission which God has entrusted to the Church to fulfill in the world ..." (c. 204 §1).

95   *Sacrosanctum concilium* 11, 14.

96   *Lumen gentium* 14.

97   USCCB, "The USCCB Committee on the Laity Report on Diocesan and Parish Pastoral Council," March 12, 2004, and CLSA/USCCB co-sponsored *Diocesan and Eparchial Pastoral Councils: A National Profile*, June 1998.

baptized faithful.[98] A rich theological literature has sprung up around the phenomenon, representing what some have called "an American consensus."[99] Out of this context the American bishops crafted the very valuable statement to guide the development of this ministry, *Co-Workers in the Vineyard of the Lord*.[100] This document raised and left unanswered many issues related to lay ministry, for example, forms of authorization, mode of installation, terms of contract, and grievance procedures.[101] Some of the issues are canonical, and the CLSA should play an active role in the exploration of these important elements, while taking care not to "set in stone" matters which are not yet ripe for settlement.[102]

Even more important than the individual issues involved is the need to envision this ministry among the other more traditional ministries in our Church, and to contribute to the full integration of lay ecclesial ministry within the larger structure of ministries. Lay ministry must find its rightful place inside the Roman Catholic *ministerium*, and we should assist with that process.

While this ministry finds its position within the panoply of ministerial roles, both ancient and modern, canonists must attend to the everyday protection of the rights and duties of lay ecclesial ministers. The healthy and fair development of lay ecclesial ministry is of vital importance to the future of our Church.

7) *Prepare for the ordination of married men to the presbyterate.*

The shortage of priests in North America is a tiresome topic, but a very serious one. It has continued for decades now, and it shows little sign of significant change. We compensated for the shrinking number of active priests by all of the obvious measures: reducing the number of associate pastors (parochial vicars),

---

98 CARA reported on July 18, 2011, that parish lay ecclesial ministers have increased to 37,929, and this number does not include those working in diocesan offices, hospitals, on campuses and many other settings. Mary Gautier and Mark Gray, "The Changing Face of U.S. Catholic Parishes," *Emerging Models of Pastoral Leadership Project, Origins* 41:12 (Aug. 18, 2011) 194-195.

99 James Coriden, "Pastoral Ministry in the Parish: A Theological Consensus and Practical Issues," *Essays in Honor of Sister Rose McDermott, S.S.J.*, ed. Robert Kaslyn (Washington, DC: The Catholic University of America, 2010) 100-123, at 103-109.

100 Subtitled *A Resource for Guiding the Development of Lay Ecclesial Ministry* (Washington, DC: USCCB, 2005).

101 Symbolic of the gradual progress toward the formalizing of the certification element of this ministry are the move of the Commission on Certification and Accreditation from a private corporation in Milwaukee to a subcommittee of the USCCB in Washington (CNS, June 20, 2011) and the formation of an Alliance for Certification of Lay Ecclesial Ministers (ACLEM) from five partner organizations (announced by National Association for Lay Ministry, June 28, 2011).

102 Contributions by Susan Wood, Lynda Robataille, and Zeni Fox in the forthcoming book, *In the Name of the Church: Vocation and Authorization of Lay Ecclesial Ministry*, ed. William Cahoy (Collegeville, MN: Liturgical Press) will help with these deliberations.

inviting foreign priests to minister here, asking priests to serve as pastors of multiple parishes, and finally, merging or closing parishes (many of which were viable and would not have been considered for closure if priests were available to pastor them).[103]

Even with these serious compensatory measures in place, many parishes still experience "Sunday celebrations in the absence of a priest," and many priests are burning out because of overwork. The lack of priests is causing grave harm to the Church, the most serious being the people's deprivation of regular eucharistic celebrations. One of the most basic rights of fully initiated Catholics is the right to participate in the Holy Eucharist (cc. 213, 843 §1, 912, 1247). The lack of persons capable of presiding at eucharistic celebrations with the faithful is a rights issue.[104]

Pope Benedict XVI, in an allocution to the Pontifical Academy of Sciences in May 2009, drew attention to "the growing awareness ... of a flagrant contrast between the equal *attribution* of rights and the unequal *access* to the means of attaining those rights. For Christians who regularly ask God to 'give us this day our daily bread,' it is a shameful tragedy that one-fifth of humanity still goes hungry."[105] The same lament can be made with regard to the "eucharistic hunger" within the Church.

Of all the proposed solutions to this crisis,[106] one frequently mentioned regarding the diocesan priesthood is the ordination of married men.[107] Because of its long history and recent revival, it seems to be an inevitable choice. It has ancient precedent, from the apostolic era to the early middle ages in all parts of the Church. It is still the more common practice in the churches of the east.

---

103 In 2000 the U.S. Church had over 19,000 parishes, now they number fewer than 17,800, a 7% decline.

The average number of registered households in those parishes has grown to 1,168. See Gautier, Gray, and Cidade, "The Changing Face of U.S. Catholic Parishes," (National Association for Lay Ministry, 2011).

104 Francis Morrisey raised this same issue in his 2010 address, "Enduring Justice for All," 7.

105 *Communicationes* 41:1 (2009) 43.

106 Dean Hoge, *The Future of Catholic Leadership: Responses to the Priest Shortage* (Kansas City, MO: Sheed & Ward, 1987). Hoge updated this study in "Addressing the Priest 'Shortage,'" *Priests for the 21st Century*, ed. Donald Dietrich (New York: Crossroad, 2006) 133-149.

107 Archbishop Edward Cardinal Egan publicly raised the issue of ordaining married men on March 10, 2009, soon after stepping down from the see of New York (CNS, March 11, 2009). The CNS article relates that Cardinal Claudio Hummes, the newly appointed prefect of the Congregation for the Clergy, made a similar suggestion in 2006.

Pope Pius XII revived the practice of ordaining married Protestant ministers who converted to the Catholic Church.[108] John Paul II approved a "pastoral provision" for such converts, mainly from the Episcopal Church, in 1980.[109] Well over a hundred married ministers from the Episcopal and other Protestant churches have been ordained as Catholic priests in the U.S. since that time,[110] and another hundred are in line for ordination under the provisions of Benedict XVI's 2009 apostolic constitution *Anglicanorum coetibus*.[111] Obviously, there are no doctrinal problems involved in the ordination of married men. It is a matter of discipline, of canonical and pastoral practice.

The CLSA has taken notice of this development over the years. A 1996 report began by referring to studies going back to 1971.[112] Resolutions were debated at the 1990 and 1991 conventions. The 1996 report covered such issues as discernment of vocations, formation, impediments, limitations on ministries, support and benefits.

Since that 1996 report and the follow-up seminar in 1997 (see note 110) our Church has learned a lot from the experiences of married deacons and from those of the married convert-priests themselves. There are canonical and practical issues which need further exploration, such as: minimum age, length of marriage, consent of wife (c. 1031 §2), remuneration or self-support options (c. 281 §3), source of funding (c. 1274), benefits for family even after priest's death or disability (cc. 281 §2, 231 §2), mobility and transfer of incardination, the effects of marital separation, civil divorce, or remarriage after death of spouse or annulment. The Society should continue its work in providing for this re-instituted form of presbyteral ministry.

---

108 Richard Hill, "The Pastoral Provision: Ordination of Married Protestant Ministers," *CLSA Proceedings* 51 (1989) 95.

109 Issued in a letter to the President of the NCCB from the Prefect of the CDF on July 22, 1980 (Prot. N. 66/77).

110 Frederick Luhmann, *Call and Response: Ordaining Married Men as Catholic Priests* (Berryville, VA: Dialogue Press, 2002) chronicles this whole development. He updated the numbers and names of the ordained converts in a letter to me dated November 22, 2010. In the same letter Luhmann told the story of Jan Kofron, a married Catholic man (not a convert) with four children, secretly ordained a priest during the Communist regime in Czechoslovakia in 1988 and conditionally reordained for the Archdiocese of Prague in 2008.

111 Cardinal Wuerl's report to the USCCB (CNS, June 16, 2011).

112 "Canonical Implications Related to the Ordination of Married Men to the Priesthood in the United States of America," *CLSA Proceedings* 58 (1996) 438-453, at 439-440. A seminar on the report was held at the following year's convention (it offered a summary of the report), and those present at the convention passed a resolution of acceptance and endorsement of the report, *CLSA Proceedings* 59 (1997) 130-135, 427.

8) *Compose and propose a fair and workable penal process.*

At last year's convention Ricardo Bass spoke with passion about our need "to be true to our canonical tradition and to our vocation in the Church" in caring for both the victims of sex abuse and those accused of abusing them. He quoted a powerful paragraph spoken by Rose McDermott eight years earlier about the shameful inadequacies of present practices and of our potential failures in our ministerial vocations.[113] The causes of the clerical sex abuse scandal go much deeper than procedures, as Pope Benedict told the Roman Curia, and we must search for ways to restore justice and charity in the Church.[114]

Here, however, I am suggesting that we do our part to repair the canonical "criminal justice system." From the preliminary investigation process (cc. 1717-1719), the judicial penal process, to dismissal from the clerical state, we should refine a set of best practices so that fairness is assured and the penal process is rendered workable, not endlessly delayed. For example, the present compulsory submission of every case to the CDF is an outrageous over-centralization, tolerable in an emergency, but an affront to episcopal authority and the integrity of particular churches once the crisis has passed. A canonical criminal process needs to be revived and employed.[115]

The Pontifical Council for Legislative Texts is developing a renewed penal process,[116] and the CLSA will certainly examine it and cooperate in its implementation. But we may need to go further, and work to assure that it results in a process that is truly serviceable in our little corner of the Church.

---

113 Ricardo Bass, "Role of Law Award Response," *CLSA Proceedings* 72 (2010) 359-361; Rose McDermott, "Role of Law Award Response," *CLSA Proceedings* 64 (2002) 435-437.

114 "We must ask ourselves what we can do to repair as much as possible the injustice that has occurred. We must ask ourselves what was wrong in our proclamation, in our whole way of living the Christian life, to allow such a thing to happen." Benedict XVI, address to Roman Curia (CNS, Dec. 20, 2010).

115 Cf. Nicholas Cafardi, *Before Dallas: The U.S. Bishops' Response to Clergy Sexual Abuse of Children* (Mahwah, NJ: Paulist Press, 2008) 149-150. One practical suggestion: create a national panel of judges with criminal trial experience from which a bishop or religious superior could choose a *terna* to try a case involving one of his priests. Experts from outside the diocesan presbyterate or institute's members should help assure objectivity and fairness.

116 Juan Ignacio Arrieta, "Proposed Reforms in Penal Procedures and the Contribution of Cardinal Ratzinger," *CLSGBI Newsletter* 166 (June 2011) 5-15. The draft text of a revised Book VI, Sanctions in the Church, is currently in circulation.

F) Final Reflections

1) *Rights as an organizing principle?*

James Provost, writing the concluding article of the Society's seminar on promoting and protecting rights in the Church twenty-five years ago (milestone number 7 above) began by asking this question: "What would be the implications in the lived experience of Catholics if protecting and promoting their rights and obligations were taken as the central concern in organizing the life of the Church?"[117]

Provost, in his creative and challenging way, explored the dimensions of the Church's life and how they would be affected if we really took the rights of the faithful as an organizing principle. In one trenchant paragraph Provost summed up what it is to be a Catholic Christian, the subject of rights and duties:

> To be a Catholic, then, is not some isolated experience; it integrates the three principles of equality, freedom and participation. Catholics live in a community of faith, worship and ecclesiastical discipline. Within that community each Catholic participates in the three-fold work of Christ: priestly, prophetic, and royal. This is a missionary work, not of individuals on their own, but of the community, since it carries out the mission God gave the Church. Each Catholic has a proper role in this mission both in the world and internal to the Church itself. Such a role is inalienable, for it comes through baptism; it is not a concession from church authorities, but is constituted as part of the very definition of "person" in the Church, and so of one's God-given rights and duties.[118]

In that sweeping, expansive interpretation of the individual person's place in the Church's mission, rights as an organizing principle is very appealing. However, in our American context I remain reluctant to endorse it as our central and controlling concern.[119]

For one thing, giving centrality to personal rights risks exaggerating the individual's interests over against those of the community, hence falling back into the trap of American individualism. Second, it sounds like an invitation to engage in the kind of adversarial litigiousness for which we Americans are famous. Finally, it appears to elevate the maintenance of the Church as institution over the accomplishment of its mission, the work to be done, the purpose of Church's existence, and the positive role each person and community must play in it. The

---

117 James Provost, "Promoting and Protecting the Rights of Christians: Some Implications for Church Structure," *The Jurist* 46:1 (1986) 289.

118 Ibid., 305.

119 Provost raised some reservations about it within the article, e.g., pp. 291-299.

focus of such an organizing principle seems inward rather than outward.

2) *Rights, Conversion, and the Holy Spirit.*

Twenty-three years ago we had a very special meeting in Baltimore. It was 1988 and the Society's fiftieth anniversary. Leonard Scott of Camden was our president and he orchestrated the celebration. At least ten bishops attended the convention, and Henry Roberts (of the *Roberts' Rules of Order* family) himself was employed as our parliamentarian.

On that august occasion Bishop James Malone of Youngstown, past president of the NCCB, addressed us on "The Canon Law Society and the Church in the United States." In a way, he did what I have just tried to do, talk about the legacy of the Society and a vision for its future, only he did it much more briefly and eloquently.

He was outspoken in praise of the work of the Society on behalf of the Church, and he singled out six of our initiatives for special mention: 1) the American Procedural Norms,[120] 2) evaluation of tribunals, 3) assistance with the code revision process, 4) due process, 5) the doctrinal responsibility project, and 6) the ongoing implementation of the new code.[121]

Bishop Malone then went on to suggest three areas of focus for our future work: 1) canonical education, and here he included bishops, priests and deacons, and lay ministers, as those in need of educating, 2) collaborative ministry, helping laity, religious, and the ordained to work together in ministry, and 3) the development of administrative tribunals in this country, and here he spoke broadly of "effective structures for the administration of justice within the Church."[122]

Bishop Malone reminded us that we are more than a professional society: "It is an association of learned Christians whose ministry it is to serve God's people." He drew attention to the quote from Paul to the Romans in our logo: "In Christ Jesus the life-giving law of the Spirit has set you free from the law of sin and death" (Rom. 8:2). He also drew attention to the new mentality (*novus habitus mentis*) that Pope Paul VI urged on those who revised and those who apply the code.

Bertram Griffin, our beloved luminary from the Northwest, responded to Bishop Malone on that occasion in 1988, and he picked up on that "new way of thinking":

---

120 Council for the Public Affairs of the Church. Rescript "Provisional Norms for Marriage Annulment Cases in the United States." July 1, 1970. *Periodica* 59 (1970) 563-592.

121 *CLSA Proceedings* 50 (1988) 26-28.

122 Ibid., 31-32.

> A new way of thinking implies a change from an old way of thinking. Change means ... a conversion experience. ... If *novus habitus mentis* were translated into Greek, it would come out *metanoia*, the word used in the New Testament for conversion, repentance, return from exile. ... This conversion experience feels like a canonical ... awakening. Canonists ... have lived for 400 years in a post-Tridentine sleep from which some of us are only beginning to awaken. ...
>
> Such [conversion] experiences are the work of the Spirit. We are powerless to bring about such a conversion using only our own resources. We can help each other awaken as we share our ongoing insights, but ultimately the degree and extent of conversion is up to God, on his timetable, in his hands. The results are in a radical sense a Spirit-inspired miracle of grace.[123]

At the end of his response, Bert closed with this prayer:

> As the wind of the Spirit blows through the Canon Law Society of America we too will gradually awaken from our post-Tridentine sleep so that we can be of better service to God and his Church. Deliver us Lord from that long sleep. Work in us that gradual awakening which only you can accomplish, grant us your peace in the midst of change, in your kindness free us from our self will and need for power and control, protect us from fear and anxiety about the future, for we wait now—we wait now—with joy and hope for the coming of our savior Jesus Christ.[124] Amen.

---

[123] "Response to Bishop Malone's Address," *CLSA Proceedings* 50 (1988) 40-41.
[124] Ibid., 51.

Major Address

Rights in the Church:
Great Expectations, Meager Results
Reverend John P. Beal

I. Introduction

On January 25, 1983, Pope John Paul II promulgated a revised Code of Canon Law, the legislative document the Church in general and canon lawyers in particular had been eagerly awaiting since the day exactly twenty-four years earlier when Pope John XXIII had announced his intention to convoke an ecumenical council and to embark on the task of revising the 1917 Code of Canon Law. As Pope John Paul II noted in the apostolic constitution *Sacrae disciplinae leges* with which he promulgated the revised code,

> The instrument which the Code is fully corresponds to the nature of the Church, especially as it is proposed by the teaching of the Second Vatican Council in general and in a particular way by its ecclesiological teaching. Indeed, in a certain sense this new Code could be understood as a great effort to translate this same conciliar doctrine and ecclesiology into *canonical* language.[1]

As a result, this revised code has often been referred to as "the last document" of the Council.

Even during this code's long period of gestation in the labors of the Pontifical Commission for the Revision of the Code of Canon Law but especially in the immediate aftermath of its promulgation, one of its most discussed, indeed heralded, features was its inclusion of most of the rights of the Christian faithful that had been identified in the documents of the Second Vatican Council. Indeed, Pope John Paul II highlighted "that which concerns the duties and rights of the faithful and particularly of the laity" as among the elements which constitute the substantial "*newness* of the new Code" and "which characterizes the true and genuine image of the Church."[2] This legal recognition of rights sharply distinguishes this revised code from its predecessor during whose regime many distinguished canonists had argued that there was simply no place for subjective

---

1   John Paul II, apostolic constitution *Sacrae disciplinae leges*, January 25, 1983: *AAS* 75 (1983) xiv. Emphasis in the original.

2   Ibid., xv. Emphasis in the original.

rights of the faithful in canon law.[3]

The catalogue of obligations and rights of the faithful has also been touted in both scholarly[4] and popular[5] venues by numerous canonists as a great leap forward for the Church's law, which promised an enhanced opportunity for the faithful to take their rightful place in the life and mission of the Church and a challenge to the canonical community to promote and protect these rights. Addressing the convention of this society in Hartford in 1982, the late James Provost compared the rights laid out in the soon to be promulgated revised Code as "diamonds in the rough," diamonds which have in the course of time "been encrusted with the accumulations of history and custom."[6] And Provost pointedly called on the members of this society "to find these rights, dig them out, and skillfully break them open so they can shine today in all their beauty."[7] Provost's talk of mining, extracting and polishing these diamonds in the rough was a heady challenge for canonists in 1982, but, by 1999, one could note a tone of resigned disappointment in Provost's voice as he and Rik Torfs asked this society's members in Minneapolis, the last CLSA convention before his death, whether "Rights in Canon Law" were "Real, Ideal, or Fluff?"[8] and concluded:

> It seems to me that the most realistic evaluation of rights in the Church is that, at the present time, they are at most an ideal. Regrettably, at times they may even qualify as "fluff." But I do not think

---

[3] The most insistent of those who denied the existence of subjective rights in canon law was Pio Fedele, *Discorso generale sull'ordinamento canonico* (Padua: CEDAM, 1941) 158-170. See also the discussion of this issue in Luigi DeLuca, "I diritti fondamentali dell'uomo nell'ordinamento canonico," *Acta Congressus Internationalis Iuris Canonici 1950* (Rome: Catholic Book Agency, 1953) 88-103 and Alfonso Prieto Prieto, "Los derechos subjectivos publicos en la Iglesia," *Iglesia y Derecho*, Semana de Derecho Canonico X (Salamanca: CSIC, 1965) 325-361.

[4] See Alvero del Portillo, *Faithful and Laity in the Church: The Bases of their Legal Status* (Shannon, Ireland: Ecclesia, 1972); Pedro Juan Viladrich, *Teori de los derechos fundamentals del fiel* (Pamplona: Editiones Universidad de Navarra, 1969); Gaetano Lo Castro, *Il soggetto e i suoi diritti nell'ordinamento canonico* (Milan: Dott. A. Giuffrè Editore, 1985); Javier Hervada, *Elementos de derecho constitucional canónico* (Pamplona: EUNSA, 1987); Juan Ignacio Arrieta, "I diritti soggetti nell'ordinamento canonico," *Fidelium Iuris* 1 (1991) 9-46); Dominique Le Tourneau, *Droits et devoirs fiondamentaux des fidèles et des laics dans l'Église*, Collection Gratianus (Montreal: Wilson and Lafleur, 2011).

[5] See James H. Provost, "Rights for Christians in the Revised Code," *New Catholic World* (May/June 1983) 110-112 and Bertram Griffin, "A Bill of Rights and Freedoms," in *Code, Community, Ministry*, ed. Edward G. Pfnausch (Washington: CLSA, 1992) 62-64.

[6] James H. Provost, "Ecclesial Rights," *PCLSA* 44 (1982) 41.

[7] Ibid.

[8] James H. Provost and Rik Torfs, "Rights in Canon Law: Real, Ideal, or Fluff?" *PCLSA* 61 (1999) 317-384.

> this should discourage canonists from the pursuit of justice, or even from attempting to provide more effective safeguards to protect and vindicate the rights of Christians. ... We are very much in a major period of transition regarding our understanding of Church, the role of individual Christians, and the place of rights in the Church. I suspect we are still at the beginning of that period, and several more generations will need to work on these issues before a new consensus begins to emerge.[9]

What happened between 1982 and 1999 to transform this enthusiastic miner, cutter and polisher of diamonds in the rough into a reluctant prophet like Moses resignedly pointing to a "place of justice, charity and peace"[10] somewhere beyond the horizon, which he would not live to see or enter? And what has happened since the revised Code of Canon Law was promulgated that has replaced the heady enthusiasm for proclaiming, protecting, and vindicating the rights of the faithful that greeted this code's appearance and that once energized these annual gatherings with something more like glum resignation?

II. Rights Consciousness in the Church: A Clash of "Social Imaginaries"

The discrepancy between what many of us in North America and elsewhere expected when the revised code's catalogue of obligations and rights first made its appearance and what we have experienced these last twenty-eight years is the result of profound differences between the social model in which we North Americans "live and move and have our being" and the one enshrined in ecclesial law and praxis.

> Among legal scholars expressions such as "social ideal" or "social model," and even "social vision," have become generally accepted ways of referring to the image of society that guide the contemporary practice of making and applying law. These images or paradigms provide the background for an interpretation of the system of basic rights.[11]

If we want to understand why the promulgation of a charter of rights of the faithful has not had the impact we anticipated, therefore, we need to move be-

---

9   Ibid., 341-342.

10 James H. Provost, "Response to the Role of Law Award," *PCLSA* 53 (1991) 343.

11 Jürgen Habermas, "Paradigms of Law," in *Habermas on Law and Democracy: Critical Exchanges*, ed. Michael Rosenfeld and Andrew Arato (Berkeley, CA: University of California Press, 1988) 13. Habermas goes on to say: "A paradigm is discerned primarily in paramount judicial decisions, and it is usually equated with the court's implicit image of society." Since the decisions of ecclesiastical tribunals do not have the value of strong precedents, the "paradigm" informing canon law must be discerned in leading administrative decisions interpreting and applying the law.

yond searching for villains among pompous prelates and not-so-enlightened despots and instead to reflect on how the social vision that sometimes explicitly, but more often implicitly, underlies our North American approach to rights differs from the one that undergirds canon law and guides its official interpretation and application. A complex of notions and intuitions about how we actually interact with one another in the social order and how we think we should interact has emerged in Western culture since the sixteenth century that departs markedly from the one that had dominated previous ages and which, in large measure, still lives on in the Catholic Church. Despite its countless manifestation and mutations, variations and versions, iterations and reiterations, this concatenation of notions and intuitions has become pervasive in Western societies in what, following the Canadian philosopher Charles Taylor, I will refer to as the modern "social imaginary."

The phrase "social imaginary" is preferable to other phrases such as "social vision" or "social model" because it does not immediately connote the sort of social theories and erudite explanations of social phenomena that are regularly spun out by philosophers and social scientists in the rarefied air of their academic ivory towers. Rather, "social imaginary" suggests something "much broader and deeper than the intellectual schemes people may entertain when they think about social reality in a disengaged way."[12] The term "social imaginary" places the focus on "the way ordinary people 'imagine' their social surroundings," something that "is often not expressed in theoretical terms, but is carried in images, stories and legends."[13] Unlike social "theories" which are usually articulated and held by a small elite, social "imaginaries" are widely shared but often implicit in everyday practice and behavior.14

> This implicit grasp of social space is unlike a theoretical description of this space, distinguishing different kinds of people and the norms connected to them. The understanding implicit in practice stands to social theory in the same relation that my ability to get around a familiar environment stands to a (literal) map of the area. I am very well able to orient myself without ever having adopted the standpoint of overview the map offers me. Similarly, for most of human history and for most of social life, we function through the grasp we have on the common repertory, without the benefit of theoretical overview. Humans operated with a social imaginary well before they ever got into the business of theorizing about themselves.[15]

---

12   Charles Taylor, *Modern Social Imaginaries* (Durham, NC : Duke University Press, 2004) 23.

13   Ibid.

14   Ibid.

15   Ibid., 26.

What then are the salient features of the modern social imaginary that almost spontaneously orients our thinking about rights and their function in our communal life both in secular society and, unless we make a conscious effort to dissociate ourselves from this imaginary, in the Church? And in what significant ways do the features of this modern social imaginary differ from the classical or traditional one that still pervades the Catholic Church and has dominated the interpretation and application of rights language in the world governed by canon law?

A. *Pou Sto? Where do the Competing "Social Imaginaries" Begin?*

1. The Modern Social Imaginary: Primacy Of The Individual

The modern social imaginary begins with the individual person. Society is conceived as being populated by a multiplicity of these individuals. These individuals are not, however, primarily the flesh and blood people with their own peculiar histories, social positions, community traditions and ethos, and relationships we encounter in everyday life. Rather, these individuals are conceived first of all as "unencumbered selves"—selves "whose personal identities are established prior to and independent of [their] ends, history and communal relations."[16] Society is established for the sake of such "unencumbered" individuals to provide them with security and to foster economic exchange and prosperity,[17] a service which "centers on the needs of ordinary life, rather than aiming to secure for individuals the highest virtue"[18] as was the case in the classical model of society stemming from Aristotle. In a preeminent way, society serves the individuals who compose it by protecting their individual rights. The rights most prized by those oriented by this modern social imaginary are those freedoms which ground "their existence as free agents,"[19] that is, those that guarantee them individual autonomy. To be moral agents shaping their own destiny, individuals must enjoy freedom from coercion by others, in matters of belief, expression and action as long as the exercise of these rights does not impinge on the same rights of others. When the exercise of these rights is assured, individuals are free, in Jefferson's phrase, to enjoy "life, liberty and the pursuit of happiness" as they individually define it for themselves.[20]

Pushed to its extreme conclusion, this identification of freedom and autonomy leads to a highly individualistic understanding of morality in which each individual is her or his own autonomous arbiter of right and wrong. Not all of the in-

---

16   David Hollenbach, "A Communitarian Reconstruction of Human Rights: Contributions from the Catholic Tradition," in *Catholicism and Liberalism*, ed. R. Bruce Douglass and David Hollenbach (New York: Cambridge University Press, 1994) 130.

17   Taylor, *Modern Social Imaginaries*, 20.

18   Ibid.

19   Ibid.

20   Ibid.

fluential articulators of the modern social imaginary have pushed the identification of freedom and autonomy to this logical conclusion.[21] "Nevertheless, there is little doubt that these understandings of human rights led modern Western culture to value autonomous freedom more highly than virtuous commitment to the common good."[22]

2. The Traditional Social Imaginary: The Primacy Of Community

The classical or pre-modern social imaginary which underlies the social teaching and ecclesiology of the Church and the canon law which derives from these sources begins its consideration of society not with the "unencumbered" individual but with the community in which individuals are "embedded." From this perspective, the isolated and "unencumbered" individual in Locke's "state of nature" or Rawls' disinterested individual "behind the veil of ignorance" is quite literally "unimaginable." Individual persons outside of the context of a community are unthinkable. "To be a person is necessarily to live in particular historical circumstances, with a particular social identity and set of relationships."[23] As a result, it is not autonomous freedom that is the essential precondition for moral agency. No, one becomes a "proper moral agent" or "a fully competent human subject."[24] only by being embedded in a community "sustained by a shared vision of the good and by communal social roles that educate us in virtue."[25] It is only in such a community that one learns how others deserve to be treated. Thus, justice or what is due to others and to ourselves cannot be determined in the abstract simply by applying universal standards of human rights to particular persons without reference to their "communal bonds, social roles, historical period and cultural traditions."[26] It is only by attending to these multiple aspects of each person's social embeddedness that we can give them their due and demand from them what is rightfully due to us. In this social milieu, moral questions ask not what our community ought to do for us but what we can and ought to do for our community.

---

21   Hollenbach, "A Communitarian Reconstruction," 131: "Locke placed constraints on freedom of self-disposition even prior to the establishment of the social contract. It must be exercised "within the bounds of the law of nature." For example, the right to private property is limited by the imperatives that there 'be enough, and as good left in common with others' and that no one appropriate more perishable goods that can be used before they spoil. Kant based all morality on the self-legislating autonomous will. But his understanding of practical reason led directly to a strongly communal notion of human beings as members of a 'kingdom of ends,' an idea with at least some echoes of the kingdom of God."

22   Ibid.

23   Ibid., 130.

24   Taylor, *Modern Social Imaginaries*, 18.

25   Ibid.

26   Hollenbach, "A Communitarian Reconstruction," 130.

In the wake of the French Revolution and the ensuing period of upheaval in Europe, the Catholic Church had a close encounter of the wrong kind with a political regime claiming to champion the "rights of man." Ever since, it has been profoundly skeptical of the way in which claims of human rights have functioned in the modern social imaginary. It is easy for us to roll our eyes at Gregory XVI's railing against the "insanity" of freedom of conscience[27] and Pius IX's condemnation of liberalism as the summary of all heresies,[28] but beneath the perhaps overheated rhetoric was a genuine concern that the more people exalted autonomous freedom, the more they treated morality as a matter of personal taste. For the Catholic tradition, the danger lurking behind the attractive façade of the modern rights agenda was and still is that it is ultimately "indifferent to the truth of all moral and religious claims."[29] That this danger was not—and is not—an illusion is attested by the subversion of a common moral vision by an individualistic understanding of morality evident in the young people recently interviewed by Christian Smith and his colleagues. For these young Americans, morality is completely a matter of subjective feeling: "the default position . . . is [that morality is] just a matter of individual taste. 'It's personal' the respondents typically said. 'It's up to the individual. Who am I to say?'"[30]

Although the Catholic Church slowly incorporated human rights into its social teaching during the century between Leo XIII's *Rerum novarum* and John Paul II's *Centesimos annos*, it has not capitulated to liberal orthodoxy in doing so. Instead, it has continued to insist with "Aristotle and Aquinas . . . that social relationships are constitutive of personality"[31] and that human flourishing requires something more than autonomy.[32] As the conciliar constitution *Gaudium et spes* insists,

> The social nature of the human beings makes it evident that the progress of the human person and the advance of society itself hinge on each other. For the beginning, the subject and the goal of all social institutions is and must be the human person, which for its part and

---

27   Gregory XVI, encyclical *Mirari vos,* August 15, 1832: *Acta Gregorii XVI*, ed. Antonius Maria Bernasconi (Rome: Sacra Congregation Propaganda Fidei, 1901) 1:169-174.

28   Pius IX, encyclical *Quanta cura* and *Syllabus complectens praecipuos nostra aetatis errores*, December 8, 1864: *ASS* 3 (1867) 168-176.

29   Hollenbach, "A Communitarian Reconstruction," 131.

30   David Brooks, "If It Feels Right..." *The New York Times* (September 13, 2001) http://nytimes.com/ 2011/09/13/if-it-feels-right.html?, accessed September 17, 2011. See Christian Smith, et al., *Lost in Transition: The Dark Side of Emerging Adulthood* (New York: Oxford University Press, 2011).

31   Hollenbach, "A Communitarian Reconstruction,"138-139.

32   See the strong critique of the role of autonomous freedom as the social norm in Joseph Ratzinger, "Freedom and Constraint in the Church," in *Church, Ecumenism and Politics: New Essays in Ecclesiology* (New York: Crossroads, 1988) 182-203.

by its very nature stands completely in need of social life. This social life is not something added on to human beings. Hence, through dealings with others, through reciprocal duties, and through fraternal dialogue they develop all their gifts and rise to their destiny.[33]

For this human flourishing to occur "more than an individualistic ethic is required,"[34] and the fundamental demands of such an ethic are accessible to human reason.[35]

While rights have figured prominently in recent Catholic social teaching, these rights are not as disconnected from correlative duties as they often have become in the secular world. Rather, "the responsibilities of social living," fulfillment of one's duties to others and to the common good of one's society, are Catholic social teaching's point of departure.[36] Rights enter the discussion not as individualistic and ultimately selfish claims on society but as "the minimum conditions for life in community,"[37] i.e., as what is required for each person to enjoy at least the "minimum level of participation in the life of the human community" consistent with his or her dignity as a member of the community.[38] Since these rights are exercised in community, they may not legitimately be exercised in a way that violates the rights of others or that jeopardizes public peace or public morality.[39] The Church does not recognize a zone of legally protected autonomy within which individuals can choose whether to act in accord with the objective norms of morality. To put it bluntly, there is never a right to do wrong, and civil authorities not only can but should enshrine the demands of public morality in legislation. Since the highest end of the Church's own law is the *salus animarum*, canon law cannot easily countenance claims that rights authorize members of the faithful to engage in behavior that is contrary to objective moral norms and that, therefore, jeopardizes their eternal salvation.

The Church's slow but selective warming to the role of human right in society was eventually followed by its recognition of rights in the Church itself. However, these rights too cannot be properly understood as individualistic claims *against* the Church but only as claims *within* the Church that empower the members of the faithful to participate in the life and mission of the Church in ac-

---

33   Vatican II, pastoral constitution *Gaudium et spes*, §25: *AAS* 58 (1966) 1045.

34   Ibid., subheading to §30; *AAS* 58 (1966) 1049: "*Quod ultra individualisticam ethicam progrediendum sit.*"

35   Ibid., §16.

36   Hollenbach, "A Communitarian Reconstruction," 141

37   National Conference of Catholic Bishops, *Economic Justice for All: Pastoral Letter on Catholic Social Teaching and the U.S. Economy* (Washington, DC: NCCB, 1986) n. 79, section title.

38   Ibid. n. 77.

39   Vatican II, decree *Dignitatis humanae*, §7.

cordance with each one's proper condition and function.[40] In the Church too, "in exercising their right the Christian faithful, both as individuals and when gathered in associations, must take account of the common good of the Church and of the rights of others as well as their own duties toward others." (c. 223, §1) Paramount among these duties of the Christian faithful is "the obligation, even in their own patterns of activity, always to maintain communion with the Church" (c. 209, §1). In cases of conflict, ecclesial communion always trumps the merely private good of an individual.

B. *Priority to the Individual Good or the Common Good?*

1. The Modern Option for the Individual Good

The primacy the modern social imaginary gives to autonomous freedom entails a commitment to insuring the freedom of individuals to choose their own "vision of the good life."[41] In a pluralistic society, there will inevitably be a multiplicity of different, sometimes inconsistent, often conflicting, and occasionally even irreconcilable visions of the good life. The emphasis the regnant social imaginary places on equality entail that no individual's vision of the good life can be given preference by society to any other individual's.

> To favor one conception of the good over another is to favor some persons over others and to treat them unequally. Thus respect for the worth of individuals requires tolerance for the different visions of the good life they hold. In this way, affirming the equality of persons is linked with being non-judgmental about what ways of life are good, at least in public and political life. In public life, all encompassing understandings of the common good must be subordinated to the importance of tolerance.[42]

Interference with an individual's private pursuit of happiness can only be justified when that pursuit impinges on the rights of others. The practical implications of this insistence on respecting the autonomy of others in their choice of what constitutes the good life are clear in the oft cited majority opinion of Justice Kennedy in the 1992 case of Planned Parenthood v. Casey, which barred governmental interference in a woman's right to choose abortion because:

> These matters involving the most intimate and personal choices a person may make in a lifetime, are central to the liberty protected

---

40   Helmut Pree, "Esercizio della potestà e diritti dei fedeli," in *I Principi per la revisione del Codice di Diritto Canonico: La Ricezione giuridica del Concilio Vaticano II*, ed. Javier Canosa (Milan: Giuffré Editore 2000) 332.

41   Hollenbach, "A Communitarian Reconstruction," 131.

42   Hollenbach, *The Common Good and Christian Ethics* (Cambridge: Cambridge University Press, 2002) 10.

by the Fourteenth Amendment. At the heart of liberty is the right to define one's own concept of existence, of meaning, of the universe, and of the mystery of human life. Beliefs about these matters could not define the attributes of personhood were they formed under the compulsion of the State.[43]

In the midst of intractably "conflicting views of what ultimately matters" and in the absence of any legitimate arbiter of these conflicts, "human rights become the conditions necessary for them to cooperate in public, while pursuing their visions of the full human good in private."[44]

Since the modern social imaginary begins with "unencumbered" individuals, those rooted in it can be tempted to see social relations as accidental accoutrements of personality and to define the problem of social life in terms of the Hobbesian dilemma of "how to induce or force the individual into some kind of social order, make him conform and obey the rules."[45] Agnostic about the knowability or even the existence of a common good, those in the thrall of the modern social imaginary can only give primacy to the good of individuals, taken singly or collectively.[46]

---

43 Planned Parenthood v. Casey, 505 U.S. 833 (1992).

44 Hollenbach, "A Communitarian Reconstruction," 134. For those imbued with the modern social imaginary, the fact of pluralism necessitates dealing with disagreements about what constitutes the genuine human good by what John Rawls has called "the method of avoidance." In other words, "we try, so far as we can, neither to assert nor to deny any religious, philosophical or moral views or their associated philosophical accounts of truth and the status of values." Avoidance of such ultimate questions is necessary because resolution of them is simply impossible. Thus, the liberal vision is ultimately agnostic about the existence of an objective common good and insistent that it is unknowable even if it exists.

45 Taylor, *Modern Social Imaginaries*, 18.

46 In the absence of any consensus about the requirements of the common good and pervasive skepticism about our ability to know this good, societies must be content to pursue policies which promote the "general welfare," "a largely economic and utilitarian concept" which "sums up the economic welfare of individual members of society into one aggregate sum" like the gross national product. Hollenbach, *The Common Good and Christian Ethics*, 7. However, the general welfare so defined not only reduces the good to economic well being but, by concentrating only on aggregates, overlooks how this economic good is distributed among the society's members. Thus, this aggregate "general" good can expand while substantial segments of society fall into poverty or otherwise left behind. As a result, some have proposed using the "public interest" as an alternative to the "general welfare" as an index of the social good. "The idea of the public interest builds upon the modern commitment to the fundamental dignity and rights of all persons. Protection of these rights is seen as in everyone's interest. Public institutions and policies that will secure these rights for all persons are thus seen as helping to realize the interests of everyone. Understood this way, the public interest is a disaggregative concept. It breaks down the public good into the effects it has on the well-being or rights of the individual

2. The Church's Option for the Common Good

The social teaching of the Catholic Church and the social imaginary out of which that teaching arises follows the classic tradition of Aristotle and Aquinas in giving priority to the common good of society to the private good of its individual members. As Aristotle insisted in the *Nichomachean Ethics*:

> For even if the good of the community coincides with that of the individual, it is clearly a greater and more perfect thing to achieve and preserve that of the community; for while it is desirable to secure what is good in the case of an individual, to do so in the case of a people or a state is something finer and more sublime.[47]

For the Catholic tradition, social connections between and among members of society are not extrinsic to but constitutive of the individual persons who make up a society. Humans can only become persons, authentic moral agents, in community. "One of the key elements of the common good of a community or society ... is the good of being a community or society at all. This shared good is immanent within the relationships that bring this community or society into being."[48]

In a society vastly larger and more pluralistic than any *polis* Aristotle could have known or imagined and even more diverse than the relatively homogeneous medieval West of Thomas Aquinas, the Church recognizes that there will inevitably be different and even at times conflicting visions of what the common good really is. Nonetheless, the Church has remained confident that those sharing a life together in community can slowly arrive at an understanding of "the good life that could not have been envisioned apart from these connections."[49] Individuals can only hope to achieve their own good while pursuing of the common good of their societies "through dealings with others, through reciprocal duties, and through fraternal dialogue."[50] Indeed, they may at times have to sacrifice the pursuit of their own personal goals and goods for the sake of the common good. As a result, their exercise of their rights cannot be unilateral demands directed at their societies but must be consistent with and promote the common good. When the exercise of individual rights, even as fundamental a right as religious liberty,

---

who make up society." Ibid., 7-8. Although the notion of the "public good" moves beyond the exclusively utilitarian and economic focus of the concept of the "general welfare," it still remains ultimately individualistic since it concerns itself only with goods that are external or extrinsic to the relationships of members of the community or society with one another. Ibid., 8.

47   Aristotle, *The Nichomachean Ethics*, 1094b. Translated by J.A.K. Thomson (London: Penguin Books, 1994) 4-5.

48   Hollenbach, *The Common Good and Christian Ethics*, 9.

49   Ibid., 18.

50   *Gaudium et spes*, §25.

is disruptive of or threatening to the common good it is the right and obligation of competent authorities to restrict or moderate the exercise of these rights.[51]

Although the teaching of the Second Vatican Council and of subsequent popes as well as the norms of the revised Code of Canon Law recognize numerous rights and obligations of the faithful in the Church, these rights too must be exercised with an eye to the common good of the Church. In secular society, charters of rights are often viewed as carving out zones for individual autonomy, protecting individuals from interference by the State, and limiting the scope of governmental authority. However, such a way of conceiving rights in the Church has met with widespread rejection. Rights are recognized in the Church to empower the faithful to participate in the life of the ecclesial community. Since they exist to serve, not to challenge, the common good of the Church, these rights cannot be legitimately exercised in ways that undermine that common good.[52] Indeed, individuals may even have the moral duty to refrain from exercising their rights if to do so would jeopardize the common good. Ecclesiastical authority exists for service to the common good of the Church. Therefore, "In the interest of the common good, ecclesiastical authority has competence to regulate the exercise of the rights which belong to the Christian faithful." (c. 223, §2)

C. *Members as Active Agents or Passive Subjects?*

1. The Modern Social Imaginary: Active Agents

Those steeped in the modern social imaginary almost spontaneously see themselves as "masters of their fates and captains of their souls" whose destinies are "not in their stars but in themselves."[53] In other words, they

> see themselves as agents, who, through disengaged, disciplined action, can transform their own lives as well as the larger social order. They are buffered, disciplined selves. Free agency is central to their self-understanding. The emphasis on rights and the primacy of freedom among them doesn't just stem from the principle that society should exist for the sake of its members; it also reflects the holder's sense of their own agency and of the situation that agency demands in the world, namely, freedom.[54]

---

51   *Dignitatis humanae*, §7.

52   Charles J. Scicluna, "'Bonum Commune Ecclesiae' As a Criterion for Regimen and the Exercise of Rights in the 1983 Code of Canon Law," in *Iustitia et Iudicium: Studi di diritto matrimonial e processuale canonico in onore di Antoni Stankiewicz*, ed. Janusz Kowal and Joaquin Llobell (Vatican City: Libreria Editrice Vaticana, 2010) 3:1267-1292.

53   Taylor, *A Secular Age* (Cambridge, MA: Belknap Press of Harvard University, 2007) 38.

54   Taylor, *Modern Social Imaginaries*, 21.

This sense of individual agency extends to the order of society itself. The modern social imaginary not only stresses the "idea of society as existing for the (mutual) benefit of individuals and the defense of their rights"[55] but views this ideal as "one not yet realized, but demanding to be integrally carried out, ... an imperative prescription."[56] Societal structures are meant to serve these ends of mutual service and mutual respect and are to be judged instrumentally on how well or how poorly they serve them. If they fail or are deficient, they need to be changed.

Implicit in this instrumental approach to social structures is a firm conviction that any

> distribution of functions a society might develop is deemed contingent; it will be justified or not instrumentally; it cannot itself define the good. The basic normative principle is, indeed, that the members of society serve each other's needs, help each other, in short, behave like the rational and sociable creatures they are. In this way, they complement each other. But the particular functional differentiation they need to take on to do this most effectively is endowed with no essential worth. It is adventitious and potentially changeable.[57]

The modern social imaginary's rejection of the notion that there is a normative order of hierarchically coordinated and complementary social roles deep in the nature of things has, on a more practical level, left those imbued with it impatient with rules no matter how hallowed and roles no matter how traditional that seem to stand in the way of achieving equality and the full flowering of rights. Since all members of society are equal, each individual should enjoy an equal voice in charting the community's direction. As a result, governance that ignores or marginalizes the governed is likely to be perceived as lacking legitimacy.

2. Traditional Social Imaginary: Passive Subjects

Traditional Catholic social teaching as it was articulated by Leo XIII and his immediate successors was nostalgic for a State that was, quite frankly, moderately authoritarian and decidedly paternalistic. After a long period of opposition and resistance, however, the Church has now made its peace with modern notions of democracy and popular sovereignty in the political realm[58] and has

---

55   Taylor, *A Secular Age*, 160.

56   Ibid., 162.

57   Taylor, *Modern Social Imaginaries*, 12.

58   See Charles Curran, *Catholic Social Teaching, 1891--Present: A Historical, Theological and Ethical Analysis* (Washington: Georgetown University Press, 2002) 146-149 and Michael Lacey, "Leo's Church and Our Own," in *The Crisis of Authority in Catholic Modernity*, ed. Michael Lacey and Francis Oakley (New York: Oxford University Press, 2011) 57-92.

adapted, sometimes begrudgingly, to the sometimes dramatic changes in social roles resulting from the marginalization of social hierarchies and the leveling emphasis on equality in the social realm. However, the Church has never backed away from its insistence that the Church's own hierarchical structure is a matter of divine law and, therefore, immutable. The Church's own self-understanding is embedded in what is essentially a pre-modern social imaginary. Although the Church frames its self-understanding in the category, imagery and language of theology rather than those of the social sciences, it is clear that the theological articulation of the ecclesial order has a profound affinity with other pre-modern social orders. Like these other orders, the Church understands its own order to be based on a Law "which has governed this people [of God] since time out of mind and which, in a sense, defines it as a people."[59] As a result, Church authorities are quick to invoke divine law or the will of Christ for his Church as a warrant for resisting encroachments of the modern social imaginary and insisting that "the Church is not a democracy."

Like the laws of other pre-modern social orders, the divine law of the Church defines it as a society whose hierarchical order corresponds to and embodies a hierarchy in the heavens. Just as Christ is head of his Body the Church so the ordained are conformed to and act *in persona Christi capitis* in teaching, sanctifying and governing the faithful on earth. The organic metaphors associated with an understanding of the Church as the Body of Christ lend themselves to seeing the Church as an organism in which functions and roles are clearly allocated and differentiated. In modern societies differentiations of roles and functions are contingent and functional; in the Church, however, they are normative and ontological.

> It is crucial to this kind of ideal that the distribution of functions is itself a key part of the normative order. It is not just that each order should perform its characteristic function for the others, ... while we keep open the possibility that things might be arranged rather differently. ... No, the hierarchical differentiation itself is seen as the proper order of things. It [is] part of the nature or form of society.[60]

The Church's commitment to this normative and hierarchical differentiation of functions in its own social order is reflected in the Magisterium's continued insistence that the difference between the priesthood of the ordained and the common priesthood of all the baptized is ontological and not merely instrumental, and its nervous warnings and interventions to head off encroachments of the non-ordained on the proper functions of the ordained in the name of equality or even on pragmatic grounds.[61] The continued dominance of a pre-modern social

---

59   Taylor, *Modern Social Imaginaries*, 9.
60   Ibid., 11.
61   See, for example, Congregation for the Clergy, et. al., instruction *Ecclesiae de mys-*

imaginary with its ontologically determined normative roles is the most plausible explanation, for example, for the recent insistence that, despite the impracticality of the rubric, ordained ministers and not lay extraordinary ministers are to purify the chalices after communion has been distributed under both species.[62]

Where such a pre-modern social imaginary prevails, the function of a society's law is not primarily to construct a just social order in which the basic rights of members are recognized and guaranteed but to conserve and, if necessary, restore the normative hierarchical order whose maintenance is itself essential for the common good of society. In such an order, concern for protecting the rights of members may not be the highest social priority but it need not be a matter of social indifference. Although the Church has not accepted the liberal vision of rights as above all guarantees of individual autonomy, it has more or less consistently viewed rights as the minimum conditions for a person's active participation in the life of his or her community so "that the true nature of the common good of the community might be more adequately understood and pursued."[63] In construing rights in this way, the Church's social teaching has implicitly acknowledged that the concrete demands of the common good, while accessible to human reason, are not already known but must be sought through dialogue and inquiry in which all the members of the community are entitled to participate and respect for the right of members is critical to their ability to participate in a meaningful way in this communal discernment.

II. Rights Consciousness in the Church: No Merely Imaginary Differences

Considered individually, these differences between the modern social imaginary that prevails in most of the Western world and is reflected in contemporary secular legal systems and the pre-modern social imaginary that continued to orient thinking in the Church and in which canon law is embedded are not sufficient to reduce the revised Code's to reduce the rights enshrined in the Church's law to mere ideals or even to rhetorical "fluff." No society however secular can long survive unless some measure of communal morality is widely accepted and serves as an effective restraint on the exercise of rights.[64] No modern secular society exempts members from sanctions for violations of laws enshrining precepts of the community's morality because they claim to act under the color of rights. No one has a right to commit murder, physical assault, offenses against property,

---

terio, August 15, 1997: *AAS* 89 (1997) 852-877.

62   *Institutio generalis Missalis romani*, April 29, 2000, §284; Congregation for Divine Worship and the Discipline of the Sacraments, instruction *Redemptionis Sacramentum*, §107, March 25, 2004: *AAS* 96 (2004) 580.

63   Hollenbach, "A Communitarian Reconstruction," 143.

64   See Charles Taylor, *Sources of the Self: The Making of Modern Identity* (Cambridge, MA: Harvard University Press, 1990) 3-24 and Jürgen Habermas, "Pre-Political Foundations of the Democratic Constitutional State," in *The Dialectics of Secularization: One Reason and Religion*, ed. Florian Schuller (San Francisco: Ignatius Press, 2006) 19-52.

and libel. Nor is respect for rights in modern societies threatened by their insistence that people carry out their duties to others and to society at large, as we in the United States are reminded every April 15.

Although those embedded in the modern social imaginary find it difficult, if not impossible, to identify their society's common good, they all recognize that individual rights, even the most fundamental of rights, are not absolute and must cede to the needs of the larger society. In the United States, for example, courts have upheld the right of governmental authorities to impinge on personal freedoms in the public interest, but they have also required these authorities to demonstrate that it really is the public interest and not mere administrative expedience or even administrative convenience that requires the abridgement of individual rights and that the government's proposed action is the least restrictive method available for securing the public good.[65] Even commitment to a hierarchically structured social order does not necessarily eviscerate the society's commitment to protecting individual right. Almost all societies, even the most democratic, develop some kind of hierarchical structure to maintain to avert anarchy and insure the maintenance of social peace, including the protection of the rights of the vulnerable. However, when commitment to public morality, duties and the common good is embedded in a rigidly hierarchical structure in which relations of complementarity override intimations of equality and in which relations of genuine reciprocity between the hierarchical authorities and the rest of society are lacking or atrophied, concern for rights easily becomes a peripheral concern or, in Provost's phrase "mere fluff.". Such is the case in the Catholic Church at the present time.

A. *Priority of Complementarity Over Equality*

The relative indifference to the rights of the ordinary faithful inherent in the pre-modern social imaginary is exacerbated when, as is the case in the Church, this imaginary is given legal articulation in the form of a code conceived and structured according to the continental European model. Of its nature, the code model of legislating tends to radicalize the dichotomy between the active governing authority and the passive governed. Long ago, Ulrich Stutz observed that, in the 1917 code, "The Church is the Church of the clergy" in which "the laity appear to enjoy only the rights accorded to protected residents, while the clergy enjoy full citizenship."[66] While the 1983 code has affirmed the fundamental equality of all the faithful and laid out a charter of rights enjoyed by all the faithful in the Church, it has also retained the code model which still juxtaposes the ordained and the non-ordained. The inherent logic of such a code is to treat the Church as a means to an end, that end being the salvation of individual souls.

---

65 See the discussion in David Alan Zwifka, *Regulation of the Rights of Individuals for the Common Good: An Analysis of Canon 223, 2 in Light of American Constitutional Law*, Canon Law Studies 552 (Washington, DC: Catholic University of America, 1997).

66 Ulrich Stutz, *Der Geist des Codex Iuris Canonici* (Stuttgart: F. Enke, 1918) 83-88.

Even the revised Code reflects a Church in which "over against the clergy, who represent the institution and administer the goods of salvation, there are only individual Christians. The starting point is found in the individual to be saved. ... and not in the Church, sacramental of salvation."[67] The result is a spiritual individualism every bit as radical as the individualism the Church's magisterial authorities regularly decry in secular society.

This individualism fostered by the legally enshrined hierarchical complementarity between governing clergy and governed faithful undermines the foundations for any structured reciprocity between the two. In other words, the Church so structured easily becomes

> One whose administration is almost entirely withdrawn from the control of its members. The relations between hierarchy and faithful are a one-way street: of governors over against the governed, of the teachers over against the taught and of the celebrants [of the liturgy] over against the spectators.[68]

Despite all the glowing rhetoric about the equality of the faithful based on baptism and the rights of the baptized in the Church, it is difficult to speak meaningfully about equality and rights in an ecclesial society in which "the laity, who represent the overwhelming majority of the baptized, are kept aloof from the decisions of some importance which affect them."[69]

B. *Priority of the Common Good*

Rights within the Church are understood not as claims of individual autonomy but as empowerments for the faithful to participate in the life and mission of the Church in accord with each one's condition and function. However, in making this transition from rights in society to rights in the Church, Church authorities have not always exhibited the same humility that Catholic social teaching has about the extent to which the concrete demands of the common good are already known to those who wield authority.

Canonical commentators have frequently noted not only that the exercise of rights in the Church must serve the common good but also that it is an essential dimension of the service character of ecclesiastical authority to serve the common good. In service to the common good, ecclesiastical authority has the duty and right to moderate the exercise of rights by the faithful in the interest of the

---

67 Hervé-Marie Legrand, "Grâce et institution dans l'Èglise: Les fondements théologique du droit canonique," in *L'Èglise institution et foi* (Brussel: Publications des Facultés Universitaire Saint-Louis, 1979) 152.

68 Legrand, 148.

69 Charles Wackenheim, "L'influence des modèles juridique sur la théologie catholique," *Revue de Droit Canonique* 39 (1989) 41.

common good. However, when the ecclesiastical authority competent to discern what constitutes the common good and its concrete requirements in particular contexts is the same authority competent to moderate the exercise of rights by subjects when they seem out of harmony with these requirements, it is easy for decisions to restrict or ignore rights to be based on merely institutional advantage or the authority's preferences or "comfort level" rather than a genuine discernment of the common good. If it illustrates nothing else, the ongoing clergy sexual abuse scandal at least shows how badly mistaken church authorities acting unilaterally can be about what constitutes the common good of the Church. Moreover, those whose exercises of rights are moderated by ecclesiastical authorities have no entitlement to be part of the process of discussion and dialogue that leads to the determination of the demands of the common good. Nor do the faithful have any very effective remedy against decisions by ecclesiastical authorities to moderate their exercises of rights. In practice, the hierarchical authorities who decide recourses against administrative acts accord enormous deference to their subordinates' discretionary determinations of the requirements of the common good, except in cases of the most egregious abuse of discretion.

When it is claimed that the common good is at issue, there has been a tendency to invest the actions of hierarchical authorities to moderate the exercise of rights of the faithful with a status analogous to that of their authentic but non-infallible statements on matters of doctrine. The faithful "are bound to adhere with religious submission of mind to the authentic magisterium of their bishops" (c. 753) not only when they teach matters of doctrine but even when they propose "prudential application[s] of church teaching based upon 'contingent and conjectural' elements."[70] In a similar way, although the faithful have the right to make their needs known to their pastors and even "according to the knowledge, competence, and prestige which they possess," to manifest to their pastors "their opinion on matters which pertain to the good of the Church" (c. 212 §§2-3), they are "bound to follow with Christian obedience those things which the sacred pastors, inasmuch as they represent Christ, declare as teachers of the faith or establish as rulers of the Church" (c. 212,= §1). In the absence of any truly independent review of decisions based on appeals to the common good, the exercise of rights by the faithful has been left in large measure to the discretion of ecclesiastical authorities.

C. *Priority of Duties Over Rights*

While the enjoyment of rights does not exempt one from fulfilling ones duties to other individuals and to society itself, the obligation of the faithful, "even in their own manner of acting ... to maintain communion with the Church" (c. 209 §1) can be, and in fact sometimes has been, cited as a justification for restricting the exercise of rights by the faithful. Church leaders, both past and present, have

---

[70] Kevin O'Rourke, "Rights of Conscience: Responding to a Bishop's Disciplinary Decision," *America* 205:3 (August 1-8, 2011) 15.

exhibited little sympathy with or tolerance for expressions of disagreement with policies and decisions of hierarchical authorities. Even when these challenges and disagreements purport to be based on rights, they are often scored as damaging to ecclesiastical *communion* and, therefore, illegitimate.[71] There is a tendency among those who are quick to invoke the demands of *communio* as a reason for squelching exercises of rights they find inconvenient or uncomfortable to see unity understood as uniformity as the paramount value of ecclesial *communio* and to insist on imposing consensus not only in doctrine but even in discipline from above instead of allowing it to emerge from below through discussion and dialogue. The Church with its penchant for articulating its self-understanding in organic metaphors needs to be wary of the dangers of excessive demands for unity. As John Gray recently observed, "A fantasy of German Romanticism..., the dream of organic social unity has always been repressive in practice. And this is not because the ideal has been wrongly interpreted. Hostility to minorities is the very logic of organicist ideology."[72]

In a legal order like that of canon law where there is no very bright line between law and morality, it is easy to drift into the sort of "legal moralism" for which disagreement with policies or decisions is construed as disobedience and or "[d]isobedience is betrayal, an offense against the community as such, and its gravity bears little or no relation to whether or how seriously particular interests are injured."[73] Where such "legal moralism" holds sway, authority in the Church may be inclined to dismiss those who exercise their rights in ways that challenge official positions or disagree with decisions of authority as disloyal and disobedient and thereby attempt to delegitimize their exercise of rights itself. As Joseph Komanchak has pointed out, invocations of *communio* sometimes do little more than "exploit it ideologically, covering with its spiritual and mystical connotations an ecclesiological theory and an ecclesial practice that do not differ substantially from the old *societas perfecta* notion."[74] This ideological exploita-

---

71   See Carlos José Errázuriz, *Justice in the Church: A Fundamental Theory of Canon Law*, Collection Gratianus (Montreal: Wilson and Lafleur, 2009) 242-243: "The very juridical good of liberty in the Church requires the juridical good of discipline, not only in order to introduce the due limits to liberty, but also in order to make liberty itself more effective.... Basically, what is at stake in discipline is first of all the great good of unity in the Church. This unity cannot be limited to what is essential (of divine law), but comprises inseparably the necessary agreement on everything that at all times and in all places is required for the good of the Church. "

72   John Gray, "The Return of an Illusion: A Review of Why Marx Was Right by Terry Eagleton and How to Change the World: Tales of Marx by Eric Hobsbawm," *The New Republic* (July 14, 2011) 27. See also Nancy L. Rosenblum, *On the Side of the Angels: An Appreciation of Parties and partisanship* (Princeton, NJ: Princeton University Press, 2008) 25-59.

73   Philipe Nonet and Philip Selznick, *Law and Society in Transition: Toward Responsive Law* (New Brunswick, NJ: Transaction, 2001) 47.

74   Joseph Komanchak, "Concepts of Communion. Past and Present," *Christianismo*

tion of *communio* can sometimes be seen in the not so subtle identification of "the Church" with its hierarchical authorities that occurs when these authorities brush aside as illegitimate exercises of rights by the faithful that challenge or question their decisions simply because the faithful have rights "in the Church" not rights "against the Church" as if hierarchical authorities were identical with "the Church" and the faithful were some kind of illegal aliens.

IV. Conclusion

As we approach the twenty-ninth anniversary of the promulgation of the 1983 Code of Canon Law, it is hard to see that the much has changed since Jim Provost addressed this society in Minneapolis twelve years ago. Now as then, "the most realistic evaluation of rights in the Church is that, at the present time, they are at most an ideal..., at times they may even qualify as 'fluff.'"[75] In retrospect, it was probably a bit naïve to think that the rights culture with which we are familiar in North American culture would materialize immediately and automatically with the appearance of a revised code. If we canonists are going to foster a rights culture in the Church, we are going to have to disengage ourselves from our own deeply ingrained social imaginaries and learn to think about rights in ecclesial society the way the Church does. To make progress we need to *sentire cum Ecclesia.*

The somewhat disappointing experience of the last several years does not mean that concern for rights in the Church was stillborn. The rights of the faithful remain embedded, indelibly embedded, in the law of the Church. The tendency of ecclesial thinking to balance rights with duties, to give priority to the common good over the individual good, and to see rights less as claims to autonomous freedom than as empowerments for participation in the life of the Church does not doom rights to being "fluff" or even mere ideals. Concern for the common good does not mean that rights are meaningless as long as there are institutions empowered and willing to subject claims that the common good requires abridgement of rights to critical scrutiny. Treating rights less as claims to autonomy than as empowerments for participation does not doom rights to oblivion as long as the community actually wants all of its members to participate actively in its life and mission in accord with their condition and function. Disagreements, especially those which deal with policy and not doctrine, are not in themselves threats to unity or to *communio* as long as all participants are open to continue the dialogue and refuse to demonize one another.

Respect for the rights of the faithful enables them to participate in the life of the Church and so promotes and strengthens ecclesial communion. As a result, it is a critical way in which we recognize the faithful as valued members of the community and allows them to see themselves as valued members. Fostering and

---

nella storia 16 (1995) 339.
75   Provost and Torf, "Rights in Canon Law," 341-342.

strengthening this sense of communion is not just a noble ideal but a practical necessity in our day. Since the nineteenth century, the Church has been active in what Charles Taylor calls "mobilizing the faithful," mobilizing them to restore Catholic life where it had been disrupted by the French Revolution, mobilizing them protect it where it was threatened by Kuturkampf, and mobilizing them to build it from scratch where it had never before existed as in North America. Whether it was to raise funds to build and maintain churches and parish plants, to found and operate educational and charitable institutions, to organize a network of social service agencies, to march and lobby on behalf of civil rights or an end to abortion, or to foster deeper piety and spirituality "the Catholic Church has unavoidably been in the business of mobilizing... , organizing and recruiting people into membership organizations with some definite purpose. But this means new forms of collective action, created by the participants themselves....[76]

More recently, the Church has been active in mobilizing the faithful not just for causes outside the Church or peripheral to its life and mission, but for activities central to its mission. The Church's teaching mission from its prestigious universities to its smallest parish religious education programs is largely in the hands of dedicated lay people; with only a few exceptions, the Church's liturgical life, the principal form in which its sanctifying mission is carried out, depends critically on the active engagement of a host of talented and dedicated "lay ministers;" even Church governance, long the last bastion of the clerical monopoly, has been infiltrated by lay professionals. Recognition and protection of the rights of the faithful is essential if this mobilization is to continue. The surest way to cause these dedicated and engaged members of the faithful to disengage themselves is by high-handed paternalism that sends the message that, despite lots of pious rhetoric to the contrary, they are not really valued members of the ecclesial community. To paraphrase Charles Taylor, there is something inherently contradictory about trying to have "a Church tightly held together by a strong hierarchical authority" that is simultaneously "filled with practitioners of heartfelt devotion."[77]

---

[76] Taylor, *A Secular Age*, 445.
[77] Ibid., 466.

Major Address

Parish Reconfiguration:
Protection of Rights of Bishops and Parishes
Very Reverend Lawrence A. DiNardo

I. Introduction

First, may I take this opportunity to express my appreciation to the Board of Governors and the Convention Planning Committee for offering me the opportunity to present a reflection on *Parish Reconfiguration: Protection of Rights of Bishops and Parishes* at this assembly of the Canon Law Society of America. The topic is significant since it touches both our personal as well as professional lives. In my own experience, the parish of my baptism, confirmation, first communion and first Mass was merged with a neighboring parish with the church being sold as possible apartments for senior citizens. In my professional life as a canonist, I have been involved not only in my own diocese but consulted with other dioceses regarding parish reconfiguration.

The closing address to this august body gathered here in Jacksonville is, as in any convention, a challenge. This is the third time that I have been invited to offer the closing address at a convention. How does one offer a reflection at a time when most of us, including this speaker, is thinking of being on our way back home to continue our work and catch up on the many issues and correspondence (e-mail and snail mail) that has been placed on our desks while we have shared a few days together updating ourselves and catching up with old friends and hopefully making new ones.

When I was first asked to offer this reflection, I wondered why me? I am not a professor of canon law, I have not written extensively in this area of the law, and I am by no means a scholar. I am, however, a continual student of the law and a practitioner of canon law for almost thirty-four years in diocesan administration, and additionally, for the past twenty-four years as a pastor in two parishes. I have been involved as a canonist in diocesan reorganization, a pastor of a parish assisting parishioners in merging with a neighboring parish and now the founding pastor of a merged and reorganized parish. It is with this background that I believe the Convention Planning Committee asked that I offer some reflections on this topic that is so important in diocesan ministry. In order that this presentation might not simply be an exercise is some philosophical or esoteric discussion, I thought that I might begin these remarks with a personal story.

In the winter of 1989 Bishop (now Cardinal) Donald Wuerl, the present Archbishop of Washington, convened what was known as the Administrative Board of the Diocese of Pittsburgh. This board was made up of the senior level administrators in our diocesan administration (e.g. the Vicars General, Episcopal Vicars, Secretariat Heads, General Counsel, and Chancellor) to discuss a topic which would eventually be a monumental moment in diocesan history. The topic for discussion was the Reorganization and Revitalization of Parishes within the Diocese of Pittsburgh.

This topic had been raised by the priest council of the diocese in the fall of 1988 when the priests presented concerns regarding the ever increasing assignment of priests to multiple pastoral assignments (two or three parishes pastored by one priest). The priest council had requested that the diocesan bishop do something about this alarming trend and "close" some of those small parishes, especially in the city and what we in Western Pennsylvania call the "river" towns. The priest council sought action on this issue and asked the diocesan bishop for some immediate relief. Thus, the purpose of the administrative board discussion was to discern whether the request had merit and, if so, how we could respond in an adequate and timely fashion.

The discussions at the administrative board, to the best of my recollection, centered on how to get this done quickly and without much fanfare. There were those who said that canon 515 §2 of the *Code of Canon Law* permits the diocesan bishop to "erect, suppress, or alter parishes" provided he "has heard the presbyteral council."[1] This simple action would seem to make the process very efficient. Just gather a list of the parishes to be suppressed, present them to the priest council, elicit their counsel and then issue decrees suppressing those parishes and the issue is resolved.

There were others, including this canonist, who questioned the wisdom of such an action. What about the rights of the parishes and the faithful of the parishes that would be proposed for closure? Another member of the staff reminded me that while the code has some procedure to vindicate one's rights in the Church, the code did not provide any procedure for the protection or exercise of those rights. Therefore, in the absence of any procedure the author of the code did not envision a process regarding exercise but only a process for vindication, known as administrative recourse.

After a lively debate about these two views of how the diocese should go about considering the issue of reorganization, the administrative board recommended to the diocesan bishop that we embark on a five year process of parish reorganization which would be entitled: *The Parish Reorganization and Revital-*

---

1   Canon 515 §2: "It is for the diocesan bishop to erect, suppress, or alter parishes. He is neither to erect, suppress nor alter notably parishes, unless he has heard the presbyteral council."

ization Project. This recommendation was accepted by the diocesan bishop and the project began in 1989 and concluded in 1994.

In this presentation I have chosen to focus on the more pragmatic aspects of parish reconfiguration. I am grateful to the work of Roch Page in his article that appeared in *The Jurist* in 2007 entitled "The Future of Parishes and the Present Canonical Legislation" [2] and an article in *Studia Canonica* by James E. Coriden in 2010 entitled "Parish Communities and Reorganizations."[3] These articles have already provided us with a wealth of material on the topic of reorganization. Borrowing from their work and from my experience in reorganization of parishes, the focus of this paper will offer several insights: (1) a review of the rights of bishops and parishes as it relates to parish reorganization; (2) the question of how does one exercise these rights within the church; and, (3) some canonical considerations in parish reconfiguration. The topic is challenging. Let us begin.

II. Rights and Obligations of Bishops

Personal experience in the reorganization process brings about various views regarding the reasons for reorganization, the need for reorganization and whether or not there are rights to be protected and if so, is there a hierarchy of rights that need to be addressed in the reorganization of parishes within a diocese. The bishop of the diocese has his own reasons why reorganization is essential and critical for the future welfare and ability to care for souls within the particular church. The parish has the belief that the care for souls can be accomplished without any change in structure and if a change is necessary let some other parish be reorganized. Finally, individual parishioners desire to maintain the parish of their family heritage, baptism, first communion, confirmation, marriage and burial. There is even the hint that the financial needs of the diocese (e.g. payment for clergy sexual misconduct) are a reason for reorganization. Within the midst of these various views, what role do rights play? Does anyone even care?

Within the present *Code of Canon Law* the rights of bishops as they relate to parish reconfiguration are not clearly defined. Attempts have been made to organize a list of the rights of the bishop that might be operative in our consideration of parish reconfiguration. Specifically, what is the role of the bishop as it relates to parish structures and more importantly the care of the particular church entrusted to him? While the code does not offer what one might call an enumeration of the obligations and rights of the bishop as it related to parish reconfiguration, a cursory glance of the canons might assist us in assembling a listing for further consideration. For example:

---

2   Roch Page, "The Future of Parishes and the Present Canonical Legislation," *The Jurist 67* (2007) 176-193.

3   James A. Coriden, "Parish Communities and Reorganization," *Studia Canonica 44* (2010) 31-52.

1. Canon 381 reminds us that the diocesan bishop possesses all the ordinary, proper and immediate power which is required for the exercise of his pastoral office.[4]
2. Canon 383 reminds us that the bishop is to show concern for all the Christian Faithful committed to his care.[5]
3. In canon 391 we are told that the diocesan bishop is to rule the particular church committed to him with legislative, executive and juridical power in accord with the norms of law.[6]
4. Canon 394 states that the bishop is to foster the various aspects of the apostolate within his diocese and to see to it that within his diocese all the works of the apostolate are coordinated under his direction.[7]
5. Canon 515 informs us that only the bishop can erect, suppress or alter parishes. The canons also indicate to us that while the parish is entrusted to a pastor as it own shepherd this is done under the authority of the diocesan bishop.[8]
6. Canon 523 clearly establishes the diocesan bishop as the one who has the authority to provide for a parish by the appointment of a pastor.[9]
7. Canon 835 places the bishop as the center of sacramental life within the particular church,[10] and
8. Canon 1276 grants to the bishop the authority to supervise the temporal

---

[4] Canon 381 §1: "A diocesan bishop in the diocese entrusted to him has all ordinary, proper and immediate power which is required for the exercise of his pastoral function except for cases which the law or a decree of the Supreme Pontiff reserves to the supreme authority or to another ecclesiastical authority."

[5] Canon 383 §1: "In exercising the function of a pastor, a diocesan bishop is to show himself concerned for all the Christian faithful entrusted to his care, of whatever age, condition, or nationality they are, whether living in the territory or staying there temporarily; he is also to extend an apostolic spirit to those who are not able to make sufficient use of ordinary pastoral care because of the condition of their life and to those who no longer practice their religion."

[6] Canon 391 §1: "It is for the diocesan bishop to govern the particular church entrusted to him with legislative, executive, and judicial power according to the norm of law."

[7] Canon 394 §1: "A diocesan bishop is to foster various forms of the apostolate in the diocese and is to take care that in the entire diocese or in its particular districts, all the works of the apostolate are coordinated under his direction, with due regard for the proper character of each."

[8] Canon 515 §2: "It is for the diocesan bishop to erect, suppress, or alter parishes. He is neither to erect, suppress, not alter notably parishes, unless he has heard the presbyteral council."

[9] Canon 523: "Without prejudice to the prescript of can. 682 §1, the provision of the office of pastor belongs to the diocesan bishop, and indeed by free conferral, unless someone has the right of presentation or election."

[10] Canon 835 §1: "The bishops in the first place exercise the sanctifying function; they are the high priests, the principle dispensers of the mysteries of God, and the directors, promoters, and guardians of the entire liturgical life in the church entrusted to them."

goods of juridic persons subject to him (parishes) and to establish particular law to regulate the administration of the temporal goods of those juridic persons.[11]

While the canons do not, in any orderly fashion, delineate the rights, duties, and obligations of the bishop in regard to parish reconfiguration, it is obvious from just this brief overview that the major responsibilities of the bishop rests with ensuring that that the ministry of word and sacrament is proclaimed and administered to the faithful through the ministry of the priest, deacons and lay ecclesial ministers. This is done by organizing the diocese is such a way so that the various resources (human and temporal) can best serve the faithful and the mission of the universal church can be advanced in the particular church which has been entrusted to his care. This becomes his primary obligation since in the end the bishop will be obligated, in accordance with the provisions of canon 399, to make a report (*quinquennial*) to the Supreme Pontiff regarding the state of his diocese.[12]

III. Rights and Obligations of Parishes

The rights and obligations of parish communities has been the subject of much discussion especially as it relates to parish reconfiguration. As Father James Coriden states in his article: *Parish Communities and Reorganizations*, "while the code developed an unprecedented list of the rights and obligations of individual Catholics, the code did not establish any equivalent list of rights and obligations for parishes or other communities." In that same article, Father Coriden attempts to develop what he calls "a sort of bill of rights."[13] While he offers a lengthy list of these rights, I would like to comment on just four which seem relevant to our discussion regarding reconfiguration.

1. <u>Right of Existence:</u> Once a faith community has been formed and recognized as a juridic person in accordance with canon 512 §3,[14] it should be allowed to remain. This principle has been further articulated by the Congregation for the Clergy in its distinction between the concept of suppression

---

11   Canon 1276 §1: "It is for the ordinary to exercise careful vigilance over the administration of all the goods which belong to public juridic persons subject to him, without prejudice to legitimate titles which attribute more significant rights to him."

§2: "With due regard for rights, legitimate customs, and circumstances, ordinaries are to take care of the ordering of the entire matter of the administration of ecclesiastical goods by issuing special instructions within the limits of universal and particular law."

12   Canon 399 §1: "Every five years a diocesan bishop is bound to make a report to the Supreme Pontiff on the state of the diocese entrusted to him, according to the form and time determined by the Apostolic See."

13   Coriden, "Parish Communities and Reorganization," 40

14   Canon 515 §3: "A legitimately erected parish possesses juridi9c personality by the law itself."

of a parish and merger of parishes.[15] It makes the point that suppression of a parish applies to the situation in which no people exist and the territory is no longer inhabited, whereas the merger of parishes implies one parish being amalgamated into another parish or two or more parishes being brought together to form a new parish to serve either the territory or communities of the previous parishes.

2. <u>Right of Information, Communication and Consultation:</u> Members have the right to know about matters that will affect their community, whether those developments come from within or outside of the parish.[16] This right of information, communication and consultation is not simply a one way street of being given information but also allowing a forum for the expression of questions, comments and discernment about the future direction of the parish community by those who will be affected by decisions made by those in authority.

3. <u>Right to Own and Use Goods and Property</u>: Parishes have the right to acquire and make use of the properties and resources they need for their pastoral care and they have a duty to care for and administer the temporal goods of the parish.[17] While one might speak of the parish and its ownership of temporal goods, the seeming issue for many parishioners is a personal claim of ownership of the parish goods. This can come about in the form of claims of restricted gifts to the parish, or a claim of individual rights involving parish property.

4. <u>Right to Vindicate and Defend its Rights</u>: The parish has the right to vindicate (assert or claim) or defend (against encroachment or denial) its rights as a parish community.[18] We have seen from the *praxis curia* that such a defense can be done by individual members of the parish but they are unable to act as representatives of the parish. The assertions made by individuals does not imply that the parish agrees or desires to seek a vindication of an alleged violation of rights but only that the individuals in the parish who have lodged an appeal of the decision of the diocesan bishop seek a remedy.

While this brief enumeration of the rights of parish communities is not meant to be an exhaustive list but just a few highlights, it does present us with one of the more complicated issues that we face as canonists which is how does one,

---

15 Letter of the Congregation for the Clergy to the Most Reverend William Skylstad, president of the United States Conference of Catholic Bishops (Prot. N. 20060481), published as "Canon 123: Regarding the Suppression and Merger of Parishes," in *Roman Replies and CLSA Advisory Opinions 2006*, ed. Stephen Pedone and Paul D. Counce (Alexandria, VA: Canon Law Society of America, 2006) 13-15. The letter clarifies the correct application of canon 123 and states that what has commonly been called "suppression" of a parish is in reality a merger or amalgamation since the faithful remain in the territory.

16 Coriden, "Parish Communities and Reorganization," 42.

17 Ibid.

18 Ibid.

whether bishop or parishes, exercise these rights and what process, if any, can be employed to ensure that the rights that we believe are granted to all the Christian faithful can be exercised in our church.

IV. Exercising Rights in Parish Reconfiguration

Rights are a very interesting topic as one looks to the *Code of Canon Law*. In the process of revision, the code commission made several major attempts to articulate not only the rights of the Christian faithful but the method by which these rights could be exercised and vindicated within the Church. The history of the *lex fundamentalis*, a topic beyond the scope of this paper, is interesting in reviewing those efforts and indicates the difficulty in bringing into the universal Church, because of the great diversity of cultures and law, a sense that without a clear delineation of a process by which one (bishop, pastor, faithful, parish) can exercise rights, how does the Church guarantee that individuals fully exercise the rights that have been granted to them in the law of the Church?

Getting back to the story which I offered at the beginning of this presentation let me offer you our diocesan response to this question. How we can assure that the parishes and by extension, the faithful be engaged in a process that will affect their spiritual lives for years to come and at the same time ensure the proper use of diocesan resources (human and temporal) to help built the kingdom of God in our particular church.

In 1989 the Diocese of Pittsburgh committed itself to informing, engaging and responding to the needs of parishes in a process of reconfiguration. This commitment of communications and collaboration was built around a five phase *Model of Reorganization*.

The first phase was known as *Parish Self-Study*, a self assessment of the vitality of every parish in light of five central elements of the church's mission in and to the world, namely, community, worship, service, education and administration. In this phase every parish was to identify what areas of parish life were important to the community, what areas of parish life the parish believed it was accomplishing, what areas of parish life needed improvement and what areas of parish life needed to be changed? This task was accomplished by a survey being sent to every registered household of every parish in the diocese (at that time about 830,000 persons). The response to the survey was about 78%, an extremely high number of returns for surveys and an indication of the importance that people placed on the process.

The second phase was known as *Realistic Envisioning and Collaborative Decision Making*, a self assessment of the vitality of each parish in light of diocesan resources (human and temporal) and diocesan guidelines. These self-assessments were first to be accomplished within the individual parish and then within a defined cluster group. The assessments were either validated or challenged by a peer review board made up of pastors and parishioners of other parishes not directly related to the cluster or parish under consideration. This resulted in some parishes being identified as in need of some form of reconfiguration.

The third phase was known as *Realistic Envisioning – Planning and Implementation*. This phase was marked by the development of parameters (e.g., number of available priests, financial constraints, present condition of church buildings, future financial costs for maintenance) for cluster planning and the development of specific plans for parish reorganization within a cluster. This phase was to prepare and document possible recommendations regarding parish reconfiguration which would be considered by the diocesan bishop. This could include several parishes being administered by one priest, several parishes being cared for by a team of priests and other lay ecclesial ministers, the merger of one or more parishes into one existing parish or the creation of a new parish from two or more parishes. The cluster planning team was responsible for preparing a plan, submitting that plan to the diocesan bishop and the implementation of the plan that would ultimately be approved by the diocesan bishop. It should be noted that in order to assist the cluster planning team, the canonical staff of the diocese had developed several critical documents to assist in the reorganization process. These included: guidelines for the scheduling of Sunday Mass; canonical guidelines for suppressing, erecting, merging and altering parishes; property disposition guidelines; financial guidelines and clergy distribution guidelines. These guidelines were complemented by other documents developed for reorganization such as: the parish complexity index, a clergy personnel profile, and a religious and lay ecclesial minister profile. All of these efforts were an attempt to provide parishioners with information that might assist them in making informed recommendations regarding parish reorganization.

The fourth phase was known as *Canonical Consultation*, a process by which the presbyteral council of the diocese would be engaged to offer counsel to the diocesan bishop regarding the recommendations that had been brought forth by the various cluster planning teams. Later in this paper, I will offer the process by which the presbyteral council was engaged in offering counsel to the diocesan bishop regarding specific recommendations.

The last phase was *Ongoing Evaluation, Revitalization and Spiritual Renewal*, a process which has not been completed to this day since we continue to evaluate our structures and parishes and make determinations as to what will best serve the needs of the church for the future.

As a footnote to the process of reorganization, when reorganization was instituted in 1989 one of the major reasons was to ensure that every parish would be served by one pastor. The mantra at that time was <u>one parish, one pastor</u>. At the beginning of the process there were 333 parishes and missions, with 333 church buildings served by 284 pastors. With the completion of reorganization in March of 1994, the diocese had 220 parishes, with 265 church buildings served by 220 pastors or team ministry. As of June 2011 the diocese now has 210 parishes served by 182 priests. Thus, once again 29 parishes are served by a priest who has another parish assignment.

While this process was by no means perfect, the purpose was to develop a method by which the bishop, pastors, parishes and the faithful could exercise the rights that we claim they have within the parish context, such as existence, hearing the word of God, receiving the sacraments, being informed and participating in decisions that affect them and given the opportunity to vindicate these rights in the Church.

V. Canonical Considerations

Any canonist who has been involved in parish reconfiguration realizes that five important canonical issues are involved in the reorganization process. These five canonical issues are: (1) the process for the suppression, erection, merging or altering parishes; (2) the process for the reduction of a church building to profane but not sordid use; (3) what constitutes the serious reasons or grave cause required in canon 1222 §2;[19] (4) the preparation and form for the issuance of the appropriate canonical decrees, and (5) the right to appeal. These five canonical issues have occupied a great deal of time for those who have been involved in a reorganization process and it would seem that some reflection on these issues might assist us in our ministry.

First, the process of suppression, erection, or altering parishes is governed by the provisions of canon 512 §2. In earlier days, the issue was the suppression of a parish or parishes and the erection of new parish to serve the parishioners of the former parishes. The rationale for this action was two-fold, first canon 515 §2 did not mention the concept of merging and canonists were concerned about careful adherence to the law and the possible subject of an appeal of a decision by the diocesan bishop and secondly, an attempt to comport with the provisions of canons 121-122[20] which established the norms for disposition of goods of

---

19   Canon 1222 §2: "When other grave causes suggest that a church no longer be used for divine worship, the diocesan bishop, after having heard the presbyteral council, can relegate it to profane but not sordid use, with the consent of those who legitimately claim rights for themselves in the church and provided that the good of souls suffers no detriment thereby."

20   Canon 121: "If aggregates of persons or of things, which are public juridic persons, are so joined that from one aggregate is constituted which also possesses juridic personality, the new juridic person obtains the good and patrimonial rights proper to the prior ones and assumes the obligations with which they were burdened. With regard to the allocation of goods in particular and to the fulfillment of obligations, however, the intention of the founders and donors as well as acquired rights mist be respected."

Canon 122: "If an aggregate which possesses public juridic personality is so divided either that a part of it is united with another juridic person or that a distinct public juridic

juridic persons. Diocesan bishops did not want to be accused of closing parishes simply for diocesan financial gain but as a necessity for the care of souls. With the letter of the Congregation for the Clergy we have come to be aware of the distinction proposed by the congregation regarding suppression and merging of parishes. What we used to call suppression is now rightly known as mergers. While the primary purpose of this clarification was to ensure that the temporal goods of the parish would be acquired not by the diocese (c. 123) but by the successor parish, in reality, the process had the same effect, the reconfiguration of to two or more parishes.[21] Critical to the discussion is the process to effectuate the merging of parishes. Since the canon speaks of consultation with the presbyteral council it seems that there are five components to this consultation: (1) convocation and notification of the members of the presbyteral council; (2) providing the members sufficient information so that they can offer proper consultation; (3) informed and free counsel to the diocesan bishop; (4) deliberation by the council and (5) appropriate written documentation about the action of the council. It is important that canonists keep before their eyes the provisions of canon 127[22] and 166,[23] which involves the convocation of a group to be consulted and the method

---

person is erected from the separate part, the ecclesiastical authority competent to make the division, having observed before all else the intention of the founders and donors, the acquired rights, and the approved statutes, must take care personally or through an executor:

1° that common, divisible, patrimonial goods and rights as well as debts and other obligations are divided among the juridic persons concerned, with due proportion in equity and justice, after all the circumstances and needs of each have been taken into account;

2° that the use and usufruct of common goods which are not divisible accrue to each juridic person and that the obligations proper to them are imposed upon each, in due proportion determined in equity and justice."

21 Congregation for the Clergy, "Canon 123: Regarding the Suppression and Merger of Parishes," 14.

22 Canon 127 §1: "When it is established by law that in order to place acts a superior needs the consent or counsel of some college or group of persons, the college or group must be convoked according to the norms of canon 166 unless, when it concerns seeking counsel only, particular or proper law provides otherwise. For such acts to be valid, however, it is required that the consent of an absolute majority of those present is obtained or that the counsel of all is sought."

Canon 127 §2, 2°: "If counsel is required, the act of a superior who does not hear those persons is invalid; although not obliged to accept their opinion even if unanimous, a superior is nonetheless not to act contrary to that opinion, especially if unanimous, without a reason which is overriding in the superior's judgment."

Canon 127 §3: "All whose consent or counsel is required are obliged to offer their opinion sincerely and if gravity if gravity of the affair requires it, to observe secrecy diligently; moreover, the superior can insist upon this obligation."

23 Canon 166 §1: "The person presiding over a college or group is to convoke all those belonging to the college or group; the notice of convocation, however, when it must be personal, is valid if it is given in the pace of the domicile or quasi-domicile or in the place of residence."

by which those who are to be called for the consultation is to be done. Strict adherence to these norms is critical for the validity of the action of the presbyteral council and ultimately the decision of the diocesan bishop.

Second, the process for the reduction of a church building to profane but not sordid use in accordance with canon 1222. What is interesting is the distinction that the code makes between a parish, found in Book II on the People of God, and a church building, found in Book IV on the Sanctifying Office of the Church. While the ordinary parishioner sees the parish and church as one and the same, the law envisions a clear distinction. A parish is established on a stable basis for a portion of the Christian faithful, under the direction of a pastor, which has been defined by some territory of some other reason. On the other hand, a church may or may not be part of a parish but a sacred building, destined for divine worship in which the faithful have a right (c. 1214) to access.[24] At the present time there seems to be a presumption that churches will remain for worship even if parishes are merged unless some grave (serious) cause exists to reduce them to profane use. While the procedure for reducing a church building follows the same procedure as the merging of a parish, the unique question is what constitutes grave or serious cause. This brings us to the next canonical consideration.

Third, what constitutes grave or serious cause necessary for the reduction of a church building to profane but not sordid use? Interestingly, the canons offer very little by way of explanation as to what constitutes grave or serious cause or even present an insight in where we might find keys to assist canonists in the proper interpretation of this canon. While decisions of church appeal courts (Sacred Roman Rota, Apostolic Penitentiary, Supreme Tribunal of the Apostolic Signatura) do not constitute *stare decisis*, the canonists can look to these courts to assist in establishing the mind of the church. In a decision of the Supreme Tribunal of the Apostolic Signatura involving an appeal case from my diocese regarding the reduction of church to profane but sordid use, the Supreme Tribunal indicated that the concept of grave cause is not to be seen as one singular cause but an aggregate of causes which might lead one to see the grave cause required by the canon.[25] The criteria for establishing grave cause presented in the brief prepared by the diocese outlined six criteria to be considered.

1. Does the church building have any historical or architectural significance which makes its reduction a cause of great scandal not only for the parish

---

24 Canon 1214: "By the term church is understood a sacred building designated for divine worship to which the faithful have the right of entry for the exercise, especially the public exercise, of divine worship."

25 Unpublished decision of the Supreme Tribunal of the Apostolic Signatura, January 18, 1997 before the College of Judges, Eduardo Davino, *ponens* , regarding Guardian Angels Church, Pittsburgh, Pennsylvania. In their decision, the Signatura stated that, "gravity arises out of convergence of factors, from which it is possible to deduce whether the issue be of a lesser moment, or rather of more than little concern."

but the community at large?
2. Was the church building dedicated or was the altar blessed? In past years, churches were not dedicated or consecrated as long as a debt existed on the church, only the altars were blessed. In reality, when the parish had a mortgage burning, many years later, the church was to be dedicated but rarely did this take place since time had passed and memories faded.
3. What are the financial constraints on the present parish that has multiple church buildings? Would the maintenance of the church building harm the ability of the parish to carry out its ministry to the parishioners?
4. Will the people have access to word and sacraments if the church building is closed?
5. Are there any individuals who claim specific rights regarding the church building?
6. Would the good of souls be impaired by the closing of the church building?

While this is not an exhaustive list of possible criteria it gives each of us some ideas of what might be considered grave cause. In the absence of a clear definition or criteria, the above might become at least a starting point for additional discussion by canonists.

Fourth, what is the proper form and execution of a decree which either merges parishes or reduces a church building to profane but not sordid use? Canon 50[26] reminds us what is important prior to the issuance of a decree such as information, documentation and hearing those who are involved and canon 51[27] states that "a decree should be issued in writing, giving, in the case of a decision, the reasons which prompted it, at least in summary fashion." In the case of merging parishes it would seem that the critical components of the decree would be the following:

1. To whom is the decree issued?
2. The overall reason(s) for reconfiguration.
3. The specific reasons in regards to this parish.
4. What happens to the parishioners of the parish(s)?
5. How have parish boundaries been altered?
6. What about the assets and liabilities?
7. What is the effective date of the decree?

In the case of the reduction of a church to profane but not sordid use, the grave causes which is applicable needs to be added to the decree as the specific

---

26 Canon 50: "Before issuing a singular decree, an authority is to seek out the necessary information and proofs and, insofar as possible, to hear those whose rights can be injured."

27 Canon 51: "A decree is to be issues in writing, with the reasons at least summarily expressed if it is a decision."

reasons for the action of the diocesan bishop. These causes need to be specific to the church building whose status is being altered and should not be generic causes since in any appeal the verification of the reasons for the actions will become an essential part of the defense on the part of the diocesan bishop.

Finally, the method of communicating to the parish the decision of the bishop is of great importance. Not only does it provide the people with the rationale that has been deduced from the entire process, of which they have been a part, but also gives the people the basis on which they may seek administrative recourse. The communication of the decree should be published both verbally and in written form to the parish and one may also choose to publish the decree in some form of diocesan communications. Whatever method is chosen needs to inform those who are directly affected that they have a right to appeal. Once again, if people are not informed of their rights, how can they exercise them let alone vindicate them before the proper ecclesiastical authority.

VI. Conclusion

While it is impossible to fully discuss this vast topic in this short reflection, this brief paper has attempted to deal with several important matters. First and foremost, the obligations and rights of bishops and parishes ultimately seek the same goal, the salvation of souls through the ministry of word and sacrament. Second, in reconfiguration a process for bishops and parishes to exercise the rights which they are given needs to be the hallmark of every reorganization plan devised by dioceses. Third, the canonical procedure, while critical, only serves to implement the process that has been determined and utilized in parish reconfiguration. Fourth, the canonical procedures are established to protect the rights of all and should be followed even if they become burdensome. Finally, process is more important that the product and those who are affected by the decisions should take part in the decisions.

I trust that this brief reflection will assist each of you in your ministry. I thank you for you kind attention.

Seminar

Obligation of the Tribunal to Report Child Abuse
Doctor Diane L. Barr

Introduction

The purpose of this talk is to address the obligations of the diocesan tribunal to report incidents of child sexual abuse. My intention is to address, in a general fashion, the civil and canonical obligations tribunal personnel have in these situations. As is my custom, I have several problems we can review at the end of this presentation to further tease out the practical issues related to this topic. My presentation is divided into four parts:

I. The Canonical Issue

As you are all well aware if you work within a tribunal, confidentiality and respect for the reputation of others is very important. Many tribunals tell their clients and witnesses that their information will be kept confidential except as required within the tribunal process. What does this mean when a tribunal receives testimony that describes sexual or physical abuse of a child by someone? Is there any obligation to report such information to civil authorities? Is this permitted under Church law? What are the practical implications of such situations?

Why Is this Important?

Tribunals have a long history of being separated from other aspects of diocesan administration. We are a secretive, quiet, hard-working bunch that attempt to sort through many personal issues for clergy and laity related to their status in the Church. This may involve laicization processes or annulment cases. It can touch those seeking to enter the seminary as well as those who want to regularize their current marriage for whatever reason. Often times this separation is a positive thing since it compartmentalizes information that could be damaging to a person's reputation, and preserves that reputation. On the other hand, any tribunal is part of a diocese or an archdiocese and that civil reality has many different consequences. It is certainly a situation with competing rights, and as the Protection of Rights is the theme of this year's convention, it is a timely topic.

Let me begin by looking at a small sample of state regulations that require child abuse reporting.

II. The Civil Law Reporting Requirements

Civil law reporting requirements will differ from state to state. I would urge you to find out what the law is in your state and how it applies to you.

Today, I will show you two different statutes to give you a taste of what we're dealing with.

Idaho Code §16-1605
"16-1605. Reporting of abuse, abandonment or neglect. (1) Any physician, resident on a hospital staff, intern, nurse, coroner, school teacher, day care personnel, social worker, or other person having reason to believe that a child under the age of eighteen (18) years has been abused, abandoned or neglected or who observes the child being subjected to conditions or circumstances which would reasonably result in abuse, abandonment or neglect shall report or cause to be reported within twenty-four (24) hours such conditions or circumstances to the proper law enforcement agency or the department."[1]

If you're wondering why I chose this statute, since I'm still licensed to practice law in Idaho I thought I'd use an example that I've studied and lived under for more than 20 years. This is an example of the mandatory reporter with an "any person" clause. This statute obligates everyone to report if they know or have reason to believe a child is being abused, abandoned or neglected. This is a very broad statute that requires everyone to look out for the abused or neglected child. That means that every tribunal worker or volunteer is subject to that obligation as part of their duties within the court.

My second example is from my current home state, Maryland.

Maryland Code §5-704
Reporting of abuse or neglect – By health practitioner, police officer, educator or human service worker (a) In general. – Notwithstanding any other provision of law, including any law on privileged communications, each health practitioner, police officer, educator, or human service worker, acting in a professional capacity in this State:

> (1) (i) who has reason to believe that a child has been subjected to abuse, shall notify the local department or the appropriate law enforcement agency; or
>
> (ii) who has reason to believe that a child has been subjected to neglect, shall notify the local department; and
>
> (2) if acting as a staff member of a hospital, public health agency, child care institution, juvenile detention center, school, or similar institution, shall immediately notify and give all information required by this section to the head of the institution or the designee of the

---

1 See http://www.legislature.idaho.gov/idstat/Title16/T16CH16SECT16-1605.htm.

head.[2]

§5-705. Reporting of abuse or neglect -- By other persons
(a) In general. –

(1) Except as provided in paragraphs (2) and (3) of this subsection, notwithstanding any other provision of law, including a law on privileged communications, a person in this State other than a health practitioner, police officer, or educator or human service worker who has reason to believe that a child has been subjected to abuse or neglect shall:

(i) if the person has reason to believe the child has been subjected to abuse, notify the local department or the appropriate law enforcement agency; or

(ii) if the person has reason to believe the child has been subjected to neglect, notify the local department.[3]

In Maryland, the criminal statute of limitations for prosecution of child sexual abuse goes back to the mid-1970s. That is to say that someone can be charged with child sexual abuse today, even though the abuse took place after 1975. As a result, reporting abuse in Maryland can have an immediate impact depending on the jurisdiction in which the abuse took place. In the past few years, several of the clergy have been criminally prosecuted under such laws. In Maryland, we err on the side of reporting.

So, looking at these statutes, who is obliged under civil law to report information about child abuse? Are you as a tribunal official required to do so? Obviously that will depend on what your state statute actually says. Sometimes it's a question of when the event occurred or where the event took place, but these parts of the question are secondary to knowing your state law and knowing it well.

III. Civil Law Obligation versus Canonical Responsibilities

The first question is whether you will ever be bound to report an allegation of child sexual or physical abuse. I would venture to say that this question will appear for you at some time in your career. Unless you want to go to jail or want to harm your diocese, you are going to be faced with what to do when an allegation comes to you. In a tribunal setting, such allegations may come up as part of a marriage case investigation (formal or informal) or in the preparation of a petition for laicization. I have had allegations come to me in a chancery setting when discussing Catholic school closings or the status of particular religious

---

[2] See http://www.lexisnexis.com/hottopics/mdcode/; see MD Family Law code §5-704.

[3] See MD Family Law Code Annotated §5-705.

orders. You simply never know where you might hear of abuse. Once you have this information, your civil and moral obligations begin and you should have a predetermined course of action that has been established for this type of situation. It is a predictable dilemma that should be evaluated, the proper course of action determined, and those bound to action trained to fulfill their obligation.

Canonical Obligations to Privacy and Confidentiality[4]

Over the last two decades, many tribunals have become more targeted in their method of marriage case investigation. Instead of asking 45 general questions about the demise of a marriage and hoping to find a ground that will somehow emerge from that dubious declaration, tribunals are now investigating specific grounds with a laser like approach. This second method tries to uncover just enough evidence to determine whether there is sufficient evidence to overcome the presumption in favor of the bond. Written questionnaires have become better organized and instructions to parties and witnesses have become specific in order to achieve better end results. Many tribunals used to avoid publishing the acts of the case to the parties because of fears that the witnesses and the other spouse would avoid being honest with the tribunal. To avoid harming personal relationships between spouses and/or witnesses, tribunals began telling those spouses and witnesses that their testimony would be shared with the parties in compliance with canon 1598. This has led to the collection of better testimony and more accurate implementation of procedures over time. Our methods have still allowed us to conform to canon 220[5] with its concerns for privacy and confidentiality by limiting who has access to what information within the tribunal itself and obtaining signed waivers from case parties.

What about reporting child sexual abuse—isn't that a violation of an individual's privacy? When it comes to the obligation of reporting allegations of child abuse, I am of the opinion that in a similar way to advising witnesses that the spouses will read their testimony, we should be advising parties and witnesses that we will be obligated to report any allegations of child sexual abuse. This way, those who actually mention these allegations will have hopefully done so deliberately, with the understanding that there could be consequences for their decision. Once they have knowingly submitted information to us, we must deter-

---

4   See articles by Edward J. Dillon, "Confidentiality in Tribunals," *CLSA Proceedings* 45 (1983) 171-181; Edward J. Dillon, "The Rights of the Respondent in Matrimonial Trials," *CLSA Proceedings* 52 (1990) 80-106; Mark Plewka, "Right of Defense in Certain Stages of the Matrimonial Process as Found in the Decisions of the Roman Rota," *CLSA Proceedings* 53 (1991) 249-262; Diane L. Barr, "Basic Civil Law Concerns for Tribunals," *CLSA Proceedings* 54 (1992) 72-86.

5   Canon 220: "No one is permitted to harm illegitimately the good reputation which a person possesses nor to injure the right of any person to protect his or her own privacy." All citations taken from *Code of Canon Law – Latin English Edition*, New English Translation (Washington, DC: Canon Law Society of America, 1998).

mine where to go from there.[6]

Protecting the Diocese

This is also a value that must be weighed in evaluating the tribunal obligation to act to report in these matters. Our own bishops have made it very clear in the *Charter*[7] and in local documents concerning Codes of Conduct and other policies that it is imperative to comply with the law and report child abuse. Any exception has been related solely to the acquisition of such knowledge by a priest under the seal of confession.

I have heard some colleagues suggest that all matters of this nature should be kept "in house" within the tribunal in order to maintain the reputation of the parties involved. No "outside" staff needs to be involved. I do not agree with this approach, given that none of us are experts in child abuse investigation and reporting. We need outside assistance to provide professional leadership in this area and also to act as a proper check and balance on our own impulses to keep things private and secret. I believe that the protection of the innocent is part of our respect for life commitment. Child abuse must be dealt with aggressively no matter where it is found. Governmental officials have tools to deal with allegations of this nature within society that we do not.

A Related Civil Case - The Rudy Kos Case[8]

As we discuss these issues it impossible not to mention the most public of civil cases that referred to supposed tribunal testimony and allegations of child sexual abuse. The Rudy Kos case from the Diocese of Dallas was covered very heavily by the secular press in the early 1990s. Then Father Rudy Kos was accused of having sexually abused at least eight boys over the period when Kos served as a seminarian and priest in the Diocese of Dallas. I'm sure a number of other dioceses have stories that also involved a priest who sexually victimized a number of young boys, but what makes this case different is that supposedly all was revealed about Kos as part of a marriage case prepared by the Diocese of Dallas tribunal. As part of the testimony in civil court it was noted that the case

---

6 See also William Bassett, "Church Records and the Courts," *America* 197:13 (October 29, 2007) http://www.americamagazine.org/content/article.cfm?article_id=10335.

7 USCCB, *Promise to Protect Pledge to Heal: Charter for the Protection of Children and Young People, Essential Norms, Statement of Episcopal Commitment*, revised June 2005 (Washington, DC: USCCB, 2006). See http://www.usccb.org/issues-and-action/child-and-youth-protection/upload/Charter-for-the-Protection-of-Children-and-Young-People-revised-2011.pdf for the full text of this document.

8 The basis of the text presented here originated with published accounts of the matter in local newspapers as well as limited discussions with the Diocese of Dallas. Newspaper accounts include David Koenig of the AP at http://www.skeptictank.org/hs/ca1.htm; the *Amarillo Globe News* had several articles, including http://amarillo.com/stories/040298/gets.shtml; http://amarillo.com/stories/012598/LG3040.001.shtml; and http://amarillo.com/stories/071198/new_dallas.shtml.

was done as a formal case. As part of the civil law trial, his former wife testified that Mr. Kos (soon to be seminarian Kos) was gay and attracted to young boys. The former wife testified that she had informed the tribunal about these issues. Having spoken with the folks at the Diocese of Dallas, this was certainly not the case. Regardless of that fact, the jury verdict in that case was over $120 million against the diocese. It was eventually settled for $23 million for eight young men. Part of the reasoning given for the verdict was that the Diocese of Dallas was presumed to have known about these allegations before they ordained Mr. Kos to the priesthood. Because of this prior knowledge, they were supposedly on notice that Mr. Kos could abuse others.

Why is this case important to us today? If the testimony of the former spouse at the civil trial was correct, it is an example of how actions of all employees of a diocese can have consequences. Any diocese receiving similar information and permitting a man to be ordained without investigating such allegations would be opening a diocese to a risk of serious liabilities. In the United States, we have already seen what difficulties the bankruptcy of dioceses can bring to the people of God.

While you and I are already very careful about the way we handle seminarian cases (I actually insist that vocation directors for clergy candidates read the entire acts of such cases so they are fully informed) we have to remember that since the tribunal is an organ of the diocese what we know will be viewed as what the bishop and other officials know about any individual abuse allegation. What we do with these allegations is regulated by law in many states (or under federal law by virtue of the child pornography laws) so what we must do to protect victims and our dioceses can be established through policies and procedures that conform to those local laws. The key to properly addressing this question is to establish these policies, educate all affected to conform to them, and then to be sure you follow the policies in place. We do have to be aware of the individual obligations we have under state laws so involving our own legal counsel in drafting these policies is key. We will talk about possible policies later in this presentation.

IV. Some Suggestions

Alright, so you now have a witness or a party giving you oral or written information that indicates there was some type of physical abuse of a child. What do you do? If all is well, you pull out your already established policy and follow it.

Develop a Policy

That policy should have been developed in conjunction with diocesan civil legal counsel, diocesan canonical counsel, the chancery office and the diocesan office or person that investigates allegations of child abuse. Why? All these persons have information that will be part of the final policy. State laws are very different from one another in this area. Some states actually protect church records or information in ways others do not. Some do not provide any protections at all. We need to know our obligations before we can provide a proper policy for our dioceses. The expertise of the professionals mentioned here will be crucial in establishing a just and conforming policy that will protect tribunal clients as well as tribunal personnel.

The policy itself should include several aspects:

- A method for taking the evaluation of the allegation outside the tribunal. This means that the final determination as to whether the allegation is to be reported should be made by someone outside the tribunal. Records of the manner in which an allegation has been handled should be kept by the person charged with reporting the allegation. There should also be some notation made in the tribunal file regarding what was done when the allegation was discovered.
- Training for Those Who Must Implement the Policy
- As with all policies, once it is established it is critical to train those with the obligation about the process and constantly test them regarding their compliance with it. Such policies usually mean some kind of change in the workplace which means there will be some resistance to the "new" way of doing things.
- Informing Parties and Witnesses of Your Obligation
- In justice and fairness, those who present evidence to you must be informed of your obligation to report abuse so those persons can make a prudent, independent judgment regarding their decision to tell you something that may trigger a reporting obligation. This usually means updating letters and documents to highlight your obligation so it is clear to the person answering the questions. Language addressing this issue should be direct and clear; no guessing should be necessary.
- Act Immediately
- When an allegation of abuse arises, deal with it immediately. Do not wait until the end of the case. You do not know who might be harmed if you wait.
- Proper Record Keeping
- If any additional information is sought, proper records should be kept regarding who did the inquiry, the information received, etc. Some notation should be made in the tribunal case regarding the reporting and action taken regarding any allegations. Appropriate records should be kept by the Child and Youth Protection Office or coordinator as determined by the policy.

A typical responsibility tree for this policy might look like the following:

- Notary/Auditor opens all testimony and discovers an allegation of child sexual abuse against someone.
- Notary brings information to the Judicial Vicar immediately.
- Judicial Vicar reviews information and contacts Youth and Child Protection representative to discuss further action.
- Judicial Vicar calls person mentioning allegation and indicates that the person

will be contacted by the Youth and Child protection representative (or diocesan attorney) to follow up and determine where to go with the allegation.
- Youth and Child Protection representative investigates and determines if reporting must be done.
- If reporting is required, a report is made by Youth and Child Protection Representative and the Youth and Child Protection representative keeps a record of the facts, when the report was made, along with any other information uncovered in the investigation.
- A brief record of what was done about the allegation is kept in the tribunal file for that case so there is no reason to address the matter a second time if court members change.

Once a policy is in place, the most important thing to remember is to adhere to this since it is now your standard for proper conduct in these situations.

Conclusion

This is an important issue for tribunals. We all want to protect those who cannot protect themselves. This is our obligation as members of the people of God. Having an appropriate policy will allow all who seek the services of tribunals to understand that obligation.

Seminar

Tips for Building Better Law Sections
Reverend John J.M. Foster

In 1988, at the fiftieth convention of the Canon Law Society of America, Robert Sanson concluded his seminar entitled "Elements of a Good Sentence" with a series of questions to assist ecclesiastical judges in evaluating their sentences as well as to promote future discussion among canonists. One of the questions Father Sanson asked was this: "Do we need a seminar on the elements of a good law section?"[1] Twenty-three years later, the Board of Governors has answered this question affirmatively.

Now we shouldn't fault the CLSA for putting off scheduling a seminar on the elements of a good law section. After all, each of us undoubtedly has a list of reasons—excuses?—for procrastinating when it comes to revising or not writing law sections for the sentences assigned by the judicial vicar.

- It takes too much time to write a new law section.
- I can't take time away from writing sentences to write or revise my law sections.
- I don't have the resources available to write or revise my law sections.
- It's easier to use the canned law sections my tribunal has always used.
- If I write a new law section, nobody is going to read it anyway.
- I wrote or revised my law sections after the 1983 code was promulgated, and the law hasn't changed since then.

Yes, tribunal officials rarely want for work. Judges always have another case (or two or ten) waiting for judgment and the sentence. Nevertheless, as we shall see, the law section is an essential element of the definitive sentence. In this seminar, I would like to propose eleven tips for building better law sections. Some of the tips are obvious to the seasoned judge. Some may focus on theory, while others will be quite practical. A few may challenge the status quo. While we will focus on law sections concerning the invalidity of marriage, a number of the tips apply to law sections for other types of cases also. In any case, my hope is that these tips will spur you to take some time to critique the law sections you use in an effort to improve them—and in so doing, improve the sentences you write as well.

---

[1] Robert Sanson, "Elements of a Sentence," *CLSA Proceedings* 50 (1988) 127.

Tip 1: Understand What a Law Section Is—and What It Isn't

Before beginning a project, it is always helpful to get one's bearings. For us, that means knowing what a law section is and what it isn't. We know that the law section is part of the definitive sentence written by the judge that brings a controversy to conclusion. We also know that the term "law section" is found in neither the Code of Canon Law[2] nor the 2005 instruction *Dignitas Connubii*.[3] Nevertheless, from the code and instruction we can deduce the function, placement, and scope of the law section. Canon 1611, 3° (*DC* art. 250 §1, 2°) states that the sentence must "set forth the reasons or motives in law and in fact on which the dispositive part of the sentence is based."[4] As for the placement of the law section in the sentence, *Dignitas Connubii*, art. 253 §3 indicates that "the dispositive part of the sentence follows these things [mentioned in §§1 and 2], preceded by the reasons both in law and in fact on which it is based (cf. can. 1612, §3)." Article 254 §1 establishes the scope:

> The sentence, avoiding both an excessive brevity and an excessive length, must be clear in explaining the reasons in law and in fact and must be based *in actis et probatis*, so that it is apparent by what path the judges arrived at their decision and how they applied the law to the facts.

By way of summary, then, the law section follows the sentence's preface and statement of facts and precedes the argument and disposition of the case.[5] It is a

---

2   *Codex Iuris Canonici auctoritate Ioannis Pauli PP. II promulgatus* (Vatican City: Librería Editrice Vaticana, 1983); hereafter cited as 1983 code.

3   Pontifical Council for Legislative Texts, *Dignitas Connubii*, Official Latin Text with English Translation, January 25, 2005 (Vatican City: Librería Editrice Vaticana, 2005); hereafter cited as *DC*.

4   1983 code, c. 1611, 3°. English translation from *Code of Canon Law, Latin-English Edition: New English Translation* (Washington, DC: Canon Law Society of America, 1998); hereafter all translations of the 1983 code will be taken from this source unless stated otherwise.

5   Writing on the parallel canon in the 1917 Code of Canon Law, Delisle A. Lemieux observed that "Paragraph 4 of this canon (1874) prescribes that the sentence be motivated. It does not specify the order of listing the motives. There are indications in the Code [cc. 1605 §1, 1871 §2, 1873 §1] from which it might be construed that the motives *in facto* are to precede the motives *in iure*. However, the reverse form is in common use" (*The Sentence in Ecclesiastical Procedure*, Canon Law Studies 87 [Washington, DC: The Catholic University of America, 1934] 83). Commenting on *DC* art. 253 §3, Klaus Lüdicke and Ronny E. Jenkins argue that the prescribed order of elements

> seems contrary to the interest of the one receiving the sentence and to the actual manner by which a judge reaches a decision. If the sentence is also to arise from a foundation in law and fact then the sentence should be formulated as an authoritative pronouncement whose foundation will not be presented in an inductive manner, but in a deductive one. That is, one would expect the judge to render a decision

concise explanation of the reasons in law that demonstrates one step in the reasoning process the judge used to reach the decision.

While the law requires that the judge spell out in the sentence the reasons in law that have been applied to the facts of the case and motivated the decision, such has not always been the case. Even though the customary practice at the beginning of the second millennium was for judges to state the reasons for their decisions in their sentences,[6] it wasn't until the First Council of Lyons (1245) that judges were required to include the reasons for their decisions in their sentences—and then only in cases involving excommunication.[7] The written inclusion of the reasons motivating the judge's decision found its way into universal law in the 1917 Code of Canon Law.[8] By mandating that judges include the reasons motivating their decisions in their definitive sentences, the legislator seeks to protect the judicial process from any abuse of discretion on the part of the judge. "If a position has to be argued and defended, often in opposition to others, then the possibility of a just sentence is greatly heightened."[9] Furthermore, as Delisle Lemieux observed,

> Although the sentence does not draw its force from the motives, nevertheless the statement of the motives is conducive to the proper administration of justice and to the development of jurisprudence and also tends to confirm the parties in their trust in the justice of

---

and then clarify why that decision was reached. This manner of proceeding would most suitably conform to the canonical (civil law tradition) expectation of judicial review. So, too, the sentence should first indicate what decision has been reached and then supply the motivation in law and fact for that outcome.

Despite the order foreseen by §3, it is not forbidden to vary the style so that the disposition of the court would be mentioned in limited form at the beginning of the second part of the sentence, with the same disposition being repeated in the third section (with a detailed indication of the *capita*). It could then be preceded by the motivation for the sentence in law and fact as indicated in the Instruction (Dignitas Connubii*: Norms and Commentary* [Washington: CLSA, 2006] 411–412).

6   See Joaquín Llobell, "Sentenza: decisione e motivazione," in *Il Processo Matrimoniale Canonico*, Studi Giuridici XVII (Vatican City: Librería Editrice Vaticana, 1988) 320; and Brian E. Ferme, "Judging Justly: The Ecclesiastical Sentence in History," *Apollinaris* 65 (1992) 532–533.

7   First Council of Lyons, *Cum medicinalis*, in *Decrees of the Ecumenical Councils*, ed. Norman P. Tanner (London and Washington: Sheed & Ward and Georgetown University Press, 1990) 1:291: "Quisquis ergo excommunicat, in scriptis proferat et causam expresse conscribat, propter quam excommunicatio proferatur."

8   See *Codex Iuris Canonici Pii X Pontificis Maximi iussu digestus Benedicti Papae XV auctoritate promulgatus* (Rome: Typis Polyglottis Vaticanis, 1917) cc. 1873 §1, 3° and 1874 §4.

9   Ferme, 536.

the sentence.[10]

By setting forth the reasons in law, the law section explains the legal criteria applied by the judge to the facts of the case.

As important as knowing what a law section is, it is important to know what it is not. A law section is not simply a listing of one or more pertinent canons from the Code of Canon Law without any comment from the judge. Neither is the law section a treatise on the specific *caput nullitatis* at issue, taking pains to cover every aspect of the defect of consent not only historically but also among Rotal auditors and commentators. Still less is the law section the forum for the judge to expound his or her pet jurisprudential ideas or to confront statements of colleagues or widely held canonical doctrine.[11] As the eminent auditor André Cardinal Jullien remarked: "The court is not a pulpit, or the sentence an avant-garde journal article."[12]

Tip 2: Know What a Law Section Contains

As noted in the first tip, neither the Code of Canon Law nor *Dignitas Connubii* provides any help in determining the content of the phrase "reasons or motives in law." Because the canon uses the Latin phrase "in iure" for the English term "law," we know that the motives certainly include law in the sense of legislation promulgated by a competent legislator, i.e., *lex*, as well as norms issued by a competent authority with executive power, i.e., *ius*. The defects of consent found in canons 1095–1099 and 1101–1103 in the Code of Canon Law are an example of *lex*;[13] while the norms contained in the instruction *Dignitas Connubii* are part of the *ius*.

As for the specific laws that are used in the law section, the judge draws them principally from the defect(s) of consent proposed in the decree formulating the doubt as well as related procedural laws. While the parties or their advocates and the defender of the bond may have presented certain laws in their respective briefs, the judge has no obligation to use them as motivations for his decision, provided that the chosen laws apply to the case.[14] While not necessary in every

---

10   Lemieux, 75.

11   See Benno Grimm, "Die Ausfertigung eines Ehenichtigkeitsurteils in Langform," *De Processibus Matrimonialibus* 2 (1995) 271.

12   André Julien. "Le juge et sa sentence," *Ephemerides Iuris Canonici* 22 (1966) 67: "le tribunal n'est pas une chaire, ni la sentence un article de revue d'avant-garde."

13   While not so much an issue in marriage cases, Matthaeus Conte a Coronata held that the laws used in a law section can be universal or particular (*Institutiones iuris canonici, Vol. III. De Processibus*, 5th ed. [Turin and Rome: Marietti, 1962] 341). See also Lemieux, 75.

14   See Lemieux, 75; and Fernando Della Rocca, *Canonical Procedure: Philosophical-Juridic Study of Book IV of the Code of Canon Law*, trans. John D. Fitzgerald (Milwau-

case, it is helpful to quote directly the applicable law.[15]

As central as the law *(ius)* is to the law section, the legal motivation consists in more than a verbatim listing of the applicable defect(s) of consent or procedural laws pertinent to the case. Sanson observes:

> A good jurisprudence is solidly grounded in theology. Good law can only follow good theology. Although a pastoral principle may not have direct juridical force, it may often provide a context and a legitimate source of interpretation.[16]

Similarly, principles articulated in the long Catholic philosophical tradition are useful in providing a proper foundation for the explanation of the law that will be applied to the facts. Thus, one finds quotations and references to the writings of the Scholastic fathers, conciliar documents, and papal magisterium in law sections. The incorporation of a text from St. Thomas Aquinas, *Gaudium et spes*, *Familaris consortio*, or a papal allocution to the Roman Rota provides not only a context for understanding the law but also a guide to its proper interpretation.

In addition to the law and to documents of a philosophical or theological nature, Rotal jurisprudence is another type of content essential for any law section. While more will be said about the nature of Rotal jurisprudence in tip four, suffice it to say here the work of the Roman Rota plays an important role in promoting "unity of jurisprudence, and, by virtue of its own decisions," providing "assistance to lower tribunals."[17]

Finally, commentaries on the law and jurisprudence as well as related issues play an important function in understanding the legal motivations on which the decision is based. It is not out of place to incorporate the relevant passages from the academic publications of Rotal judges, who write not in their official capacity as prelate auditors but as scholars of the law. Similarly, commentators on the canons dealing with the defects of consent or procedural law expound and clarify the law. At the same time, judges should not limit themselves to canonical commentators. Experts in psychology, medicine, culture, civil law, etc. can provide insights from their own specialties that can illumine a substantive or procedural norm.[18]

---

kee: Bruce Pub. Co., 1961) 282.

15 See John Jukes, OFM Conv., "The Quality of Sentences," *CLSGBI Newsletter* 81 (1990) 20.

16 Sanson, 123.

17 John Paul II, apostolic constitution *Pastor bonus*, June 28, 1988, art. 126: *AAS* 80 (1988) 892. English trans. in *Code of Canon Law, Latin-English Edition: New English Translation*, 721; hereafter, all translations of *Pastor bonus* will come from this source.

18 See Jukes, 20; Manuel J. Arroba Conde, CMF, *Diritto Processuale Canonico*, 2nd

Before we proceed further, a word is in order concerning the response the judge is to give to that which is contained *in iure*. Canonists are well aware that judges must have moral certitude to render an affirmative decision in the case before them (c. 1608 §1). Canon 1608 §2 states: "The judge must derive this certitude from the acts and" those things that are proven (*ex actis et probatis*). It is precisely from those things *ex actis et probatis* that the judge draws the reasons or motives in fact on which the decision rests. In other words, the reasons or motives in law are drawn from the applicable law, magisterial documents, Rotal jurisprudence, and writings of learned commentators and specialists, and the reasons or motives in fact come from the acts and those things proven therein. If the law requires judges to have moral certitude concerning the latter, what is their response to the former? Blessed Pope John Paul II answered this question in his 1980 allocution to the Roman Rota:

> The judge's duties toward the law are, therefore, serious and multiple. I will mention only the first and most important one, which, moreover, implies all the others: faithfulness! Faithfulness to the law—to divine, natural and positive law, and to canon law, substantial and procedural.[19]

Noting that the pope did not "apply the concept of moral certainty to the *quaestio iuris*,"[20] Joaquín Llobell illustrates the problem that would arise if moral certitude were to be connected with the legal question:

> To describe the primary attitude of the judge regarding the "quaestio iuris" on the basis of moral certainty, might imply that the juridic norm is considered open to interpretation as diverse as the positions of hypothetical parties that attempt—in their specific procedural mission of reconstruction of the "quaestio facti"—to affirm the validity and the nullity of a same marriage.[21]

---

ed. (Rome: EDIURCLA, 1994) 429; Sanson, 122-123; and Josef Weber, "Die Ausfertigung eines Ehenichtigkeitsurteils in Kurzform," *De Processibus Matrimonialibus* 2 (1995) 280.

19 John Paul II, Allocution to the Tribunal of the Roman Rota, February 4, 1980: *AAS* 72 (1980) 177; English translation from William Woestman, *Papal Allocutions to the Roman Rota: 1939-2002* (Ottawa: Saint Paul University, 2002) 163.

20 Joaquín Llobell, "La genesi della sentenza canonica," in *Il processo matrimoniale canonico*, Nuova edizione riveduta e ampliata, ed. P. A. Bonnet and C. Gullo, Studi Giuridici 29 (Vatican City: Librería Editrice Vaticana, 1994) 706. The full text reads: "Il fatto è che il Papa non applica il concetto di certezza morale alla *quaestio iuris*, rendendo opportuna la riflessione su talune conseguenze deducibili."

21 Joaquín Llobell, "La sentencia canónica en las causas de nulidad matrimonial," *Ius Canonicum* 29 (1989) 161: "Describir la primordial actitud del juez respecto a la «quaestio iuris» en base a la certeza moral, podría implicar que la norma jurídica se considera susceptible de interpretaciones tan diversas como las posturas de hipotéticas partes que

While judges enjoy a certain degree of autonomy in identifying the *quaestiones iuris* that will be applied to the facts of a case, they are called to fidelity in understanding and using the law in reaching their decisions. The law is what it is and how it has been interpreted by the magisterium, Rotal jurisprudence, and scholars (see cc. 17 and 19). Judges cannot approach the law like they approach the facts, i.e., seeking moral certitude about whether they agree with canon X or the interpretation given to it by the Rota. This is not to say, of course, that judges abdicate their own duty of interpretation. Rather, as servants of the law, judges make their interpretation within the parameters found in canons 16–19.[22]

Tip 3: Recognize How the Law Section Functions Within the Sentence

Good content alone does not make a good law section. The content must be organized and structured properly. Indeed, how the law section is organized will determine how the argument is developed. Organization and structure begin with recognizing how the law section functions within the sentence.

Commentators have long noted that the entire sentence has the structure of a syllogism.[23] The power of the syllogism, James Gardner observes, is that "once the premises are assented to, the logical force of the syllogism precludes any subsequent denial of the conclusion toward which the syllogism inexorably drives; one who has agreed to the premises is trapped."[24] In the definitive sentence, the

---

intentan—en su específica misión procesal de reconstrucción de la «quaestio facti»—afirmar la validez y la nulidad de un mismo matrimonio."

Pius XII noted in his 1942 allocution to the Roman Rota that the moral certitude of judges "si appoggia sulla costanza delle leggi e degli usi che governano la vita umana" (*AAS* 34 [1942] 339).

22   Sanson, 121, observes: "The judge knows the principles of interpretation given in canons 16, 17 and 19. Although in a strict sense only the legislator gives an authentic interpretation of law for the whole ecclesial community, a very important part in clarifying the sense of the law is given to the judge. The interpretation is authoritative for the parties. The judge interprets law by examining similar laws, the purpose of the law, circumstances, and the mind of the legislator. The law is viewed in text and context of the proper meanings of the words, with due regard for parallel passages. The judge decides a case using general principles of law observed with canonical equity, the jurisprudence and praxis of the Roman Curia, and the common and constant opinion of learned persons."

23   See Lemieux, 3; Fernando Della Rocca, *Istituzioni di Diritto Processuale Canonico* (Turin: Unione Tipografico Editrice Torinese, 1946) 299–300; R. Navarro Valls, "Los fundamentos de la sentencia canonica," *Ius Canonicum* 15 (1975) 310; Ignatius Gramunt and Leroy Wauck, "The Judicial Declaration of Consensual Incapacity," in *Canons and Commentaries on Marriage*, ed. Ignatius Gramunt, Javier Hervada, and Leroy Wauck (Collegeville, MN: The Liturgical Press, 1987) 188; Mario F. Pompedda, "Decision-Sentence in Marriage Trials: Of the Concept and Principles for Rendering an Ecclesiastical Sentence," *Quaderno Studio Rotale* 5 (1990) 96; Llobell, "La genesi della sentenza canonica," 697; and idem, "La sentencia canónica en las causas de nulidad matrimonial," 153–155.

24   James A. Gardner, *Legal Argument: The Structure and Language of Effective Advo-*

law section is the major premise; the argument section forms the minor premise; and the dispositive section is the conclusion. At its most basic, then, an affirmative sentence on the ground of partial simulation *contra bonum sacramenti* would play out the argument in this syllogistic form:

Syllogism	Sentence Structure	Argument
Major Premise	*In Iure*	Marital consent that excludes the *bonum sacramenti* by a positive act of the will is invalid.
Minor Premise	*In Facto*	The petitioner excluded the *bonum sacramenti* by a positive act of the will.
Conclusion	*Dispositio*	Therefore, the petitioner's marital consent is invalid.

The motivations in law can be distinguished by the various elements found in the defect of consent formulated as the doubt in the case. In other words, the law section will examine these elements:

- The content of the *bonum sacramenti*
- What it means to exclude the *bonum sacramenti* from consent
- The requirements for a positive act of the will
- How this type of exclusion is proven.

While the first three elements are found in canon 1101 §2 in a general way and in the formulation of the doubt specifically, the fourth element is necessarily an implicit element required by the nature of the judicial process. Each of these elements will become major premises in its own syllogism, where the minor premise will come from a proven fact in the acts leading to a conclusion. Another way of looking at the entire law section, then, is the compilation of the major premises from the all nested syllogisms in a logical, narrative whole.

Because the only way an argument can be attacked is to attack one of the premises, it is necessary that each major and minor premise in each nested syllogism be grounded.[25] A premise cannot be accepted as true simply because the author says so. Major premises obtain certainty either by authority or by content.[26] (Minor premises obtain certainty from proven facts contained the acts of the

---

cacy, 2nd ed. (Newark, NJ: LexisNexis, 2007) 6.

25   See ibid., 27.

26   Working from the perspective of United States civil law, Gardner understands that certainty by authority refers to premises grounded in constitutional, statute, or case law. Certainty by content relies on test, step, and factor analysis (see ibid., 37–48). Because the canonical system does not operate under a system of binding precedent, Gardner's two types of certainty have been adapted in this analysis.

case.) Grounding by authority comes from citing the law, which, by its nature, is to be obeyed. Indeed, no one—including the judge—can overrule the law. For example, the major premise that the petitioner excluded the *bonum sacramenti* by a positive act of the will is grounded in authority by citing canon 1101 §2. It is not unusual, however, for the formulation of the law to be complex. As noted above, the doubt and argument derived from canon 1101 §2 contain three elements. These elements provide "tests" or conditions that must be proven for the requirements of the law to be satisfied or not. Not only do the tests organize the law section but they also provide a structure for the argument section.

Because the law can be vague at times, a major premise can also be grounded in the certainty of content provided by citing Rotal jurisprudence or respected experts. More will be said about the nature and function of Rotal jurisprudence in the next tip. Concerning the use of respected experts, canon 19 states that "the common and constant opinion of learned persons (*doctorum*)" can assist in resolving a case if a legal norm is lacking. One frequently finds in Rotal sentences direct quotations from or references to eminent canonists, psychological and medical professionals, and others to support a proposition or interpretation because these opinions are themselves proposed in reasonable arguments. One benefit of grounding a major premise in Rotal jurisprudence or the opinion of experts is seen in the guidance given for identifying and clarifying tests and factors not expressly stated in the law. For example, canon 1103 states that only grave fear invalidates consent. Yet it was a 1943 decision *coram* Heard[27] that held that grave fear can be either absolute or relative. In this or any factor analysis, Rotal jurisprudence lists various traits that are relevant to a specific issue, not all of which are required for the test to be proven.[28]

Finally, it must be remembered that, though a major premise may be grounded in either authority or content, its certainty does not mean the source is infallible or irreformable. Perhaps an older law was referenced as the authority. Rotal jurisprudence may have changed or developed on the issue. Respected experts may have other valid opinions. It is precisely this potential lack of absolute certainty that provides an opening for attacking the argument in a counterargument.

Tip 4: Understand the Role Played by Rotal Jurisprudence

After the law itself, Rotal jurisprudence is the most important source of material for the law section. It is imperative, then, that judges understand the nature and purpose of Rotal jurisprudence vis-à-vis the crafting of the law section. Ecclesiastical laws are interpreted according to canons 17, 18, and 19. Among the sources canon 19 provides for resolving a *lacuna legis* is the "jurisprudence

---

27   C. Heard, January 21, 1943: *RRDec* 35:62.

28   In addition to factor analysis, Rotal jurisprudence has identified "tests" for proving defects of consent, e.g., the tests of antecedence and severity vis-à-vis the psychic cause required in canon 1095, 3°.

and practice of the Roman Curia." This provision of law led Cardinal Mario Pompedda to conclude:

> As the reference is exclusively to the jurisprudence of the Roman Curia, and since in this matter [i.e., marriage cases] the Tribunal of the Rota is uniquely competent, it follows that by jurisprudence we must mean that which flows from the jurisdictional activity of the same Roman Rota.[29]

Rotal jurisprudence, then, is the collective suppletory law provided by the prelate auditors of the Apostolic Tribunal of the Roman Rota. Each Rotal judge does what any judge must do when no provision of law applies to the case at bar:

> he, since it is his duty to judge and decide the case, must on his own create the norm to apply and he himself must fulfill the role of legislator relative to the unanticipated situation which confronts him. He must do this, however, in accordance with criteria already established in the legal system, thus preventing any abuse on his part.[30]

Even though the Rota plays an important role in assisting tribunals with the interpretation of the law, its decisions do not create binding precedents that must be followed by lower courts.[31] This lack of binding precedential value, however, cannot be construed to mean that Rotal sentences lack authority. The collection of the suppletory laws—this jurisprudence—found in Rotal sentences "has not only a moral, but also a properly juridic authority because it juridically and ef-

---

29   Pompedda, 95. See also John Paul II, Allocution to the Tribunal of the Roman Rota, January 23, 1992, n. 4: *AAS* 85 (1993) 142: "Ancora e proprio nell'ambito della interpretazione della legge canonica, particolarmente ove si presentano o sembrano esservi «lacunae legis», il nuovo Codice—esplicando nel canone 19 ciò che poteva essere desumibile anche dall'omologo canone 20 del precedente testo legislativo—pone con chiarezza il principio per cui, fra le altre fonti suppletorie, sta la giurisprudenza e prassi della Curia Romana. Se poi restringiamo il significato di tale espressione alle cause di nullità di matrimonio, appare evidente che, sul piano del diritto sostantivo e cioè di merito, per giurisprudenza deve intendersi, nel caso, esclusivamente quella emanante dal Tribunale della Rota Romana." Monsignor Ernesto Fiore, dean of the Roman Rota, referenced this notion four years earlier in his greeting to the Holy Father before the latter's 1988 allocution to the Rota: "Ma quando specificamente si tratta di un Tribunale Apostolico quale è la Rota Romana, la giurisprudenza rappresenta quanto meno una fonte suppletoria della legge canonica già nei casi di lacune della legge stessa (cfr. can. 19)" ("Indirizzo di Omaggio al S. Padre," *Monitor Ecclesiasticus* 113 [1988] 172).

30   Mario F. Pompedda, "Jurisprudence as a Source of Law in the Canonical System of Marriage Legislation," in *Marriage Studies: Reflections in Canon Law and Theology*, vol. 4, ed. John A. Alesandro (Washington, DC: Canon Law Society of America, 1990) 111.

31   A Rotal sentence—like that issued by any tribunal—"does not have the force of law and only binds the persons for whom and affects the matters for which it was given" (c. 16 §3). See also Pompedda, "Jurisprudence as a Source of Law," 112.

ficaciously influences the *interpretation* and concrete application of the law."[32] This is precisely what *Pastor bonus*, art. 126 means when it states that, "by virtue of its own decisions, [the Roman Rota] provides assistance to lower tribunals."[33] At the same time, the common understanding of the suppletory laws provided by the Rota "contributes enormously to the creation of *uniformity* in the interpretation and practical actuation of the law."[34]

Any discussion of the nature of Rotal jurisprudence would be remiss if it neglected Sanson's observation underscoring its collective nature.

> We also know that a single Rotal auditor is not an authority in and of himself, that there are different schools of interpretation in the Rota, and that Rotal jurisprudence has continuously developed. A judge may even be misled by using an older Rotal interpretation which may be based on outdated theology, psychology, or even canon law. Nevertheless, Rotal jurisprudence has a unifying function as well as an exemplary one, and its authority is not from one or a few decisions but a manner of judging which is consistent in many decisions over a period of time.[35]

Richard Barrett agrees: "Rotal jurisprudence acquires a firmness when the majority of the Auditors concur on some aspect of the general interpretation of laws and their application to determinate circumstances."[36]

When it comes to Rotal jurisprudence, however, the rubber meets the road when tribunal officials—whether judges, defenders of the bond, or advocates—ask the question: how do I know if the views expressed in this Rotal sentence are Rotal jurisprudence?—at least as understood here. Llobell proposes authenticity, actuality, and the provisional nature of a normative character as three criteria for determining the binding force of Rotal jurisprudence.[37] What any one Rotal

---

32   Pompedda, "Jurisprudence as a Source of Law," 117; emphasis in the original.

33   *Pastor bonus*, art. 126; *AAS* 80 (1988) 892.

34   Pompedda, "Jurisprudence as a Source of Law," 117; emphasis in the original. See also *Pastor bonus*, art. 126; *AAS* 80 (1988) 892.

35   Sanson, 121.

36   Richard Barrett, "Reflections on the *Bonum Coniugum*," *Monitor Ecclesiasticus* 124 (1999) 515, n. 5.

37   Llobell, "La genesi della sentenza canonica," 715–716: "La giurisprudenza rotale avrà quindi valore vincolante per i casi simili, regolati dalla legge in modo lacunoso sia dall'ordinamento latino che orientale quando riunirà i seguenti requisiti:

"a) *Autenticità* derivante dall'inequivocabile autorevole dichiarazione (forse della stessa Rota) di essere pronunciata in un preciso senso per riempire una puntuale lacuna di legge. In assenza di tale formale garanzia, bisognerà ricercare se vi sia *uniformità morale* da parte delle decisioni rotali. Una tale uniformità sarà riscontra-

ponens writes in a sentence, then, can be considered binding to the extent that (1) it comports with the jurisprudence found in other sentences by the same and different auditors, (2) it is current, i.e., it has not been subsequently modified, and (3) it continues to fill a *lacuna legis* until such time as a competent authority decides to act normatively.

Tip 5: Use Current Rotal Jurisprudence

The jurisprudence of the Rota covers not only the defects of marital consent but also various procedural issues that arise in the course of the ordinary contentious process. Recent CLSA conventions have offered seminars that examined force and grave fear and error of quality of a person[38] as well as error that determines the will[39] and defective convalidation.[40] What I propose to do, then, is examine the current jurisprudence of the Rota on two defects of consent: the grave defect of discretion of judgment concerning marriage (c. 1095, 2°) and partial simulation *contra bonum coniugum* (c. 1101 §2). I have chosen these particular defects of consent because (1) jurisprudential developments in the former—a ground still frequently used by the Church's marriage courts—may have been overlooked by busy tribunal officials, and (2) the last decade has seen significant developments in the latter at the Rota.

A. *Grave Defect of Discretion of Judgment (c. 1095, 2°)*

Canon 1058 establishes the principle that "all persons who are not prohibited by law can contract marriage." The marital impediments found in canons 1083 to 1094 state when a person is juridically unqualified (*inhabiles*) and, therefore, prohibited from entering marriage. Also prohibited from marrying are those who are incapable (*incapax*) according to each of the numbers in canon 1095.

---

bile—in senso positivo—quando provenga dall'attività di distinti ponenti e turni; e—in senso negativo—quando non ci sia un atteggiamento discordante da parte delle decisioni rotali.

"b) *Attualità* di questa giurisprudenza, poiché è noto che, nello straordinario sforzo della Rota per sviscerare le esigenze di validità e capacità consensuale, si sono adottati alcuni criteri successivamente modificati dallo stesso Tribunale apostolico.

"c) *Provvisorietà del carattere normativo* della giurisprudenza rotale. La natura nomopoietica cesserebbe nel momento in cui sia dato un intervento specificamente legislativo circa l'oggetto concreto. Con tale intervento del legislatore non si darebbe più la condizione indispensabile per la forza nomopoietica autonoma della giurisprudenza rotale, cioè l'esistenza di una lacuna di legge."

38   See John G. Johnson, " '...Into Something Rich and Strange': Some Changes in Rotal Jurisprudence Inspired by the 1983 Code of Canon Law," *CLSA Proceedings* 70 (2008) 158–176.

39   See John P. Beal, "Determining Error: Hot New Ground or Recycled Old Ground?" *CLSA Proceedings* 71 (2009) 62–89.

40   See Augustine Mendonça, "Defective Convalidation," *CLSA Proceedings* 70 (2008) 193–236.

Canon 1095, 2° states that persons "who suffer from a grave defect of discretion of judgment concerning the essential matrimonial rights and duties mutually to be handed over and accepted" are incapable of establishing marriage. I would like to focus briefly on two aspects of this *caput nullitatis*: the notion of discretion of judgment and how it can be defective, i.e., the cause of the defect.

1. Discretion of Judgment

Ignatius Gramunt and Leroy Wauck defined discretion of judgment as the "ability or power to discern particular goods and make particular judgments by differentiating and assessing those goods."[41] As a psychological power, the discretion of judgment is comprised of three elements: cognitive knowledge, evaluative knowledge, and internal freedom. A recent sentence *coram* Pinto, himself citing Mario Pompedda, summarizes what is required for discretion of judgment.

> We are able to consider that discretion or maturity of judgment entails three aspects in ordinary Rotal jurisprudence, that is three well-defined elements: a sufficient intellectual cognition concerning the objects of consent; the achievement of a sufficient evaluation proportionate to marriage or more precisely, a critical knowledge; and finally, internal freedom, that is the capacity to deliberate with sufficient evaluation of the motives with freedom of the will from any determining interior impulses.[42]

Rotal jurisprudence has come to understand the term "discretion of judgment" to mean maturity of judgment.[43] The term maturity, however, has different meanings. In his 1987 Rotal allocution, John Paul II warned against experts not formed in a Christian anthropology. For these experts, "*psychic* maturity which is seen as the *goal* of human development ends up being confused with *canonical* maturity which is rather *the basic minimum* required for establishing the validity

---

41   Ignatius Gramunt and Leroy Wauck, "'Lack of Due Discretion': Incapacity or Error?" *Ius Canonicum* 32 (1992) 537.

42   Mario F. Pompedda, "Ancora sulle nevrosi e personalità psicopatiche in rapporto al consenso matrimoniale," in idem, *Studi di diritto matrimoniale canonico* (Milan: Giuffre, 1993) 56, quoted in *c.* Pinto, March 24, 2000: *RRDec* 92 (2000) 270: "Possiamo ritenere che la *discretio* o *maturitas iudicii*, implica nell'ordinaria giurisprudenza rotale tre aspetti, cioè tre elementi ben definiti: una sufficiente *conoscenza intellettuale* circa l'*oggetto* del consenso;—il raggiungimento di una sufficiente *valutazione proporzionata* al connubio, ossia una conoscenza critica;—e infine la *libertà interna*, cioè la capacità di deliberare con sufficiente valutazione dei motivi e con autonomia della volontà da qualsiasi impulso interno determinante." English trans. by Richard F. Reidy, "The Grave Defect of Discretion of Judgment Necessary to Establish the Invalidity of Marriage Under Canon 1095, 2°" (JCL thesis, The Catholic University of America, 2010) 40.

43   See Augustine Mendonça, "Consensual Incapacity for Marriage," *The Jurist* 54 (1994) 494.

of marriage."[44] So important is this point, that the pope repeated it the following year:

> As I noted last year, the misunderstanding can arise from the fact that the expert declares that a party is incapable of contracting marriage, while referring not to the minimum capacity sufficient for valid consent, but rather to the ideal of full maturity in relation to happy married life.[45]

But it is not only experts who confuse or misunderstand these uses of the term maturity. The parties and witnesses who participate in our tribunal processes do not understand maturity in its canonical sense but rather in its commonly used psychological sense. It ought not surprise us, then that people—understanding maturity as some state reached later in life rather than earlier—respond to our questions like this:

- "Even though Jim was a successful businessman, he was immature."
- "Of my three daughters, Allison was the least mature."
- "I was more mature when I married my present husband than when I married [the Respondent] twenty years ago."

If most people—experts included—see maturity as some future state of development or growth, we would hope that the petitioner has matured in the twenty years since her first marriage. But her declaration of this fact does not prove that she was either psychologically or canonically immature at the time of the first marriage. As used in Rotal jurisprudence since 1987, then, discretion—i.e., maturity—of judgment refers to the canonical minimum required of a party for contracting marriage. In other words, to say that a party's discretion of judgment was gravely defective is to say that he or she did not possess the minimum ability to make a judgment to enter marriage. It should be noted that the law presumes that parties to marriage possess this canonical minimum of discretion of judgment at puberty.[46]

---

44 John Paul II, Allocution to the Tribunal of the Roman Rota, February 5, 1987, n. 6: *AAS* 79 (1987) 1457; trans. Woestman, 194; emphasis added in translation.

45 John Paul II, Allocution to the Tribunal of the Roman Rota, January 25, 1988, n. 9: *AAS* 80 (1988) 1183; trans. Woestman, 201.

46 See 1983 code, c. 1083. See also Ignatius Gramunt and Leroy Wauck, "The Legal Rule of Consensual Incapacity," in *Canons and Commentaries on Marriage*, ed. Ignatius Gramunt et al. (Collegeville, MN: The Liturgical Press, 1987) 166–167 and 170–174; John P. Beal, "Diriment Impediments Specifically [cc. 1083–1094]," in *New Commentary on the Code of Canon Law*, ed. John P. Beal, et al. (New York/Mahwah, NJ: Paulist Press, 2000) 1282–1284; Juan Ignacio Bañares, Commentary on canon 1083, in *Exegetical Commentary on the Code of Canon Law*, ed. Ángel Marzoa et al., Ernest Caparros, gen. ed. for the English language edition (Montreal: Wilson & Lafleur, 2004) 3/2:1170–1171; and Pedro-Juan Viladrich, "Matrimonial Consent," in *Exegetical Commentary on the Code of Canon Law*, 3/2:1229–1230.

2. Discretion of Judgment That is Defective

Judges are fond of noting that canon 1095, 2° is silent as to the cause of the defect of discretion of judgment. John Paul filled this *lacuna legis* for each of the numbers in canon 1095 in his 1987 Rotal allocution:

> For the canonist the principle must remain clear that only *incapacity* and not *difficulty* in giving consent and in realizing a true community of life and love invalidates a marriage... . The hypothesis of real incapacity is to be considered only when an anomaly of a serious nature is present, which, however it may be defined, must substantially vitiate the capacity of the individual to understand and/or will.[47]

It is not just any psychic anomaly but rather a *grave* psychic anomaly that is required as the cause of the defective discretion of judgment. As the pope explained in his 1988 allocution, the psychic anomaly must be grave because "the normal human condition in this world also includes moderate forms of psychological difficulty" and "only the most severe forms of psychopathology impair substantially the freedom of the individual."[48]

Since 1987, John Paul II's understanding that a grave psychic anomaly must be the cause of defective discretion of judgment has not only been accepted into Rotal jurisprudence[49] but also included in the *ius* of the Church. Article 203 §1 of the 2005 instruction *Dignitas Connubii* states that the judge is to have the assistance of an expert in cases involving a "defect of consent because of a *mentis morbum* or (*vel*) because of the incapacities described in can. 1095." The latter phrase "or because of the incapacities described in can. 1095" is new with the instruction and modifies canon 1680. In his 2009 allocution to the Rota, Pope Benedict XVI reaffirmed the teaching of his predecessor as expressed in *Dignitas Connubii*.[50]

It is precisely the presence of a grave psychic anomaly that distinguishes cases where parties *could not* exercise discretion of judgment concerning marriage from those where they *did not* exercise such discretion. Gramunt and Wauck explain:

---

47 John Paul II, 1987 allocution, n. 7; *AAS* 79 (1987) 1457; trans. Woestman, 194; emphasis in the original.

48 John Paul II, 1988 allocution, nn. 6 and 7; *AAS* 80 (1988) 1182; trans. Woestman, 199–200.

49 See Mendonça, "Consensual Incapacity for Marriage," 506; *c.* Boccafola, June 23, 1988: *RRDec* 80 (1988) 428-429; and *c.* Faltin, April 6, 1995: *RRDec* 87 (1995) 275 and 279.

50 See Benedict XVI, Allocution to the Tribunal of the Roman Rota, January 29, 2009: *AAS* 101 (2009) 126.

> A person who labors under some disorder which prevents him or her from making a particular assessment concerning the desirability of this particular marriage (with its essential rights and obligations), cannot arrive at the practical judgment involved in matrimonial consent. This, however, is *not to be confused* with error of judgment or "poor judgment," since a *mistake* in judgment concerning the character of one's spouse or the circumstances surrounding the marriage does not mean incapacity. A person who is psychologically capable can rectify the mistakes or draw greater good from them, but a person who *lacks the fundamental psychological make-up* is simply not able to be committed to the "essential matrimonial rights and obligations to be given and accepted."[51]

From this very brief—and, admittedly, incomplete—review of the current state of Rotal jurisprudence concerning the grave defect of discretion of judgment concerning marriage, one can see the developments in this defect of consent in the past quarter century. It is not uncommon, however, to find law sections that do not include any of the developments examined here. Indeed, a few cite no Rotal sentences since the years leading up to the promulgation of the 1983 code! One is left to wonder how a just decision can be rendered when the reasons in law on which it is partially based do not acknowledge—let alone incorporate—developments in the law and jurisprudence.

B. Partial Simulation *contra bonum coniugum* (c. 1101 §2)

With the 1983 code's inclusion of the *bonum coniugum* as an end of marriage and the ordination to the *bonum coniugum* as an essential element of marriage, canonists and Rotal jurisprudence began to explore what these terms meant juridically. In the first two decades following the promulgation of the 1983 code, Rotal jurisprudence examined the nature of the *bonum coniugum* with an application to cases involving the incapacity of a party to consent to marriage, specifically canon 1095, 2° and 3°. Representative of this understanding is a 1999 sentence *coram* De Lanversin, which itself makes use of earlier work by the Rotal auditor Francesco Bruno.

> 14. ... However, if someone is radically incapable of self-giving, by reason of some psychic disorders [*sic*], his/her material consent is to be held as void because of the total ineptness of such act to pledge genuine interpersonal relations ordered to promote the moral, spiritual and social good of the spouses.
>
> 15. "Interpersonal communion is not confined to sex but presumes the capacity for love and self-giving by which some personal goods are communicated in order to build up the good of the spouses and

---

51 Gramunt and Wauck, "The Legal Rule of Consensual Incapacity," 175; emphasis in the original.

attain the ends of marriage. The radical incapacity to establish interpersonal relations prevents the good of the spouses, for it makes it impossible to assume and fulfill conjugal duties" (*coram* Bruno, sent. 16 December 1988, RR. Dec., vol. 80 [1988], p. 748, n. 5).[52]

Eventually, though, canonists and the Rota began to consider if and how the ordination to the *bonum coniugum* of canon 1055 §1 could be an autonomous ground of invalidity according to canon 1101 §2. The thinking runs along these lines: Canon 1055 §1 describes the marital covenant—*matrimonium in facto esse*—as a partnership of the whole of life (*consortium totius vitae*). This covenantal partnership of the whole of life, the canon tells us, "is by its nature ordered to the good of the spouses and the procreation and education of offspring." Two conclusions can be drawn from this doctrine. First, the *bonum coniugum* cannot be identified with the partnership of the whole of life. For, if that were true, then exclusion of the good of the spouses would amount to total simulation. Second, because the marital consortium is ordered to the *bonum coniugum*, the good of the spouses is an end of marriage, which exists outside the marriage. Cormac Burke's position, then, makes perfect sense: because the *bonum coniugum* exists outside marriage (as an end), no one has a right to it.[53] What a spouse does have a right to, however, is for his or her marriage to be ordered toward the good of the spouses. The ordination to the *bonum coniugum*, just like the ordination to the *bonum prolis*, is an essential element of marriage[54]—and thus internal to the marriage. For this reason, the exclusion of the ordination to the good of the spouses from a party's consent by a positive act of the will invalidates marriage.

While Burke argued that cases of partial simulation *contra bonum coniugum* are rare and should generally be considered under the three Augustinian *bona*,[55] the Roman Rota has judged more than a handful of cases on this ground since 2000.[56] The law section of Civili's 2000 sentence traces the notion of the *bonum*

---

52   *Coram* DeLanversin, May 15, 1997: *RRDec* 89 (1997) 389–390; English trans. in *Monitor Ecclesiasticus* 124 (1999) 469; adapted.

53   See Cormac Burke, "Progressive Jurisprudential Thinking," *The Jurist* 58 (1998) 445–447.

54   "Ordinatio enim matrimonii ad bonum coniugum est revera elementum essentiale foederis matrimonialis, minime vero finis subiectivus nupturientis" (*Communicationes* 15 [1983] 221).

55   See Burke, 450–478.

56   In a May 2009 paper given at the Eastern Regional Conference of Canonists in Rockville Centre, NY, Augustine Mendonça ("Recent Rotal Jurisprudence on Exclusion of *Bonum Coniugum*," 1–2) identified eight sentences from the Rota on the exclusion of the good of the spouses: *c.* Pinto, June 9, 2000: *RRDec*. 92 (2000) 460–468, English trans. in *Studia canonica* 39 (2005) 271–288; *c.* Civili, November 8, 2000: *RRDec* 92 (2000) 609–620, English trans. in *Studia canonica* 39 (2005) 309–330; *c.* Serrano, January 23, 2004, English trans. in *Philippine Canonical Forum* 10 (2008) 321–338; *c.* Turnaturi, May 13, 2004: Prot. N. 18.766 (unpublished), English trans. in *Studies in Church Law* 2 (2006)

coniugum from the mutual assistance found in canon 1013 §2 of the 1917 code through *Casti connubii*, *Gaudium et spes*, and *Familiaris consortio*. From the latter document, Civili highlights the following text of John Paul II:

> This conjugal communion sinks its roots in the natural complementarity that exists between man and woman, and is nurtured through the personal willingness of the spouses to share their entire life-project, what they have and what they are: for this reason such communion is the fruit and the sign of a profoundly human need.[57]

The auditor observes that the *bonum coniugum* comprises two essential elements: each spouse is a human person, and the man and woman possess equal personal dignity within the conjugal relationship.[58] Civili concludes:

> A positive act of the will against the ordination of marriage toward the good of the spouses is verified when the will of those who marry is directed contrary to both the human and Christian commitment for a continued growth in communion toward a more fruitful unity of bodies, hearts, minds and wills. This daily growth cannot occur unless one, by respecting the dignity of the other, gives him/herself to the other with total love that is unique and exclusive. Human dignity is based on fundamental human rights. Therefore, one who intends by a positive act of the will not to recognize the fundamental rights of the other, excludes the good of the spouses.[59]

Quoting Sebastian Villegiante, the 2004 sentence *coram* Turnaturi puts a finer point on the nature of the exclusion:

> One who wants marriage, but wants it only to use the person of the spouse for the exclusive purpose of obtaining his or her goods and fortune, *per se* does not exclude or cannot exclude the other goods, but such a person certainly does not give rise to a dual and equal interpersonal relationship ordered to the common good of their own perfection in the quality of spouses. The good of the spouses is not realized as a whole, if it is torn away from other goods, because it is

---

297–321; *c.* Ferreira Pena, June 9, 2006, English trans. in *Studia canonica* 42 (2008) 503–523; *c.* Monier, October 27, 2006: Prot. N. 17.557 (unpublished), English trans. in *Studia canonica* 43 (2009) 243–260; *c.* Verginelli, March 16, 2007 (unpublished); and *c.* Arokiaraj, March 13, 2008; English trans. in *Studia canonica* 42 (2008) 525–540.

[57] John Paul II, apostolic exhortation *Familiaris consortio*, November 22, 1981: *AAS* 74 (1982) 101, quoted in *c.* Civili, November 8, 2000, n. 3: *RRDec* 92 (2000) 611; *Studia canonica* 39 (2005) 313.

[58] *Coram* Civili, nn. 4 and 5; *RRDec* 92 (2000) 611–613.

[59] Ibid., n. 6; *RRDec* 92 (2000) 613; *Studia canonica* 39 (2005) 319–320.

the matrimonial institution in itself which, from the time of creation, is above all ordered to the good of the spouses....[60]

In light of his review of the Rotal sentences judged on the exclusion of the ordination to the *bonum coniugum*, Mendonça summarizes the notion of the good of the spouses in this way:

> The true meaning of *bonum coniugum* is the perfection or wholesome growth of each spouse and of both spouses together within the context of the conjugal communion. A man and a woman are joined together to perfect each other both in their earthly existence and in the pursuit of their eternal salvation. This spousal perfection embraces every aspect of a human being, namely the physical, emotional, sexual, moral, spiritual, and social dimensions. Each spouse has the right to his or her perfection in all these aspects of human life.[61]

For busy tribunal officials, knowing the content of a defect of consent is only half the battle. Advocates, defenders, and judges also want and need to know what types of behavior, characteristics, and motivations can serve as proof in these cases. Like any type of simulation, an invalidating exclusion of the *bonum coniugum* happens only by a positive act of the will, which can be explicit or implicit. Moreover, the simulation is proven by either the direct method—i.e., by a judicial or extrajudicial confession, corroboration of witnesses, and a *causa simulandi* that outweighs the *causa contrahendi*—or the indirect method—in the absence of any type of confession of the simulator, proofs drawn from the circumstances and motives before, during, and after the marriage. Because it would be rare that a party explicitly excludes the ordination to the *bonum coniugum* from his or her marital consent,[62] cases involving this type of partial simulation will use the indirect method of proof.

Among possible motives for excluding the ordination to the *bonum coniugum*, one can identify an aversion to one's spouse, malice (including the revenge postulated by the famous Jemolo case[63]), and personal advantage. Taking her lead from Turnaturi's 2004 sentence, Lynda Robitaille states that people do

> marry for their own benefit. They do not marry to build a partner-

---

60   S. Villeggiante, "Il '*bonum coniugum*' e l'oggetto del consenso matrimoniale in diritto canonico," *Monitor Ecclesiasticus* 120 (1995) 307, quoted in c. Turnaturi, May 13, 2004, n. 10; *Studies in Church Law* 2 (2006) 308.

61   Mendonça, "Recent Rotal Jurisprudence on Exclusion of *Bonum Coniugum*," 11.

62   See Lynda Robitaille, "Exclusion of the *Bonum Coniugum*: Interpreting and Assessing Evidence," *CLSGBI Newsletter* 157 (2009) 107.

63   See Lawrence G. Wrenn, "Refining the Essence of Marriage," in idem, *The Invalid Marriage* (Washington, DC: CLSA, 1998) 202–203.

ship, to form a couple with another. They marry for themselves, for their personal good, because there is something they perceive that they want from being 'married,' yet they are not willing to put themselves out in any way for anyone other than themselves.[64]

Judges and other officials who have served any time at all in a tribunal have undoubtedly seen a case or two that contains motives such as Robitaille describes. Yet these cases may have been judged on a grave defect of discretion of judgment or an inability to assume the essential obligations of marriage—and not an exclusion of the *bonum coniugum*.[65] Canon 1095 would be the appropriate ground if a grave psychic anomaly renders a person's discretion of judgment gravely defective. But should the psychological expert not diagnose a psychic anomaly or diagnose an anomaly that is not grave, and there is proof of a positive act of the will excluding the *bonum coniugum*, then simulation is a possible answer.[66]

Since cases involving an exclusion of the good of the spouses will often make use of the axiom "actions speak louder than words," tribunal officials are interested in the types of behavior that might indicate a positive act of the will—albeit implicit—to exclude the *bonum coniugum*. Robitaille has identified several such indicators:

- People who have never had to work or sacrifice for anything in their lives;
- People who expect to receive everything they want, the way they want it;
- People who view the world superficially, i.e., for its wealth, beauty, material goods;
- People who enter a lifelong, faithful and fruitful commitment yet expect that the marriage will not demand anything of them that they do not choose to give.[67]

Ultimately, Robitaille says, persons who exclude the ordination to the good of the spouses want and choose to enter a "unilateral partnership." The challenge for tribunal officials today is not only to understand how the Rota has embraced and used this ground of invalidity but to recognize it in the cases that come before our courts.[68]

---

64 Robitaille, 98.

65 See ibid.

66 Robitaille, 110, draws the following conclusion: "If, however, the person wants only his or her own good through selfishness, self-centeredness, or a non-recognition of the worth of the other as partner, then it is not a case of incapacity, it is a case of exclusion: the person chose his or her own good over that of the spouses together. This is an act of the will: a choice against the good of the spouses."

67 The listing here is adapted from Robitaille, 106.

68 See ibid., 110.

Tip 6: Incorporate Updated Procedural Law

It is not enough for tribunal officials to keep up to date on the substantive issues concerning the various defects of consent found in the Code of Canon Law. As important as the content of each defect of consent is, equally important is the procedural law that governs which proofs can be admitted to the trial and how the proofs are to be used. The laws that direct the use and interpretation of proofs, for example, can and should be applied to the facts of the case. For this reason, judges and other officials will want to incorporate current procedural law in their law sections. The 2005 instruction *Dignitas Connubii* has provided several clarifications and elaborations of the procedural law governing marriage trials. Two are worthy of a brief examination here.

A. *The Confessions of Parties*

Ecclesiastical processes admit various types of proofs: declarations of the parties, the testimony of witnesses, reports of experts, documents, and presumptions (see cc. 1526–1586). Unlike the former law,[69] canons 1536 §2 and 1679 of the 1983 code and *Dignitas Connubii*, art. 180 see the declarations of the parties as having probative value. Of the types of declarations that parties might make in a marriage trial, the confession is singled out. Yet it is precisely the object of the confession that has been modified by the instruction. The development of the procedural norms concerning the confession of a party is seen clearly when the texts of canon 1535 and *Dignitas Connubii*, art. 179 §2 are placed side-by-side. Emphasis has been added to underscore the instruction's elaboration of the law.

1983 code, c. 1535	*DC* art. 179 §2
A judicial confession is the written or oral assertion of some fact *against oneself* before a competent judge by any party *concerning the matter of the trial*, whether made spontaneously or while being questioned by the judge.	However, in causes of the nullity of marriage a judicial confession is understood to be a declaration, made in writing or orally, before a competent judge, spontaneously or at the questioning of the judge, by which a party asserts a fact *regarding oneself that is opposed to the validity of the marriage.*

Following the jurisprudence of the Rota, *Dignitas Connubii*, art. 179 §2 establishes a different understanding of a confession in marriage trials.[70] The import of this development for tribunal officials is that the object of the confession has been changed from a statement of a party against himself or herself to a statement by a party concerning himself or herself and against the validity of the

---

69 See Sacred Congregation for the Sacraments, instruction *Provida Mater*, August 15, 1936: *AAS* 28 (1936) 337: "Depositio iudicialis coniugum non est apta ad probationem contra valorem matrimonii constituendam."

70 See Lüdicke and Jenkins, 305.

marriage.[71] Because "the weight of a confession rests on the presumption that a person would not normally speak against his/her interests in trial,"[72] the fact that the confession in marriage trials concerns the party and is against the invalidity of the marriage places the focus on the marriage and not the party's interest (i.e., for or against the declaration of invalidity) in the process.

To illustrate this point, take the example of the petitioner who alleges an exclusion of children on her part. If the petitioner declared before the judge that she handed over the right to acts per se apt for the generation of offspring (c. 1101 §2), she would be making a confession as understood in canon 1535—though not *DC* article 179 §2—because her statement contravenes her interest in having the marriage declared invalid but not the invalidity of the marriage. On the other hand, in the case of the respondent in favor of a declaration of the invalidity of his marriage due to *dolus* on the petitioner (c. 1098) his admission that he intentionally deceived the petitioner does not contravene his position at trial (c. 1535) but does speak against the validity of the marriage (*DC* art. 179 §2).

B. *The Use and Role of Experts*

Judges, defenders of the bond, and advocates are well aware of the requirement of canon 1680:

> In cases of impotence or defect of consent because of mental illness (*mentis morbum*), the judge is to use the services of one or more experts unless it is clear from the circumstances that it would be useless to do so; in other cases the prescript of can. 1574 is to be observed.

Understanding the canon's use of the term *mentis morbum* to mean a psychopathology in the psychiatric sense, tribunal officials have liberally taken advantage of the exception clause ("unless it is clear from the circumstances that it would be useless to do so") to forego getting an expert's report, especially in cases involving a grave defect of discretion. In light of John Paul II's 1987 and 1988 allocutions and Rotal jurisprudence, article 203 of *Dignitas Connubii* has elaborated on when the use of an expert is to be employed in marriage trials.

> In causes concerning impotence or a defect of consent because of a *mentis morbum* or (*vel*) because of the incapacities described in can. 1095, the judge is to employ (*utatur*) the assistance of one or more experts, unless from the circumstances this would appear evidently useless (cf. can. 1680).

By adding the phrase "or (*vel*) because of the incapacities described in can.

---

71   See ibid. and Johnson, 166, n. 41.

72   Roch Pagé, "The Instruction *Dignitas Connubii*: Selected Issues" (paper presented at the Western Region Canon Law Convention, San Jose, CA, March 1–3, 2010).

1095," the instruction recognizes that the psychic anomalies required to prove cases using canon 1095 are broader than the psychopathologies called *mentis morbum*.[73] In other words, because canon 1095 cases require some psychic anomaly, article 203 mandates the normative use of an expert.

It is also worth noting that experts do more than simply bring their particular expertise to bear on the facts of a case as required by law. As a 1998 response of the Apostolic Signatura states,

> The services of experts in such cases are to be employed not only because they have been prescribed by law, but especially because such services are an instrument of proof, which, as happens in most cases, the judge cannot ignore in order to derive moral certainty "from the acts and proofs", so as to be able to pronounce sentence in favour of the nullity of a marriage.[74]

Judges and advocates, then, should welcome the assistance of experts inasmuch as they serve as another means of proof in what might otherwise be a case with insufficient proofs from other sources.

That exceptions to the principle stated in canon 1680 and article 203 §1 exist is clear not only from the clause "unless from the circumstances this would appear evidently useless" but also from the verb form used in the code and instruction. In each case, the text states that "the judge is to employ" (*iudex ... utatur*) one or more experts in the aforementioned cases. By using the deponent verb *utor, uti* in the third person subjunctive mood, the code and instruction establish

---

73   See Antoni Stankiewicz, "Some Indications About Canon 1095 in the Instruction *Dignitas Connubii*," in *Studies on the Instruction* Dignitas Connubii, ed. Patricia M. Dugan and Luis Navarro, Gratianus Series (Montréal: Wilson & Lafleur Ltée, 2006) 43: "This was seen as supporting the opinion that rejected such an obligation in cases under canon 1095—especially those dealing with the serious defect of discretion of judgment and with the incapacity for matrimonial obligations (c. 1095, nn. 2°–3°), because there was no mention to canon 1095 in canon 1680." While Stankiewicz references Wrenn, 30 as representative of those who hold this opinion, the auditor's statement corrects the view proposed more recently by Pagé, 16: "This new prescript does not mean that for each of the three incapacities of can. 1095, the judge is obliged to request an expertise. Can. 1680 remains in force when stating that 'in cases of defect of consent because of mental illness, the judge is to use the services of one or more experts unless it is clear from the circumstances that it would be useless to do so.'"

74   Supreme Tribunal of the Apostolic Signatura, response, June 16, 1998, n. 4: Prot. N. 28252/97 VT, in *Forum* 9/2 (1998) 54. See also Mario F. Pompedda, "Inability to Assume the Essential Obligations of Marriage," in *Incapacity for Marriage: Jurisprudence and Interpretation*, Acts of the III Gregorian Colloquium, ed. Robert M. Sable (Rome: Pontificia Universitas Gregoriana, 1987) 208: "For the ecclesiastical judge, the *peritia* represents one of the elements of proof, but not the sole element of proof which the law accords to the judge to arrive at a decision. The *peritia* is one of the means to arrive at the truth."

the normative way of acting, all the while recognizing that the ideal might not be achieved in particular cases.[75] It cannot be forgotten, moreover, that exceptions to the law—whether recognized explicitly or implicitly—are subject to strict interpretation (c. 18).

What types of cases have been identified in jurisprudence or by commentators as exceptions to the norm of *Dignitas Connubii*, article 203 §1? The Apostolic Signatura has identified two exceptions.

> An expert report about the psychic state of a party can seem to be "evidently useless" in order to prove the nullity of a marriage: a) when, even if the matter in hand is not «an expert report» in the technical sense, in the acts there exists a document or testimonial, which is so qualified, that it provides sufficient relevant proof to the judge; b) when from proven facts and circumstances, without any doubt, there appears either a lack of sufficient use of reason or a serious lack of discretion of judgement or an incapacity to assume the essential obligations of marriage. The reason is that in this case the nullity of the marriage can be declared on account of an evident lack of consent, without the need of a carefully drawn up diagnosis of the psychic cause due to which there exists that defect. However, in such cases the judge can ask the expert to explain some document or fact, which exists or is alleged in the acts.[76]

A third exception is recognized among commentators. For example, Lüdicke and Jenkins write that an expert's report is not required

> when the proofs are so conclusive that a report from an expert becomes superfluous. This applies above all in causes ... based on c. 1095, 1°, but for which insufficient facts have been adduced to indicate a basis for the ground.[77]

In other words, if the specific defect of incapacity will be given a negative decision because it lacks any basis in the facts presented, the judge would not need to obtain an expert's report to substantiate this.

A second development with regard to procedural law and experts concerns more explicit norms regulating the interaction of tribunal officials and experts. *Dignitas Connubii*, art. 209 goes into some detail concerning what the judge is

---

75 See John M. Huels, *Liturgy and Law: Liturgical Law in the System of Roman Catholic Canon Law* (Montréal: Wilson & Lafleur, 2006) 235.

76 Supreme Tribunal of the Apostolic Signatura, response, n. 5; *Forum* 9/2 (1998) 54–55.

77 Lüdicke and Jenkins, 346.

to ask the expert in the decree of appointment and how the expert is to respond.

>§1. In causes of incapacity, according to the understanding of can. 1095, the judge is not to omit (*ne omittat*) asking the expert whether one or both parties suffered from a particular habitual or transitory anomaly at the time of the wedding; what was its seriousness; and when, from what cause and in what circumstances it originated and manifested itself.
>
>§2. Specifically:
>
>1° in causes of *defectus usus rationis*, he is to ask (*quaerat*) whether the anomaly seriously disturbed the use of reason at the time of the celebration of the marriage; and with what intensity and by what symptoms it manifested itself;
>
>2° in causes of *defectus discretionis iudicii*, he is to ask (*quaerat*) what was the effect of the anomaly on the critical and elective faculty for making serious decisions, particularly in freely choosing a state in life;
>
>3° finally, in causes of incapacity to assume the essential obligations of marriage, he is to ask (*quaerat*) what was the nature and gravity of the psychic cause on account of which the party would labour not only under a serious difficulty but even the impossibility of sustaining the actions inherent in the obligations of marriage.
>
>§3. The expert in his opinion is to respond (*respondere debet*) to the individual points defined in the decree of the judge according to the precepts of his own art and science; he is to take care (*caveat*) lest he exceed the limits of his task by giving forth judgements which pertain to the judge (cf. cann. 1577, §1; 1574).

In addition to general questions that the judge is to ask the expert, the norm also provides specific areas of inquiry for each of the numbers of canon 1095. The expert is to be given a copy of the acts and other pertinent documents so he or she can accomplish the task assigned by the judge (*DC* art. 207 §2). The report of the expert is itself to be an argument that makes the case for his or her professional opinion.[78] *Dignitas Connubii*, art. 212 prescribes that, upon receiving the expert's report, the judge weighs the conclusions, giving the reasons why the expert's opinion is to be accepted or not.[79] Pompedda has detailed more precisely

---

[78] See *DC* art. 210 §2. Pompedda, 213 states: "We must accustom ourselves, then, to require the *peritus* to present an opinion that is argumentative, an opinion that evidence his/her reasons and motivations both from the Acts and from the principles of the psychological sciences."

[79] Mario Pompedda lamented: "Regrettably medical opinions often are assumed into the sentences of ecclesiastical tribunals without that necessary 'critical filtering' which is part of the judge's task."

how the judge weighs this intervention.

> To evaluate an expert's report means:
>
> —To take into account the deductive principles used in the report and the methods followed by the *peritus* or expert in the report;
>
> —To determine which facts or *indicia* in the acts have lead [*sic*] the experts to reach an opinion; whether these facts are truly demonstrated from the acts or from a specific medical examination;
>
> —To affect what may be called an effort at translating the expert's report from a psychological plane to a juridic plane;
>
> —To examine and then to accept only those conclusions of the expert which both are founded on widely-accepted scientific reasonings and are founded in the constant principles of rational psychology.[80]

Finally, *Dignitas Connubii* gives a role to the defender of the bond vis-à-vis the expert in canon 1095 cases. Article 56 §4 entrusts these functions to the defender:

- To ensure that the questions proposed are clear and do not exceed the expert's competence;
- To see if the expert's opinion uses a Christian anthropology and scientific method, pointing out to the judge anything in favor of validity;
- To indicate to the appellate court anything improperly evaluated by the lower judge.

The details found in the 2005 instruction concerning the use and role of experts in marriage cases manifest developments in procedural law since the promulgation of the 1983 code. Because the motives *in iure* include issues of process as well as substance, judges must not only be aware of these developments but also include them in their law sections.

Tip 7: Know the Audience Who Will Read the Sentence

The definitive sentence contains the reasoned decision rendered by a judge in response to a doubt formulated on the basis of the petitioner's *libellus* and respondent's reaction. Along with the defender of the bond, the petitioner and

---

"In the first level, it is this 'critical filtering' which brings with itself a *correct interpretation* of the reasonings inspired by psychoanalytic criteria and then more generally by psychological-testing or phenomenological structures. However at the next stage the judge must 'sift out' only those elements which are juridical in character. For the purposes of the decision, some of these elements will have canonical relevance, others will not" ("Decision-Sentence in Marriage Trials," 92).

80 Pompedda, "Decision-Sentence in Marriage Trials," 92.

respondent form the first audience of the judge's legal reasoning.[81] Inasmuch as the parties are not experts in canon law, Lüdicke and Jenkins assert that the legal reasoning "concerning the impugned marriage is to be expressed in a way that can be understood."[82] Indeed, the petitioner and respondent should be able to understand why the court decided as it did so that the aggrieved party can vindicate his or her rights by means of a complaint of nullity or appeal.[83] What this undoubtedly means for the petitioner and respondent is that the law section serves a catechetical function.[84] The parties to marriage trials include not only faithful Catholics but also ambivalent and hostile Catholics. Non-Catholic Christians and non-Christians also participate in marriage trials. A clearly written law section can be a teachable moment and correct some of the misinformation that exists in the world about the Catholic understanding of Christian marriage. As important as sensitive, cautious, and clear language is in communicating the motives in law for an affirmative decision, such care is needed even more when the decision is negative.[85]

Of course, writing for the parties does not negate the fact that the sentence, including the law section, will also be read by at least one tribunal at the appellate level. Lest the higher court conclude that the judge possesses a faulty understanding of the motives *in iure*, law sections should not water down the finer points of the pertinent defects of consent or procedural law simply in an effort to aid the comprehension of the parties. With a little effort, the proper balance can be found between the precise, technical legal language required for the appellate court and the clear, accessible—yet still correct—language that enables the parties to exercise their rights knowledgably.

Tip 8: Organize the Law Section Logically

The eminent canonist Francis Roberti said that the law section is a systematic explanation of the juridic principles that serve to define the question.[86] Unfortunately, Cardinal Jullien's observation shows how far practice can be from theory:

---

81 Canon 1615 requires that the sentence be published to the parties either by giving it to the parties or their procurators or by sending it to them. The right of the parties to obtain a copy of the sentence is reinforced by the precept of c. 1634 §2 in which the appellate judge can bind the lower judge to fulfill the obligation of c. 1615. For an interesting examination of how canon 1615 is implemented in select U.S. tribunals and the underlying reasons, see Susan Mulheron, "Publication of the Definitive Sentence in a Marriage Nullity Case: An Analysis of Canons 1614-1615 and Tribunal Practice in the United States" (JCL thesis, The Catholic University of America, 2011).

82 Lüdicke and Jenkins, 414.

83 See Weber, 276.

84 See Grimm, 266–267.

85 See ibid., 267.

86 Francesco Roberti, *De Processibus*, vol. 2 (Rome: Apud Aedes Facultatis Iuridicae ad S. Apollinaris, 1926) 187.

The *in iure*, instead of being a sober and precisely documented exposition of the central point of law, is a bad treatise of law, charged with unnecessary detail, loaded with fragments of jurisprudence, which are not really adapted to the case: the necessary fact is lacking or is embedded in a sterile abundance.[87]

Earlier tips have shown that the law section contains pertinent statements of the substantive and procedural law as well as excerpts of conciliar or papal teaching, Rotal jurisprudence, and commentaries by experts. The argument formulated by the judge has identified the "tests" and/or factor analysis that prove whether or not moral certitude has been reached concerning the petitioner's claim. How can a judge bring organization and structure to these various pieces?

In organizing the law section, a good rule of thumb seen in the law sections of the Rota is to work from the general to the specific. Oftentimes, the law section begins by stating the doctrinal foundations about marriage. Canons 1055, 1056, or 1057 may be quoted in whole or in part. Relevant sections from *Gaudium et spes, Familiaris consortio* or other magisterial documents can provide context for the juridic doctrine that serves as the foundation for the specific norms coming later. Of course, any quotations from conciliar and papal documents should be relevant to the law and facts of the case at bar. Focus is lost, for example, when the law section quotes several sentences from *Gaudium et spes* concerning the procreation of children for a case adjudicated on an exclusion of fidelity.

The doctrinal foundation then segues into the heart of the legal motivation—the explication of the specific defect of consent at issue in the case. Beginning with the quotation of the pertinent canon, the defect of consent is explained. Whether the explanation is structured according to the major premises of the nested syllogisms used to formulate the argument or the "tests" and factor analysis identified in the law or Rotal jurisprudence, the law section continues to move from the general to the specific. For example, a law section about simulation could begin by explaining the notion of simulation in general before moving to show how simulation is done (i.e., by a positive act of the will). Next might follow a statement that distinguishes partial simulation from total simulation. Finally, comes the exposition of the content of the specific type of simulation at issue.

The defect of consent should be developed in view of the concrete facts of the particular case to be decided. Interesting but extraneous points only take the reader's attention away from the tightly constructed argument the judge is fashioning. Using the ground of partial simulation *contra bonum prolis* as an il-

---

87   Jullien, 30: "*L'in jure,* au lieu d'être une exposition sobre et justement documentée du point central de droit, sera un mauvais traité de droit, chargé de détails inutiles, surchargé de fragments de la jurisprudence, qui ne sont pas vraiment adaptés au cas: le nécessaire fait défaut ou est noyé dans une abondance stérile."

lustration, if the point at issue is the permanent exclusion of the right to acts per se apt for the generation of offspring, there is no need for the law section to go into detail about the notion of a temporary exclusion. The law section is not a legal treatise; it need not examine every aspect of the defect in detail.

The last major piece of the law section is the exposition of how the defect of consent is proven. In addition to the 1983 code and *Dignitas Connubii*, Rotal jurisprudence will be especially helpful in providing the pertinent material concerning the types and methods of proof for every defect of consent. In simulation cases, the law section should lay out the basic distinction between the direct and indirect methods of proof. For cases involving an incapacity to consent, some attention will be given to the requirement for using an expert, and—if one was not used in the case—when one is not required.

As the exposition of the defect of consent and the means of proof unfolds in the law section, references to other norms, to Rotal jurisprudence, and to experts will be made to support the assertion. These references can be made either by direct quotation, paraphrase, or simply a source citation. Any direct quotations used should be translated into the language of the sentence. Quotations in Latin or a modern language foreign to the petitioner and respondent frustrate their understanding of the legal motives on which the judge's decision rests. Generally the original language of the quotation is not given, unless it is a question of a particular word or phrase. Of course, the source of the quotation or paraphrase (including the translator, if known) must be given. While it is unlikely that a party will desire to track down a source cited in the law section, the advocate, defender of the bond, or an official of the appellate tribunal might try to do so. Providing an accurate citation is not only good scholarship and a courtesy to the reader but also bolsters the argument. After all, if the source of the assertion cannot be located, then the statement is not grounded. Consequently, the argument loses at least some of its force.

Tip 9: Use Variable and Invariable Segments

Unlike Rotal auditors, few judges working in first or second instance have the time to write a new law section for each case. This reality, however, does not exempt the judge from enumerating the particular motives in law that have been applied to the facts of the case.[88] To include irrelevant legal issues in the law section can not only bring confusion to the parties reading the sentence but also incite ill feelings that might prompt a lack of confidence in the ultimate decision. For this reason, so-called canned law sections speak about the law only in a general way and do not argue the law with an eye toward the specific facts of the case. In addition, these generic law sections do not advance the jurisprudence either in the local tribunal or at the appellate level.

---

88   Jukes, 20.

Notwithstanding this ideal, all is not lost for the busy judge. This tip proposes that judges write law sections with invariable and variable segments. Using a law section for canon 1095, 3° as an example, the invariable segment would provide an exposition on the canon itself and the conditions set forth in Rotal jurisprudence. Not only would the distinction between difficulty and impossibility be discussed but so would the elements of antecedence and severity with regard to the psychic cause that is required in the canon. Depending on the case, this invariable segment could be used in most sentences requiring a law section on this defect of consent. Variable segments would then be written on each of the specific psychic causes that come before the judge. This is important for the legal motivation because the nature and effect of alcohol dependence on the inability to assume the essential obligations of marriage differ from those of dependent personality disorder or bipolar disorder, etc. Simulation is another ground that lends itself to having invariable and variable sections. Today's word processing software makes it easier than ever to cut-and-paste variable segments into their proper place in the law section.

Tip 10: Pay Attention to the Details

The Divine Name is invoked not only when the collegiate tribunal meets to deliberate (c. 1609 §3) but also at the beginning of each definitive sentence (c. 1612 §1). Tribunal officials, then, can agree with the aphorism "God is in the details."[89] The saying, which means that details are important, draws attention to the finer points that sometimes are overlooked in writing the sentence, including the law section. Recalling a few of these issues can improve the law section and sentence.

Attention to formatting and style express the professionalism of the judge and the tribunal. Because the law section is an integral part of the definitive sentence, it should look like it in terms of formatting and style. The font and font size of the law section should be the same as the other parts of the sentence. Headings and subheadings should have the same appearance as those used in the other sections of the sentence. Consideration given to these details subconsciously increases the reader's confidence that the judge has competently applied the correct law to the facts of the case.

A reader's confidence in the decision is likewise reinforced when the sentence is accurate. Before publishing the sentence, the judge must review the direct quotations taken from the law, jurisprudence, and acts to ensure that each has been reproduced faithfully. Of course, any paraphrased material must comport with the original text. Similarly, citations must be checked to guarantee that references to books, articles, definitive sentences, etc. are accurate. Few things are as

---

89   Gustave Flaubert is generally attributed as the author of the statement "Le bon Dieu est dans le détail" (see Gregory Titelman, *Random House Dictionary of Popular Proverbs and Sayings* [New York: Random House, 1996] 119).

maddening to researchers as not being able to find a source because the citation is in error. The judge must also see that the names of the parties, witnesses, court officials, et al. are spelled correctly.

Finally, errors in grammar, spelling, syntax, etc. can be corrected by careful proofreading of the sentence. If it is not possible to put the drafted text aside for a few days to approach it anew, a judge should find a competent proofreader to review the text for typographical errors and other mistakes.

Ruggerio Aldisert, chief judge emeritus of the U.S. 3rd Circuit Court of Appeals, has noted the following about judges. What he says applies to ecclesiastical judges also.

> A judge is a professional writer. Whether the judge writes well or poorly, he or she writes for publication. By force of circumstances, everything he or she does in the conduct of his or her office must be expressed in words, preferably—but alas, not always—with a high degree of clarity and precision. Other writers may have the assistance of elegant typography and graphic illustration. The judge is armed with the figurative pen.[90]

Because ecclesiastical judges are professional writers, they must be knowledgeable about the *ius vigens* and jurisprudence as well as grammar, spelling, syntax, and other related topics. The parties and appellate tribunals will form an impression of the judge not only from what he or she says but how he or she says it.

Tip 11: Stay Up-to-Date
The law is not static; neither is the jurisprudence that interprets it. For this reason, tribunal officials—indeed, all practicing canonists—cannot view continuing education as a luxury—or worse, as not applying to them. Who among us would go to a doctor who did not stay abreast of the latest developments in medicine or to an accountant who refused to stay current with tax law? Lacking any specific requirements for ongoing education for canonists in universal or particular law, how can the busy tribunal official remain current on marriage and procedural issues?

Read. Even though the publication of volumes seems to be getting further behind, *Decisiones seu Sententiae*, published annually by the Roman Rota, is essential for the ecclesiastical jurist. Fortunately, recent Rotal jurisprudence is being published in various vernacular languages. In English, Rotal sentences can be found in *Studia Canonica* (Ottawa), *Studies in Church Law* (Bangalore),

---

[90] Ruggerio Aldisert, *Opinion Writing*, 2nd ed. (Bloomington, IN: Author House, 2009) 103.

the Canon Law Society of Great Britain and Ireland's *Newsletter*, *Philippine Canonical Forum* (Manilla), and *Forum, A Review of Canon Law and Jurisprudence* (Malta, 1990–2006). Before the end of 2011, the CLSA will publish a volume of Rotal sentences in English translations approved by the auditors who wrote them.[91] In Spanish, Rotal sentences can be found in *Anuario Argentino de Derecho Canónico* (Buenos Aires) and *Revista Mexicana de Derecho Canónico* (Mexico).

Participating in seminars and workshops on tribunal issues is another fruitful way to remain current on various issues concerning marriage and procedural law. Not only do tribunal officials have the opportunity to hear what the current thinking is on the defects of consent but they also can engage in conversation with colleagues to learn from one another.

Conclusion

The law section is a principal component of the definitive sentence because it lays out the motives in law on which the decision is based. So important is the law section that canon 1622, 2° prescribes for the remediable nullity of the sentence if "it does not contain the motives or reasons for the decision." Of course, motives might not be contained in the sentence for two reasons. First, the motives can be absent from the sentence. Pompedda noted: "The omission (total defect) of motives is equated with an absolute insufficient reasoning, such that very useless, incongruent and contradictory reasonings are adduced from the sentence that in no manner can either explain nor [*sic*] confirm the dispositive resolution given in the sentence."[92] This situation can occur, for example, when the sentence contains no law section at all, or, more likely, when a case considers the invalidity of a marriage on multiple grounds and a law section on one of the grounds is missing from the sentence.

Second, the sentence may well contain legal motives, but they might be erroneous. Citing Coronata and Reiffenstuel, Lemieux held that "if in the enumeration of the motives *in iure* there is an evident and certain error against the provisions of law and the erroneous motives are the sole basis of the decision, then the sentence is invalid."[93] Likewise, William Doheny stated: "if false or palpably irrelevant reasons and motives are alleged there would presumably be grounds for [a] complaint of nullity or an appeal."[94]

---

91 See *Rotal Jurisprudence* (Washington, DC: CLSA, 2011).

92 Pompedda, "Decision-Sentence in Marriage Trials," 97. See also Lüdicke and Jenkins, 406. Because c. 1622, 2° is unchanged from c. 1894, 2° of the 1917 code, see also Lemieux, 75; and William J. Doheny, *Canonical Procedure in Matrimonial Cases*, 2nd ed. (Milwaukee: The Bruce Publishing Co., 1948) 1:483 and 517.

93 Lemieux, 76.

94 Doheny, 1:517. See also Della Rocca, *Canonical Procedure*, 282, n. 21.

The Christian faithful and others who approach our tribunals expect and deserve a critical examination of their ecclesiastical status and a just decision in their cases. Law sections built on the solid foundation of the law and jurisprudence that are organized logically and are understandable to both the parties and appellate tribunal do more than provide legal reasons to answer the question of a party's marital status; they also teach what the Church believes about Christian marriage. With the recent emphasis on the new evangelization, perhaps our law sections can be another tool to announce the Gospel of Christ's faithful and indissoluble bond with the Church sacramentalized in the marriage between a baptized man and woman.

SEMINAR

BISHOPS AND RELIGIOUS: RIGHT RELATIONSHIPS FOR ECCLESIAL MISSION
Sister Sharon L. Holland, IHM

At the beginning of an evening question and answer period with religious, the query came: "Do we *have* any rights?" The religious may have believed that I knew the situation which gave rise to the question; or, may have chosen not to explain it publicly. It could have evoked a very short answer: "yes". Or, it could have launched me into a very long discourse.

Was it the right question? When a person or a group feels seriously aggrieved by an act of authority, it is certainly a legitimate question. Canonically speaking, it requires serious analysis before moving to formal administrative recourse (c. 1733 §1). Sometimes deeper issues will also surface. Together with the concrete expression of rights, there are questions of the respective responsibilities of the parties, the common good and ecclesial communion.

A brief case can serve as an illustration.

A pontifical religious institute of women had closed an apostolate in the Archdiocese and had put their convent up for sale. This was done in consultation with the Archbishop and with his full agreement. Given a bad economy, there had been no offers on the property for some months. Then the Sisters were contacted by the local Muslim community which was prepared to make a good offer for the building to be used as a school. Negotiations began. Rumours and agitation in the neighbourhood also began and the Archdiocese received complaints. The people of the local parish and neighbourhood were fearful and had become hostile to the rumoured sale proposal. The Archbishop asked for a meeting with the Sisters, and urged them to reconsider the sale for the sake of harmony in the Church and to avoid further deterioration of relations between Christians and Muslims.

- Do the Sisters have a *right* to sell their property? (c. 634)
- Do the Sisters require the consent of the Archbishop to sell? (c. 638 §3)
- Did the Archbishop have a *right* to ask the Sisters to reconsider? (c. 383)
- What responsibilities may be motivating the Sisters?
- What responsibilities may be motivating the Archbishop?
- What are the primary values you would consider in seeking a solution?

In the current climate in the Church, where an exaggerated sense of protecting the good name of the Church has been cited as a part of the scandal of child abuse[1], one chooses words carefully in speaking of prudent judgment and the common good. However if we lose balance in the opposite direction we risk trampling on other rights.

This Seminar's broad title reflects the desire to speak of rights and responsibilities in terms of bishops and religious being mutually involved in the one mission of the Church. We will review briefly the rights and duties of each, consider the types of cases which risk putting them into conflict, and share some simple strategies for avoiding unnecessarily turning to either authoritative condemnations or administrative recourses.

Theological Underpinnings of the Law

It is becoming more and more common for authors to speak and write of right relationships and of dialogue in the Church. Actually, as you well know, the 1983 code seeks to provide for such relationships even if they cannot be legislated.

In *Sacrae Disciplinae Leges*[2], we were reminded of the right relationship of law to the rest of ecclesial life.

- Law serves the purpose of creating an order in the ecclesial society in which the primary elements of faith, grace and charisms—especially charity—can organically develop. The law was revised in order to enable it to be better serve the Church's saving mission. (*SDL,* p. xxix)
- The characteristics of a true image of the Church include those stating that all members of the people of God participate in its 3-fold mission of teaching, sanctifying and governing, and consequently, all have both duties and rights. (*SDL* pp. xxx)
- Likewise, the Preface to the Latin Edition of the 1983 code, reiterated the principles for revision of the code which had emanated from the 1967 Synod of Bishops.[3] These two offer a foundation for a right balance of obligations and rights.

Principle 1 reaffirmed the "juridic character" of the new code, as required by the social nature of the Church. For a proper sharing in the life and goods provided by the Church, "the code must define and protect the rights and obligations

---

1   In the Holy Father's letter to the people of Ireland, one of the causes of the present problem cited is: "A misplaced concern for the reputation of the Church and the avoidance of scandal, resulting in failure to apply existing, canonical penalties and to safeguard the dignity of every person." Benedict XVI, "Pastoral Letter to Catholics of Ireland on Priestly Sex Abuse," n. 4 (March 19, 2010) *Origins* 39/42, 682-687.

2   John Paul II, apostolic constitution *Sacrae disciplinae leges* (January 25, 1983). Page references are to the *Code of Canon Law, Latin-English Edition: New English Translation* (Washington, DC: CLSA, 2001).

3   The full text of this preface is found in the *Code of Canon Law, Latin-English Edition*, xxxiii-xliii.

of each person towards others and towards the ecclesiastical society" insofar as these pertain to divine worship and the salvation of souls.

Principle 3 then added, that insofar as possible, the law "besides the virtue of justice, is to take cognizance of charity, temperance, humaneness and moderation, whereby equity is to be pursued…".

Principle 6 addressed the status of the persons involved:

> On account of the fundamental equality of all members of the Christian faithful and the diversity of offices and functions rooted in the hierarchical order of the Church, it is expedient that the rights of persons be appropriately defined and safeguarded.

It was assumed that this principle would result in an exercise of authority more clearly understood as service and in an avoidance of abuse.

Principle 7 called for procedures for the protection of subjective rights, including administrative procedures of recourse. This, as you are aware, is a particular area where the canons fell short of the hopes of the Synod Fathers.

Based on the theology of Vatican Council II and these principles, the Latin code now has four distinct lists of obligations and rights: those of all of the Christian faithful (cc. 208-223) those of the laity (cc. 224-231), those of clerics (cc. 273-289) and those of religious institutes and their members (cc. 662-672). Many others are scattered throughout the code, however, and those often are more applicable to our cases than the canons in the lists.[4]

Carrying Forward the Mission Together

---

[4] Early in the code revision process, there were drafts developed for a "constitution" type document, applicable to the entire Catholic Church—East and West—called the *Lex Ecclesiae Fundamentalis*. Included were the canons on these rights of all (cc. 10-25). In the 1971 synod, with 1313 bishops attending, the *concept* of an *LEF* was approved but with only 61 satisfied with the text *as it was* then.

The subsequent 1978 draft of the Latin code contained a list of obligations and rights of all of the faithful which would be suppressed if the *LEF* was published. By the time of a final plenary meeting on the code in 1981, it was clear that the *LEF* would not be promulgated, and certain canons had to be inserted in the final revision of the *CIC*. See John Alesandro, "Introduction," in *The Code of Canon Law: A Text and Commentary*, ed. James Coriden et al. (New York/Mahwah, NJ: Paulist Press, 1985) 7.

The *Code of Canons for the Eastern Churches* (*CCEO*) now contains the parallel list of rights and obligations of all of the Christian faithful (cc. 7-26), as well as distinct lists of rights and obligations of patriarchs (cc. 78-101), of eparchial bishops (cc. 190-211), and of clerics (cc. 367-393). There is no parallel listing for religious, but various obligations and rights are established throughout the canons.

The code places an accent on the role of every baptised person in promoting the mission entrusted to the Church by Christ (e.g. c. 208, c. 210). The whole people of God, in the complementarities of offices, roles and functions, is called to go forward in communion, spreading the Gospel. Since we are a human society carrying out this divine mandate, the canons seek to provide for this harmonious ordering. Our focus here is on bishops and religious.

The Comprehensive Role of the Bishop in the Ecclesial Mission

A diocesan bishop is the shepherd or pastor of a portion of the people of God (c. 369). As a successor of the Apostles, through the Holy Spirit, he is teacher of doctrine, priest of sacred worship and minister of governance. These roles must be exercised in hierarchical communion (c. 375). The diocesan bishop has all ordinary, proper and immediate power necessary for his pastoral function (c. 381 §1), a function which is described as extending to *all* of the persons within his territory. His listed responsibilities for pastoral care, promotion of vocations, ministry of the word, holiness of life, sacramental ministry, governance and administration of goods, and the unity of the Church, are extraordinarily demanding (cc. 383-393). His oversight of all apostolates in the Diocese (c. 394) is a particular point of intersection for our consideration of the works, rights and obligations of religious within the particular Church.

Participation of Religious in the Ecclesial Mission

The canons on religious are further illustrative of the interplay of the authority roles, rights and duties which can promote right relationships for mission between bishops and of religious superiors. A superior general "holds power over all the provinces, houses, and members of an institute," to be exercised according to proper law (c. 622). Even if not a cleric, his or her authority is now recognized in the canons as a sharing in the ecclesiastical power of governance (c. 596 §§1, 3).

The essential context for the exercise of this role is the "just autonomy of life, especially of governance" which is acknowledged for each institute, whether pontifical or diocesan (c. 586 §1). This means that institutes "possess their own discipline in the Church and are able to preserve their own patrimony intact..." The proper patrimony referred to is that of canon 578 addressing the mind and designs of founders for the nature, purpose, spirit and character of each institute. This autonomy of life is referred to again in the canons describing both institutes of pontifical right (c. 593) and those of diocesan right (594).

The relationship between the religious institute and the particular church begins when an institute, with the previous written consent of the diocesan bishop, establishes a house in the diocese. The religious superior is then the competent authority to erect the house (c. 609 §1). Both the bishop and the religious will have taken certain factors into consideration before the decision was made:

- Will this be to the advantage of the church and of the institute?
- Will the religious be able to carry out their religious life properly according to their purposes and spirit?
- Is it prudently judged that the needs of the members can be provided for in this place? (c. 610)

When consent is given to religious to establish a house in the diocese, a number of rights are included by the code itself. These, in effect, further acknowledge the just autonomy of life of the institute. The religious may

- live according to the character and purposes of the institute;
- carry out the works proper to the institute unless particular conditions have been set;
- a clerical institute may have a church and exercise sacred ministry, observing other applicable norms of law (c. 611).

Particular conditions might be set to avoid a duplication of ministries being carried out already by other religious. The bishop and the superior will have discussed the needs of the church, in light of the charism of the institute.

In light of these principles, a case can be considered.

A diocesan institute of women, dedicated primarily to the contemplative life has its headquarters in a large diocese of Mexico and has subsequently received permission to establish a house in a U.S. diocese. The superior general later sought the consent of your bishop to erect a house in the diocese. Because the see was vacant, the diocesan administrator verbally welcomed the sisters to come. The sisters arrived in good faith, apparently unaware that he most probably was not authorized to give the consent (c. 134 §3)[5] and that, in any event, it had to be in writing. By the time the new bishop was appointed and installed, the sisters were living on a property received from a benefactor and were hoping to build a separate novitiate. Religious at a nearby college were tutoring some of the new sisters in English and providing them some extra food and supplies. Being essentially contemplative, they hoped to earn a living by production of a popular ethnic food.

The new bishop sends you, as his vicar for religious, to sort out the facts and make recommendations. What will be your major concerns in seeking to observe canonical norms and pastoral concern? What information do you need?

---

5 Canon 427 §1, although giving broad power to the diocesan administrator, limits this by "excluding those matters which are excepted by their nature or by the law itself." Canon 134 §3 states: "Within the context of executive power, those things which in the canons are attributed by name to the diocesan bishop are understood to belong only to a diocesan bishop and to the others made equivalent to him in can. 381, §2, excluding the vicar general and episcopal vicar except by special mandate."

We have seen that the consent to establish a house in a diocese, brings with it the right to live the particular life of the institute and to carry out the works proper to it. There are always these two dimensions – life and mission. Before discussing works, the code itself emphasizes the witness value of the consecrated life as the primary apostolate of all religious (c. 573). The code, taking up the teaching of the council, urges an integration of life so that all action is imbued with the religious spirit and the whole life is imbued with apostolic spirit. Action flows from intimate union with God and strengthens that union (c. 675 §§1-2). More recently, in the apostolic exhortation following the 2008 Synod on the Word, Pope Benedict XVI spoke of the consecrated life as "a living 'exegesis' of God's word."[6]

Bishops and Religious: Collaboration in Mission

In the canons dedicated to the apostolate of religious institutes, there is a clear call for what today we call "right relationships" for mission. The final paragraph of canon 675 focuses directly on the relationship of religious with the Church. The apostolic action of religious, "to be exercised in the name and by the mandate of the Church is to be carried out in the communion of the Church" (c. 675 §3). Because the Church has erected the religious institute and approved its constitutions, the work done by the members is said to be *in the name of the Church*. With the approval of its constitutions, an institute's founding vision for mission, becomes an *ecclesial mandate*. Ecclesial *communion* is the logical consequence. Vatican II and countless subsequent documents touch upon the broad areas of communion which canon 205 synthesizes as communion of faith, sacraments and governance.

Canon 678 §1 states the principle that religious are subject to the authority of the bishop in the care of souls, the public exercise of divine worship, and in other works of the apostolate. In the exercise of the apostolate they are also subject to their own superiors. Religious are to faithfully observe the institute's way of life and the bishops too are to urge this if necessary (c. 678 §2). In recent years this has presented a serious challenge to clerical religious who are asked to sacrifice community life and the promotion of a particular spirituality in order to provide one man for a diocesan parish.

Finally, this same canon urges collaboration:

> In organizing the works of the apostolate of religious, diocesan bishops and religious superiors must proceed through mutual consultation (c. 678 §3).

Canon 680 urges cooperation and coordination between institutes, and be-

---

6   Benedict XVI, post-synodal apostolic exhortation *Verbum Domini*, n. 83 (September 30, 2010) *Origins* 40/27, 416-455.

tween institutes and secular clergy, always respecting the proper character and purpose of individual institutes. The two-fold authority under which religious minister, points out the interrelated rights and duties of bishops and of religious superiors more clearly than do the various lists of rights and obligations.

For the local level, the canons make further specific provisions. Works entrusted to an institute remain under the authority and direction of the bishop and the relationship is regulated by a written agreement (*conventio,* c. 681). The spelling out of the nature of the work, the number of religious, the finances and norms for the termination of the agreement, can avoid unnecessary tensions. When an individual is being appointed to diocesan office, both authorities must be involved: the bishop appoints, but only after presentation by or approval of the religious superior. Either authority, however, may remove the religious, simply informing the other (c. 682).

Both authorities again are involved when a bishop, for grave cause, wishes to prohibit a member from residing in the diocese; the superior must be invited to act first and the Holy See must be informed (c. 679). Likewise, if the bishop, during his pastoral visitation to apostolic works in the diocese discovers abuses, he may make provision on his own authority only if the superior fails to act (c. 683).

These provisions seem reasonable enough, and in general they are, but our thoughts quickly go to recent cases. We think of Phoenix, of St. Louis, of the Apostolic Visitation of U.S. women religious, of bishops and religious superiors in handling clerical sexual abuse accusations. What we know for sure about all of these cases is that we don't know everything. I would like to suggest that we also must keep aware of where our own prejudices lie. As canonists, we seek the facts available to us and try to analyze the canonical dimensions of the situation but we also are human beings, bringing with us our own positive and negative experiences.

Finding the Best Path Forward

As we analyze the facts, rights and duties of particular cases, we may find ourselves acknowledging that there was, in fact, a right to act, but asking if there was not another solution. There may, at times be cause for administrative recourse (cc. 1732-1739), but again, we may question if it is the best way forward. Is recourse necessary for the restoration of justice or is the goal retaliation at the expense of right relationships within the Church?

Canonists generally have studied a great deal about procedures. I want here to share some other insights into ways of respecting mutual rights and obligations in carrying forward the mission of the Church. I have shared these with religious leadership and with lay leaders in ecclesial apostolates. They sound simple, but of course we all know that human relationships are never just simple. These are some ways suggested for maintaining relationships within the diocese; they seem addressed to the religious, but obviously they are impossible unless there is responsiveness in kind on the part of the bishop and/or the responsible diocesan officials.

- *Be known*: Personal contacts when there are no particular issues can go a long way toward maintaining good relationships. Visits to a new bishop, invitations to congregational celebrations and participation in diocesan celebrations or events serve to establish or strengthen mutual acquaintance and relationship in a positive atmosphere. Some bishops welcome these contacts; some do not find time.
- *Quality participation*: Gatherings convened by vicars for religious for an exchange between diocesan and religious leaders can offer the possibility for deeper mutual understanding of the needs of the local church and the apostolic initiatives of religious institutes. The declining number of dioceses with vicars or delegates for religious, apparently for economic reasons, is a cause for concern.
- *Timely communication*: Matters involving change in a religious apostolate in the diocese or involving one of its members usually needs timely dialogue. This can be on the initiative of either authority: bishops, in deciding to close parishes or schools or to terminate the services of a religious in a diocesan office; religious superiors, in deciding to close or restructure a work of the institute or to withdraw religious from diocesan works or positions. The operative word is *timely*, with the assurance and expectation of confidentiality as needed in the case.
- *Try to stand in the other's shoes*: Bishops often find themselves under considerable pressure to maintain their reputation for orthodoxy with Rome, other bishops, and supportive laity. Religious often feel negatively judged and extremely vulnerable to episcopal decisions in which they may or may not have been involved. Manifest mutual concern for the Church's mission in the local church can be a constructive beginning point.
- *Prepare meetings well*: Knowledge of the local realities can help in determining the persons best equipped to participate in meetings regarding the apostolate of religious. Consider who is best informed and most articulate for representing the religious institute and who is designated by the diocese to deal with such matters on behalf of the bishop. Whether the topic is a new initiative, change, termination, alienation of religious property or the restructuring of apostolic works and their sponsorship, the right persons and information are essential. Sufficient clear, factual material should be provided to the bishop or the religious superior in advance, according to the matter at hand. Then it is the expectation that all will have studied the materials beforehand. Expertise and confidence, together with respect and openness to listen and understand all sides of a question, go a long way toward solutions.
- *Plan the follow up*: Sometimes a further meeting will be needed; sometimes there will be a timeline for an agreed upon letter or document. There may be need for subsequent meetings with an agenda resulting from unfinished busi-

ness of the previous one. If a matter is of media interest, if at all possible, issue a joint press release.

Conclusion

Why is it that we are experiencing more frayed relationships in the Church today? Perhaps those of us consciously involved in the life of the Church prior to Vatican Council II should be least surprised if today there is a certain pulling back. Dramatic changes were initiated by the council and enthusiastic initiatives toward their realization were undertaken. It would be interesting to make a comparative study of the post-Tridentine era, taking into account today's accelerated modes of world-wide communication.

In recent years, certain lay theologians have reflected on the evolving implications of Vatican II's ecclesiology and reactions to the implementation of or the refusal to implement the role of laity in the life and mission of the Church.[7] Author and Harvard professor of theology Bradford Hinze has published a study which, I believe, sheds an important light on why the kind of dialogue we frequently seek to encourage in the Church is also somewhat suspect.

In his 2006 publication *Practices of Dialogue in the Roman Catholic Church*[8], Hinze identifies "aims and obstacles, lessons and laments" gleaned from the examination of a wide variety of dialogic experiences in the Church since Vatican Council II. The chapter detailing the preparation, celebration and follow-up of the 1976 initiative of the U.S. Conference of Catholic Bishops referred to as "Call to Action" is illustrative. Long and extensive in planning and preparation, this very ambitious call to dialogue in the U.S. Church, demonstrated the tremendous potential for the broad involvement of all in ecclesial affairs. Inadvertently, it also revealed a parallel weakness.

Hinze points out how the experience of the Call to Action seemed to suggest to participants that everything, including doctrine, was subject to dialogic decision making. Thwarted in efforts to promote change on contentious doctrinal or moral issues, some laity have become disillusioned with the Church's new efforts at consultative processes, and some bishops have pulled back from asking the opinion of this disillusioned faithful. Contemporary authors continue to point out as problematic the code's provision for consultative processes, but not for the involvement of laity in decision making.

---

7   Examples would include Richard R. Gaillardetz, *By What Authority? A Primer on Scripture, the Magisterium and the Sense of the Faithful* (Collegeville, MN: Liturgical Press, 2003) and Paul Lakeland, *The Church: Living Communion* (Collegeville, MN: Liturgical Press, 2009).

8   Bradford Hinze, *Practices of Dialogue in the Roman Catholic Church: Aims and Obstacles, Lessons and Laments* (New York: Continuum, 2006).

Such experiences, of course, raise the issue of how to successfully engage in dialogue within the Church, dialogue called for, in fact, by Paul VI in his first encyclical.[9] This is essential to the building of ecclesial communion but obviously must respect the specific roles, rights and responsibilities of each participant. The bishop, as teacher of the faith cannot put doctrine to a vote, but he can listen and learn from the concerns and anguish of those most affected by particular theologically based practices. Indeed the rights of the Christian faithful call upon all to recognize the role of bishops in teaching and governing the Church, but also the right to make known their needs (c. 212 §§1-2). The same canon gives broad recognition to the right and duty of all to express their opinions to their pastors and to others of the Faithful in matters where they have expertise, and keeping in mind the common good. You can imagine the debate that went into each phrase of that text.

> According to the knowledge, competence, and prestige which they possess, they have the right and even at times the duty to manifest to the sacred pastors their opinion on matters which pertain to the good of the Church and to make their opinion known to the rest of the Christian faithful, without prejudice to the integrity of faith and morals, with reverence toward their pastors, and attentive to common advantage and the dignity of persons (c. 212 §3).

Like the bishop, the religious superior cannot renounce his or her right and duty to govern the institute in its rightful autonomy and to promote the life and mission of the members. The just autonomy is lived in ecclesial communion when the rights and duties of all are respected and points of conflict are worked through in patient dialogue.

And so, "Do we have rights?" Yes, everyone…rights to be protected and respected by all. And we have responsibilities to be fulfilled. These two frequently are in tension, one which we hope can be creative tension worked through in charity and truth for the higher good.

In pursuit of this ideal, supported, but not automatically produced by the canons, I frequently return to a phrase from *Christus Dominus*:

> There should be the closest possible coordination of all apostolic works and activities. This will depend mainly on a supernatural attitude of heart and mind grounded on charity.[10]

---

9   Paul VI, enclyclical *Ecclesiam Suam*, August 6, 1964: *AAS* 56 (1964) 609-659.
10   Vatican II, decree *Christus Dominus* 35.5, October 28, 1965: *AAS* 58 (1966) 692.

Seminar

Restoring and Reintegrating a Priest Falsely Accused of Sexual Abuse of a Minor
Reverend Monsignor Daniel F. Hoye

When I was asked to give this seminar on restoring an accused priest to ministry I joked that it could be a very short presentation because so few priests have been restored. Nevertheless, in a convention dedicated to the protection of rights, it is appropriate to reflect on the rights, or lack there of, of priests falsely accused of sexually abusing a minor.

What I plan to do today is

1. Introductory Remarks
2. Review Policies and Applicable Canons
3. The Scope of the Issue
4. Case Studies
5. A Communication Strategy for Restoring the Cleric
6. Observations about the Role of an Advocate in the Preliminary Investigation.

1. Introductory Remarks

The sexual abuse of minors by anyone is a terrible crime. When it is done by a cleric it is truly reprehensible. When I speak of restoring a cleric to ministry, I am not talking about restoring one who has abused a minor; rather I am speaking of restoring one whose guilt has not been established by means of a canonical process. I think that it is true that many accused clerics are guilty as charged. But that is not always the case. Like many of you, I have had clients who were innocent. For one reason or another, false accusations were made. The question being addressed here is how we restore these men to public ministry.

It should be noted that while the cleric may not be guilty of sexual abuse, there may be other factors that render him unfit at this time for public ministry. There may be psychological issues, addictions of one form or another, personality disorders, etc. Not every cleared priest can be put back into public ministry. But some can be.

I am limiting the scope of my remarks to diocesan priests. Religious have different options of keeping an accused cleric, even a guilty cleric, within the religious family but not have him exercise public ministry. I have no experience whatsoever in working with religious priests. My focus today is putting a falsely accused diocesan priest back in public ministry. Again, each case is different. A cleric may be cleared but may not want to be given an assignment. Perhaps he is beyond retirement age. Some older priests who have been cleared just want to retire in good standing and that is perfectly understandable.

Some have been so traumatized by the process that they do not want to assume any public ministry. They suffer from a form of Post Traumatic Stress Disorder and just cannot engage in public ministry. While many dioceses have support for the victim of sexual abuse, and rightly so, few if any have a built in support system for clerics who have been falsely accused. In my opinion, they should.

I have to make it clear in the beginning that I am far from a scholar in the field of canon law. I am a practitioner, and a part time one at that. I am a full time pastor of a large parish on Cape Cod, MA. Like many of you, I backed into this whole field of penal law.

I do recall when we were going over the penal law section of the 1917 code, the professor told us we would review the material but probably would never uses these canons in our lifetime. How could we have known what would develop? We more senior canonists had to teach ourselves. The CLSA has been helpful in providing workshops and encouraging experienced advocates to offer workshops on how to be a canonical advocate to a cleric who has been accused of sexual abuse of a minor. Rick Bass, Paul Golden, Pat Lagges, Fred Easton, Dan Smilanic and others are to be commended for sharing their expertise. After getting my JCL way back in 1975, I recently completed my very first canonical trial involving this issue. I guess learning never stops.

So, if you are looking for a scholarly presentation today, you might want to leave now!

Like many of you I learned the penal process by doing it. Among the cases I have dealt with were four priests who have been restored to ministry; one was restored twice, having been accused of abuse by another person after he had been restored. In a short while I will share with you my experience with these priests.

I suspect that many of you in this room have similar experiences. I hope that during our discussion you will share your thoughts

2. Policies and Canons

The chief applicable law on restoration is found in the *Essential Norms* published in 2002.[1] As can be expected with the circumstances surrounding the draft-

---

1   For the text of these norms and an accompanying *Charter* articulating the bishops' key pastoral concerns and commitment to addressing this issue, see USCCB, *Promise to*

ing of *Essential Norms*, the emphasis in the document is on the accuser and the process that is followed in investigating his/her complaint. The cleric and his rights get little attention.

Essential Norms have undergone two revisions since promulgated in 2002.[2] In the 2006 revision we read in Article 13:

> "Care will always be taken to protect the rights of all involved, particularly those of the person claiming to have been sexually abused and of the person against whom the charge has been made. When an accusation has been shown to be unfounded, every step possible will be taken to restore the good name of the person falsely accused."

This norm has remained the same since the 2006 revision when "an accusation has been shown to be unfounded" was substituted for the original "an accusation has proved to be unfounded."

Essential Norms is law for the United States. As we know, the issue of sexual abuse has exploded in Ireland and other countries in Europe. In order to guide the drafting of the equivalent of our *Essential Norms* for other episcopal conferences, the Congregation for the Doctrine of the Faith issued guidelines in a Circular Letter published on May 16, 2011.[3] While not directly applicable to the United States, it is interesting to note what the CDF says regarding accusations and return to ministry:

> The accused cleric is presumed innocent until the contrary is proven. Nonetheless the bishop is always able to limit the exercise of the cleric's ministry until the accusations are clarified. If the case so warrants, whatever measures can be taken to rehabilitate the good name of a cleric wrongly accused should be done.[4] ... Unless there are

---

Protect Pledge to Heal: Charter for the Protection of Children and Young People, Essential Norms, Statement of Episcopal Commitment, revised June 2005 (Washington, DC: USCCB, 2006).

2 The *Essential Norms* were granted *recognitio* for three years by the Congregation for Bishops on December 8, 2002, taking effect on March 1, 2003. On March 1, 2005 the Holy Father approved an extension upon request of the USCCB and at the recommendation of the Congregation for Bishops. A revised version of the *Essential Norms* was approved in June 2005. *Recognitio* was granted on January 1, 2006, and the norms were promulgated on May 5, 2006.

3 Congregation for the Doctrine of the Faith, May 3, 2011, "Circular Letter to Assist Episcopal Conferences in Developing Guidelines for Dealing with Cases of Sexual Abuses of Minors Perpetuated by Clerics." The text of the letter is available on the Vatican website: http://www.vatican.va/roman_curia/ congregations/cfaith/documents/rc_con_cfaith_doc_20110503_abuso-minori_en.html.

4 Ibid., General Considerations, I.d.3.

serious contrary indications, before a case is referred to the CDF, the accused cleric should be informed of the accusation which has been made, and given the opportunity to respond to it.[5] ... The return of a cleric to public ministry is excluded if such ministry is a danger for minors or a cause of scandal for the community.[6]

The United States norms, in my opinion, need to be revised again to standardize the right to respond to an accusation. More about this later, but I have been involved in cases where the cleric is told little or nothing about the details of the accusation and is forbidden to conduct an investigation on his own. Neither the cleric nor his advocate is permitted to read the file or submit a brief to the diocesan review board.

I stress that this is not the case with every diocese but it is in some. Since the preliminary investigation could possibly lead to the laicization of the cleric, the law should require the cleric to have an advocate during the preliminary investigation. Further, that advocate should have access to the entire file including the *acta* going to the review board and the advocate should be invited to submit a brief to the review board prior to the board making a recommendation to the ordinary.

I also note that contrary to *Essential Norms*, the Circular Letter does not argue for a "one strike and you are out" policy.[7] Ministry is to be excluded "if such ministry is a danger for minors or a cause of scandal for the community."[8] This gives some latitude to the ordinary. Whether this would be politically doable in the United States is highly questionable. Nevertheless, we have seen that there are degrees of sexual abuse.

Is it possible that one day we can introduce the principle of proportionality into our norms? I hope so but it would be a huge hill to climb.

Sacramentorum sanctitatis tutela, issued in 2001 and slightly revised on July 15, 2010, is the major piece of universal legislation for the handling of sexual

---

5   Ibid., II.

6   Ibid., III.i.

7   *Essential Norms* 8: "When even a single act of sexual abuse of a minor by a priest or deacon is admitted or is established after an appropriate process in accordance with canon law, the offending priest or deacon will be removed permanently from ecclesiastical ministry, not excluding dismissal from the clerical state, if the case so warrants (CIC, c. 1395 §2; CCEO, c. 1453 §1)." The footnote to this norm indicates that "Removal from ministry is required whether or not the cleric is diagnosed by qualified experts as a pedophile or as suffering from a related sexual disorder that requires professional treatment."

8   Circular Letter, III.i.

abuse cases.[9] Surprisingly it has no reference whatsoever to restoring a priest who has been cleared.

Relevant Canons:[10]

Canon 220: No one is permitted to harm illegitimately the good reputation which a person possesses nor to injure the right of any person to protect his or her own privacy.

Canon 221 §1: The Christian faithful can legitimately vindicate and defend the rights which they possess in the Church in the competent ecclesiastical forum according to the norm of law.

Canon 1390 §2: A person who offers an ecclesiastical superior any other calumnious denunciation of a delict or who otherwise injures the good reputation of another can be punished with a just penalty, not excluding a censure.

Canon 1390 §3: A calumniator can also be forced to make suitable reparation.

Canon 1717 §2 (regarding a preliminary investigation of a delict): Care must be taken so that the good name of anyone is not endangered from this investigation.

Canon 1723 §1: The judge who cites the accused must invite the accused to appoint an advocate according to the norm of can. 1481, §1 within the time limit set by the judge.

§2: If the accused does not make provision, the judge is to appoint an advocate before the joinder of the issue; this advocate will remain in this function as long as the accused does not appoint an advocate personally.

3. Scope of the Issue

When I started to do research for this project I sent a survey to 188 (arch) dioceses. I must admit it was not a successful effort. Only 41 responded and only a handful had restored a falsely accused priest to ministry and almost all those restored were never publicly named. Some responses simply stated that they would not share any data with me.

I made the decision not to report on the results of the survey for this seminar

---

9   For an historical introduction to the norms from the CDF, the list of modifications in the revised *SST* norms, and a Latin and English text of the *SST* norms, see *Roman Replies and CLSA Advisory Opinions 2010*, ed. Sharon Euart, et al. (Washington: CLSA, 2010) 66-92.

10   All English translations of canons are taken from *Code of Canon Law, Latin-English Edition: New English Translation* (Washington, DC: CLSA, 1998).

because I did not think the low number of responses warranted it.

I did discover that for the last five years, the USCCB Office of Child Protection has reported the results of the annual CARA survey of (arch)dioceses concerning allegations of sexual abuse of minors by diocesan clergy. This data includes the number of new allegations of abuse for the year and the number of accused priests who were restored to ministry. The numbers indicate that we do not have much experience in restoring priests:

Year	New Accusations	Restored to Active Ministry
2006	635	12
2007	599	11
2008	178	9
2009	398	6
2010	428	5
Total	2,238	43

(Source: Center for Applied Research in the Apostolate Annual Surveys 2006-2010)

While the dates of accusations and restoration may overlap at time, it can be said that less than 2% of accused diocesan clerics were restored in the last five years. That is a pretty low number but for those 43, their restoration is significant.

4. Case Studies

Over the last ten years or so I have been involved in four cases where the accused cleric was found not guilty in one way or another and was restored to ministry. Four is not many but those four are about 10% of the total who were restored. Without giving names, let me describe for you some of the cases. I want to tell you that I have the permission of three of the four priests to share their stories. Unfortunately, the fourth priest has died. I sent those who were living a draft of my remarks and all said they did not object to me telling you about them.

In the first case, since no public announcement was made about the accusation, no public announcement was made about the priest's restoration. He simply started to function in a public manner. No one but a few close friends ever knew about it. The case involved a retired priest. He was simply informed that an accusation had been made and that until the matter was resolved he could not wear clerical clothing nor exercise public ministry. The accusation came in the form of a single letter from an attorney. I am not sure why no public announcement was made but perhaps the policy of public announcements was not yet developed by the diocese in question.

The priest just made excuses why he could not help out pastors who were looking for assistance. Six months went by before the cleric approached me for assistance.

I discovered that the diocese had done absolutely nothing to investigate this matter. "We are busy" was the excuse. I wrote a few letters and finally the diocese called the cleric and said they were dropping the charge. Apparently the diocese contacted the attorney who made the accusation and he informed them that he no longer represented the accuser with whom he only met once when he agreed to write the letter making the accusation. He had not heard from the person since. Months of agony for the accused could have been shortened had the diocese been more responsive.

Another case I had was quite different. A priest had served as a chaplain at a specialized school. He along with several religious women was accused of sexually abusing students. The case was criminally pursued in the courts and after more than a year the case was dismissed.

The diocese then began its own investigation and eventually the priest was cleared. He was already retired but had lived in a rectory and used to celebrate public Masses. When the accusation was made, his ministry was restricted and he could not wear clerical dress. He also had to move out of the rectory. When he was restored, a press release was issued and an announcement was made in the parish and he was welcomed back with open arms.

While the diocese did issue a press release, I found that a common experience is that the media gives much less attention to a restoration than to an accusation. With the exception of the first case I mentioned, the media gave minimum attention to a restored priest. Bad news sells; good news does not.

The clerics I have worked with were welcomed by their communities. One is regularly picketed by a victims support group but with little impact on the parish. I think a lot has to do with the relationship the priest has with his parishioners. If they have known the priest for some time and they trust him, they are grateful that he has been cleared.

None of the priests I worked with were accused of molesting multiple victims over many years. While I do not think such a priest would ever be cleared and restored, if he were, his restoration would certainly be different than the ones I dealt with.

While the restoration of this retired priest should have been the end of the story, unfortunately it was not. He was accused by a different person a year or so after he was restored. Once again he was put on leave and had to move out of the rectory. Once again there was substantial media coverage about the accusation. The priest had a wide circle of supporters who even were willing to pay for a private investigator. The diocese strongly opposed this. They basically threatened the priest to stop investigating the matter.

This is like the district attorney being the only one to investigate an alleged crime and the attorney for the accused totally unable to look into the matter. While I can understand the need for the diocese to investigate, I fail to understand why the accused cleric cannot look into the matter and even have his team interview those who are willing to talk to them.

While the priest was eventually told he was exonerated and a press release was issued, the diocese did not want him functioning until they knew whether or not a prominent civil attorney would pursue the matter in a civil fashion.

The diocese's press release stated that he was cleared and was awaiting a new assignment. Since he was already retired, I was not sure what that meant but I did know the diocese did not want him celebrating public masses. He was allowed to move back into the rectory and to wear clerical clothing, but the diocese wanted to keep him off the radar screen lest the civil attorney followed up with a civil suit and then the diocese would have to remove him a third time while the civil process played out.

While I argued strongly that this was not right, I lost and the priest was in limbo for another few months. The stress was too much and the priest was hospitalized for depression. While he eventually returned to the parish he said he could no longer take the pressure of public preaching. While the people accepted him, he did not do well and died a relatively short time after he was restored the second time.

Another case involved a priest who was accused of a single act of abuse some forty years ago. Unfortunately the same attorney I alluded to in the last case named this priest in a civil suit, but associated him with two other priests who seem to have been guilty of abusing minors. My client adamantly denied any abuse.

Without going into all the details, the case dragged on for a couple of years and eventually was settled with the diocese paying the victim but stating that Father x denied he abused the accuser. During this time the priest was restricted in ministry. His case argues for the importance of support from brother priests. He had a wonderful support system that kept him going.

I don't think the diocese ever knew this but the priest would go back to his parish on a semi-regular basis to check the mail and to see what was going on.

The administrator had no problem with this. The priest even met several times with his pastoral council!

I would not recommend this approach but there were no protests from parishioners.

Finally the diocese reinstated the priest but once again there was only a press release that the media picked up on in a very minor way.

It took an extraordinary amount of time to bring the case to a conclusion. In January of a certain year the review board recommended that he be reinstated. It was not until April that he was informed of the decision to clear him but it was three more years before he went back to the parish. The delay was caused by the priest not being willing to settle the civil suit brought by an attorney.

His acceptance by the parishioners was wonderful and he is pastor of the same parish to this day. Once again, his case demonstrates the willingness of a parish to believe in someone whom they trust. He had been their pastor for many years and the accusation simply did not fit with the man they knew.

By the way, he was pastor where the retired priest I just spoke about lived. Talk about double jeopardy! Two priests from the same parish falsely accused and both removed from the parish around the same time and both eventually restored.

I have to say that this particular diocese was not open to the involvement of an advocate at the stage of the preliminary investigation, an investigation I emphasize that took several years to complete. I was never allowed to see the file. I was not allowed to submit a brief to the review board. I did write some letters to the CDF but not once did I get even as much as an acknowledgement.

When I was president of CLSA I had an opportunity to meet with Cardinal William Levada, Prefect of the Congregation for the Doctrine of the Faith, and two other officials. I mentioned that it was frustrating to write to the Congregation and not even receive assurance that the letter was received. The lower officials present stated that it is their policy to deal only with bishops. Cardinal Levada said that at least an acknowledgement of the receipt of the letter would be appropriate, but I do not think that has ever happened. Perhaps your experience is different and I would welcome hearing about this when we have our discussion.

The last case I will report on was a positive experience with a diocese that was quite open to my involvement as the advocate for the accused. He was a retired priest who was accused of sexual abuse that allegedly took place thirty years ago in a different state. Because of civil law, the statute of limitations had not yet expired.

The diocese made the accusation public through press releases and statements to all the parishes in which the priest served. Because of the civil implications, the diocese could not investigate until the matter was resolved by civil authorities. Eventually the district attorney said he would not bring charges and the diocese began its own investigation. The diocesan investigator allowed me to see the report that was to go to the review board and welcomed an advocate's brief. Unfortunately, the board did not recommend that the priest be restored and the ordinary accepted this recommendation.

The matter was referred to CDF and a canonical trial took place. The priest had the means to hire a private investigator. If you have ever done this, you know it is expensive. But the investigator uncovered lots of material that called into serious question the credibility of the accuser. The priest was found not guilty and the ordinary agreed to restore him.

Once again the diocese issued a release and unlike the widespread coverage that occurred when he was accused, very little was made of it. In fact, when I googled the priest's name several weeks after he was restored, only the coverage of the accusation was found. After several weeks, a few references to his clearance finally appeared. As I said, the priest was retired but has done some supply work and seems to have been well received. He too had forty-plus years of a good reputation to help people accept the accusation as a false one and welcome the priest back to active ministry.

5. Communication Strategy

I think every diocese should have a written communication strategy on how to deal with an accusation and how to deal with restoring a priest to active ministry. I believe some have these strategies but many simply say in the policies that "everything should be done to restore the good name of the priest."

A communication strategy for the restoration might include these items:

- Issue a press release to all local media, including printed press, TV and radio
- Follow up with local media by the diocesan communications director to try to facilitate wider coverage of the restoration
- Have the letter announcing his return to ministry read in all the parishes where the letter removing him from ministry was read
- Post an announcement on diocesan website, Facebook, and Twitter
- Have a diocesan official go to the parish(es) and speak at all Masses if this was done when the accusation was made
- Celebrate a rite of welcoming at the major Mass on a weekend

I believe that all of this should be done in consultation with the cleared cleric. He may not want anything more than a simple announcement that he has been cleared. If already retired, he may just want to go off into the sunset. I also believe that the diocese should offer counseling to the cleared cleric. He has been traumatized and may well need some professional assistance as he begins to exercise public ministry again.

6. Preliminary Investigation

From my experience, I think there should be some modifications in the *Essential Norms* to insure the right of defense and to put some time restrictions on the process.

It has been my experience with different dioceses that the accused's right to the help of an advocate during the preliminary investigation is uneven to say the least. While the advocate's role is clearly outlined in the canonical trial, there are no rights given to the advocate in the preliminary investigation.[11] Often the diocese will encourage the accused cleric to seek canonical advice but then the diocese does not invite or permit the advocate to review the entire file and to submit a brief to a review board.

Theoretically, the priest's case could be sent to CDF for forced laicization without any word from his canonical advocate. While I have been told by others that CDF will require the input from an advocate, right now that is not part of the *Essential Norms*. It should be.

I believe the advocate should have similar rights in the preliminary investigation as he has in a penal trial. He should be able to review all the evidence before a report goes to the review board and should be able to submit a brief or actually appear before the review board as it deliberates the matter.

As I have said previously, the role of the advocate in the preliminary process should be mandated along the line of canon 1723.[12] I also think there should be a time frame within which the diocese needs to complete its investigation. I have been involved with cases that drag on for years. The accused cleric was removed from ministry and was in a virtual limbo until a resolution took place.

---

11   *Essential Norms* 6: "When an allegation of sexual abuse of a minor by a priest or deacon is received, a preliminary investigation in accordance with canon law will be initiated and conducted promptly and objectively (CIC, c. 1717; CCEO, c. 1468). During the investigation the accused enjoys the presumption of innocence, and all appropriate steps shall be taken to protect his reputation. The accused will be encouraged to retain the assistance of civil and canonical counsel and will be promptly notified of the results of the investigation." The norms state that the accused has the right to counsel, but the rights and role of that counsel are not specified in the norms.

12   Can. 1723 §1: The judge who cites the accused must invite the accused to appoint an advocate according to the norm of can. 1481, §1 within the time limit set by the judge.

§2: If the accused does not make provision, the judge is to appoint an advocate before the joinder of the issue; this advocate will remain in this function as long as the accused does not appoint an advocate personally.

Perhaps a norm could read that "the preliminary investigation should be completed within three months time unless circumstances are such that a limited extension of a month is granted."

As I said in the beginning, this is not intended to be a scholar's view of restoring a falsely accused cleric to public ministry. Rather, this seminar is the sharing of one canonist's experience.

Like many of you, I have dealt with clerics who clearly were guilty of abusing minors. Thankfully, I was also involved with several who were not guilty. Their lives were turned upside down and I was grateful to have been helpful in getting things turned right side up.

SEMINAR

TRIBUNAL, SEMINARY, CLERGY AND PERSONNEL FILES: IS THERE AN ABSOLUTE RIGHT TO PRIVACY? A CIVIL AND CANON LAW PERSPECTIVE
Rita F. Joyce

This presentation covers four of the common types of files found within the diocese. It should be noted that some of the material presented may also be applicable to records found in religious institutes. The canonical aspects will be presented through the lens of civil society and the civil court systems in which we function.

In the time allotted we will discuss a broad understanding of what these records are. We will look at government protections that might be available. What specific regulations might be protective of information contained in these files? Are there outright bars to the release of information? What typically are in these files, in other words, what is collected and what is ultimately retained? What have civil courts done with requests for materials in church files? What defenses might be available? Finally some old and new civil cases will be reviewed to see what we can learn from them. This is admittedly a lot of information to cover and it can be dry, but hopefully there will some points made that can be helpful to you in your practice of law in the Church.

Government Protections:
What protections of our information does government offer? We continually hear about Health Insurance Portability and Accountability Act (HIPAA) and an "alphabet soup" of other government acts or regulations such as the Family Medical Leave Act (FMLA), Americans with Disabilities Act (ADA), Freedom of Information Act (FOIA), and various other types of privileges such as attorney/client, doctor/patient, counselor/patient, and priest/penitent. Is information collected really private? Can the government or the Church keep this information secret? The answers are varied and complex. There are some protections that we all learned in our civics/social studies classes. For example, the Fourth Amendment to the United States Constitution provides that there must be probable cause for a warrant to allow a search or a seizure of one's person, property, papers and "effects." Specifically, the Fourth Amendment provides as follows: "The right of the people to be secure in their persons, houses, papers, and effects, against unreasonable searches and seizures, shall not be violated, and no war-

rants shall issue, but upon probable cause, supported by Oath or affirmation, and particularly describing the place to be searched, and the persons or things to be seized." The government protects its citizens from search of their personal documents without a proper, legitimate reason.

Privileges are attached to attorney/client, clergy/penitent, and doctor/patient relationships for very obvious reasons. In Pennsylvania, for example, in order to have protection by the clergy communicant protection, the communication must be made: a) in confidence; b) made to a member of the clergy; c) made for spiritual purposes.[1] If communication is made to a member of the clergy, even if it is for counseling or solace, it does not get the protection of privilege unless motivated by spiritual or penitential considerations.

HIPAA privileges apply only in very limited circumstances. The privacy privileges are applicable to health care providers, heath care clearing houses, and a health plan. So, when a bishop worries that he is being required to turn over HIPAA- protected materials collected in a tribunal proceeding or contained in seminary or priests' files in some type of litigation, it is unlikely that HIPAA applies. This is not to imply that records are not confidential, but if one is a health plan or a health care provider, HIPAA does not help. As an example, the Diocese of Pittsburgh is self-insured as a health plan; therefore the diocese was obligated to adopt a written privacy policy to which it must adhere.

Information gathered for FMLA, which is applicable to employers of fifty (50) or more persons, is confidential and employees within the diocese have an expectation to privacy of medical information contained therein. When documentation is completed to justify up to twelve (12) weeks of unpaid leave to care for a family member, that information as to the medical aspects of the file are confidential. This can be protected from "discovery" in a legal process. The act requires that all confidential medical information is kept separate from routine regular employee files. The same regulations apply to medical information contained in the employee's files that pertain to the ADA. The act provides that information obtained regarding medical conditions or history of the applicant that is collected and maintained must be done on a separate form and kept in a separate medical file that is considered and treated as a confidential medical record. This must be tempered by the type of legal process in which one is involved. If the employee is personally involved in bringing a malpractice suit, information in the medical file cannot be protected from use in court.

Contents of these records/files:

I. *Tribunal*
For the canonical process for a declaration of nullity of a marriage, what must

---

1   *Commonwealth v. Stewart*, 690 A.2d 195 (Pa. 1997).

the tribunal collect and retain?

The tribunal obtains the initial petition, the application with facts supplied by the parties, both petitioner and respondent in the marriage, a complaint of nullity (*libellus*), statements of witnesses, briefs by the advocates, observations of the defender of the bond, transcription of the oral testimony, judicial decrees, proofs of service, the definitive sentence, the decree of the court of second instance, and sometimes counseling or medical records, all provided with an expectation of confidentiality. Also included in the file are the civil marriage records, baptismal certificates, marriage license, divorce decree, church investigations, and questionnaires for both parties if they were married in the Catholic Church and completed pre-nuptial investigations.

Persons who come to the tribunal come with the expectation that only those persons directly concerned with their case will have access to this sensitive and personal information (c. 1455). After a decision is rendered and has been ratified by the second instance court, the files may be preserved in some fashion, electronically or otherwise, and eventually peripheral documents are usually shredded, except for the definitive sentence, which must be kept perpetually. All of this is contingent upon the particular diocese's retention policy.

A reasonable question to ask is: can a court become entangled in sorting out a canonical process with its particular standard of proof, moral certitude? Courts are unused to this standard, as the courts recognize standards of proof "beyond a reasonable doubt," or proof by a "preponderance of the evidence." Of all four file types that are discussed in this presentation, tribunal records have the strongest argument for non-disclosure. The entire purpose of the tribunal process is to admit someone to the sacraments or to clarify someone's standing in the Catholic Church and nothing more.

The easiest and cleanest argument can be made about the non-accessibility to tribunal proceedings and records. To support this thesis, I rely upon William Bassett in *Religious Organizations and the Law*, who places the discussion about church records in the following context: "Church discipline, like theology is essentially interpreted within a context of belief, totally outside the cognizance of the courts."[2] Church discipline is understood in light of religious language. In other words, *if* it is a matter of our Church discipline, i.e. as clarifying someone's status in the Church certainly is, then civil courts tread on dangerous grounds to become involved in our Church process.

There is no civil purpose to a tribunal petition for a declaration of nullity. There is no civil effect that is gained from an affirmative decision. The key to

---

2   William Bassett, et al., *Religious Organizations and the Law* (Eagan, MN: West Publishing, 2010) section 7.52.

this argument is that the purpose of gathering the material is solely for an ecclesiastical process to reunite the parties to the Catholic faith, thus it can have no civil consequence.

Also, there is no right of an individual to access peripheral documents such as permission letters that might be attached to the granting of a marriage dispensation. Therefore, if the parties to the case have no right to access these documents, how can there be a right of another to do so, even a civil court?

II. *Clergy Files/Seminary Files*

Canons that pertain to seminaries are canons 232 through 264. They provide a broad overview of the obligation to have seminaries, what qualifications a seminarian must have, spiritual life, subjects to be taught, and what is necessary for priestly formation. The canons refer to the theological underpinnings of seminary formation from Vatican II, *Christus Dominus*, from papal documents such as *Presbyterorum ordinis*, and *Pastores dabo vobis*, etc. There is guidance in the canons about the program of instructions for college (minor) seminaries in the most general sense that "training and education ought to be on par with that of their peers."[3]

A. Seminarian files: Canonical Contents

Only three canons deal with files or records with specificity. Canons 240-242 deal with records in the very broad sense. Two other canons (1050-1051) direct that certain requirements are in place for ordination, and canon 1036 provides that the seminarian write in his own hand that he wishes to be promoted to orders. It can be presumed that the requirements of the latter three canons must be kept in the files of the seminarian. However, in the canons there is no comprehensive listing of documents or records to be kept in the files of the seminarian. Because the information is extrapolated from many other canons, more time is allotted to piecing together the contents of seminary files than is allotted to the contents of tribunal or clergy files.

Canon 240 §2 directs that various professors are to be consulted when a candidate is admitted to orders or is to be dismissed (implying that *obviously* recommendations are placed in the files of seminarians) but that spiritual directors and confessors are never to be asked their opinions.[4]

---

3   Richard G. Cunningham, "Commentary on Canon 234," in *New Commentary on the Code of Canon Law*, ed. John P. Beal et al. (New York/Mahwah, NJ: Paulist Press, 2000) 307.

4   Canon 240 §2: "When decisions are made about admitting students to orders or dismissing them from the seminary, the opinion of the spiritual director and confessors can never be sought."

Canon 241 is the first tangible reference to specific material that is to be kept. A seminarian must submit documents of the reception of baptism and confirmation and "any other things required by the prescripts of the program for priestly formation."

Additionally, this same canon tells the bishop that he is to admit only those candidates who are "judged" qualified to dedicate themselves to the ministry, and he is to consider their human, moral, spiritual, and intellectual qualities, their physical and psychic health and their intentions.[5] This would require that medical, psychological/psychiatric information is gathered as well as retained, and also that grades and tests that demonstrate academic achievement are reviewed and likely also retained.

Canon 242 empowers each conference of Catholic Bishops to develop a program of priestly formation that prescribes among other things evaluations, letters of recommendation from pastors, teachers, academic records, and standardized testing. Some even require a personal essay on the candidate's vision of priestly ministry and why the candidate chooses this as a life's vocation. Also, if a person was dismissed from another seminary, then testimony of the previous seminary rector is required to be included in the paperwork. This is mandatory and must be done in every instance.[6]

The result of interviews and evaluations by medical doctors and other professionals are used for examination of the applicant's health while psychological assessments are used to judge motivation. And, if a candidate was previously married and had a declaration of nullity of marriage, then documentation and special permission is also needed.

---

5   Canon 241 §1: "A diocesan bishop is to admit to a major seminary only those who are judged qualified to dedicate themselves permanently to the sacred ministries; he is to consider their human, moral, spiritual, and intellectual qualities, their physical and psychic health, and their correct intention.

§2: Before they are accepted, they must submit documents of the reception of baptism and confirmation and any other things required by the prescripts of the program of priestly formation.

§3: If it concerns admitting those who were dismissed from another seminary or religious institute, testimony of the respective superior is also required, especially concerning the cause for their dismissal or departure."

6   Canon 242 §1: "Each nation is to have a program of priestly formation which is to be established by the conference of bishops, attentive to the norms issued by the supreme authority of the Church, and which is to be approved by the Holy See. This program is to be adapted to new circumstances, also with the approval of the Holy See, and is to define the main principles of the instruction to be given in the seminary and general norms adapted to the pastoral needs of each region or province.

§2: All seminaries, both diocesan and interdiocesan, are to observe the norms of the program mentioned in §1."

Canon 1036 directs that the candidate for ordination to either the diaconate or presbyterate present to the bishop in his own hand a signed statement attesting that he will receive the orders freely and will devote himself perpetually and at the same time he asks to be admitted to the order of either the diaconate or the presbyterate.[7] Obviously, then this is another document that one would expect to be in a permanent file.

Canon 1050 provides that for a person to be ordained testimonials are necessary to verify that educational studies are completed, and that the diaconate was conferred.[8] This is again evidence that these documents must be kept in the seminarian's files.

Canon 1051 requires testimonials of the rector of the seminary that testifies to sound doctrine of the candidate, and good moral aptitude for ministry among other requirements. If the candidate is not of the bishop's own diocese, in other words, not his subject, then he needs permission and documentation from the bishop of the other diocese where the man is to be incardinated in order to be able to validly ordain. These permissions, the dimissorial letters, attest that all of the documents mentioned in canon 1050 are in place.[9]

---

7   Canon 1036: "In order to be promoted to the order of diaconate or of presbyterate, the candidate is to present to his bishop or competent major superior a declaration written in his own hand and signed in which he attests that he will receive the sacred order of his own accord and freely and will devote himself perpetually to the ecclesiastical ministry and at the same time asks to be admitted to the order to be received."

8   Canon 1050: "For a person to be promoted to sacred orders, the following documents are required:

1° a testimonial that studies have been properly completed according to the norm of can. 1032;

2° for those to be ordained to the presbyterate, a testimonial that the diaconate was received;

3° for candidates to the diaconate, a testimonial that baptism, confirmation and the ministries mentioned in can. 1035 were received; likewise, a testimonial that the declaration mentioned in can. 1036 was made, and if the one to be ordained to the permanent diaconate is a married candidate, testimonials that the marriage was celebrated and the wife consents."

9   Canon 1051: "The following prescripts regarding the investigation about the qualities required in the one to be ordained are to be observed:

1° there is to be a testimonial of the rector of the seminary or house of formation about the qualities required to receive the order, that is, about the sound doctrine of the candidate, his genuine piety, good morals, and aptitude to exercise the ministry, as well as, after a properly executed inquiry, about his state of physical and psychic health;

2° in order to conduct the investigation properly, the diocesan bishop or major superior can employ other means which seem useful to him according to the circumstances of time and place, such as testimonial letters, public announcements, or other sources of information."

The Rector of the college seminary in Pittsburgh explained that the diocese maintains a checklist of everything that is needed in the application process and requires each candidate to complete an application packet that would have the following types of materials in the file:

1. Seminary application
2. Summary of a canonical interview with the rector that asks questions which might show a person ineligible (impeded) from the exercise of orders, such as: did he ever attempt suicide, or drug overdose, participate in an abortion, or voluntary homicide, is he mentally ill, had ever committed heresy, apostasy or schism, attempted marriage, self-mutilated himself, or has he attempted to act as a priest or a bishop while being neither, or who operated under some canonical penalty.
3. The results of an interview that inquires about the understanding of celibacy, whether the person has ever engaged in any kind of activity that could be construed to be misconduct, whether the person is a new convert to the faith, etc.
4. A spiritual biography essentially detailing how the candidate has seen the presence of God in his life.
5. Three psychological tests
6. Proof of insurance
7. Necessary baptismal and confirmation certificates
8. Evidence of legal residency
9. Transcripts from all educational institutions
10. Letters of recommendation from three parishioners, the pastor, and two other priests
11. Evidence of compliance with the Safe Environment Policy of the diocese
12. All grades and evaluations of the seminary faculty

Additionally when a person goes on to the theologate, copies of all important documentation are made and forwarded to that seminary, with the originals being retained in the diocesan seminary where the candidate is to become incardinated. All evaluations, grades, and remarks of the faculty of the major seminary are retained in that seminary's files, but copies of all materials are also forwarded to the diocesan seminary where the seminarian is to become incardinated. The major seminary acts as an agent for the bishop who will eventually ordain the seminarian.

The most important evaluation prior to orders is done at the time of the deaconate ordination, because at that point the relationship of the seminarian to the diocese changes and both the diocese and the seminarian acquire certain legal and canonical rights to each other.[10] Incardination takes place at the ordination to

---

10   Canon 266 §1: "Through the reception of the diaconate, a person becomes a cleric and is incardinated in the particular church or personal prelature for whose service he has

the deaconate; therefore, there is a careful examination which takes place at the seminary or other suitable place. These evaluations and results of the examinations are kept in the seminarian's permanent files. These questions asked of the seminarians are generally uniform and would be very similar from diocese to diocese.

In our diocese, all files are retained by the seminary until one year after ordination, when extraneous materials that relate to admissions might be destroyed and the balance of the file is sent to the diocesan clergy office to be made part of the priest's file.

Best practice is that retention schedules for these documents be clear and unambiguous. The Diocese of Pittsburgh retention schedule for the seminary notes: photographs, college or pre-theology application papers, pastor recommendations for entrance into the seminary, pastoral evaluation forms and transcripts and routine correspondence are to be retained for one year after ordination *and then destroyed*. Practice is that fewer things are destroyed and more are retained. All other records are to be incorporated into the priest's personnel files one year after ordination. The retention schedule also includes, in addition to the application, similar to a personnel file, copies of sacramental records, the seminarian contract, and assignments. The Diocese of Pittsburgh's retention schedule also retains files of those seminarians who have dropped out for a period of twenty-five years in case they apply to another program.

B. Clergy Files: Contents

There are no separate canons that deal with the content of routine clergy files. There are two canons that deal with the secret archives (cc. 489 and 490). Diocesan policy will establish what a diocese determines to keep. As a result of litigation that has embroiled the Church for over twenty years, it is more difficult to argue that anything that is kept in a clergy file is kept for purely Church purposes. When medical information or records for psychological treatment are contained in the files, one *can possibly argue* those specific areas can be kept protected under privacy laws or HIPAA-type related laws. As was stated initially, HIPAA has very limited application to the diocese or to ordinary files unless the diocese provides a self-insured health plan for employees or acts as an intermediary between employees and health care providers. *These files are akin to personnel files and the right to absolute protection of these files was lost in court a long time ago.*

In *Hutchison v. Luddy*,[11] the court in Pennsylvania distinguished between documentation that involves interchurch doctrine and those documents that are "merely" personnel files. The Pennsylvania Superior Court granted broad dis-

---

been advanced."

11   414 Pa. Super. 606 A2d 905 (1992).

covery to a victim of clergy sexual abuse regarding the personnel files of all priests in the Diocese of Altoona-Johnstown who had been accused of similar misconduct, which included canonically protected materials in the "secret archives." The court held, after an in camera review, that these files did not contain any confidential communications of a spiritual nature that would be protected by the statutory clergy-communicant privilege. The court stated: "This privilege protects 'priest-penitent' communications; it does not protect information regarding the manner in which a religious institution conducts its affairs or information acquired by a church as a result of independent investigations not involving confidential communications between priest and penitent."

See *Commonwealth of Pennsylvania v. Stewart*,[12] involving the Diocese of Allentown, now the leading case where a church has been forced to disclose personnel records maintained in confidence on an ordained priest. The Pennsylvania Supreme Court held that the files of a priest who had been killed by the defendant were not statutorily privileged, absent an in camera demonstration that they contained communications of a spiritual nature by the priest.

The Courts of Illinois, Massachusetts, New Jersey, and Pennsylvania have all found these records admissible.[13] The case of *Roman Catholic Archbishop v. Superior Court*[14] illustrates how broadly the processes for compelled disclosure of priests' files may sweep. In this particular case, the Superior Court allowed the enforcement of grand jury subpoenas despite objections raised under the clergy-penitent privilege, the psychotherapist-patient privilege, and the Free Exercise and Establishment Clauses of the First Amendment.

In summary, what can be stated about these files is that typically clergy files are clergy personnel files. They contain general information such as educational background, the transferred seminary file, documents and dates of ordination, letters of appointment, letters of recommendation, and personal correspondence to and from the diocesan bishop and the Clergy Personnel Office. Correspondence to and from the diocesan bishop is only retained until the death or transfer of the diocesan bishop. After the death of a priest, in the Diocese of Pittsburgh, retention of the personnel file in the office is two years and then it is permanently placed in the diocesan archives.

Clergy restricted files have a permanent retention in the Diocese of Pittsburgh.

---

12   547 Pa.277, 690. 2d 195, 93 A.L.R.5th 741(1997) 597 (1994).

13   See *Michael B. v. Superior Court*, 103 Cal. App. 4th 1384, 127 Cal.Rptr.2d. 454 (2d. Dist. 2002); *People v. Campobello*, 388 Ill.App.3d 619, 284 Ill. Dec 654, 810 N.E.2d. 307, 123 A.L.R. 5th 761 (2d Dist. 2004); and *Society of Jesus of New England v. Commonwealth*, 441 Mass. 662, 808 N.E.2d 272 (2004).

14   *Roman Catholic Archbishop of Los Angeles v. Superior Court*, 131 Cal. App. 4th 417, 32 Cal.Rptr.3d 209 (2d Dist. 2005).

They are retained in the Clergy Office until two years after death of the priest; these files then are moved permanently to a restricted archive *within* the diocesan archives.

What is placed in the clergy restricted files must be handled very carefully in light of the litigation facing the Church today. In 2003, the Diocese of Pittsburgh adopted a policy concerning the contents of clergy restricted files. A sample of a policy is attached as a reference. After careful analysis in my own diocese, we have taken the position that this policy is civilly sound from a defensive perspective. However, some may argue that it flashes in the face of the requirements of canons 489 and 490, the secret archives canons mentioned above.

Canon 489 provides for the secret archive: "§1 In the diocesan curia there is also to be a secret archive, or at least in the common archive there is to be a safe or cabinet…in it documents to be kept secret are to be protected most securely. §2 Each year documents of criminal cases in matters of morals, in which the accused parties have died or ten years have elapsed from the condemnatory sentence, are to be destroyed. A brief summary of what occurred along with the text of the definitive sentence is to be retained." Therefore, the canon directs destruction of the file after ten years with retention of only a short summary. After death everything including the summary is to be destroyed. Canon 490 provides that only the bishop of the diocese is to have the key to the above files.[15]

The canons on secret archives are not new, and have been part of the law of the Church in the 1917 code. The concepts were carried over into the 1983 code. The secret archives are to hold all materials pertaining to a penal or criminal trial in the Church. They are to hold papers that granted dispensations for occult marriages—for marriages celebrated in secret. Canon 1133 states: "A marriage celebrated in secret is to be recorded only in a special register which is to be kept in the secret archive of the curia."

The law of the Church did not envision that there would be civil or legal implications to crimes that were tried in the Church courts. The drafters understood that these Church trials would be infrequent and would deal with very sensitive issues that could damage the reputation of a priest, but that this misbehavior was within the framework of the Church, and not society as a whole. It was never the intention of the secret archives to handle and maintain priest personnel files!

In today's climate, strict adherence to these two canons make the diocesan attorney's (both civil and canonical) job more difficult for reasons that are self-

---

15   Canon 490 §1: "Only the bishop is to have the key to the secret archive.

§2: When a see is vacant, the secret archive or safe is not to be opened except in a case of true necessity by the diocesan administrator himself.

§3: Documents are not to be removed from the secret archive or safe."

explanatory. At the first hint of civil or criminal litigation there must be directions given to preserve all documents and to destroy nothing, or else the diocese runs a risk of a charge of spoliation or destruction of evidence. Strict adherence to canon 489 will direct that the documents must be destroyed to not damage the reputation of the priest.

These two canons were written for a different time and in a different context, with no imagination that they could ever be construed to apply to sexual abuse allegations of today, or to place the Church at odds with civil society.

III. Personnel Files

These files contain applications for employment, a resume, commendations, proof of citizenship (I-9 Forms), disciplinary actions, income tax declarations, absence reports, vacation, sick and bereavement leave information, release of information for allowance to conduct background checks, letters of recommendation, etc.

If any medical or psychological information is collected and maintained, it must be secured separately and confidentially. In the Diocese of Pittsburgh, our Notice of Privacy Practices provides a disclaimer that states: "Permitted Use and Disclosure of Medical Information About You—As Required By Law. We will disclose medical information about you when required to do so by federal, state or local law. For example, we may disclose medical information when required by a court order in a litigation proceeding such as a malpractice action."

Defenses available:

Canon 1455 is one of the best defenses, in that judges and tribunal personnel are always bound to observe secrecy, if revelation of some procedural act could bring disadvantage to the parties. Additionally, discussions are to be secret, votes and opinions secret and if disclosure of proofs will endanger the reputation of others, then witnesses, experts, advocates and parties can be bound to secrecy.[16]

Explanation of what is in the internal and the external forum can be used as a defense.

---

16   Canon 1455 §1: "Judges and tribunal personnel are always bound to observe secrecy of office in a penal trial, as well as in a contentious trial if the revelation of some procedural act could bring disadvantage to the parties.

§2: They are also always bound to observe secrecy concerning the discussion among the judges in a collegiate tribunal before the sentence is passed and concerning the various votes and opinions expressed there, without prejudice to the prescript of can. 1609, §4.

§3: Whenever the nature of the case or the proofs is such that disclosure of the acts or proofs will endanger the reputation of others, provide opportunity for discord, or give rise to scandal or some other disadvantage, the judge can bind the witnesses, the experts, the parties, and their advocates or procurators by oath to observe secrecy."

The Free Exercise Clause and the protection from governmental interference and excessive entanglement, sometimes called "the church autonomy doctrine," is also a primary defense.

Cases where tribunal records have been defended:

The key issue is whether there a civil purpose or purely an ecclesiastical purpose? In tribunal cases as we know, the purpose of the process is to solely search for truth, to adjudicate the rights of the parties, reunite parties separated from the Church to the Church, and to make reception of the Eucharist possible. Therefore, how can a civil court interfere in these purely ecclesiastical matters? It should be noted that if the information is available through less intrusive means, they must be used.

Reference is made to a recent Pennsylvania case argued successfully in the Diocese of Scranton in the Court of Common Pleas of Monroe County, *Commonwealth vs. Eleanor Nicolosi*.[17] The defendant filed a petition to compel production of the tribunal file of her husband for the "annulment" of his first marriage. Mrs. Nicolosi was charged with homicide in the death of her husband whose body was found on their property. The diocese argued canon 1455 concerning the secrecy of these documents. The judicial vicar testified in an affidavit:

> Proceedings to determine the nullity of the sacrament of marriage serve important religious and spiritual ends for the individuals involved and for the Church. Ecclesiastical tribunals in such matters are bound by Canon Law of the Roman Catholic Church to treat such matters in the utmost confidence. The integrity of the ecclesiastical proceeding is in large measure dependent upon its confidentiality, particularly the candor and the confidentiality of the communications made within this sacramentally related forum. The parties and the witnesses to an ecclesiastical proceeding expect that this confidentiality will be honored, and this expectation is also an essential element of the proper functioning of the religious exercise.

The attorneys for the Diocese of Scranton argued: "Communications were made to the ecclesiastical tribunal for none other than a wholly spiritual purpose, the declaration of the nullity of reception of one of the sacraments of the Church. The ultimate act of the diocesan tribunal declares the spiritual status of the parties. This spiritual status is of utmost concern to the parties as well as to their shepherd."

The court in Monroe County recognized that the nullity process related only to the sacrament of matrimony (as the judicial vicar explained it) and its spiritual consequences and effects and that clergy members involved in the process serve

---

17   *Commonwealth vs. Eleanor Nicolosi* (2004) n. 420.

in a spiritual capacity, thereby allowing the (clergy, priest, minister of the gospel) privilege to apply.[18] Eventually, Mrs. Nicolosi was found guilty.

In a case out of Kansas City decided in April 2011,[19] the Archdiocese of Kansas City in Kansas filled a motion to intervene because the subject matter concerned a claim for defamation based on statements made by the defendant during ecclesiastical nullity proceedings. The archdiocese filed an *amicus* brief as part of the proceedings. The parties were married in 1993 in a Catholic ceremony. They subsequently divorced in 2007 and the defendant in this case filed a petition for a declaration of nullity in 2009. In connection with the process, the defendant made a written statement as part of her petition. In the statement it is alleged that she made false and damaging statements of fact regarding her ex-husband's behavior and psychological state, including that he was diagnosed as bipolar. The judge in the case framed the issue as: "Whether a defendant can be held civilly liable for an alleged tort committed while engaged in religious tribunal proceedings."

The court asked whether ecclesiastical proceedings are *quasi* judicial, and if so, are statements made during those proceedings entitled to a) absolute immunity, b) qualified immunity, or c) if they enjoy any privilege at all. Further the judge asked: "Can a Kansas court be bound by ecclesiastical law or view, and can Kansas law restrict ecclesiastical proceedings as they relate to non-Church members (the plaintiff in the case was not Catholic), as obviously the answer has broad implications.

After a detailed analysis of whether the Archdiocese of Kansas City has any interests that differed from the defendant's interests, the court decided that the statements made in the tribunal proceeding were privileged as made pursuant to the defendant's First Amendment right to Free Exercise of her religion. The court further stated that: "An individual's right to engage in the free exercise of his or her religion is protected by the First Amendment. To hold otherwise, would require individuals to defend themselves in civil court for statements made during required religious proceedings, even if the statements are later determined to be true."

Ryan v. Ryan held that documents given by the wife to her priest while seeking an annulment were protected by the priest penitent privilege.[20]

An older case that serves as a springboard for other courts to hold that records and testimony must be protected is the *Cimijotti v. Paulsen* case.[21] Ultimately,

---

18 *Commonwealth v. Stewart*, 547 Pa.277, 690 A.2d 195, 200 (1997).
19 *Purdum v. Purdum*, n. 09CV 10056, Div 2, KSA Chapter 60.
20 642 N.E. 2d 1028 (Mass 1994).
21 219 F. Supp. 621 (ND. Iowa 1963), 230 F. Supp. 39, 41 (N.D. Iowa 1964).

the case went to the 8th circuit where the granting of the summary judgment was upheld. Another case concerned a federal district court and a suit by the former husband of the defendant for slander and conspiracy to damage his reputation and his property.[22] The ex-husband joined two other women as co-defendants. The alleged wrongful acts occurred during the time that the couple was married, and it involved statements made to Catholic priests in the course of a Church proceeding brought by the ex-wife for Church sanction of her action for separate maintenance and divorce.

Initially the court ruled that the priests to whom the communications had been made could not be forced to disclose the substance of those communications, absent a showing of malice. The court stated:

> To allow slander actions to be based solely upon statements made to the Church before its recognized officials and under its disciplines and regulations would be a violation of the First Amendment. The law withdraws from the State any exertion of restraint on free exercise of religion. The freedom of speech does not protect one against slander, yet a person must be free to say anything and everything to his Church, at least so long as it is said in a recognized and required proceeding of the religion and to a recognized official of the religion. This does not mean that in some instances it may not have to be disclosed, but nonetheless the person must not be prohibited, by fear of court action either civil or criminal against his person or property, from actually making the communication. Also the court is not holding that it would not be actionable if communicated to other third persons. Likewise, it might be actionable if made outside strictly religious activities.

Affidavits:

Affidavits assist in the presentation of the argument to the courts. Monsignor William King of the Diocese of Harrisburg provided the affidavit in the *Purdum* case.[23] Attached for reference is the affidavit of Very Reverend Anthony Generose of the Diocese of Scranton, that was used in the *Nicolosi* case.[24]

Conclusion

A sustainable argument should and could likely be made successfully to preserve the confidentiality of tribunal records, because of the fact that they are strictly for a Church purpose with no civil effect. The faithful have a right to privacy if what they seek is strictly Church oriented or for a Church purpose. Confidentiality is a *sine qua non* of the spiritual exercise of the tribunal inquiry

---

22   340 F. 2d 613 (8th Cir. 1965).
23   *Purdum v. Purdum*, n. 09CV 10056, Div 2, KSA Chapter 60.
24   *Commonwealth vs. Eleanor Nicolosi* (2004) n. 420.

into and determination of the nullity of a Catholic sacramental marriage. The confidentiality assures the integrity of the proceeding and encourages if not guarantees the full and fair exposition of the pertinent facts. Without the protection of confidentiality, the candor and openness of the parties could well be compromised. To breach the sacred trust of confidentiality, through compelled disclosure of important information, would burden the free exercise of the religious and spiritual nature of the tribunal process and the life of the Church.

The argument to withhold the contents of most of the files for clergy and seminarians would be less likely to be successful because these records are akin to personnel files. The law is established that personnel files are discoverable and admissible into evidence in court proceedings.

Best practices are to be sure that the contents of the files are orderly, follow whatever the retention policy is for that specific office, review the retention policy every five years to insure that it is still appropriate for the office, and consult with the diocesan canonist and diocesan attorney to insure that the files are in compliance with canonical or legal requirements with respect to the files in question.

Appendices
- Clergy Restricted Files SAMPLE
- Affidavit of Reverend Anthony Generose, *Commonwealth of Pennsylvania v. Eleanor Nicolosi*, n. 420 Criminal 2004.

APPENDIX A
Sample Protocol Regarding Content of Clergy Restricted Files

Office of Vicar for Clergy
Subject: Content of Restricted Files Clergy
Purpose:
These Guidelines are established to secure the proper maintenance of clergy files particularly in dealing with sensitive matters related to the clergy and their ministry to the faithful.

Applicability:
Office of the Vicar for Clergy

Definitions: General Guidelines:
Clergy Personnel Restricted Files are created as the repository for reports and relevant documents relating to problems involving serious issues in the life of a priest or deacon and the exercise of his ministry.

As a general guideline the contents of the file should be comprehensive enough to fully detail the nature of the problem and the response taken by the Diocese of_____.

Contents of the File:
- The file is to contain documents that are clear and unambiguous. Where possible, a summary of the problem is to be made at certain critical stages and signed and dated by the person writing it. The summary is to detail facts and not conclusions.
- The file must contain a copy of a "Restricted Release of information" signed by the priest allowing a treatment facility or a treating professional to release information to the Diocese of_____, including reports of counselors or psychotherapists if treatment was rendered.
- The file is to contain copies of the correspondence from the Vicar for Clergy to the treating facility, if applicable.
- The file must contain a copy of a signed complaint if applicable.
- The file must contain copies of correspondence sent to any third party in the review of the matter.
- The file must contain the proceedings and the recommendations of the Diocesan Review Board if applicable.
- The file must contain a copy of the Compliance Sheet that indicates if the file is in compliance with the *Charter for the Protection of Children and Young People*.
- In addition to the above materials, the file must contain copies of all letters of

warning (canonical warnings) if any, all precepts that were issued, if any, and all decrees signed by the proper diocesan officials, showing compliance with internal Church policy and canon law.

Access to Files:

The contents of these files are restricted for use by the Secretary or Vicar for Clergy the Director of Clergy Personnel, and the Diocesan Assistance Coordinator.

Responsibility for Maintenance of Files:

The ultimate responsibility for the maintenance of the files is with the Vicar for Clergy. The files are to be maintained consistent with the Diocesan Retention Schedule for that Office.

Effective Date: _____
Amended: _____

APPENDIX B
Affidavit of Reverend Anthony Generose

In the Court of Common Pleas
Monoroe County
Commonwealth of Pennsylvania v. Eleanor Nicolosi, Defendant

No. 420 Criminal 2004

Affidavit of Rev. Anthony Generose

Rev. Anthony Generose, being duly sworn according to law, deposes and states as follows:

1. I am an ordained priest of the Roman Catholic Diocese of Scranton, Pennsylvania. I am a trained canon lawyer of the Roman Catholic Church and serve the Diocese of Scranton as Officialis-Judicial Vicar. In that capacity I act as presiding judge in all matters coming before the diocesan tribunal, including the matters involving the nullity of the sacrament of marriage. I am authorized to speak on behalf of the Catholic Diocese of Scranton in this matter.
2. On October 12, 2010, counsel for the Defendant in the above-captioned matter filed a Petition to Compel Production of Records, seeking an order directing the Bishop of the Diocese of Scranton to produce "the Francis Nicolosi Annulment file dated in or about 1995."
3. Thereafter, on November 8, 2010, Defendant's counsel caused a Subpoena to be issued to the Bishop of the Diocese of Scranton, directing him to appear before the Court on November 19, 2010, and to bring with them the following items:
    "Church Annulment File of Francis S. Nicolosi, including but not limited to Annulment Questionnaire [sic] and information/documents signed by Eleanor Nicolosi."
4. Proceedings to determine the nullity of the sacrament of marriage serve important religious and spiritual ends for the individuals involved, and for the Church. Ecclesiastical tribunals in such matters are bound by the Canon Law of the Roman Catholic Church to treat of such matters in the utmost confidence. The integrity of the ecclesiastical proceeding is, in large measure, dependent upon its confidentiality, particularly the candor and the confidentiality of the communications made within this sacramentally-related forum. The parties and witnesses to an ecclesiastical proceeding expect that this confidentiality will be honored, and this expectation is also an essential element of the proper functioning of the religious exercise.
5. The principal role of the marriage nullity proceeding is to effect a desired

and proper spiritual state of being for the parties involved. It does not relate to all the civil law status of any marriage, but rather only to the sacrament of matrimony and its spiritual consequences and effects. All documents and all testimony received in connection with the proceeding are devoted to this ultimate end. As spiritual shepherd to its adherents, the Roman Catholic Church is bound in fidelity to its duty to God to perform that role in the manner best suited to the spiritual salvation of the souls with which it is entrusted. The sacred trust of confidentiality is an essential element in the performance of that role.

6. To disclose the items demanded by the Motion to Compel Production and the Subpoena in this case would be to breach the religious confidences vested in me and in the Diocese of Scranton, t the detriment not only of my own ministry and that of the Church, but to the detriment of the parties and witnesses involved, and to the detriment of all those individuals throughout the Church who partake in such exercises with the expectation that the confidentiality of what the Church's theological beliefs describe as the spiritual "internal forum" will be preserved as inviolate, in a manner similar to communications made under the seal of confession. Such a breach would violate the highest ecclesiastical law of the Roman Catholic Church, the Church's Canon Law.

7. The religious integrity and confidentiality of marriage nullity proceedings must be preserved even if a party to a proceeding, or a witness who participated in such a proceeding, should somehow seek: to waive the confidentiality of his or her own communications made within the context of that proceedings. The church's requirement of confidentiality must be held out as absolute in order to assure the candor and spiritual integrity of all communications made within this forum.

8. I have read the contents of the Motion for Protective Order and to Quash Subpoena and the Memorandum in Support of that Motion being submitted contemporaneously with this Affidavit by the Diocese of Scranton and I endorse all of the statements made therein and incorporate those statements into this Affidavit.

Further the Affiant Sayeth Not.

A shore Memorandum of Law accompanied the Affidavit.

Seminar

Simulation: New Lyrics to an Old Tune
Very Reverend Anthony L. Kerin

Audio Cue: Australian National Anthem first verse.

That is a fine way to commence proceedings. We use the national anthem to mark special occasions with a national dignity, at civic and sporting events and podium presentations at international competitions such as the Olympic Games. In Australia over many years now there has been a concerted effort to encourage athletes representing the nation, to sing along with the tune. Now many more people are able to sing the anthem.

The anthem is most often sung by a choir or a soloist and yet at other times it is just an instrumental tune that is played. Everyone familiar with the tune knows it is the national anthem and so even without the words, the essential sentiment is still conveyed. There are some problematic words in it such as 'girt'. Not a common everyday word. A bit like 'consubstantial' it is not a word for everyday conversation.

For the purposes of this seminar, let's start with a question. Is it the tune and the words or just the tune alone that makes it a performance of the national anthem?

This is the analogy I am using for this talk today. When the tune alone is played, are the words implied? Does the tune evoke the lyrics? And if so which lyrics, for sometimes we mishear the lyrics. Misheard lyrics have their own corner of the internet with thousands of pages listing humorous alternatives to the original words penned by the song writers.

Misheard lyrics may be the result of a mistake, sometimes made by a person confident in the firm belief that they are the correct words as they heard them, regardless of the fact that they are not what was sung by the artist nor intended by the songsmith. These people are in error but unaware of it.

There are those who would attempt the anthem but cannot hold a note, seem to be tone deaf, sing flat or for any number of other reasons underperform. Are they lacking capacity? Should they take the Lee Marvin approach to singing? Then the anthem becomes a recitation.

It is altogether different when the person deliberately rewrites the words, even to the point of parodying the original song. They are using the original tune with a modified lyric to amuse themselves and/or others. These people are partially simulating the song, remaining faithful to the tune but substituting the words.

There is yet another variation. There are those who would substitute the original tune and sing the original lyrics to an entirely different melody, albeit one with the same meter. These might be seen as totally simulating the song.

If an anthem is so substantially altered, is it still the National anthem? Or has it changed into something else altogether?

Audio Cue: *Australian Anthem – to the tune of Working Class Man*.
Some might consider this to be disrespectful, perhaps a little too working class for the national tune. But what should we say about the merits of someone who presents a more pious intention?

Audio Cue: *Australian Anthem – to tune of Amazing Grace*.
Consider someone who sings the words of the anthem to the tune of Amazing Grace. It is hardly a disrespectful intention.

	Atonal	Tune	Melodious
Exact Words	☑ Lyrics ☒ Tune "*Poem*"		☑ Lyrics ☑ Tune "*Real Anthem*"
Lyrics		☒ Lyrics ☒ Tune "*Different Song*"	☒ Lyrics ☑ Tune "*Parody*"
Humming	☒ Lyrics ☒ Tune "*Not a Song*"		☒ Lyrics ☑ Tune "*Misheard Lyrics*"

The question remains. Is it the melody or the lyrics or both that is essential for a valid performance of the national anthem? By analogy, let us explore the performing of marriage consent.

But first I offer a disclaimer. I do not intend to make a studied analysis of Rotal decisions concerning the ground of simulation in this paper. There are many fine articles that do precisely that[1]. My intention here is to explore what happens

---

1 See John G. Johnson, "Total Simulation in Recent Rotal Jurisprudence," *Studia canonica* 24 (1990) 383-425;

William H. Woestman, "Simulation Revisited," *CLSA Proceedings* 65 (2003) 241-256; Lynda Robitaille, "Simulation, Error Determining the Will, or Lack of Due Discretion?" *Studia canonica* 29 (1995) 397-432;

when altogether separate ideas and concepts are juxtaposed in the hope of gleaning a new insight that may, in good time and with due reflection, perhaps assist our thinking about such grounds for nullity as canonically employed in Church Tribunals.

But first I would like to revisit some prior learnings. How do we know what we know? And how do we decide what we do?

Epistemology:

In 2006 I gave a paper at the Canberra Conference of the Canon Law Society on Error determining the will[2] and in many ways this paper is a follow on from that presentation. It is worth our while to go back over what I said at that time about the knowing of knowing and the dynamics as we understand them of the interaction between the intellect and the will.

The traditional epistemology underlying canon law dates from a time before the separation of the human sciences. From antiquity until the end of the Middle Ages one common method unified the various sciences as they studied human nature. Theology, Philosophy, Metaphysics and Psychology, such as it was at the time, all reflected upon the human condition in a similar manner and with a similar method. This unified vision of human nature, perhaps given most complete expression in the investigation and findings of St. Thomas Aquinas published as the *Summa Theologiae*, lost influence and recognition with the divergence of the human sciences in the modern era.

In the Thomistic view, the intellect is considered as separate and distinct from the will. The intellect is the domain of knowledge, which is recognized as experienced by the senses. The senses are both external (taste, sight, smell, feel) and internal[3] (common sense, imaginative sense, estimative sense or judgment, memorative sense). The will is the domain of appetite,[4] that is, the power by which we are inclined towards some thing or some action. It is consequent upon knowledge and is therefore a rational appetite. It is inclined towards the good, or at least the apparent good. In error it can be inclined toward wrong masquerading as good.

This Thomistic overview of mankind was eclipsed by an increasing specialisation in the various sciences and their attendant new and differing investigative approaches. Philosophy began to exhibit a tendency to overstate the significance

---

John P. Beal, "Determining Error: Hot New Ground of Nullity or Recycled Old Ground?" *CLSA Proceedings* 71 (2009) 62-89; Margaret A. Ramsden and Gerald T. Jorgensen, "Sources For Canon 1101, §2: Total Simulation," *Marriage Studies V: Sources in Matrimonial Law*, ed. Gerald T. Jorgensen (Washington, DC: CLSA, 2004) 115-126.

2   Tony Kerin, "Determining Error," *CLSANZ Proceedings* (2006) 37.

3   *Summa Theologiae* I, 78, 4, ad 2.

4   *Summa Theologiae* Ia, 80, 1.

of human reason. Theology increasingly set aside the human condition in favour of exploring more supernatural and less concrete considerations. Psychology, with its scientific method consciously and deliberately expunged any reference to metaphysics, so as to seek for itself a neutral autonomy, based on objective and verifiable facts not influenced by values or morality. The human being is of course a combination of all these aspects and we ignore or exaggerate any individual factor at our peril. We are most human when all these aspects are in balance.

The field of canon law is best served by lawyers who are conscious of these developments and their divergence. We can then better seek a synthesis of the human sciences to aid our understanding of mankind's behaviour and thinking.

Bernard Lonergan[5] proposed just such an approach with a transcendental method as an anthropological vision of mankind common to the philosophical and social sciences. He outlines the levels of function of the intellect and will in their knowing and deciding.

1. Experience
2. Practical understanding (insight)
3. Critical reflection and Judgment
4. A decision about what to do

The first three levels correspond to the knowing and discerning which Thomistic theory would call the 'speculatively - practical' judgment and they reside in the intellect. The fourth level is the 'practical – practical' judgment and this level is a function of the will.

By way of an example, imagine a football fan sitting in the family room watching the big game on television.

1. Experience: First he acknowledges his experience. He says to himself "I feel hungry". It may be that his experience was prompted by a fast food commercial or that he has not eaten for some hours. The important point is that he senses his hunger.
2. Practical understanding (insight): His previous experiences lead him to the insight that when he feels hungry, the remedy is to eat something.
3. Critical reflection and Judgment: He reflects that he should perhaps prepare something to eat. To this point he is still in the family room and his thinking is still in the intellect.
4. Decision / Action: The decisive action he now takes is to leave the family room and enter the kitchen to cook something. He cannot cook anything in front of the television and he cannot decide anything in his intellect. He

---

5 Bernard Lonergan, *Method in Theology*, 2nd ed. (New York: Herder, 1973) 13-14.

physically needs to move to the kitchen and mentally his thinking needs to move to the will.

This example is exaggerated for the sake of the argument. The truth be known, most of us have an open plan kitchen / sitting room and we move from one to the other without entering a new room. Likewise, the knowing / deciding processes are less clearly defined in reality and we certainly find ourselves moving back and forth from the intellect to the will continually throughout the process of each decision.

How is this football fan's decision making (will) influenced by his intellect? Well for a start his appetite is whetted by his experiences. His choice of what to cook is determined by his experience of the commercial products to which he is exposed, his previous experience in food preparation, his skill in cooking or lack of it and the provisions in his pantry. Whether he decides on baked beans or toast or filet mignon is not simply down to his desire. It is determined to a great extent by his current circumstances, such as the availability of ingredients, the length of time until the game resumes after the half time break, the degree of his hunger and his competing desire not to miss the game.

We can apply this same analysis to the decision to marry. A person experiences a calling to companionship. It may be inspired by motives that range from altruistic love through to sheer loneliness. The insight comes with an understanding that a partnership would be a remedy not just for concupiscence. Critical reflection moves the person to consider marriage. Thus far the thinking is entirely in the intellect, but it moves to the will when the decision to propose marriage is made.

The availability and choice of partner, the previous experience of other's marriages including those of parents and relatives, the recognition of one's own needs, capacities and motivation all contribute to the appreciation of the marital commitment. The exercise of discretion of judgment in making the decision to marry is influenced and in most cases, determined by the thinking in the intellect that precedes the act of the will that establishes the irrevocable consent. One can only will to commit to that type of marriage that one knows, appreciates, comprehends and thus embraces.

Bernard Lonergan argued that his description of these four component stages in our knowing is a common feature that affords meaningful dialogue between distinct sciences. For our benefit it offers a bridge between canon law, philosophy and psychology. Lonergan's description of the functioning of the intellect and will outlines how the speculative practical judgement (knowing and discerning) involving experience, insight and critical reflection can be affected by emotional influences and speculative beliefs and even erroneous ideas, but that such influences remain in the intellect. The fourth level of deciding to act consequent upon the function of the intellect is the practical – practical judgement. This is an act of the will.

Lonergan considers that there are three facets to this act of the will[6]. He calls them 1) will - the ability to make decisions, 2) willing – the act of deciding, and 3) willingness – the predisposition to decide one way more than the other. The emotional influence, which may be present in the knowing and discerning, most often enters the will or deciding as this biased predisposition.

The Interrelation of Grounds of Nullity:

Attitudes and intentions influencing marriage consent are many and varied. In each nullity case, the court is attempting to describe and define in canonical terms, the intentions and actions of people whose lives are not usually neatly confined to canonical categories. Courting couples are rarely canonically conscious in their deliberations. However, where we can apply the facts of the case to the law and determine with moral certitude a canonical argument for invalidity, then nullity can be declared. We must remember that we are using categories and descriptions to define the actions of couples who gave no canonical thought to what they were doing. Applying such a jurisprudential overlay to the reality as lived by a couple is very much a later addition and the actions of a couple may not neatly fit one ground or another.

For this reason I propose in this seminar to try to imagine possible ways of graphically displaying the interrelation of various grounds for nullity. I emphasize that such a schematic representation of a couple's consent to marriage will not be of itself a proof of nullity, but rather it is an aide to assist a judge to refine his thinking on how such a consent might be or not be valid in a given case. It is not, I emphasize again, a matter of drawing a graph and presenting this as proof of nullity. It is rather a matter of imagining the graph to assist the judge in giving some form to the argument for or against nullity in the sentence to be written.

Comments from the parties reveal their thinking and if we can identify where such thoughts reside in the intellect and will, we are well on the way to defining the invalidity or otherwise of their consent. A person who says "I didn't used to believe in divorce, but then I got married" is telling something of his or her thinking. Such an expression would not confirm an invalidating error or partial simulation for it is clearly an opinion arrived at after the wedding day. This acceptance of divorce is after the event and so could not have influenced, let alone determined the consent. But if a person says "If I didn't believe in divorce, I could never have gotten married" then here the thinking of the person indicates either a pre-condition, a partial simulation or a determining error. Is this a conditioned consent? When might it become partial simulation? Or is it an erroneous intellect determining the will?

These questions got me thinking about the inter connection. Is there a way we can map what is taking place so that we might better understand the thinking of

---

6   Bernard Lonergan, *Insight: A Study of Human Understanding* (London, 1958) 623.

the parties in a given nullity case. We know that grounds such as partial simulation, unfulfilled condition and error determining the will have an overlap and might merge into one another depending on the perspective of the description.

When a person appears to consent to a marital union but expressly intends to exclude marriage or its essential properties from the consent, then that consent is invalid[7]. The traditional proof of this simulation was the identification of the positive act of the will purposefully and consciously excluding marriage or an essential property from this consent.

But people who hold marriage to be dissoluble, such as some non-Catholics, would struggle to make such a positive act of the will. Why would a person who holds marriage to be dissoluble take the trouble to overtly express a positive intention to reject indissolubility? The distinction between an explicit positive act of the will and an implicit exclusion, just as invalidating but the result of a pervading intention of non inclusion began to appear. As the jurisprudence developed after 1983 around the new canon 1099 on error determining the will, this new juridic figure for invalid consent, without the conscious act of the will, was variously described as error in the intellect imposing itself on the will, implicit simulation or unfulfilled condition.[8] In subsequent jurisprudence, the positive act of the will has sometimes not been so explicit and there are numerous cases where the act was implicit, folded into the lifestyle, attitude or behavior of the person, and not so obviously pronounced.

It is sometimes evident when a party replaces the *consortium vitae* with some other value such as legitimacy for children or qualifying for inheritance as the principal object of their consent. It may be argued that in some cases they even fail to include marriage itself in their consent.

Some Rotal judges have argued that error in the intellect is a form of conditioned consent that cannot be fulfilled since it errs about a quality that is essential to marriage. Monsignor Lawrence Wrenn[9] made a useful distinction suggesting that in the 1940's Rotal judges believed that error only rarely influenced the will to the degree necessary such that a positive act of the will excluded an essential property of marriage[10]. But when it did the error brought about a simulation. The object of consent is erroneously conceived. But in later Rotal decisions[11] we see the error determining the will such that the intending itself is erroneous. Here it

---

7   Canon 1101 §2.

8   Elissa Rinere, CP, "Error which Causes the Contract," *Studia canonica* 38 (2004) 81.

9   Lawrence G. Wrenn, "Sacramentality and the Invalidity of Marriage," *The Jurist* 60 (2000) 219-220.

10   C. Heard, *RRDec* 32 (1940) 110.

11   C. Sabbatini, *RRDec* 56 (1968) 927-928.

is not the object of the consent that is in error but the consenting itself.

Francis Morrissey,[12] has recently described the debate concerning canon 1099 and whether it is a new ground of nullity or not. He mentions that Cardinals Navarette and Grochelewski hold that this canon simply consolidates decades of jurisprudence on *error pervicax*. On the other hand Bishop A. Stankiewicz, P. Viladrich, R. Brown. L. Wrenn and A. Mendonca see this canon as a new and autonomous ground of nullity. Morrissey offers a further clarification by highlighting that where a person is aware that his or her lifestyle and beliefs are contrary to what the Church understands as marriage, then it is simulation. But where the person is unaware of this, it is a case of error determining the will.

Do we need a positive act of the will for a partial simulation of marriage? Is not an implicit desire to exclude some essential property sufficient to partially simulate the consent?

If it is a matter of an unfulfilled condition then such a condition needs to be consciously placed. Where one erroneously perceives marriage not to possess some essential property, why would one place such a condition? If one held no precautionary doubts then there is no reason to place any condition upon the consent. Stankiewicz[13] makes the Thomistic distinction between speculative error and practical error. Mere exposure to erroneous opinions does not necessarily lead to an invalid consent. I might speculate marriage to be dissoluble yet still will my marriage to be permanent.

Practical error involves the applying of the erroneous notion to this marriage itself. It is not simulation he says but the willing of a pseudo marriage where the object of the marriage consent is different from what the Church would expect.

Lynda Robitaille in a most enlightening study of the "Bologna Hippy Case"[14] draws on Gus Mendonca's analysis of the Rotal sentences to arrive at an interesting conclusion. Namely, the demonstration that Lack of Due Discretion need not come from a mental illness or anomaly, but it can arise from a lifestyle or cultural influence.

The case concerns Titus, a baptized Catholic who at age 16 became a hippy, rejecting society's view of marriage and replacing it with a concept of free love. At 19 years he met Bertha, aged 17. In the summer of '65 she became pregnant and at the behest of her parents they wed on 7 February 1966. Bertha was eight

---

12   Francis Morrissey, "Error Determining the Will," presented at the 2011 CLSGBI Conference, p. 11.

13   C. Stankiewicz, April 25, 1991: *RRDec* 83 (1991) 280-290.

14   Lynda Robitaille, "Simulation, Error Determining the Will, or Lack of Due Discretion? A Case Study," *Studia canonica* 29 (1995) 397-432.

months pregnant. The couple separated in July that same year.

The Tribunal of first instance in Bologna found negative on an intention *contra bonum sacramenti*. An appeal to the Rota saw Stankiewicz add the ground of Simulation as in first instance and find affirmative on 23 July 1982. The second instance for this ground was a third instance hearing coram Davino on 20 March 1985. This court found affirmative on the ground of lack of due discretion, although it quoted extensively from the arguments and proofs of the Stankiewicz decision. With two affirmatives but on different grounds the case went to Serrano in fourth instance, and this time the court found the two decisions to be conforming. The same facts were recited as proof of Simulation in second instance and of Lack of Discretion in third instance. This was sufficient for Serrano to find for conformity. So much for the previously axiomatic belief that simulation and lack of discretion are mutually exclusive.

Like all the sacraments, marriage may be described by its Matter and its Form. The Matter of most other sacraments is the bread, wine, oil, or water, while the Form is the words of conferral by the celebrant. In the Latin Church's sacramental theology[15] the Matter of the sacrament is the couple themselves, and they are also the celebrants of the sacrament; the gift of self, given and accepted, by each and to the other. The Form of marriage is the exchange of vows and there are essential elements that must be expressed in such vows for those couples bound to a catholic form of marriage. Couples marrying in Eastern rite churches are not required to express vows.

For couples not bound to Catholic form the requirements are simply that their consent not expressly exclude the essential properties. Church Tribunals presume validity[16] and a valid intention on the part of any non-catholic man and woman who desire to commit their lives to each other, however they may express it.

Catholic couples are presumed to want marriage as the Church intends it. Their request to contract marriage in a Catholic ceremony is usually sufficient to establish this desire on their part. For a catholic party to a union to contract marriage other than as the Church understands it requires a deliberate effort to simulate, at least partially, his or her consent to the marriage. Pre-nuptial inquiry forms and the counseling of Catholic celebrants in preparing the couple for the wedding demand that the essential properties are at least canvassed with every couple seeking a Catholic wedding.

However, there is increasing evidence that more and more couples do not consent to marriage as the Church understands it. There is abundant evidence

---

15 In the Eastern Churches, the matter is the couple but the celebrant is a priest (not a deacon) and the form is the crowning ceremony.

16 Canon 1060.

that couples marry not as the Church understands it, but rather, as other people do. Thus many such couples seek out a civil union rather than a Church wedding. They would normally have to know what the Church expects, to simulate the consent. If they are Catholic and bound to form, such a wedding would lack canonical form before it was ever investigated on the grounds of simulation.

Let us map these various intentions to begin with as various kinds of impaired consent.

Error: That is where someone says, "I want a marriage as I understand it". I don't know that I am wrong. I am not even aware that I am in error. I want what I consider to be marriage.

Condition: "I want a marriage but I want it on my terms." These are the ground rules for this union. If they are not fulfilled, then the marriage is off.

Partial Simulation: "I want marriage but without the children, or without the permanence or fidelity." Woestman has argued that a *contra bonum coniugum* case is identical to the simulation of marriage itself and the lack of Rotal decisions on this ground is because cases which might fit such a decision were heard on total simulation[17].

Total Simulation: "I want a wedding but I don't want a marriage". They want a wedding for some other effect such as residency, a work permit, inheritance or legitimacy for offspring, but they do not want a lifelong union of man and wife. It is certain that they do not want a marriage. The reason they are prepared to undergo a wedding is unrelated to the usual intentions we might associate with a marriage.

How do these grounds relate to one another? I propose we return to the categories of Aquinas with his Intellect and Will, albeit with Lonergan's refinements. What might valid consent look like?

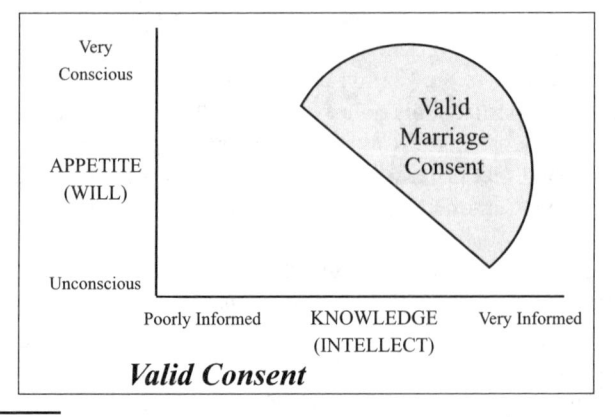

Valid Consent

---

17   Woestman, op.cit., 255.

If we graph the Intellect on the x axis and the Will on the y axis, a valid marriage consent might be represented like this. I suggest that valid consent is an area of the graph rather than a point because no two couple's consents are the same but anything that finishes in the area of well informed and consciously willed, suffices for a valid consent. The extreme right end of the x axis might be the province of couples who have courted for years, and know each other very well, but possess no appetite for the commitment that marriage demands. The top extreme of the y axis is perhaps the realm of those impetuous types who though poorly informed about marriage and each other, are quick to marry and perhaps even marry again in serial relationships. These extremes are both outside the parameters of valid consent.

- Traditionally Rotal jurisprudence has distinguished between total simulation and partial simulation.
- Total simulation occurs when the content of marital consent itself (cc. 1055 §1; 1057) is excluded through a positive act of the will[18].
- Partial simulation - some essential property or element of marriage is excluded through a positive act of the will.
- Total simulators may be aware that a marriage does not exist while partial simulators may believe that a subjectively defined marriage does exist.

Generally, total simulation is considered to be deliberate decision to undergo a wedding but not to bind oneself to marriage. Are mature, rational and thoughtful people the only ones capable of simulating? Lynda Robitaille raised this question[19] as she sought to break down some of the stereotypes established by jurisprudence traditionally understood. John Johnson also queried whether all simulators were aware of this disparity in their thinking and actions[20]. In summary, total simulators are thought to know what they are doing and the consequences of those actions. They make a positive act of the will, either explicitly or implicitly, to intend a wedding while pretending a marriage.

Partial simulators intend a marriage, even if it is a union tailored to their own perceptions, excluding the properties they consider dispensable. Hey may do so due to lack of understanding of the essential nature of those properties. They may act without awareness of the consequences of their actions.

So now we take a look at impaired consent. The poorly informed, unconscious consent of someone inadvertently in error would appear at the bottom left of the graph. The very informed, very conscious traditional understanding of total simulation of marriage is up in the top right area where we previously saw valid consent, not because it is valid, but because it requires the same clarity of

---

18 Ramsden and Jorgensen, 115.
19 Robitaille, op cit.
20 John Johnson, "Simulation—Recent Jurisprudence," *Studia canonica* 24 (1990) 390.

thought, knowledge and intention to totally simulate as it does to place a valid binding consent. Traditionally there is no lack of discretion in a total simulation of consent. They are intending a wedding but pretending a marriage. But as we have seen in the Bologna case, examples of cases where the simulation was implied rather than conscious are starting to appear.

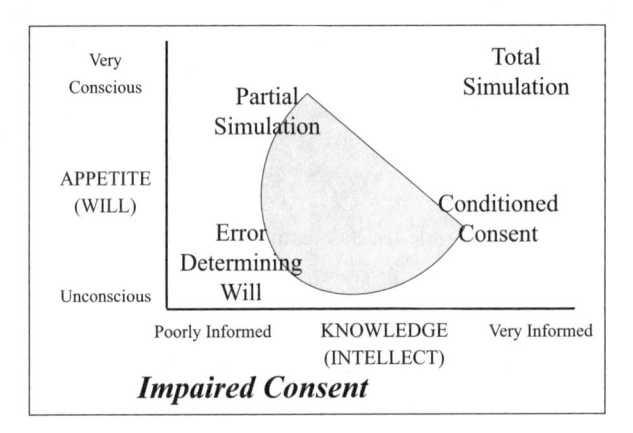

```
                    |  Very                        Total
                    |  Conscious    Partial        Simulation
                    |             Simulation
                    |              ⌒⌒⌒⌒⌒
        APPETITE    |           /         \
         (WILL)     |          |           \
                    |           \          Conditioned
                    |            Error      Consent
                    |         Determining
                    |  Unconscious  Will
                    |_____
                       Poorly Informed  KNOWLEDGE    Very Informed
                                       (INTELLECT)
```

Impaired Consent

Conditioned consent is more a feature of the willing being impaired. There is clearly an informed knowledge required to place the condition, but the capacity to consciously commit is impaired with such cautionary doubt that some condition is imposed.

On the other hand, partial simulation requires more of a conscious commitment, albeit to a less than well informed object of consent. The object of marital consent is diminished by the exclusion of some essential quality or property.

And in the middle we have the cloud of lack of discretion of judgment. This area of the graph represents consent that is impaired by ill informed knowledge in the intellect failing to motivate a sufficiently conscious commitment in the will. The consent in these cases sometimes exhibit indications of partial simulation or conditioned consent and sometimes even ignorance or error. Mostly in these instances there is a lack of clear indications of thought patterns or method.

The third section of canon 1095 regarding incapacity for marriage cannot appear on this graph of impaired consent, because in those cases there is no consent. In such a case the person does not possess the capacity to elicit a consent.

If we interpret the sentences of the various grades in the Bologna case we can see that some judges estimated the knowing and willing of Titus slightly differently. Stankiewicz saw this fellow's consent to have simulated, for he wanted a wedding to appease the parents in law, but could not entertain the concept of a binding marriage and within 5 months returned to the "free love" lifestyle of his culture. Davino saw it slightly differently. Titus was possessed of a diminished appetite for commitment that saw him lack discretion concerning the essential rights and duties of marriage.

We have noted how couples not bound to the Latin Church form of marriage do not have to pronounce marriage vows to marry validly. This highlights the significance of the wording of vows for couples who are bound to that form. The fashion of writing their own vows, like the signing of a pre-nuptial agreement, may not necessarily prove an invalid consent. To the degree that it modifies the marriage consented to, it is material to a nullity investigation, but we must also acknowledge the attitudes of young people today, who have every expectation that life is full of options and that they can pick and choose what they are comfortable with.

In the FOCCUS Pre Marital Inventory Instrument statement number 142 says "I could not under any condition remain married to my spouse if he/she were ever unfaithful to me". It is a trick question and it is fascinating as a facilitator of the FOCCUS instrument, to discuss this with couples. The preferred response is Disagree. Yet in a majority of couples both parties Agree with this statement. In most cases they are not so much imposing a condition on their consent, but seeking to send a message to their partner that they consider fidelity an important feature of this intended union. Perhaps they feel that if they didn't agree with it, their partner might get the wrong idea. It causes great discussion which is, of course, the purpose of the instrument in the first place.

We do well to analyze the significance of comments and actions made by couples when marrying, for they reveal to us the mysteries of their thinking. My own hope is that the graph we have devised here might prove useful to judges in the task of applying the lived reality to the categories of the law in our tribunals. As we address the consenting of the parties we might consider where it might fit on the x and y axis in terms of understanding of marriage and commitment to willing that understanding. The plot that results may then offer an indication of what ground might be best applied in judgment. As I said, it is not a proof, but an aide to clarifying the argument that might motivate a morally certain sentence. I would now welcome any comments, refinements or cautions you might have to offer.

Seminar

The Holy See and the Protection of US Clergy Rights: A Historical Perspective
Reverend Kevin E. McKenna

I love being a pastor of an urban cathedral parish – let me count the ways: I love the nine and ten year olds from the neighborhood who occasionally run into our cathedral and love to play with our large immersion baptismal font, play with the light control panel in the sanctuary and then sing rap over the ambo microphone. I like being the pastor of the cathedral where a woman will make an occasional appearance after the 1st mass of the day, walking down the aisle singing a gospel hymn at the top of her voice before exiting through a side door. I love being the pastor of a cathedral where a man wearing much jewelry will remove a corporal from the altar after mass, liturgically rinse it in the baptismal font and then carefully place it over the arm of the statue of the Blessed Mother in the sanctuary.

I also love taking sabbaticals.

But let me be clear – I have been greatly blessed to pastor a beautiful city community with a wonderful staff, many talented and gifted parishioners who willingly and extravagantly share their time, talent and treasure to help build and grow our community, a community that is extremely diverse in its make-up, with numerous refugees that have come to join us in our diverse community of multiple different ethnicities and rainbow hues.

But I still love taking a sabbatical – which I did not too many years ago.

I had grown to admire especially those members of our society who have undertaken as a ministry proper advocacy for those disenfranchised of their rights for one reason or another. I decided to spend my sabbatical learning about our forbears in canonical ministry who by their efforts, although working with a different ecclesiastical law, one which was contemporary to their time, still showed us the way by their studious research, study and non-compromising advocacy for those they felt were being treated unjustly.

I spent many delightful hours at the University of Notre Dame's library and archives, the archives of other dioceses and the archives of the Propaganda Fide, or as it is now known, Congregation for the Evangelization of Peoples. What a narcotic – quiet hours of reading and research!

My research introduced me to some professional and non–professional canonists, self-trained practitioners, as well as some bishops from outside of the United States who came to observe and make recommendations about much needed improvement in relations between priests and their bishops, relations which had been badly damaged in the late nineteenth century due to some perceived deprivation of rights, with clergy morale at an all time low.

But my greatest discovery is that these individuals, working to defend rights, in a wonderful way presaged and obviously impacted the ministry of succeeding canonists and our Canon Law Society which has committed itself to form canonists "marked by a zeal for justice in the Church, aware that while each individual must sacrifice for the common good, true communion is advanced only when the dignity and fundamental rights of each person are held to be inviolable."[1]

I began to see quite an amazing similarity between the work of these nineteenth century canonical lights and the work of some of our own canonists today. I would like to share with you today what I hope is the fruit of that research and perhaps some wisdom that has been bequeathed to us by our canonical ancestors.

In October of 2002, Cardinal Giovanni Battista Re, then Prefect of the Congregation for Bishops in Rome, issued in the name of the Vatican a response to the American bishops concerning the *Essential Norms for Diocesan/Eparchial Policies Dealing with Allegations of Sexual Abuse of Minors by Priests, Deacons and or Other Church Personnel.*[2] These norms had been hastily assembled by the U.S. bishops in their June Plenary meeting in Dallas, Texas, to respond to the tragic developments concerning the sexual abuse of minors by clerics in the U.S.[3]

Although an urgent response was needed, some canon lawyers had raised concerns about the lack of due process for accused clergy in the norms. Questions emerged, including issues about the removal of clergy after an allegation

---

1   Canon Law Society of America, "Code of Professional Responsibility," www.clsa.org/?page=04codeofrespons.

2   Letter of Cardinal Prefect Giovanni Battista Re of the Congregation for Bishops (October 14, 2002): "Answer to the 'Essential Norms for Diocesan/Eparchial Policies Dealing with Allegations of Sexual Abuse of Minors by Priests, Deacons, or Other Church Personnel,'" www.vatican.va/roman_curia/congregations/cbishops/documents/rc_con_cbishops_doc_20021018_re-usa_en.html.

3   United States Conference of Catholic Bishops, "Essential Norms for Diocesan/Eparchial Policies Dealing with Allegations of Sexual Abuse of Minors by Priests, Deacons and or Other Church Personnel," in *Promise to Protect Pledge to Heal* (Washington, DC: USCCB, 2003).

before any substantive investigation had been made; the lack of a clear definition of sexual abuse; the right of the accused and accuser to their good reputation while investigations were underway; and disregard for any prescription (in some ways similar to civil law "statute of limitations").

Cardinal Re's letter pointed to some of these same issues, observing that the application of the policies adopted at Dallas could be the "source of confusion and ambiguity."[4] He noted the difficulty in reconciling the provisions of the Dallas norms with the universal law of the Church, especially when the terminology used was "vague or imprecise."[5]

Contributions of the Mixed Commission

As a result of the later intervention by a mixed commission of American bishops and curial officials, some safeguards for due process were provided. The revised norms clarified the status of the important work of the review board, the group that the bishop is to consult regarding allegations of sexual misconduct.[6] Qualifications for service on this board are enumerated, a term is established, and they are *defined* as a "consultative body" to the bishop.[7] The norms underscored the need for each diocese ("eparchy" for Eastern Catholics) to have a written policy on the sexual abuse of minors by priests, deacons and other church personnel and to be in conformity with the requirements of the universal law of the Church.[8] The observance of prescription is included, although the bishop can petition the Congregation for the Doctrine of the Faith, as we know, for a dispensation, "while indicating appropriate pastoral reasons."[9] The norms clarified "psychological testing," sometimes utilized by bishops to establish the guilt of an accused. As norm 7 states, the alleged offender "may be requested to seek, and *may be* urged *voluntarily* to comply with an appropriate medical and psychological evaluation at a facility mutually acceptable to the diocese/eparchy and to the accused."[10] The definition of sexual abuse has been somewhat clarified, but there is no provision for a gradation of penalties according to possible offenses. Although the bishop/eparch is reminded of his possible use of executive power to remove clerics from office, remove or restrict faculties and limit the exercise of ministry, he is likewise reminded that in exercising this broad administrative

---

4   Letter of Cardinal Prefect Giovanni Battista Re.

5   Ibid.

6   United States Conference of Catholic Bishops, "Essential Norms for Diocesan/Eparchial Policies Dealing with Allegations of Sexual Abuse of Minors by Priests, Deacons and or Other Church Personnel," in *Promise to Protect Pledge to Heal*, Revised Edition (Washington, DC: USCCB, 2006).

7   Ibid., nn. 4-5.

8   Ibid., n. 2.

9   Ibid., n. 8.

10 Ibid., n. 7.

power, recourse is available to the cleric..[11] It is also mentioned that care will always be taken to protect the rights of all parties involved when an accusation has been made.[12] If an accusation has proven to be unfounded, "every possible step will be taken to restore the good name of the person falsely accused."

After the revised norms received the *recognitio* of the Congregation for Bishops in December of 2002, some canonists and others continued to critique the norms regarding the seeming inconsistency of the concepts, propositions and positions contained in the new norms to canonical tradition. Father Ladislas Örsy, for example, in his article "Bishops' Norms: Commentary and Evaluation" provided a critical commentary on the meaning of the individual norms within the broader context of the life and beliefs of the Church and its need to have structures that prevent corruption and promote growth.[13] The esteemed theologian, the late Cardinal Avery Dulles, in an article that was published in 2004, wrote passionately about the need for a revision of the Dallas Charter and the "Essential Norms," believing that in "their effort to protect children, to restore public confidence in the church as an institution, and to protect the church from liability suits, the bishops opted for an extreme response."[14]

Although these serious concerns were voiced concerning the revised norms by canonists and others, the intervention of the Holy See, in calling for revisions in the original norms and in calling for the mixed commission, was seen by many canonists as most helpful.

The purpose of this presentation will not be to examine in any detail the revisions that took place after the review by the Holy See and the work of the Mixed Commission. Nor will it proffer any evaluation or assessment of the revisions. Rather, citing the dynamics of the participation of the Holy See in the drafting of legislation that involves clergy discipline and norms for the United States, I would like to provide some background from American Catholic Church history that will demonstrate the important role that Rome has played in moderating or even adjusting American procedures in the hopes of bringing disciplinary norms and procedures into a conformity with the universal legislation of the Church. I would also like to use this presentation as an opportunity to introduce you, if you have not met them, to some canonists and writers in the field of canon law from the nineteenth century, ones whom I believe are worthy of study and gratitude for their service to the Church in the United States, as well as to the Universal Church.

---

11 Ibid., n. 9, footnote 6.

12 Ibid., n. 13.

13 Ladislas Örsy, "Bishops' Norms: Commentary and Evaluation," *Boston College Law Review* 44 (2003) 999-1030.

14 Avery Dulles, "Rights of Accused Priests: Toward a Revision of the Dallas Charter and the 'Essential Norms,'" *America* 190:20 (June 21-28, 2004) 19.

Prior Roman Intervention

In June of 1853, the Holy See had assigned Archbishop Gaetano Bedini to investigate the status of the Church in the United States. Increasingly concerned about a variety of issues, including the rise of lay trusteeism and anti- Catholic nativist movements, the visit would also provide Rome with a first hand account of the tensions between bishops and their priests. It would also give Rome the opportunity to sound out the hierarchy in the United States about the possible appointment of a permanent apostolic delegation. Many priests pinned their hopes on the appointment of an apostolic delegate, firmly believing an objective eye would better represent their concerns and interests with Rome.

Bedini had been sent to the United States on his way to his official posting in South America. On the surface, Bedini's trip was described as a courtesy visit to the President and to the citizens of the United States on his way to Brazil and there is no record of the bishops ever being notified of any contrary intention. However, Propaganda had prepared a set of instructions for Bedini's visit including the observation of the state of religion in the United States and in particular the conduct of the clergy and any abuses of which he might become aware of. He was also to bring any such abuses to the attention of the bishops and then report his findings to the Holy See. Propaganda also instructed Bedini to sound out the bishops about the possibility of the appointment of an apostolic delegate and to explore the possibility of more uniformity in governance among the various ecclesiastical provinces, the conversion of slaves and Indians, and the continuing ethnic conflicts that were rife.[15] Unfortunately, the visit took place during a period of severe anti-Catholicism and therefore he had some hostile encounters. Mobs in Cincinnati and Wheeling converged on the respective cathedrals protesting his appearance. He had to eventually leave the country under tight security, "smuggled aboard the three-master Atlantic in New York harbor and spirited out of the country."[16]

Bedini did however manage, at the conclusion of his seven month visit, to file a comprehensive report of his observations of the Church in the United States which was sent to the Congregation for the Propagation of the Faith. The report provided a detailed description of the Church. His observations touched upon the "Catholic Religion in General," the "American Bishops," the "American Clergy" and the "Religious Orders."[17] He also sent a shorter report (*relazione*) that treated the question of the possible establishment of a permanent Papal Nunciature in Washington, D.C., a topic that he had been requested to examine by Rome during

---

15   James F. Connelly, *The Visit of Archbishop Gaetano Bedini to the United States of America, June 1853 – February 1854* (Rome: Gregorian University, 1960) 14.

16   James Hennesey, *American Catholics: A History of the Roman Catholic Community in the United States* (New York: Oxford University Press, 1981) 125.

17   Connelly, 191.

the course of his stay.[18]

Bedini noted that, on the whole, the bishops were satisfied with their priests, with an occasional exception. He referenced a tension that the later visitor, Bishop George Conroy, would also discuss with the Holy See. It appeared to Bedini that a major *lacuna* in the American Church was a lack of pastoral stability for the clergy. "It seems that the priests during their ministry do not have the full guarantee of security which Canon Law gives them, and their position may be changed from one moment to the next. There are no parishes but missions, and so, the priests assigned to them, find themselves in such a precarious position that they always fear an immediate change."[19] Bedini was reluctant to evaluate this situation since he thought, for some reason, that to do so would be imprudent. "There are pros and cons."[20] He did not know how difficult it was for priests to work hard, "to build churches and schools at great sacrifice, to gain the good will of the parishioners and then suddenly to be transferred by the unexpected inclination of the bishop."[21]

The exact implications and ramifications of Bedini's visit and report are not evident. However, tensions in the United States between bishops and their priests continued to simmer.

James Alphonsus McMaster (1820 – 1886), the editor of the national religious newspaper, *The Freeman's Journal*, and a convert to Roman Catholicism, was a vociferous critic of the manner in which priests were being treated in mid – nineteenth century United States. He had been a strong advocate of papal supremacy and used his newspaper columns to challenge any American bishops who did not endorse the doctrine of papal infallibility during the First Vatican Council. He was also a strong supporter of States' rights and was imprisoned without indictment in 1861 due to his strongly written attacks on President Lincoln after the president had appealed for troops after the attack of Fort Sumter. His journal also temporarily lost its mailing privileges. It was said that it was never difficult to discern McMaster's views on any topic – he shared them openly and with enthusiasm!

In an article that appeared in the *Freeman's Journal*, October 3, 1868, he took on an issue that would consume him – the cause of clergy rights. In an editorial he penned entitled "Do Not Dioceses Suppose Parishes?" he deplored the lack of canon law used in regulating the conduct of clergy and the relations of

---

18   Ibid.

19   "The Report of Gaetano Bedini, Archbishop of Thebes, to His Eminence Cardinal Fransoni upon the Nuncio's return from the United States of America," in Connelly, 218 (1180 r).

20   Ibid.

21   Ibid., 221 (1181 v).

the bishops toward their clergy. He affirmed his allegiance to the official teachings of the Church in writing in this regard, and he entered the fray with great reluctance personally wishing that he could ignore the issue. But he felt morally obliged because "the great question is how it affects, and will affect the interests and principles, of our great Catholic community."[22] He went on to attack in this article the decision that had been promulgated at the conclusion of the recently completed Second Plenary Council of Baltimore, that the question of a change in the status of priests in the United States raised at the Council be postponed for at least another twenty years (or perhaps forever) – that the title of "mission" in America be maintained (rather than parish). Such a status, argued McMaster, created an anomaly. For example, some of the oldest churches which were identified as "quasi-parishes" were, in some instances, larger than some *dioceses.* "Why, in some of our city churches," McMaster wrote, "more money is spent in maintaining the chromatic music of the choirs, than the Episcopal revenues in some of these inchoate dioceses."[23] He was not at all arguing against the creation of new dioceses. Rather, he complained, should we not be erecting *parishes* instead of missions? "Why can there be no legitimate parishes, in a land with so many legitimate *Bishops*?" [24] For McMaster, the granting of the title "pastor" by the bishops to priests in the United States would be for them a step towards more recognized rights for clergy in the United States. As he again pointed out: "We deeply regret not finding, so far as we have read [the statutes of the Second Plenary Council of Baltimore] any provision for a wronged priest to vindicate his *right* to a justification before his own Bishop, and to a standing, on trial, and acquittance, in his own Diocese. We sincerely hope we may be mistaken, and that someone will, charitably, set us straight."[25] McMaster believed that his editorial was merely a reflection of a "certain degree of ventilation" that was taking place among clerics about the general discipline of the clergy at that time. He received much support from priests who responded with a deluge of letters, reinforcing his concerns with personal testimonies.

One of the respondents to McMaster's observations who would carry the torch to an international audience was Eugene O'Callaghan, a priest of the Diocese of Cleveland. Born in Kanturk, Ireland in 1831, the youngest of six children and the son of a wool spinner, he arrived in the United States in 1847 and ultimately entered Notre Dame at South Bend and then St. Mary's Seminary in Baltimore and was ordained to the priesthood in 1859. Taking up the cause that he had read in McMaster's editorial and fueled by extensive discussions conducted in a priests' study group he had formed, he composed a long letter, written under the pen name "Ecclesiasticus," to the editor of the *Freeman's Journal.* O'Callaghan agreed with McMaster that the issues and questions of clergy rights

---

22   *Freeman's Journal*, Oct. 3, 1868.
23   Ibid.
24   Ibid.
25   Ibid.

should be discussed in a thorough but respectful manner. However, he chose as his "weapon of choice" the "canons" of the Church. "Our Right Rev. and Most Rev. prelates, however unjustly, expose themselves to the suspicion that they are unwilling to introduce Canon Law," he wrote, "because they must govern legally, not arbitrarily."[26] He was supporting McMaster's thesis that the Church in the United States deserved to be recognized no longer as a *mission* church but rather should have the status of a fully grown church subject to canon law.

> Must we yet be regarded as a missionary field? We have grand cathedrals, sumptuous and numerous churches, well settled congregations, a numerous clergy, and a well established and influential hierarchy. Must we yet be regarded as a missionary country? Why is there, at least, not some approach made towards Canon Law? Why do not our venerable prelates make a move toward the introduction of those time honored and salutary laws?[27]

Such an approach, Ecclesiasticus (O'Callaghan) preached, would bring peace to the troubled waters of the time. "Thus would innumerable difficulties, now necessarily existing, be settled and our esteemed prelates would wonderfully contribute not only to the happiness of their people, but also would to the peace and comfort of their own minds."[28]

Encouraged by the *Freeman's Journal* editor, O'Callaghan began a work that would consume his energy amidst his pastoral duties and lend him a national pulpit. He wrote a series of twelve articles to the *Journal*, under the name "Jus" mostly written in advocacy for the implementation of canon law in the United States. In the course of time, he addressed almost every topic related to priest-bishop tensions, including the need for canon law, the suspension of priests without due process, and tenure for pastors. The articles of "Jus" were always featured on the front page of the *Freeman's Journal* normally under the headline "The Status of the Clergy."

According to O'Callaghan, the reason for the morale problems that plagued the priests in the United States was the inability or the unwillingness of the bishops to use canon law. He again and again returned to the theme he had hammered at as "Ecclesiasticus." Since the United States at the time was considered to be still a missionary outpost and subject to Propaganda Fide, the bishops had been given great leeway in the handling of clergy issues. The bishops saw this as an appropriate arrangement for a church that was still maturing and in need of flexibility in management. As previously seen, this was an arrangement that the editor McMaster thought no longer operable. With so many flourishing churches,

---

26   *Freeman's Journal*, November 7, 1868.

27   Ibid.

28   Ibid.

universities, colleges and religious houses, Jus complained: "In the presence then of such a state of things, to retain the Missionary discipline of the Church is like wrapping a full grown man in swaddling clothes and feeding him on pap."[29] In addition, this arrangement was not helpful to the enculturation of the Catholic Church into the American culture, Jus complained. The lack of due process afforded priests was a scandal, he claimed, to Protestants, perpetuating the illusion of a church that was inimical to the values of a democracy. "It cannot be denied," he wrote, "that the abnormal relation of our Bishops to our priests and laity seems to justify the Protestant opinion that the Church is the enemy of liberty."[30] Although the Church in the United States was dynamic and growing, the internal structure and ordering had not taken place. It was even alienating Catholics. "This arbitrary rule gradually weakens the faith of shallow-minded and uninstructed Catholics, while our enemies are ever on the alert in representing the Church to them as the enemy of liberty and pointing to these high-handed acts of arbitrary will, to justify their charges."[31]

Jus received such an outpouring of support from priests who devoured his pungent observations in the *Freeman's Journal* that he decided to take further action beyond just the writing about priestly woes. Through one of his articles he cajoled his priestly readers, with the support of the editor, to sign a petition to be rendered to the Holy See. The demands would include: a bill of rights for priests, including stability for every priest with a pastoral office of at least seven years and punishment limited to temporary suspension unless judged for a greater penalty by special judges accepted by the priests at an annual synod. "Any manifestation of their [priests of the U.S.] desire, couched in humble and respectful language, breathing the spirit of charity, professing unalterable attachment to the Holy See, and supplicantly petitioning for law and protection would, I have no doubt, receive a favorable hearing in Rome and move the heart of the Saintly Pius IX."[32] Although O'Callaghan voyaged to Rome in 1869 to appeal personally against his own removal from a parish in the Diocese of Cleveland, no such petition was every submitted. Jus wrote his last article on February 26, 1870, satisfied he had completed his mission – although with no visible changes in procedures or discipline – and bringing to the attention of the Church in the United States and beyond the plight of the American clergy and what he had termed "arbitrary rule."

In 1878, another official visit to the United States by an observer from the Holy See was arranged. Bishop George Conroy of the Diocese of Ardagh in Ireland had been serving as temporary Apostolic Delegate to Canada. He had requested the opportunity for some extended time in the United States for a re-

---

29 *Freeman's Journal*, December 12, 1868.
30 Ibid., July 17, 1869.
31 Ibid.
32 Ibid., November 20, 1869.

spite from his duties and time away to help him deal with serious personal health concerns. Propaganda instructed him to use his time in the United States for a review of the Church in the States. Although he had a much shorter visit than Bedini's, Conroy nevertheless made an extensive tour, including Cincinnati, St. Louis, and San Francisco. Like his predecessor, he also made observations about the problems in the relations between bishops and priests, while providing information to Rome about the possible establishment of a permanent delegation in the United States.

The deteriorating relationships between the clergy and the bishops occupied a great amount of attention in his report. Again, some of the same pastoral issues that had been noted by Bedini were still present, if not worsening. "He was careful to state that the priests had not rebelled against episcopal authority or unduly displayed their ill-temper by their actions, except in some very rare cases. He had noticed, nevertheless, 'a certain rumbling [sordo] discontent among the clergy which could easily open the door to some serious scandal.'"[33]

Perhaps Conroy's negativity can be attributed to the continued deterioration by the time of his visit in the relationship between many of the bishops and their priests. As Conroy testified: "It should not cause surprise, therefore, that the clergy has begun to lose the respect due to the episcopacy. This is true of the clergy in almost every part of the country. It seems to me that these complaints, though too harsh in form, are not unreasonable in their basis."[34]

The other great concern of Conroy's regarding the bishop and priest relationship was again, the seeming lack of the use of canon law in dealing with disciplinary matters. The clergy, as Conroy observed, where greatly annoyed at the developments that took place at the 2nd Plenary Council of Baltimore regarding the right accorded them to change priests' assignments at will.

> To tell the truth, a conflict on this ground was inevitable, the respective rights of the bishops and of the pastors being so incompatible. The bishop interpreted the Synod of Baltimore in a way that removed from the pastor all right to permanence in his parish and made him a mere vicar of the bishop. The pastor, on the contrary, especially for the past five years, while conceding to the bishop that the pastor is removable *ad nutum*, insists upon the bishop's obligation of not removing him from his parish *sine causa*.[35]

---

33 Ibid.

34 Ibid.

35 Robert Trisco, "Bishops and Their Priests in the United States," in *The Catholic Priest in the United States: Historical Investigations,* ed., John Tracy Ellis, (Collegeville, MN: St. John's University Press, 1971) 201.

But Conroy was also critical of the actions of the priests, that they were at times disingenuous about their rights since they were not consistent in their approach:

> Many of these priests who have taken their appeals to the Holy See have returned victorious to their parishes; and since some of them were anything but respectable in their lives, their triumph roused the indignation of the bishops, even against the Holy See. Some pastors claim every right for themselves [...] while to their wretched flocks no right is granted; but perhaps it will be true that to attack the bishops means to defend the Church.[36]

Conroy goes on to quote a "respectable" priest who had written to him about the controversy between bishops and priests:

> We shall not have peace in this country until the relations between bishops and priests shall be established and made clear according to the norms of the provisions of canon law, which is desired so much by all of us. Today priests have no rights at all; they can be chased from their posts at whim while the bishops exercise a veritable tyranny over them.[37]

Conroy concluded from his conversations with bishops, and more particularly with priests, "How much everyone wants a clear and precise rule on the canonical position that the American pastors occupy."[38] As we shall soon note, this clarification by the Holy See soon was forthcoming.

Conroy was to spend some time during his visit in the United States with Richard Burtsell, of the Archdiocese of New York, a former classmate from their time together at the Propaganda College in Rome where they studied for the priesthood. While preparing for ordination, Burtsell had spent some time studying ecclesiastical history and canon law. He became conversant in proper canonical procedures and processes, and upon his return to the United States and assignment in pastoral ministry, he became a firm advocate for the canonical rights of priests. This interest in canonical procedures and the rights of priests was fueled by his participation in the "Accademia,"[39] a group so–named by the Arch-

---

36 Ibid.
37 Ibid.
38 Ibid.
39 The Accademia had begun as an approved theological society of the Archdiocese of New York in 1865. It followed a model that was similar to a society of scholars established by Cardinal Manning in London. It was established in the Archdiocese by Jeremiah Cummings, the first American graduate of the Urban College in Rome, and Henry Brann, another graduate of the college, as a forum for continuing theological education

diocese of New York chancery, alumni of the Propaganda who gathered regularly for scholarly theological discussions about the issues of the day. As a Church historian notes, commenting on the conversations that Conroy had with Burtsell and other former classmates: "It is not surprising that the delegate showed more sympathy for the priests than for the bishops in his report."[40]

The exact influence of the report of Conroy to the Propaganda is not easily discerned. But on July 20, 1878, the Sacred Congregation for the Propagation of the Faith issued an instruction, the *Method to be observed by the Bishops of the United States, in taking cognizance of, and adjusting the criminal and disciplinary causes of clergyman.*

This Instruction was modeled on a similar instruction that had been prepared by the Congregation for England to deal with similar issues.[41] The American Instruction consisted of two parts: an introduction and a procedure to be followed. The introduction was critical of the efforts that had been made by the American bishops in their handling of disciplinary matters. In addition to treating the development of the use of certain procedures in the United States, it commented on the sloppiness of procedures followed: "It is moreover to be deplored that it not rarely happens, that many, and indeed necessary things are wanting in the statements sent, and when all things are considered that grave doubts often arise as to the trust to be placed in or refused to the documents brought forward in these cases."[42]

The procedure that was now to be used was built on a procedure first utilized formally in the United States developed by the Provincial Council of St. Louis in 1855. Patterned on the process found in the decrees of the Council of Trent, the procedure included the bishop (or the diocesan vicar general, if so delegated) selecting two or three priests who served as assessors in examining any proofs or witnesses in the case and giving counsel to the bishop who was the ultimate judge in the proceeding. The Instruction of 1878 included the five priest assessors (at least three) who would serve as an investigative commission. Their role

---

for priests. It was soon opened to all priests of the Archdiocese. It disbanded after a year due to a complaint that it was dominated by too many former students from the Urban College. However, by 1866, Thomas Farrell, pastor of St. Joseph's Parish in New York, had resumed the theological discussions and the society was re-instituted. See Robert Emmett Curran, "The New York Accademia and Clerical Radicalism in the Late Nineteenth Century, *Church History*, 47:1 (March 1978) 48-65.

40   Trisco, 202.

41   *Modus procendi in consilio capiendo a Concilio investigationis priusquam finaliter deiiciatur rector missionaries*, *Acta et Decreta Sacrorum Conciliorum Recentiorum Collectio Lacensis,* III (Freibur-Breisgau: Herder, 1875) columns 960–961.

42   "Dolendum autem est, non raro evenire, ut transmissis actis plura, eaque necessaria desiderentur atque perpensis omnibus, gravia saepe dubia oriantur circa fidem documentis hisce in causis allatis habendam vel denegandam" *Acta Sanctae Sedis XII* (1879) 88.

was more investigative, attempting to determine the veracity of the testimony and witnesses participating so that the bishop could give a just verdict to the case and an impartial sentence if the cleric were found guilty of the allegations.[43] The process was not enthusiastically received by many American bishops, some of whom were concerned that they had not been consulted in the formulation of the process used. Bishop Bernard McQuaid of Rochester, on his *ad limina* visit to Rome in 1878, expressed candidly his fears that this new legislation "would inflict very great injury to the Church in this country."[44] Bishop Michael Corrigan of Newark (later Archbishop of New York) similarly castigated the decree, disparaging that even priests were opposed to it, since, he believed, its use will give great notoriety to such trials "and [...] failings cannot be covered up as in the past."[45] Canonists such as Burtsell, reflecting back on the impact of the procedure, reservedly welcomed it as a step in the right direction for the needed protection of priests' rights, but complained concerning the manner in which the procedure was used (when used at all.) For example, he complained that advocacy for the accused was often denied or that the accused was not permitted to select his own advocate for the case. "Any priest in good standing called upon by the accused to aid him should at once be accepted by any fair-minded judge; and the rejection of any one as counsel without a very serious reason is very strong evidence that passion, dislike, and prejudice, not zeal for souls or God's glory, are at the bottom of the charges made."[46] Appreciated, however, was that the accused was notified in detail about the nature and proofs of the case. He could even challenge the witnesses' testimony through the presider of the Commission.

The response of the American bishops to this procedure and to the observations that had been made about their relationship to their priests by Conroy (which may have influenced Propaganda in issuing this process), was mostly negative, as could be expected. The bishops, as has been seen, were always sensitive to Roman visitors and perceived threats to their autonomy and "deemed themselves competent to keep the Holy See faithfully informed of their own affairs."[47]

---

[43] For an outline of the procedure of the Instruction, see Kevin McKenna, "Clerical Penal Procedures in the United States in the Nineteenth Century and the Instruction of 1878," *The Jurist* 70 (2010) 186–205.

[44] Frederick Zwierlein, *Life and Letters of Bishop McQuaid, Vol. II* (Rochester, New York: Art Print Shop, 1926) 173.

[45] Zwierlein, *Letters of Archbishop Corrigan to McQuaid and Allied Documents* (Rochester, New York: The Art Shop, 1946) 22.

[46] Richard Burtsell, *The Canonical Status of Priests in the United States* (New York: John J. O'Brien, 1887) 54.

[47] Gerald P. Fogarty, *The Vatican and the American Hierarchy From 1870 to 1965* (Stuttgart: Anton Hiersemann, 1982) 17.

A Judicial Commission to Assist the Bishop

The Instruction established a "Judicial Commission" in each diocese, consisting of five priests chosen at a diocesan synod, "most worthy and, as far as possible, well versed in canon law." Their principal duty was to examine disciplinary cases of priests against whom the bishop sought to bring charges. If the bishop contemplated removal of the priest from office, the cleric could not be deprived of his position unless at least three of the commissioners had been employed by the bishop to examine the case and their counsel had been heard. The commission would receive from the bishop's vicar general (or other appropriate delegate) a summary of the case in writing, with a transcript of the evidence. The accused would be cited by the bishop to appear before the commissioners with prepared answers to the proofs that had been gathered. The accused would be invited to speak and could bring with him any appropriate exculpatory materials. After this appearance, the Commission would deliberate, each councilor providing a separate written opinion with the reasons for his decision. However, if doubts still remained, witnesses could be called on the same day or later. Witnesses for the prosecution, after having been examined by the Commission, could be interrogated by the accused. The Commission would again deliberate and send their findings to the bishop for his decision. Should the bishop or the accused decide to appeal, it would be sent to the metropolitan archbishop, who would proceed in the same manner, with his own Commission.

Many priests in the U.S. welcomed this intervention from the Vatican. In some ways, they were now judged by a jury of their own peers (the Commission), who had a decisive, and possibly determinative role to play in reviewing testimony and evidence. They were grateful that another court (metropolitan) could review their appeal, with the possibility left open for an appeal to Rome. They also were grateful that they had an opportunity to present a defense, and canonists argued successfully for the presence of an advocate for the accused at these proceedings on the basis of natural equity.

Reform Derailed

In meetings in Rome between some of the U.S. archbishops and officials of Propaganda preparing for the Third Plenary Council of Baltimore, this latest Instruction was seen to be in need of revision. One archbishop (Michael Corrigan of New York) expressed concerns about the presence of "laymen" who were now serving as defense counsel for priests instead of clerics. He worried that "artful, cunning, crafty, and evil advocates would be chosen who would strive by every stratagem to upset the judgment of the bishop."[48] Some relief, however, was to be given to clergy by the Third Plenary Council of Baltimore (1884) including the possible appointment of "irremovable rectors" with certain restrictions and norms concerning dismissals and transfers.

---

48 *Jurist* 11 (April 1951) 310.

Rome As Another Set of Eyes

The Vatican has sometimes acted as "another set of eyes" for solutions to problems in local churches, as was seen in the Church in the U.S. in the 1870's. After receiving complaints about the lack of procedure used in dealing with transfers and removals from office, the Holy See responded with a process in 1878 which was continuously revised until the Code of 1917. As has been seen, the 1878 procedure highlighted the work of the priest assessors, who principally assisted the bishop in a review of the charges and evidence against a cleric. The missionary rector was to appear before the commission which would read his prepared answer to the charges, with the cleric available to answer questions. He would have the option of presenting witnesses. He would be given the opportunity to hear testimony presented to the Commission (should the Commission deem it prudent), and the accused could question the witnesses himself.

In more recent times, examining the legislation after a two year trial use of the *Essential Norms* in the United States, they were slightly revised, with the insights and assistance of the Holy See, including the addition of a statement that "during the investigation, the accused enjoys the presumption of innocence and all appropriate steps will be taken to protect his reputation."[49]

The terrible scourge of sexual misconduct against the young has left a horrific blight upon the clergy. Inexcusable behavior regarding supervision has eroded the confidence of many members of the Christian community in the institutional Church. It can be reasonably hoped that a just application of approved disciplinary procedures, and the observance of the rights of all people involved in any allegation of inappropriate clerical behavior or sexual misconduct, will be scrupulously observed. Perhaps as the penal processes continues to be reviewed, as in 1878, some creative solutions may be offered for balancing the protection of the common good and the defense of the rights of the innocent. Hopefully, whatever emerges in terms of procedures in this matter will assure that clergy accused of sexual misconduct are properly prosecuted and punished if guilty, and also respect due process by providing protection for the rights of all – including the accused who might even possibly be proven innocent.

---

[49] "Essential Norms" (2006) n. 6.

Seminar

Drafting the Definitive Sentence: Law and Craft
Reverend Monsignor Mark A. Plewka

In order to set the stage for this seminar, I would like to begin with a quotation from the eminent canonist Mario Cardinal Pompedda. The quotation concerns the person of the judge. "The Judge must not only be endowed with a sufficient scientific preparation (canonical) but he must be capable of practical judgment. He must also have some experience of both reality and of human nature. He must have a sagacious intelligence."[1] The purpose then of this seminar is both to provide some "scientific preparation," as well as some practical directives on how to craft the definitive sentence in a formal marriage case that is both canonically correct, to the point, and pastorally sensitive.

I intend to divide this presentation into two parts. The first part will deal with the *remote* preparation for the drafting of the sentence. In this first part of the presentation I wish to focus on two concrete items that have been employed in our tribunal, which have proved very beneficial in setting the stage for a good trial and ultimately for a good sentence. In the second part of the presentation I wish to focus on the canons that treat of the nature and elements of the definitive sentence, as well as on concrete examples of the application of these canons to the composition of the definitive sentence itself.

Let us begin by recalling what a sentence is. Canon 1868 of the 1917 *CIC* provides a more fulsome definition than what can be found in the more attenuated expressions in the 1983 code or in *Dignitas connubii* (cf. c. 1607 and art. 246): "A sentence is a legitimate pronouncement by which a judge resolves a cause proposed by the litigants and treated in a judicial manner."[2] I would like to highlight two items mentioned in the canon, namely, litigants—or as we usually say petitioners and respondents—and treatment in a judicial manner. The definitive sentence in a formal marriage case should be the result of a process in which, ideally, both parties have been involved. In regard to remote preparation for the possible maximal involvement of the parties, providing both of them with clear

---

1   M. F. Pompedda, "Decision-Sentence in Marriage Trials: Of the Concept and Principles for Rendering an Ecclesiastical Sentence," *Quaderni dello Studio Rotale* 5 (1990) 93.

2   1917 *CIC* c. 1868 §1: "Legitima pronuntiatio qua iudex causam a litigantibus propositam et iudiciali modo pertractatam definit, sententia est: eaque interlocutoria dicitur, si dirimat incidentem causam; definitiva, si principalem."

and sufficient information about the trial is critical. This can be accomplished by sending the parties, when the case has been accepted, a document that explains in clear and concise language the formal process and its important stages. The intent of such a document would be to inform the parties about their rights and responsibilities in the formal process, so that they can clearly understand what they are undertaking. This document should be designed to assist the parties to become aware of the stages of the formal process so that they can actively, directly, and personally participate in the proceedings. In short, the parties should be provided with a "user-friendly road map."

At this point, I wish to spend some time highlighting some concrete items that should be contained in such a "road map." The first is a clear and concise definition of a declaration of marital invalidity. A declaration of marital invalidity, popularly termed an annulment, is a decision by a Church court that morally certain proof is had that the marriage in question is not valid, that is, that it was entered into invalidly. The reason for providing this definition is because, with regard to the popular understanding of what takes place in the ecclesiastical courts, there is a lot of "heat" but precious little "light." As most tribunal practitioners are aware, in the popular imagination "annulments" are usually understood as "church divorces" for marriages that turned out badly, or they are also understood as ecclesiastical permissions slips allowing a person to receive Holy Communion. Correcting at the outset of the trial, these popular but erroneous ideas, can go a long way in facilitating and insuring a procedurally and canonically correct process in which the parties can be involved.

The second item should be an explanation of the various court personnel and their respective roles. For example, an explanation of the role of the advocate: an advocate is the person appointed by the petitioner or the respondent to assist the party in presenting and arguing their case. Or an explanation of the role of the defender of the bond: the defender of the bond is the person who proposes everything which can be reasonably brought forth in favor of the validity of the marriage and against the granting of a declaration of invalidity.

The third item should list the various stages of the trial and their time limits should be clearly set forth. Mention should also be made that the parties will be notified in writing at each significant stage of the process.

The first stage of the trial is the acceptance of the petition for trial and the citation of the respondent. This stage starts the clock running, and with the respondent cited the case becomes "locked in" and becomes the property of the tribunal before which it has been lodged.

The second stage is the joinder of issue (*contestatio litis*). This takes place fifteen days after the citation of the respondent. This is the stage at which the judge sets the grounds of invalidity to be adjudicated in the case. The grounds for which a formal trial for a declaration of invalidity can be conducted are many and varied. Sometimes petitioners and advocates propose many, yet incompatible, grounds. It is the duty of the judge to determine the precise ground, which might be applicable and worth adjudicating.

The third stage of the trial is the instruction of the case. Ten working days after the joinder of issue the judge decrees that the testimonies of the witnesses, proposed by the petitioner and/or the respondent, and other proofs are to be gathered by the tribunal. The parties to a marriage case, ideally, should be informed of the date that the gathering of the proofs commenced. As tribunal practitioners are aware, this is the stage at which delays are frequently encountered. Sometimes witnesses claim that they have never received the citation from the tribunal for testimony. Some witnesses supply little or no real information. Some witnesses claim to have supplied testimony when they have not done so. Some witnesses just fail to cooperate. Since the burden of proof in a marriage case rests with the petitioner, and not the tribunal, it is important that the parties be informed concerning the situation of witness testimony in their cases.

The fourth stage of the trial is the publication of the acts. When all of the proofs seem to be gathered, the judge informs the parties that they have the peremptory right to inspect the acts of the case. This is not an absolute right but, rather, one which is subject to the procedures and limitations of canon law. The purpose of publication is twofold. Firstly, so that the parties can know the proofs upon which the sentence will be based, and secondly, so that the parties can determine, based upon the inspection, whether they should propose additional proofs. *DC* art. 233 §1 determines that the judge in the decree of the publication of the acts is to determine a time limit for such inspection. Two weeks, that is, ten working days has proved to be an equitable time limit for the parties to inform the tribunal that they wish to inspect the acts of the case.

The fifth stage of the trial is the conclusion and opening of the discussion and definitive sentence. After the time for the inspection of the acts has lapsed, the judge issues the decree of conclusion and opening of the discussion, thus closing the case to further evidence. The parties are notified of this decree. During this time, the defender of the bond presents a written argument, based upon the law and the facts, proposing all reasonable arguments for the validity of the marriage and against the granting of a declaration of invalidity. All are notified that the judge hopes to render a decision within the next thirty days. The judge then writes the definitive sentence. The definitive sentence is a document that contains the reasons, based upon the law and the facts, for the decision in the case. In the definitive sentence the judge decides whether morally certain proof of the invalidity of the marriage is had on the grounds set at the joinder of issue. If the judge rules in the affirmative to any one of the grounds set at the joinder of issue, then he has ruled in favor of granting a declaration of invalidity. If the judge rules in the negative to all of the grounds set at the joinder of issue, then he has ruled against the granting of a declaration of invalidity. The parties and the advocate(s) are notified of the decision and their rights of appeal.

Other things noted in our "road map" document have proved valuable. For example, a paragraph about who is responsible for the cost of a report of an expert, when necessary, or a paragraph about the time limits for a formal case (a year in first instance and six months at second instance), or a paragraph about other actions such as the *vetitum*, renunciation or abatement.

Providing the parties with a document at the beginning of the process that details the stages of the process and other items has been invaluable in my experience. It is an example of true transparency—instead of "heat" the parties are provided with "light." It encourages the parties to participate in the case by being able to monitor the progress of the case. In my experience, since the parties have been notified throughout the trial of the various stages, there are fewer telephone calls to the tribunal from the parties inquiring about the status of the case. Also, supplying the parties with a document that details the steps of the trial and the various time limits, serves to keep the tribunal "on its toes" so to speak in seeing that the cases are moved along expeditiously.

A second document that has proved useful is what we have termed the acknowledgment form. When a case has been accepted for trial, the petitioner and their advocate are notified. Included in the letter of notification of acceptance is a document entitled acknowledgment form. This form contains three questions for the petitioner. The first lists the names of the court officials assigned to the case and asks whether the petitioner has any objections to the proposed officials. The second question asks whether there are any significant sources of proof that have not been previously indicated. The third item lists the alleged grounds of invalidity that have been proposed in the *libellus* by the petitioner and the advocate. The last question asks whether the petitioner has received the document entitled *The Formal Process for a Declaration of Invalidity*, i.e. the "road map," and whether they have read it. A longer acknowledgment form is sent to the respondent, highlighting the way in which they can participate in the trial, either by a personal interview or by composing a written declaration following a prepared outline format.

These two documents, that is, the *Formal Process for a Declaration of Invalidity* and the acknowledgment form serve the purpose of insuring that the parties have some basic and accurate knowledge of what the trial entails and, hopefully, these two documents can engage them in such a way that they fully participate in the trial.

The "road map" and the acknowledgment form are two concrete means for insuring that the judicial process is conducted in a canonically correct manner. They have served us well. My point here is that it should be clear that it is only after a proper trial has been conducted that a proper sentence can be written.

Now in this second part of the presentation, I first want to treat of the current canon law about the definitive sentence. I wish to turn our attention to canon 1611, which treats of the nature and elements of the sentence. For our purposes, numbers one and three of canon 1611 are the most important. Canon 1611: "The sentence must: 1° decide the controversy deliberated before the tribunal with an appropriate response given to the individual doubts."[3] It might be asked how the controversy is decided. The sentence settles the controversy by ruling on the various doubts that were determined in the joinder of issue. Rev. Msgr. Craig Cox astutely notes the following in the CLSA commentary: "The requirement that the sentence settle the controversy also provides an important principle for the crafting of a judicial sentence. The argument of the sentence must be focused on the specific doubt or doubts (*dubium* or *dubia*), and not wander into unnecessary discussions of related but irrelevant information learned during the trial. A sentence will be much more convincing to the extent that its author focuses precisely on a response to the specific controversy."[4]

Another tool that can assist in crafting the sentence is the manner in which multiple doubts to be resolved can be formulated. Instead of joining the issue on multiple grounds, all of which will need an appropriate argumentation and reply, I suggest that the doubts be formulated subordinately (*subordinate*). For example, the first doubt may be framed as whether morally certain proof of invalidity is had upon the ground of force or fear, in accord with canon 1103, exercised against the man, petitioner. Failing this first ground, whether morally certain proof is had of the invalidity of the marriage on the ground of grave lack of discretionary judgment, in accord with canon 1095, 2° on the part of the man, petitioner. Should the first ground receive an affirmative decision, the subordinate ground can be answered in the following manner: "Since at the joinder of issue the doubts to be resolved were formulated in a subordinate fashion, there can only be the following reply. In answer to the proposed doubt whether proof of the invalidity of the marriage is had upon the ground of grave lack of discretionary judgment, in accord with canon 1095, 2°, on the part of the man, petitioner, I find *non proponi*, that is, it is not to be proposed." A qualified but more nuanced support for this position can be found in the commentary on *Dignitas connubii* by Prof. Dr. Klaus Lüdicke and Rev. Msgr. Ronny E. Jenkins.[5]

Canon 1611, 3°: The sentence must "set forth reasons or motives in law and

---

3   All English translations of the 1983 Code of Canon Law are from *Code of Canon Law, Latin-English Edition: New English Translation* (Washington, DC: CLSA, 1998).

4   Craig A. Cox, in *New Commentary on the Code of Canon Law*, ed. John P. Beal et al. (New York/Mahwah, NJ, Paulist Press, 2000) 1720.

5   Klaus Lüdicke and Ronny E. Jenkins, *Dignitas Connubii: Norms and Commentary* (Alexandria VA: CLSA, 2006) 406.

in fact on which the dispositive part of the sentence is based." Once again the words of Craig Cox: The sentence "must contain a reasoned argument in which the evidence adduced in the instruction phase is analyzed in light of the law and jurisprudence to justify the tribunal's decision. It is not enough for the sentence to simply assert a conviction; it must demonstrate the reasoning which led the judges to reach moral certitude. A judicial argument, then, is much more than a summary or recapitulation of the testimony and other evidence. The sentence must establish the canonical bridge linking the specific facts of the case with the relevant law in order to support the decision."[6] In short, the sentence is a reasoned argument in which the evidence is evaluated and weighed. It is not intended to be a dissertation upon the personalities of the parties.

Dignitas connubii in article 254 now provides the judge with a concrete admonition of how the sentence should be composed. "The sentence, avoiding both excessive brevity and an excessive length, must be clear in explaining the reasons in law and in fact.... The presentation of the facts, however, as the nature of the matter requires, is to be done prudently and cautiously, avoiding any offense to the parties." It should be noted that article 254 has no parallel in the Code of Canon Law. It first appeared in the *primum schema* of February 22, 1999, and with some minor textual reworking it is what we have in the promulgated version of *Dignitas connubii*.

It should be noted that there are two audiences for whom the sentence is being written, namely, the parties as well as the judges of second instance. Concretely this will mean that there will be terms or concepts in the sentence with which the parties may not be familiar. For example: judicial confession, *causa contrahendi*, or *contra bonum prolis*. The judge need not eschew the use of these terms, but nevertheless the reasoning in the sentence needs to have clarity. The use of Latin along with at least a translation should be considered. Prudence and caution dictate that not everything learned in the course of the trial need be put into the sentence. This also means that one's manner of expression in the sentence needs to be balanced and temperate. In all of these things, the judge needs to have a "sagacious intelligence" to balance all these factors. I should like to note that all of this will come with experience and practice, study and critique.

Let us now turn our attention to the formalities and solemnities of the sentence (cf. canon 1612 and *DC* art. 253).

A sentence has four parts, namely, an introduction, a *species facti* (i.e. fact section), an *in iure* (i.e. law section), and an *in facto* (i.e. argument section). Should one need a model of how a sentence should begin one can see the model put forth by Rev. Lawrence Wrenn.[7] Likewise the first sentence in the annual

---

6   Cox, 1720-1721.

7   Lawrence Wrenn, *Judging Invalidity* (Washington, D.C.: CLSA, 2002) 92-93.

volumes of the decisions of the Roman Rota can be consulted.

Canon 1612 §1 determines that after the invocation of the divine name—*In Nomine Domini. Amen* suffices for this—the sentence must express in order the judge or tribunal, petitioner, respondent, procurator, and their domiciles along with the names of the defender of the bond. This can be accomplished in one paragraph that need not exceed a half a page of typed script.

Next comes the *species facti*, that is, the fact section. I like to divide the *species facti* into two parts. The first part, "procedural history," is the processual *iter* of the cause. In the first paragraph of this section I include the names of the parties, their baptismal status and ages at the time of the wedding, along with the date and place of marriage. Additionally, mention is made of the number of children born to the union, the length of common life, the date of the divorce, which party sought the divorce, and by what civil jurisdiction it was granted. In the following paragraph I indicate the name of the party who lodged the *libellus*, the date on which the case was formally accepted along with the title for competency. In the third paragraph I indicate that the respondent was properly cited and whether or not they cooperated in the trial. In the following paragraphs the date of the joinder of issue is given along with the formulation of the *dubium* or *dubia*. The date that the instruction of the case was undertaken is provided. The date of the publication of the acts is given along with an indication of whether the parties availed themselves of their peremptory right to inspect the acts of the case. The date for the conclusion and opening of the discussion is noted. The first part concludes with the notation that the defender of the bond has returned his written animadversions.

One may ask why spend the time doing this. It is done because it is tied to the document, that is, the "road map" that was sent to the parties at the beginning of the trial. The parties, in effect, can put the sentence alongside the "road map" and see that the tribunal has conducted the trial as it has been described and that what they have been led to expect has been fulfilled.

The second section of the *species facti* is what I title the "marital history." In this second section I provide the following information: the date and place of birth of the parties and a brief indication of family background, such as the number of siblings and whether the family was intact or divorced. I then indicate how the couple met and what attracted them to one another. Mention is made of how the subject of marriage arose and whether there were any problems in the courtship. I may describe the wedding and any unusual thing that may have happened on that day. I briefly indicate the problems in the union that led to the divorce. This second section, the marital history, is usually no longer than half a page. In summary, then, the introduction together with the *species facti* generally will take no more than two pages.

The next major section of the sentence is the *in iure*. This can begin with a citation of the applicable canon for invalidity. The mere four words, "lack of due discretion," are not enough for a law section. Likewise, a brief indication referencing the law sections to be found in the tribunal's personal collection of law sections is not adequate. In our day, when there are plenty of resources concerning canonical jurisprudence, it is a mistake not to have a clear law section. Besides, this is a requirement mentioned in *DC* art. 250: "The sentence must present the arguments or reasons, in law and in fact, on which the dispositive part of the sentence is based." Once again the determination of how much material to place into the *in iure* is a matter of balance and experience.

The next major section of the sentence is the *in facto*, i.e. the argument. This, I believe, is the most crucial and sensitive part of the sentence. I would like to briefly spend some time demonstrating how to begin this section. Then, I will move on to a treatment of three different headings of invalidity as they might appear in the *in facto* part of the sentence. These will be lack of due discretion, simulation, and force or fear.

The first paragraph of the *in facto* can begin in the following manner: "We now turn to an enumeration of the proofs produced in the case. The petitioner supplied a written marital history and the judge took the petitioner's formal declaration in person at the tribunal." Next I list the number of witnesses proposed by the parties and who supplied testimony in the case. If it is a case in which the report of an expert is required, I note that the *peritus* has supplied a report. Next, mention is made of the first *dubium* to be resolved.

The key to actually composing a cogent and reasoned *in facto* is to be aware of and attend to the standard jurisprudential touch stones that need to be established from the evidence for the case to be considered proven. For us today, the first *dubium* will be lack of due discretion, in accord with canon 1095, 2°. One can set the stage for the resolution of this ground by providing a careful law section or by some jurisprudential remarks placed into the *in facto* section itself. In the *in facto* section, I sometimes place the following: "Due discretion of judgment, or rather the lack of it, as a heading of matrimonial invalidity, touches upon the process of consent itself. In this process one must know, evaluate, and freely choose the essentials of matrimony. However, if any part of this process is gravely defective, and the operative word is *gravely*, then the consent furnished is inefficacious, that is, invalid. It must be remembered that discretion of judgment must be directed to the essentials of matrimony, that is, to the *bona matrimonialia*. For it is only the essentials of matrimony, that is the goods of indissolubility, fidelity, the procreation and education of children, and the good of the spouses, which provide the measure for evaluating the sufficiency of consent. Likewise, it must also be remembered that one need not have the discretionary abilities of the proverbial rocket scientist in order to enter into marriage validly. After all, marriage is the usual vocation for most human beings, one to which most are naturally inclined."

Next I like to quote either from a presentation given at the third Gregorian Colloquium or from the doctoral dissertation of Raymond Cardinal Burke, JCD. This is because he clearly sets out the two jurisprudential pillars of a lack of due discretion case, namely, witness testimony which brings forth signs that call into question a person's discretionary abilities, and the expert opinion:

> We need to look for signs before the marriage, at the time of the marriage, and after the marriage which uncover the history of the development of the person. The argumentation in any cause for "lack of discretion of judgment" is always going to have a historical quality to it because the development of the person is being described.
>
> Many times it can happen that there are only signs after the marriage, but from those signs we can begin to interpret situations prior to the marriage which cohere with what those signs after the marriage indicate. Here is where the help of an expert is particularly needed.[8]

Let it be remembered that "a serious condition affecting the intelligence and freedom of a person cannot help but have given signs of its presence at some time to some persons. The witnesses called should bring forth reports of these signs. The coherence of the two proofs, expert opinion and testimony of witnesses, will be the chief sources of moral certitude for the judge."[9] Having set the stage, so to speak, I then cull from the witness testimony the concrete signs that do call into question the discretionary abilities of the party, for example, drug and alcohol use. Having listed the signs, I then conclude with the following, in these or similar words. "The judge is satisfied that the witnesses have indeed brought forth signs which do call into question the freedom, more specifically, the internal liberty of the party at the time of consent."

Next, in the sentence, I turn my attention to the report of the expert. Handling the report of the expert in the definitive sentence, especially if it has been reserved in accord with canon 1598 §1, is a matter of some delicacy. In this regard, it is well to remember that one of the functions of the sentence is to weigh and evaluate the evidence. Does this piece of evidence contribute to the solution of the case? And if it does, why is it of value? Here, then, is an example of what minimally should be mentioned. "We now turn to an evaluation of the report of the *peritus*. The judge accepts the report of the *peritus*. It is solidly based upon

---

8   *Incapacity for Marriage: Jurisprudence and Interpretation*, ed. Robert M. Sable (Rome: Pontifica Universitas Gregoriana, 1987) 133-134.

9   Raymond L. Burke, *Lack of Discretion of Judgment Because of Schizophrenia: Doctrine and Recent Rotal Jurisprudence*, Analecta Gregoriana, vol. 237 Series Facultas Iuris Canonici: sectio B, n. 47 Diss. Rome, 1984 (Roma: Editrice Pontificia Università Gregoriana, 1986) 136.

well-established facts found in the acts of the case and is cogently presented. The *peritus* gives a finding that is well in accord with rotal jurisprudence as being causative of defective discretion. Likewise it serves to establish for the judge the necessary "gravity" as mandated by the norm of canon 1095, 2°. Thus the judge is satisfied that the *peritus* has brought forth the necessary second jurisprudential touchstone in a lack of due discretion case, namely, credible expertise."

Please note that I did not use the word diagnosis. In a definitive sentence, one need not quote from latest *Diagnostic and Statistical Manuel of Mental Disorders*. Sometimes in the line that mentions that the finding is well in accord with rotal jurisprudence I will briefly cite some rotal decision that specifically mentions the psychological debility, though, this is certainly not required or necessary. Also, if one has psychological expertise that has been derived from custody evaluations or police reports, then one can be a bit more expansive in the sentence.

I would like to note, however, that it is not enough merely to line up the signs from the witnesses and the report of the *peritus* and then conclude immediately for invalidity. I think it is important to locate the lack of discretionary ability in either an inability to evaluate or in a lack of internal liberty in the party at the time of consent. And from my experience, it is more often than not that in a lack of due discretion case, the defect is found in a lack of internal freedom at the time of consent. So please allow me to explain how this is handled in the definitive sentence.

I provide an understanding of lack of internal freedom by quoting at length from the book by James Ross Spence:

> Regarding internal freedom of choice, that freedom of the will is necessary which enables a choice to be made between marrying and not marrying, between, marrying this person and marrying that person. There must be a choice, something to be determined, and the capacity to determine it.
>
> Man has free will, but it is not a freedom without limits. He is influenced in his tastes and attitudes by the society in which he lives, by the people with whom he mixes. He usually assumes the standard of the environment of his upbringing; he bears the influence of his own personal history, with its pleasures and pains. These influences all act on his emotions. Free will does not mean the absence of influences, or impulses; rather, free will means that these influences and impulses do not determine the will. The average person recognizes these influences, and compensates for them, or keeps them within manageable bounds.
>
> A man who is substantially subject to his emotions often has an

> under-developed or over-developed psychic condition, a part of his personality that has lost its balance of influence, its equilibrium in the normal harmony of the psyche. That condition can create a psychic need which calls forth an emotion in response. That emotion may distort the faculty of knowing or willing.
>
> [Such a person] who decides to marry may have a grave lack of knowledge, either of marriage or himself, and may make a gravely erroneous judgment in his assessment of himself in that marriage. In this way the emotions affect the intellect.
>
> Similarly [such a person] may know what marriage is, but cannot, because of the disorder, choose between alternatives. Such a person behaves reflexively or impulsively, moved by unconscious forces. He makes no decision to marry; circumstances take over. In this way the emotions affect the will.
>
> It is clear then that the will must act freely in making a decision. The question which next confronts the canonist is how much interference with the freedom of the will is required to render invalid a decision to marry? This again is a matter where the circumstances must be examined individually. What is established in the jurisprudence is that the interference must gravely affect the capacity for the formation of the human act of consenting to marry. It is, therefore a grave interference with the operation of the will that renders consent to marriage null.[10]

Having cited Spence, I resolve the *dubium* in the following manner. "It is clear to the judge from the evidence produced in this case that the petitioner was so enthralled to his/her emotions at the time he/she entered into matrimony that his/her act of consent was a reflexive and impulsive one moved by unconscious forces, and not the required *actus humanus* necessary for valid and sufficient consent. Therefore, in answer to the proposed doubt whether proof of the invalidity of the marriage is had upon the ground of grave lack of discretionary judgment, etc."

Now let us turn our attention to cases of simulation. The key jurisprudential touchstones in such a case are the judicial confession, and the *causa simulandi* and *causa contrahendi*. Standard jurisprudence makes clear that primary proof in a simulation case is the judicial or extra judicial confession of the simulator. However, what can be done if such is lacking? In this situation I rely upon a sentence of Msgr. Kenneth Boccafolla, which I quote directly into the sentence.

> The judge frankly admits that this case is a very difficult one for solution. And this is all the more so on account of the lack of the ju-

---

10 James Ross Spence, *Consent to Marriage in a Crisis of Personality Disorder* (Rome: Editrice Pontificia Università Gregoriana, 1985) 47-48.

dicial confession of the alleged simulator. However, the judge takes direction from the following quote in a case *coram* Boccafola:

"Proof of total simulation is difficult, because it can often be proven only by indirect means; in fact, it becomes more difficult if the party simulating the pretense should assert the contrary. However, as we can read in a sentence *c*. Felici, *RRD* 48 (1956) 403: "The confession of the simulating person need not necessarily be done with words; *it is sufficient if it be done by deeds—which may be more eloquent than words—as long as they are several, certain, and univocal*; provided also that they demonstrate in the common understanding that the contracting party in no way wanted to oblige himself/herself to the bond of marriage. This is all the more true when the simulating party could not manifest the simulation in words, because the reason pushing the person to simulate his or her consent is present" (*RRD* 88 [1996] 381).

I then go on to explicate a pattern of behavior on the part of the alleged simulator which clearly indicates that the simulator in no way intended to bind himself/herself to marriage itself or one of its essential but rather by a positive act of the will—implicit or explicit, actual or virtual—elected to exclude marriage or one of its essentials. Following this, I explicate the *causa contrahendi* and the *causa simulandi*. I frequently located the *causa simulandi*, that is, the motivation for simulation in the *indoles*, that is, the very character of the alleged simulator.

Let us now turn our attention to force or fear cases. This canon on force or fear contains within its formulation the necessary jurisprudential touchstones. Canon 1103: "A marriage is invalid if entered into because of force or grave fear from without, even if unintentionally inflicted, so that a person is compelled to choose marriage in order to be freed from it." In other words, the judge must establish from the evidence that the fear was extrinsic, grave—at least subjectively so—and causative. This usually does not present a problem if the case is well instructed. In addition, if the marriage took place before the advent of the 1983 *CIC* then the formulation of the force or fear canon, c. 1087 of the 1917 *CIC*, must be dealt with.[11] In other words, the issue of whether the fear was just or unjust has to be dealt with. A single paragraph can be employed in a force or fear case to sum up the conclusion. "The judge finds that the evidence produced in this case fits the template of a classic reverential force and fear case. And likewise it meets the four jurisprudential criteria established by canon 1087 of the 1917 *CIC*. Was the fear extrinsic? Yes, it was. It came from the mother of the petitioner who pressured her daughter. Was the fear grave? Yes, it was, and

---

11   1917 *CIC* c. 1087: §1: Invalidum quoque est matrimonium initum ob vim vel metum gravem ab extrinseco et iniuste incussum, a quo ut quis se liberet, eligere cogatur matrimonium.

§2: Nullus alius metus, etiamsi det causam contractui, matrimonii nullitatem secumfert.

this almost in the absolute sense of that word. Was it causative? Yes, it was. The petitioner has testified that she felt she had no other choice but to marry. This too is supported by witness testimony. And, lastly, was the fear unjust? Yes, it most certainly was. And this is because the freedom to freely choose one's state in life, which is a fundamental human right, not to say a canonical right (cf. c. 219), is denied."

Let us now turn our attention to the conclusion of the definitive sentence. Article 257 §2 of *DC* states that "Information is to be provided at the time of the publication of the sentence regarding the way in which an appeal is to be placed and pursued, with explicit mention being made of the faculty to approach the Roman Rota besides the local tribunal." After I have resolved the *dubium*, I end my sentences with the following:

> In accord with canon 1615, I order the publication of this sentence by mailing a copy of it to both the Petitioner and the Respondent.
>
> In accord with canon 1625 and canon 1628, the Parties are notified that this sentence may be challenged by a complaint of nullity or by an appeal to the Metropolitan Tribunal of the Archdiocese of Denver or by an appeal to the Roman Rota.
>
> Should either Party appeal this sentence to the Metropolitan Tribunal of the Archdiocese of Denver that Party is hereby notified that he/she will be responsible for the entire cost of such an appeal. Initial cost for such an appeal is one hundred dollars ($100.00).
>
> Should either Party appeal this sentence to the Roman Rota that Party is hereby notified that he/she will be responsible for the entire cost of such an appeal. Initial cost for such an appeal is approximately eight hundred and fifty dollars ($850.00).
>
> In accord with canon 1630, the Parties are notified that an appeal must be filed before the Judge who pronounced the sentence within the peremptory time limit of fifteen available days (*tempus utile*) from the notification of the publication of the sentence.
>
> In accord with canon 1682, I order that this sentence which has declared the invalidity of the marriage, be sent *ex officio* to the seat of our appellate tribunal, that is, the Metropolitan Tribunal of the Archdiocese of Denver in Denver, Colorado along with any appeals from the Parties, should any be received.

While some sentences maybe longer or shorter, in the main, I find that a well-crafted, complete and thorough sentence in a formal marriage case need not exceed seven to eight pages.

Let us now turn our attention to the publication of the sentence itself. This is governed by the norm of canon 1615 and *DC* article 258. The texts of the *CIC* and *DC* are substantially the same: "The publication or communication of the sentence is to be made either by giving a copy of the sentence to the parties or their procurators, or by sending it to them in accord with art. 130 (cf. can 1615)," that is, by sending them a copy of it in the mail or by other secure means.

This requirement of the law has come in for some criticism by canonists. "A legally well-argued sentence does not communicate the whole picture of the broken relationship. It uses language that may be hard for the parties to understand. Its narrowly focused analysis of the broken relationship from the point of view of the Church's law and jurisprudence may be experienced as cold, harsh, foreign, or insensitive by the parties who lived through those tragic circumstances and whose emotions may still be rubbed raw. Thus, in marriage nullity cases, merely impersonally mailing the sentence to the parties often is counterproductive and even hurtful."[12]

While acknowledging these concerns, I would like to speak from personal experience. The Tribunal of the Diocese of Pueblo has been publishing its sentences to the parties by mailing them a copy since 1989. In the vast majority of cases, we hear nothing in reply from either the petitioner or the respondent. However, sometimes we do hear from the parties.

In a case adjudicated in the affirmative in 1990 on the ground of lack of due discretion on the part of the woman petitioner, both she and her former spouse were sent copies of the definitive sentence. The case was a particularly difficult one. The man respondent was opposed to the granting of an affirmative and actively opposed the petitioner's claim, even going so far as to fly in from out of state to be interviewed. Also, there were the blunt psychological reports from therapists of the petitioner, which the woman herself supplied and which were employed in the composition of the definitive sentence. After the case was finished, I received the following thank you note from the petitioner: "I never got the chance to thank you for helping me obtain an annulment. I know it was tedious work. I pray for you and the fine and careful work your office does." This is not the only thank you note that we have received. There have been others, although not many.

We have also received some angry replies from respondents. In a more recent case that ruled in the affirmative to the woman petitioner's grave lack of discretionary judgment, we received a two and half page typed reply from the man respondent, after he had received a copy of the first instance sentence. Of interest for our seminar today is the following from that reply: "I thank you for respecting my request for communication of the outcome, despite my protests to formally submit to this proceeding as I have stated in prior mailings and maintain

---

12   Cox, 1724.

still to this day and to eternity as much as I can proclaim. I also applaud your thorough effort to substantiate your decision and provide that in a documented form for my understanding and review."

The respondent then went on, not to appeal the sentence, but to attempt to undercut the right of the Catholic Church to judge such cases, even of non-Catholics, and to challenge the psychological premises employed—terming them "somewhere between the *De anima* of Aristotle up to Maslow and Rodgers." When he received notice that the court of second instance had granted a second confirming affirmative, his note was quite a bit shorter: "I hereby declare that your declaration is bias (*sic*) and full of balony (*sic*) in accordance with justice and natural law." My point here is that the definitive sentence engaged him and, according to his rights, he took it seriously enough to attempt to rebut it in writing. That sentence fulfilled its task of adequately providing the reasons in law and in fact for the decision.

There are a number of values to be gained in publishing the definitive sentence to the parties. The first is the fulfillment of the law itself, as noted in canon 1615, not an unworthy goal. Secondly, if only the dispositive part of the sentence is given to the parties, then prescription does not obtain. In other words, the sentence will remain open to challenge at any time. Publishing the sentence also has the benefit of prodding judges and tribunals to pursue and use other grounds of matrimonial invalidity. After all who wants to write the same sentence all the time? Lastly, a well honed and careful sentence demonstrates that the parties are being treated as adults. It seems to me that this is one of the few times in the Church when persons are given the reasons in writing for why they are being treated as they are. In short, this is an exercise in transparency.

I would like to close my presentation where I began, that is, with another quotation from Cardinal Pompedda: "The ministry of the judge rendering a sentence is a service that, if well understood, confers upon the judicial ministry all of its nobility and all of its validity."[13] This nobility of purpose is one of the goals that all of us involved in tribunal ministry should strive for in crafting our definitive sentences in marriage cases.

Appendix
- The Formal Process for a Declaration of Invalidity of Marriage

---

13   Pompedda, 93.

APPENDIX
The Formal Process for a Declaration of Invalidity of Marriage

Introduction

This document is written for persons who have a formal marriage case pending before the Tribunal of the Diocese of Pueblo. This document lists only the most important stages of the formal process. The intent of this document is to inform the Parties about their rights and responsibilities in the formal process so that they can clearly understand what they are undertaking. This document is designed to help the Parties become aware of the stages of the formal process so that they can actively, directly and personally participate in the proceedings.

Declaration of Invalidity, a Definition and Values

A Declaration of Invalidity, popularly called an annulment, is a decision by a Church Court that morally certain proof is had that the marriage in question is not valid, that is, that it was entered into invalidly. It is a decision that at the time of the wedding ceremony there was a radical defect present that rendered the consent furnished inefficacious, that is, invalid. Thus, a Declaration of Invalidity is not a Church divorce for a marriage that turned out badly. It is not a decision allowing persons to receive Holy Communion nor is it a statement of forgiveness or blame. The primary purpose of the formal process is to provide a forum in which a person may seek to vindicate their right to marry in the Catholic Church. Some persons are offended that the process for obtaining a Declaration of Invalidity is conducted in a judicial setting. Nevertheless, it is conducted in a judicial setting to assure fairness and objectivity.

The Catholic Church seeks to uphold two values in this process, namely, the dignity of the human person and faithfulness to the teachings of Jesus about divorce and remarriage. The Catholic Church holds that when two persons make the matrimonial pledge of "for better for worse, until death," that the couple has given their word. And the Church holds the bride and groom to their word. For the Church holds that most persons have the ability to make the permanent commitment of marriage. In this the dignity of the human person, and their right to make choices, is upheld. Also the Catholic Church seeks to remain faithful to the teachings of Jesus about marriage and divorce.

The Catholic Church holds that all marriages, even of non-Catholics, are more than the mere public witnessing of the private consent of the Parties, to be entered into and broken at will. Therefore, the Catholic Church holds that all marriages, even of non-Catholics, are valid until the contrary is proven. The burden of proving the invalidity of a marriage rests with the Petitioner, not the Tribunal.

Personnel

The person who actively seeks a Declaration of Invalidity is termed the Petitioner. The former spouse, the other Party, is termed the Respondent. An Advocate is the person appointed by the Petitioner or the Respondent to assist that Party in presenting and arguing their case. Any properly authorized cleric or lay person of the Diocese of Pueblo may function as an Advocate before the Tribunal. The Tribunal is run by the Judicial Vicar. Other personnel in the Tribunal include associate Judges, Defenders of the Bond, Notaries and Auditors. The Defender of the Bond is the person who proposes everything which can be reasonably brought forth in favor of the validity of the marriage and against the granting of a Declaration of Invalidity.

Acceptance of the Petition

When a petition for a Declaration of Invalidity has been received and the Tribunal has securely established its jurisdiction, and the case appears to have merit, then the Tribunal commits itself to investigate the case. The Petitioner and Advocate are then notified that the case has been formally accepted for investigation. The acceptance of a case for investigation is not a guarantee that a Declaration of Invalidity will be granted. Rather the acceptance of a case is a statement that a formal trial will be conducted. Included with the notification letter of acceptance are two other items: 1) this document entitled The *Formal Process for a Declaration of Invalidity of Marriage*; 2) the Acknowledgment of Petitioner form. The Petitioner should answer the questions on the Acknowledgment of Petitioner form and return it to the Tribunal immediately.

Citation of the Respondent

On the same day that the Tribunal formally accepts the case for adjudication, it writes to the former spouse. Included with the citation letter are four other items: 1) the Acknowledgment of Respondent form listing, among other items, the court personnel and the alleged ground(s) of invalidity; 2) an outline form for the Respondent to follow in composing a written declaration; 3) this document entitled *The Formal Process for a Declaration of Invalidity of Marriage*; 4) a pamphlet entitled *Why the Church is Granting More Annulments*. The cooperation of the Respondent is asked for, either by a personal interview or by a written statement. Frequently, the Respondent elects not to cooperate in the process. Sometimes the Respondent participates in the process and actively seeks to oppose the Petitioner's claim that the marriage is invalid. At other times, the Respondent is just as eager to obtain a Declaration of Invalidity as the Petitioner. The Respondent is afforded the right to offer names and addresses of knowledgeable and willing witnesses in support of their claims in the process.

Once the Respondent is properly cited, the case is "locked in" and becomes the property of the Tribunal before which it was lodged. The Tribunal actively seeks to protect the rights of all Respondents. For this reason the Respondent must always be cited and notified at certain critical stages of the process.

Joinder of Issue

The Joinder of Issue is held fifteen days after the Citation of the Respondent. The Joinder of Issue is the stage at which the Judge sets the grounds to be investigated. The setting of the grounds is based upon the petitions and responses of the Parties in the case. The grounds for which a formal trial for a Declaration of Invalidity can be conducted are many and varied. Sometimes Petitioners and Advocate(s) propose many, yet incompatible, grounds. It is the duty of the Judge to determine the precise grounds, which might be applicable and worth adjudicating in the case. Both Parties and Advocate(s) are notified of the Joinder of Issue.

Instruction of the Case

Ten working days after the Joinder of Issue, the Judge decrees that the Instruction of the Case is to begin. This is the stage at which the testimonies of the witnesses and other proofs are gathered by the Tribunal. Among the most important sources of proof in a marriage case is the testimony of knowledgeable and willing witnesses. The Tribunal directly contacts the witnesses who have been named by the Parties. They are given two weeks to furnish testimony either in person, at the Tribunal, or by written affidavit. Full and adequate witness testimony is absolutely essential in a marriage case. Delays are frequently encountered at this stage. Sometimes witnesses claim they never received the citation for testimony from the Tribunal. Some witnesses supply little or no real information. Sometimes witnesses write mere letters of recommendation instead of narrating the facts. Some witnesses fail to have their written affidavits properly notarized. Sometimes witnesses claim to have sent a written affidavit to the Tribunal when, in fact, they have not done so. Some witnesses just fail to cooperate.

When notified that the Instruction of the Case has begun, the best way for the Parties to avoid delays is to contact their witnesses immediately to insure that they cooperate fully with the Tribunal's request for testimony. Since the burden of proof rests with the Petitioner and not the Tribunal, the Parties should urge their witnesses to come to the Tribunal in person to provide testimony if possible. However, if a witness is not able to come personally to the Tribunal, then the Parties should tell the witness to follow the outline form provided for them and to be detailed and lengthy in their written testimony and to give examples.

A good witness is a person who is knowledgeable about the personalities of the Parties, the decision to marry, the courtship and the subsequent history of the marriage. Frequently one's parents and brothers and sisters are good witnesses because they usually know about all the necessary areas.

Interview of the Petitioner

At some time during the Instruction of the Case a personal interview between the Judge and the Petitioner is held. This interview, or formal declaration, is conducted in privacy. It is taped and later transcribed. This formal declaration of the

Petitioner is one of the sources of proof in formal marriage cases. This interview lasts about twenty or thirty minutes. Some Petitioners are a little nervous at this interview. Some Petitioners are offended at what they feel is a mere rehashing of what they wrote in their written marital history. Nevertheless, this interview is never a waste of time, for the information gained at this interview can be critical and decisive. At the end of the interview the Petitioner is free to ask any questions about the progress of the case.

Evaluation by a Psychological Expert

When Canon Law requires it, after all of the testimonies and interviews are completed, the case is sent to a Court appointed psychological expert for evaluation. The Petitioner is liable for the cost of this evaluation, which is usually $150.00. The report of the expert is considered an important source of proof in marriage cases.

Publication of the Acts

When all of the evidence seems to be in, the Judge issues the Decree of the Publication of the Acts and notifies the Parties and the Advocate(s). At this stage of the process the Parties may review, at the Tribunal, the materials in the case file. This is not an absolute right. It is subject to the procedures and limitations of Canon Law. The Parties are notified that they have ten working days to inform the Tribunal that they wish to inspect the acts. At the time of Inspection the Parties and the Advocate(s) may propose new and additional proofs. The case file is always open to the legitimately mandated Advocate(s) of the Parties.

Decree of Conclusion and Opening of the Discussion and Definitive Sentence

After the time for the inspection of the acts has lapsed, the Judge issues the Decree of Conclusion and Opening of the Discussion, thus closing the case to further evidence. The Parties and Advocate(s) are notified of this decree. During this time the Defender of the Bond presents a written argument, based upon the law and facts of the case, against the granting of a Declaration of Invalidity. All are notified that the Judge hopes to issue a decision in the case within the next thirty days. The Judge then writes the Definitive Sentence. The Definitive Sentence is a document containing the reasons, based upon the law and the facts, for the decision in the case. In the Definitive Sentence the Judge decides whether morally certain proof of the invalidity of the marriage is had on the grounds set at the Joinder of Issue. If the Judge rules in the affirmative to anyone of the grounds, then he has ruled in favor of granting a Declaration of Invalidity. If the Judge rules in the negative to all of the grounds, then he has ruled against the granting of a Declaration of Invalidity. The Parties and Advocate(s) are notified of the decision and their rights of appeal

Automatic Appeal

If an affirmative decision is granted by the Tribunal of Pueblo, the case must be automatically sent to the Metropolitan Tribunal of the Archdiocese of Denver for review. If the Metropolitan Tribunal grants a second conforming affirmative decision, thus upholding the decision of the Tribunal of Pueblo, then the Declaration of Invalidity can be issued. The Parties and Advocate(s) will then be notified.

Time Limits

Canon Law determines that the time limit for a formal marriage case only begins when the Tribunal has formally accepted the case for investigation. Canon Law determines that formal cases should be settled within one year at the local Tribunal and six months at the appellate Tribunal. Most of our cases are completed within these time limits. Some cases do take longer.

Other Actions

Vetitum Sometimes, even if a Declaration of Invalidity is granted, the Judge will place a prohibition, that is, a *vetitum*, on one or both Parties preventing them from entering into another marriage in the Catholic Church until certain conditions have been fulfilled. The Party is notified of these conditions. A Party who is under a prohibition cannot set a date or arrange for a new marriage until all of the conditions for lifting the prohibition have been fulfilled.

Renunciation Sometimes the Petitioner is not able to produce the evidence necessary to prove the invalidity of the marriage. Instead of issuing a negative definitive sentence, the Judge may ask the Petitioner to withdraw their case. This has the advantage that at some future date additional evidence might be forthcoming, which would allow the Petitioner to reopen the case.

Abatement Sometimes the Petitioner loses interest in pursuing their case or sometimes the Petitioner refuses to cooperate with the Tribunal. In these situations, the Judge can issue a Decree of Abatement, which relieves the Tribunal of further investigating the case and issuing a definitive sentence. The case is then closed and placed into the archives of the Tribunal.

Future Weddings

Only after two concordant affirmative decisions have been granted, and a Declaration of Invalidity is issued, may the Parties plan a new marriage. No priest may promise a date, nor may any couple set or arrange a date for a new marriage before receiving the final decree.

SEMINAR

HOME-SCHOOLED CHILDREN AND THE RIGHT TO THE SACRAMENTS IN THE *CODE OF CANON LAW*
Margaret Romano-Hogan

As anyone who has ministered in a parish knows, the time of preparation of young people for the reception of the sacraments of reconciliation, Eucharist, and confirmation, is wonderful. There is nothing quite like the excitement of first Communion day. Even older youth anticipate with pleasure the time they will be sealed with the gift of the Holy Spirit. As anyone who has ministered in a parish also knows, this time can be beset with difficulties and conflicts that require the wisdom of Solomon to resolve. Besides the usual issues regarding the ceremonies themselves, there has arisen in our day the question of what sort of preparation can be required for children to receive the sacraments; specifically, whether children can be required to attend parish catechetical and sacramental programs in order to receive these sacraments. This brief – and I say brief because the question is broad and complex[1] – discussion of the Church's teaching on the matter of catechesis, especially sacramental catechesis, will hopefully point to an answer rooted in her own understanding of the whole matter of catechesis.

In this endeavor I intend to illustrate what seem to me to be the issues which must be addressed. Nothing said here should in any way be taken to accuse anyone of bad faith with regards to the matter. It does seem to me, however, that there is much good-faith confusion and incompleteness with regards to the issue, which it is my goal to clarify in this discussion. The methodology I will follow here is to look at the pronouncements of the Church, including those of the Supreme Pontiffs, on the various issues involved.

I. The Second Vatican Council

As any good canonist knows, the *Code of Canon Law,* promulgated in 1983 [hereafter 83 *CIC*], must be understood and interpreted in the light of the teaching of the Second Vatican Council.[2] Hence our first question must be: How does

---

1   I am indebted to Rev. Mark A. Gurtner for providing me with a copy of his unpublished JCL thesis, "Canonical Factors to be Weighed with Regard to the Formulation of Diocesan Norms for Preparation for First Eucharist for Home-Catechized Children", submitted to the Faculty of the School of Canon Law of The Catholic University of America in 2005.

2   Cf. John Paul II, Apostolic Constitution *Sacrae disciplinae leges,* January 25, 1983:

the council treat the question of catechesis? How does it treat the question of the agents of catechesis? How does it treat the question of the rights and duties of parents regarding the catechesis of their children?

As many have remarked, the ecclesiology of the Second Vatican Council is one in which the role of the Church's bishops, always in communion with the Supreme Pontiff, comes into greater relief. Thus we would expect to find in the council's documents some indications of the Church's understanding of the role of the bishops in catechesis, and we do.

a) *Lumen gentium*

The documents of the Second Vatican Council are fairly explicit with regard to the bishop's duty regarding catechesis. *Lumen gentium,* the Dogmatic Constitution on the Church gives us a fairly explicit picture of how the Church is, by divine will and design, ordered.[3] Even though much more will be said in *Christus dominus*, the Decree on the Pastoral Office of Bishops in the Church, one finds in *Lumen gentium*, most especially in Chapter III, some clear statements regarding the office of the bishop. In episcopal consecration, the duties of teaching and ruling are conferred upon the bishop and he takes the place of Christ such that when he acts as teacher, shepherd and priest he is acting *in eius persona*, that is, in the person of Christ (*LG* 21). The bishops are the successors of the apostles and in the college of bishops the apostolic college is perpetuated; together with the Supreme Pontiff and never apart from him, they have *supreme and universal authority over the Church* (*LG* 22; emphasis added). The bishop receives his mission of teaching from Christ himself (*LG* 24) and preaching the gospel is one of his more important duties (*LG* 25). The bishops govern their dioceses not only with their words,

> But over and above that also by the authority and sacred power which they exercise exclusively for the spiritual development of their flock…This power, which they exercise personally in the name of Christ, is proper, ordinary and immediate, although its exercise is ultimately controlled by the supreme authority of the Church… In virtue of this power bishops have a sacred right and duty before the Lord of legislating for and of passing judgment on their subjects, as well as of regulating everything that concerns the good order of divine worship and of the apostolate (*LG* 27).

Nor are the bishops to be regarded as vicars of the Roman pontiff (*LG* 27). I

AAS 75/2 (1983) vii-xiv. English Translation can be found in *Code of Canon Law Latin-English Edition* (Washington, DC: Canon Law Society of America, 1998) xxvii-xxviii.

3   Vatican II, decree *Lumen gentium*, November 21, 1964: *AAS* 57 (1965); English translation in *Vatican Council II: The Conciliar and Post-Conciliar Documents*, ed. Austin Flannery, 2nd ed. (Northport, NY: Costello Publishing, 1996) [hereafter *LG*].

would argue that it is clear that the role and authority of the bishop in regulating the life of the particular Church of which he is head is envisioned by the council to be very substantial, at least in what pertains to his duty regarding teaching, which includes evangelization *and* catechesis.

In Chapter IV, *Lumen gentium* also speaks of the role of the laity, by which the council means those not in Holy Orders and those not in religious state approved by the Church (*LG* 31). The vocation of married partners is to be witnesses of faith and love of Christ to one another and to their children. In the next chapter of the document, entitled *The Call to Holiness*, the council states that Christian married couples should train their children in Christian doctrine and evangelical virtues (*LG* 39). However, the council has already spoken clearly that "Like all Christians, the laity should promptly accept in Christian obedience what is decided by the pastors, who as teachers and rulers of the Church, represent Christ" (*LG* 37).

b) *Christus dominus*

Christus dominus, which was promulgated approximately a year after *Lumen gentium*, repeats and expands on much of what is found regarding the office and duties of the bishops in that earlier conciliar document.[4] "By virtue, therefore, of the Holy Spirit who is given to them bishops have been constituted true and authentic teachers of the Faith, and have been made pontiffs and pastors"(*CD* 2). One hears very clearly in the statement the echo of *Lumen gentium's* description of how the bishop, presiding in God's stead over the flock, shepherds that flock in which he is teacher of doctrine, minister of sacred worship, and holder of office in government (*LG* 20). Individual bishops, under the authority of the Supreme Pontiff, in the name of God, care for their flocks as their proper, ordinary and immediate pastors, sanctifying and governing them (*CD* 8a and 11). The proclamation of the gospel is a principal duty of the bishop (*CD* 12).

According to *Christus dominus* the bishop's role in catechesis is not negligible. He is to be especially concerned about catechetical instruction, whose goal, the council says here, is to develop in men (and women), a living, explicit and active faith, enlightened by doctrine (*CD* 14). There is to be a close collaboration and coordination of all the apostolic works under the direction of the bishop (*CD* 17); certainly catechesis would fall under the category of "apostolic works." Among those who cooperate with the bishop in his pastoral task is the parish priest[5] whose catechetical duty is explicitly mentioned (*CD* 32, 2).

---

4   Vatican II, decree *Christus Dominus*, October 28, 1965: *AAS* 58 (1966) 673-696; English translation in *Vatican Council II: The Conciliar and Post-Conciliar Documents*, ed. Austin Flannery, 2nd ed. (Northport, NY: Costello Publishing, 1996) [hereafter *CD*].

5   In the United States the equivalent term would be "pastor," not simply a priest who works in a parish.

However, the wealth of the teaching of the Second Vatican Council is not exhausted in *Lumen gentium* and *Christus dominus*. What do other conciliar documents say about catechesis?

c) *Gravissimum educationis*

Gravissimum educationis,[6] the Declaration on Christian Education, "promulgates some fundamental principles concerning Christian education especially in regard to schools" (*GE*, Preface). The Council makes the bold statement that all Christians have a right to a Christian education, which is clearly envisioned as a formation for Christian living in the world. Pastors have a grave obligation to ensure that a Christian education is enjoyed by all the faithful, especially the young (*GE* 2).

But it is the third article of this document, we will see, that pertains to our purpose here, especially as it tends to stir up a bit of controversy. It will be helpful to quote it:

> As it is the parents who have given life to their children, on them lies the gravest obligation of education of their family. They must therefore be recognized as being primarily and principally responsible for their education.[7] The role of parents in education is of such importance that it is almost impossible to provide an adequate substitute (*GE* 3).

The document goes on to describe this duty of the parents:

> It is therefore the duty of parents to create a family atmosphere inspired by love and devotion to God and their fellow-men ... The family is therefore the principal school of the social virtues which are necessary to every society ... (A)bove all it is in the Christian family that children should be taught to know and worship God and to love their neighbor ... In it they will have their first experience of a well-balanced human society and of the Church.... Through the family children are gradually initiated into association with their fellow-men (*sic*) in civil life and as members of the people of God...

> The task of imparting education belongs primarily to the family, but it requires the help of society as a whole. Civil society...should rec-

---

6   Vatican II, declaration *Gravissimum educationis*, October 28, 1965: *AAS* 58 (1966) 728-739; English translation in *Vatican Council II: The Conciliar and Post-Conciliar Documents*, ed. Austin Flannery, 2nd ed. (Northport, NY: Costello Publishing, 1996) [hereafter *GE*].

7   What is here translated as "responsible for their education" is "*educatores*" in the Latin text.

ognize the duties and rights of parents...and provide them with the requisite assistance." Insofar as the common good requires it, the civil society can establish its own schools. Education is in a very special way the concern of the Church (*GE* 3).

What emerges from foregoing, and indeed from the tenor of the document itself, is that *Gravissimum educationis* is a document about education, *and not primarily about catechesis*, even though catechesis is seen as a means for the Church to exercise its educational function (*GE* 4). If the section quoted extensively above is situated in the context of the whole document it becomes clear that what the Church is concerned to do herein is to establish the right of the parents, free from any coercion *by the civil society*, to choose the *school* (*GE* 6) in which their children will receive that sort of human education that it is the right of every person to receive (*GE* 1). The council also wishes to make clear that while the civil society has a proper role in regulating schools, it cannot claim a monopoly such that the only schools which may exist are those sponsored by the same civil authority (*GE* 6). Much of the rest of the document talks about the various types of Catholic institutions of learning which are to be provided.[8]

d) *Apostolicam actuositatem*

The Decree on the Apostolate of Lay People, *Apostolicam actuositatem*, discusses the absolutely critical role of the laity in the mission of the Church, and the distinctiveness of their particular vocation.[9] The priestly, prophetic and kingly office has been entrusted to the apostles and their successors by the Lord, and they exercise it in His name and by His power. But the laity also share in this office, albeit in way distinct from that of the bishops (*AA* 2). To the laity belongs the distinctive task of renewing the temporal order (*AA* 7) and the family has a special and necessary role to play in this regard. For example, the Christian couple has a particular and important role. They are to be the first to pass on the faith to their children and to educate them in it, and to form them for Christian life. But Christian couples have duties which, when fulfilled, have effects which reach beyond the family, for example, the duty to witness to the indissolubility of marriage, the duty to witness to the right and obligation (*ius et officium*) of parents to give their children a Christian upbringing, and the duty to witness to the dignity and legitimate autonomy of the family. The family is the primary vital cell in society, and is a domestic sanctuary of the Church (*domesticum sanctu-*

---

8   Even so, the council does seem to give preference to schools as a means of education: "Among the various organs of education the school is seen as of outstanding importance" not just for the intellectual formation it offers, but by "providing for friendly contacts between pupils of different characters and backgrounds it encourages mutual understanding" (*GE* 5).

9   Vatican II, decree *Apostolicam actuositatem* [hereafter *AA*], November 18, 1965: *AAS* 58 (1966) 837-864. English translation in *Vatican Council II: The Conciliar and Post-Conciliar Documents*, ed. Austin Flannery, 2nd ed. (Northport, NY: Costello Publishing, 1996).

arium Ecclesiae); the whole family is to worship liturgically and carry out works of charity and hospitality, as a family (*AA* 11).

However, this activity of the laity, like any other activity of the Body of Christ, is not carried out independently of the hierarchy. The hierarchy must direct the exercise of the apostolate to the common good of the Church, and see to it that doctrine and order are safeguarded. This connection is so vital that, while different apostolates have different relationships with the hierarchy, no enterprise may lay claim to the name "Catholic" if it does not have the approval of legitimate ecclesiastical authority.[10] And there are those instances in which "the hierarchy entrusts the laity with certain charges more closely connected with the duties of pastor: in the teaching of Christian doctrine…In virtue of this mission the laity are fully subject to superior ecclesiastical control in regard to the exercise of these charges" (*AA* 24).

The Council returns to the theme of the role of parents when it discusses the matter of those who train others for the (lay) apostolate. Parents have the task to prepare their children from an early age to discern God's love for all, and to teach them to have concern for their neighbor's needs. "Children must be trained, besides, to go beyond the confines of the family and take an interest in both ecclesial and temporal communities…Their integration into the local parish community should succeed in bringing them the awareness of being living active members of the people of God. Priests, for their part, should not lose sight of this question of training for the apostolate…" (*AA* 30). Formation, it would seem, includes this integration into the local parish community.

e) *Dignitatis humanae*

Dignitatis humanae,[11] the Declaration on Religious Liberty would seem to take a somewhat new direction regarding parents' rights vis-à-vis their children's religious upbringing. This document confirms that the family has the right to organize its own religious life in the home under the control of the parents, and to decide the form of the religious upbringing of their children (*DH* 5). However, from the rest of this section of *Dignitatis humanae*, it is clear that a familiar refrain is playing: the "institution" over and against which the parents enjoy this right is the *civil society*. Parental rights are violated if children are forced to attend classes which are not in agreement with the religious beliefs of the parents or if there is but a single compulsory system of education from which all religious instruction is excluded. And it must be remembered that the Second

---

10   Including, I would claim, a catechesis which is not approved by legitimate ecclesiastical authority.

11   Vatican II, declaration *Dignitatis humanae*, December 7, 1965: *AAS* 58 (1966) 929-941. English translation in *Vatican Council II: The Conciliar and Post-Conciliar Documents*, ed. Austin Flannery, 2nd ed. (Northport, NY: Costello Publishing, 1996) [hereafter *DH*].

Vatican Council met during a time when the Cold War between communism and the free world was at its height, when religious (and civil) rights were being trampled in the name of the "Workers' Paradise." This context must be considered when coming to a correct understanding of this document.

f) *Gaudium et spes*

And finally we come to the final document of the council, the great *Gaudium et spes*, the Pastoral Constitution on the Church in the Modern World.[12] In the second part of the document, entitled "More Urgent Problems," is found some of the council's most explicit teaching regarding marriage and family matters, especially as regards the dignity and holiness of matrimony and the fruitfulness of married love. This "celebration" of the Sacrament of Matrimony may perhaps sound timeworn to the contemporary ear, but the articulation of it fell fresh and green on the ears of many at the time it was written. The council speaks of the ordering of marriage and married love to the procreation and education of offspring; this great gift of children is the crowning glory of marriage. After discussing the gifts given to the couple in this sacrament, the council goes on to discuss the salutary effects, on the entire household, of the example and prayer of the spouses. And here is found once again, a statement of the role of the parents in the religious development of their children: "(When) spouses are given the dignity and role of fatherhood and motherhood, they will eagerly carry out their duties of education, especially religious education, which primarily (*imprimis*) devolves on them" (*GS* 48). Instruction about the "dignity of married love, its role and its exercise" is to be given to young people, in a timely and suitable fashion, above all in the heart of their own families, to prepare them for courtship and marriage (*GS* 49). And finally, civil authority should consider it a "sacred duty" to acknowledge the true nature of marriage and the family, to protect and foster them (*GS* 52).

So, what does the Second Vatican Council say about catechesis? Understanding this is critical to understanding the *Code of Canon Law* which flows from it.

i) The diocesan bishop has a primary, God-given duty to order whatever pertains to the life of the local Church. This includes catechesis.

ii) The council clearly affirms the obligation and duty of parents to provide for the education of their children, especially for their religious education. In fact, certain types of formation cannot take place, at least not well, outside the home.

iii) When the council speaks of the "rights of parents" regarding the education

---

12   Vatican II, pastoral constitution *Gaudium et spes*, December 7, 1965: *AAS* 58 (1966) 1025-1115. English translation in *Vatican Council II: The Conciliar and Post-Conciliar Documents*, ed. Austin Flannery, 2nd ed. (Northport, NY: Costello Publishing, 1996) [hereafter *GS*].

of their children, it is clear that the council is affirming that parents have a right to choose an *education* that will respect their religious beliefs, over against a totalitarian system of compulsory education. The principle of subsidiarity is invoked in this context (*GE* 3). However, it must be remembered that in the documents of the council, education and catechesis are not the same thing, as is clear from the different ways in which these two topics are treated.

Given conciliar documents, therefore:

iv) There does not seem to be a right established by the council whereby parents might legitimately act against the directives of their bishops regarding catechesis of their children.

v) Any sort of "catechesis" which does not enjoy the at least tacit endorsement of the diocesan bishop cannot call itself Catholic.

II. From the Second Vatican Council to the new Code of Canon Law

We turn now to the teachings of the Church's magisterium expressed in the documents found in the time between the close of the Second Vatican Council and the promulgation of the new *Code of Canon Law* in 1983. While it may be possible to argue that these documents do not constitute "law" strictly speaking, they certain are indicative of the mind of the legislator and thus invaluable as a tool for understanding what is set forth in the council, and later in the 1983 *Code of Canon Law*.[13] And in these documents this dependence of catechesis on the direction of the local bishop is set forth clearly.

a) *General Catechetical Directory*

The first document to treat explicitly of matters pertaining to catechesis is the *General Catechetical Directory*, from the Sacred Congregation for Clergy.[14] This document, promulgated on April 11, 1971, has as its intent

> To provide the basic principles of pastoral theology—these principles have been taken from the Magisterium of the Church, and in a special way from the Second General Vatican Council—by which pastoral action in the ministry of the Word can be more fittingly directed and governed... Moreover, the specific task of applying the principles and declarations contained in this Directory to concrete situations properly belongs to the various episcopates, and they do this by means of national and regional directories, and by means of catechisms and the other aids which are suitable for effectively

---

13   Note how many of the fonts of the 83 *CIC* refer to conciliar and post conciliar documents.

14   Sacred Congregation for Clergy, *General Catechetical Directory*, April 11, 1971: *AAS* 64 (1972) 97-176; *CLD* 7:834-839 [hereafter *GCD*].

promoting the work of the ministry of the word" (*GCD Proemium*).

Indeed, catechesis is something which is shared by the whole Church. "Furthermore, the witness given by the life of both the catchiest and the ecclesial community contribute very much to the efficacy of catechesis" (*GCD* 32). Precisely because the witness of this community is so critical, "(I)t is clear how necessary it is that the ecclesial community, *according to the mind of the Church and under the guidance of her bishops,* (emphasis added) remove or correct things that mar the appearance of the Church and constitute an obstacle for men (sic) to embrace the faith" (*GCD* 35; cf. *GS* 19). "The catechist acts not in his or her own name, but "in the name of the Church he or she acts as a witness of the Christian message" (*GCD* 76). "There is to be profound cooperation between catechists and parents" (*GCD* 79).[15]

However, the document highlights the role of bishops in catechesis. The document was created as a response to the directive found in *Christus dominus* n.44, and the first step in its creation was consultation with episcopates throughout the world (*GCD Proemium*). The primary focus of the document is practical – assistance to episcopates around the world with the creation and production of catechisms and catechetical documents – but as mentioned above, the task of doing so properly belongs to those various episcopates. "The Directory is chiefly intended for bishops, Conferences of Bishops, and in general all who *under their leadership and direction* (emphasis added) have responsibility in the catechetical field" (*GDC Proemium*).[16] It is the bishops who "make authentic judgments regarding expressions of that deposit (of Faith) and the explanations which the faithful seek and offer" (*GDC* 13). The document continues, "Shepherds of souls should always keep in mind the obligation they have of safeguarding and promoting the enlightenment of Christian existence through the word of God for people of all ages and in ail historical circumstances" (*GCD* 20). (Again, there is

---

15 However, the document seems to envision the time when children are first prepared for sacraments as a time when they begin to relate "directly" to the Church, and not only through the "mediation" of the family (*GCD* 79).

16 The renewal envisioned by the *GCD* is not to be achieved primarily by increasing the "amount" of catechesis "delivered." "(T)hose who are unable to understand the depth of the proposed renewal, as though the issue here were merely one of eliminating ignorance of the doctrine which must be taught. According to the thinking of those people, the remedy would be more frequent catechetical instruction. Once the matter has been considered that way, that remedy is immediately seen to be altogether unequal to the needs. In fact, the catechetical plan is to be thoroughly renewed, and this renewal has to do with a, continuing education in the faith, not only for children but also for adults"(*GCD* 9). Also, "The function of catechesis, however, cannot be restricted to repetition of traditional formulas; in fact, it demands that these formulas be understood, and be faithfully expressed in language adapted to the intelligence of the hearers, using even new methods when necessary. The language will be different for different age levels, social conditions of men, human cultures, and forms of civil life (cf. *DV* 8; *CD* 14)" (*GCD* 34).

a reference to the Decree on Bishops from Vatican II, *Christus dominus,* this time to n.14) Finally, the "Catechetical Office, therefore, which is part of the diocesan curia, is the means which the bishop as head of the community and teacher of doctrine utilizes to direct and moderate *all the catechetical activities* (emphasis added) of the diocese. No diocese can be without its own Catechetical Office" (*GCD* 126). Thus it is clear from the very beginning of the document that bishops have a pre-eminent role in catechesis in their dioceses.[17]

b) *Evangelii nuntiandi*

We turn now to the Apostolic Exhortation *Evangelii nuntiandi*, promulgated by Pope Paul VI after the 1974 Synod on Evangelization, and near the close of the Holy Year of 1975.[18] While the whole document may be said to express the "heart" of the Holy Father regarding evangelization, it would seem at first glance that his specific concern is with catechesis, what *Catechesi tradendi*[19] will later call a "moment" of evangelization (*CT* 18) can be found in number 44. Catechesis must include fundamental teachings; its goal is to form patterns of Christian living. In sum, it is a teaching which leads to living.[20]

However, it is in Section VI, entitled *The Workers for Evangelization*, that the mind of the Holy Father regarding the evangelizer's role (and, by extension, the catechist's, since catechesis is a form of evangelization) is revealed even more profoundly. Evangelization is a profoundly ecclesial act. No evangelizer acts in virtue of a mission which he or she attributes to himself or herself or by a personal inspiration, but in union with the mission of the Church and in its name (*EN* 60). And no one is master of one's own evangelizing, with a power to carry it out according to individualistic criteria.[21]

The Holy Father continues by describing the roles that various members of the Church play in the task of evangelization. In union with the Successor of Peter, the bishops receive through episcopal ordination the authority to teach in the Church (*EN* 68). The primary and immediate task of the laity is not to build up the ecclesial community but to evangelize the world (*EN* 70). The family, the domestic Church, should have various aspects of the whole Church, and

---

17 "The Supreme Pontiff, PAUL VI, by a letter of his Secretariat of State, n. 177335, dated March 18, 1971, approved this General Directory together with the Addendum, confirmed it by his authority and ordered it to be published" (*GCD*).

18 Paul VI, apostolic exhortation *Evangelii Nuntiandi*, December 8, 1975: *AAS* 58 (1976) 5-76 [hereafter *EN*].

19 John Paul II, apostolic exhortation *Catechesi tradendae*, October 16, 1979: *AAS* 71 (1979) 1277-1340 [hereafter *CT*]. English translation in *L'Osservatore Romano* English ed., November 12, 1979, n. 607.

20 Ibid., 44. Even here the Holy Father notes the role of the bishops in guiding the preparation of particular catechetical directories.

21 *EN* 60.

the members evangelize each other, and together become evangelizers of other families (*EN* 71). The task of parents and teachers is to help their children and students discover the truth (*EN* 78).

c) *Catechesi tradendi*

In *Catechesi tradendi* the Church is blessed with the first of Pope John Paul II's "formal," as it were, discussions of the question of catechesis, issued a year to the day of his election as Successor of Peter. *Catechesi tradendi* reaffirms the *General Catechetical Directory* as the basic document for encouraging and guiding catechetical renewal (*CT* 2), at least at the time of the former's promulgation. *Catechesi tradendi* is itself, it would seem, a sort of commentary on and fruit of the work of the fourth general assembly of the Synod of Bishops, whose theme was catechesis, especially of children and youth. There are certain aspects of this document that are especially relevant to the topic at hand.

Catechesi tradendi makes clear what the Holy Father calls the "Christocentricity" of catechesis. Every catechist must transmit the teaching and life of Christ, and refrain from presenting "opinions and options" personally held as if they expressed Christ's truth (*CT* 7, 30). But this teaching is not abstract, it is rather the communication of the living mystery of God. The apostles, who were called by Christ rather than themselves (*CT* 10) transmitted to their successors (i.e., the bishops) the task of teaching and also associated many others with them in this task (*CT* 11).

In what seems to be some of the clearest and strongest language on the subject, the Holy Father confirms that the Church has always viewed catechesis as a sacred duty and an inalienable right. "(E)very baptized person, precisely by reason of being baptized has the right to receive *from the Church* (emphasis added) Christian instruction enabling him or her to enter on a truly Christian life" (*CT* 14). This task has a priority in the Church (*CT* 15) and at differing levels, the pastors have the chief responsibility for it (*CT* 16).[22]

Catechesis, while not identical with evangelization, is a distinct moment within it (*CT* 18). It is aimed at developing a mature faith in the person who has initially accepted the person of Jesus Christ and given Him complete adherence in life (*CT* 20, 25). Catechesis is aimed at this development more that at the original proclamation of the gospel, even though in practice children often arrive for catechesis without any sort of initial evangelization and "catechesis" finds itself charged with arousing the heart to faith (*CT* 19).

The Holy Father goes on to describe those in need of catechesis, and how those needs are met. The ones who needs are met first in the home are infants and

---

22 After discussing the role of priests and religious in this apostolate, the document says simply that "On another level, parents have a unique responsibility" (*CT* 16).

very young children (*CT* 36). But by the time of the reception of the sacraments, the document seems to assume that the child will not continue to be exclusively catechized in the home:

> For the child there comes soon, at school and in Church, in institutions connected with the parish or with the spiritual care of the Catholic or state school not only an introduction into a wider social circle, but also the moment for a catechesis aimed at inserting him or her organically into the life of the Church, a moment that includes an immediate preparation for the celebration of the sacraments (*CT* 37).[23]

In the penultimate section of the document, entitled, *The Task Concerns Us All*, the Holy Father sets forth his teaching on the role played by his "beloved brothers and sons and daughters" (*CT* 63), i.e., all the members of the Church. And it is clear that all have different but complementary roles to play.[24]

The Holy Father minces no words when it comes to the bishop's responsibility in their dioceses concerning catechesis:

> You are beyond all others the ones primarily responsible for catechesis, the catechists par excellence...(L)et the concern to foster active and effective catechesis yield to no other care whatever in any way...This concern...should also lead you to take on in your diocese, in accordance with the plans of the episcopal conference to which you belong, the chief management of catechesis (*CT* 63).

He then goes on to describe the responsibilities of others vis-à-vis catechesis, including priests, religious and lay catechists. Interestingly, the next *locus* of catechesis he mentions is not the family, but the parish. The Holy Father wishes to stress that "the parish community must continue to be the prime mover and pre-eminent place for catechesis" (he mentions this not once but twice in this section) and it must function as a sort of home for the baptized where they are fed and sent out to their apostolic works (*CT* 67).

When the Holy Father does discuss the family's role in catechesis, it is clear that that role is not the same as the bishops' nor the parish's role. The family's catechetical activity has a "special character, which is in a sense irreplaceable." Rather than the more formal sort of catechetical activity which occurs in the parish, the family educates in faith when the members help each other to grow through the witness of their own lives, and in the day-to-day life lived in ac-

---

23 Interestingly, in this paragraph no mention is made at all about the role of the family in catechesis.

24 It is interesting to note that the structure of this section of the document, nn. 63-71, is quite similar to that in *Evangelii nuntiandi,* nn. 66-73.

cordance with the Gospel. In fact, Christian parents must reinforce in the family setting the more methodical teaching received elsewhere. And under extraordinary conditions, yes, they must prepare themselves to be their children's own catechists. But this is obviously not seen as the norm, at least in this document (*CT* 68).

It would appear, thus, that at the beginning of his pontificate, Pope John Paul II had a very explicit teaching the right of the baptized to receive catechesis from the Church, about the role and responsibility of the bishop regarding catechesis, and similarly, about the place of catechesis in the parish.

d) *Familiaris consortio*

Familiaris consortio, promulgated a little over two years after *Catechesi tradendi,* is not primarily a document about catechesis.[25] It is a document about the family. However, because "the very institution and of marriage and conjugal love is ordained to the procreation and education of children" (*FC* 14) it is not surprising to find some discussion regarding the role of the parents and family in the education of children.

In *Familiaris consortio*, the Holy Father recalls the teaching of the Second Vatican Council that parents are the "first and foremost (*primi et praecipui*) educators of their children. Their role as educators is so decisive that scarcely anything can compensate for their failure in it" (*FC* 36). This right is described as "essential," as "original and primary," and as "irreplaceable and inalienable and incapable of being entirely delegated to others or usurped by others" (*FC* 36). But the sort of education the Holy Father (and the Second Vatican Council) is referring to is a particular one: the creation of a family atmosphere so animated with love and reverence for God and others that a well-rounded personal and social development with be fostered among the children (*FC* 36). Parents must train their children in the essential values of human life; it is the first and fundamental school of social living (*FC* 37). The family is a school of love, of God and others. For Christian parents the sacrament of marriage consecrates them to share in the specifically Christian education of their children, and makes of their educational role a "ministry" of the Church for the building up of its members (*FC* 38). In the family the gospel is "transmitted and radiated" (*FC* 49). Parents have the right to choose an education in conformity with their religious faith (*FC* 40). As regards sex education, this is a basic right and duty of parents and must be carried out under their guidance (*FC* 37).

However, *Familiaris consortio* continues "(t)he family is the primary but not the only and *exclusive* (emphasis added) educational community." The commu-

---

[25] John Paul II, Post-synodal Apostolic Exhortation *Familaris Consortio,* November 22, 1981: *AAS* 73 (1981) 81-191 [hereafter *FC*]. English translation in *L'Osservatore Romano* English ed December 21-28, 1981, n. 715. .

nity aspect of the human person, "both civil and ecclesiastical – demands and leads to a broader and more articulated activity resulting from the collaboration between the various agents of education. All these agents are necessary…" (*FC* 40). The service rendered by Christian parents is essentially ecclesial, and insofar as it is, it must remain in communion and collaborate with all the other evangelizing and catechetical activities in the diocese and parish (*FC* 53).

One of the great contributions of *Familiaris consortio*, therefore, is a deeper and more profound explication of that right and duty of education that does belong to parents in a most excellent way, a kind of education that cannot be delegated to others – an education in which children come to know, love and have a living experience of human values and the values of the Gospel, and in a special way the value, beauty and ultimate purpose of human sexuality. And because it is an ecclesial service, this education, which parents have a right and duty to carry out, must be accomplished in communion with local Church.

e) *Charter on the Rights of the Family*

The *Charter on the Rights of the Family*, a document of the Pontifical Council on the Family, was "(p)resented by the Holy See to all persons, institutions and authorities concerned with the mission of the family in today's world October 22, 1983."[26] Its creation was a response to the Synod of Bishops celebrated in 1980 which explicitly recommended that a Charter of the Rights of the Family be drawn up and circulated to all concerned.

A look at the articles of this *Charter,* which deal explicitly with education (articles 5 and 7) reveals some familiar language regarding the rights and duties of parents. Another look, this time at the footnotes, indicates why the language is familiar. With very few exceptions (and in fairness, we must mention one of the exceptions is a reference to the 1939 encyclical of Pius XI, *Divini illius magistri*), all of the footnotes reference the documents of the Second Vatican Council, or *Familiaris consortio*. Thus, if the *Charter* is to be interpreted in harmony from the sources from which it draws, it cannot but be understood to present the same understanding as that of the council and *Familiaris consortio*.

III. 1983 Code of Canon Law

In the 1983 *Code of Canon Law* the fruit of the reflections of the Second Vatican Council, and the Church's experience after the council, have found their way into the Church's universal law for the Latin Rite.[27] And so, what does the 83 *CIC* have to say about the matters under discussion here? How does the Code treat the question of catechesis? How does it treat the question of the agents of catechesis? How does it treat the question of the rights and duties of parents regarding the

---

26   Holy See, *Charter of the Rights of the Family* (Vatican City: Vatican Polyglot Press, 1983).

27   Cf. previous footnote number 13.

catechesis of their children?

However, before answering the questions about the 83 *CIC*'s provisions for catechesis, it will be necessary to examine the expressions of the very ecclesiology undergirding the 83 *CIC*, specifically, the role of the diocesan bishop in the life of the local church. For catechesis is an ecclesial activity, an apostolate. What does the 83 *CIC* say about the role of the bishop in the apostolic activity of the local Church?

There can be no question that the 83 *CIC* envisions the direction of specifically ecclesial activities to rest, ultimately, with the diocesan bishop. Lay persons have a function proper to themselves, but that proper function is, so to speak, *ad extra*, it is the infusion of the values of the Gospel into the temporal order. Lay persons can and do *cooperate* in the bishop's role of teaching, sanctifying and governing the local Church, but it is not a task that flows from their specific role as lay persons. That the bishop is "in charge" of all the activities of evangelization, having been given the *munus docendi, regendi et sanctificandi* through his episcopal consecration, is clearly stated in several places in the 83 *CIC* (cc. 375, 756 §2). As part of his pastoral care for the whole life of the Church in his diocese (c. 381), the bishop has a particular vigilance over catechesis; for example it belongs to him to *edicere* norms (c. 775 §1) regarding how it is carried out in his diocese. All the Christian faithful are bound to maintain and foster the communion of the Church, and by extension, with the local bishop into whose care the responsibility for the local church has been entrusted. All the Christian faithful are bound to follow the bishop's norms for catechesis (c.774 §1); since he is to regulate the life of the Church in his diocese this can extend not only to what is taught but how it is taught, since the Christian life which catechesis intends to kindle is not limited to the learning of formulas.

But what of the role of others in catechesis? The 83 *CIC* discusses the roles of various others in the work of evangelization, and specifically, of catechesis. The pastor of the parish (*parochus*) has a crucial role to play, especially in sacramental catechesis and discernment of readiness for the first reception of penance and Eucharist. Religious men and woman have a role. And there is, above all, the role of the parents and family.

What are the specifics of this role, however? How is it carried out? The council documents, and the post-conciliar documents, give pride of place to the role of the family in the care and education of children by the parents and in the family. The code mentions, among the rights of the lay Christian faithful, the *gravissimum* obligation and right parents have of educating their children; they are to especially care for their Christian education according to the teaching handed on by the Church (which indicates that the bishop is in charge of evangelization and catechesis; not just doctrine but also life [c. 212]). In the chapter of the code which concerns catechesis it is clear that the parents' role is a very profound, rich, and irreplaceable one – they are *obliged*, above any others' responsibility, to form their children in faith and Christian life by word and example (c.774 §2). In the section on Christian education (which the 83 *CIC* seems to view as distinct from catechesis; the sections are physically separate in the code and catechesis is found as an element in the Ministry of the Word, while Christian education seems to be a distinct sort of enterprise) parents are indeed bound by the obligation and enjoy the right to educate their children and also have the right (*ius*) to chose the means by which this is carried out (c. 793 §1).

A careful reading, in text and context, and according to the proper (and canonical) use of the words involved (c. 16), indicates clearly, it would seem, that the obligation and right not only to educate but also to choose the means of education of their children mentioned in canon 793 cannot be applied with broad strokes to the parents' rights and duties regarding catechesis. The canons are separated in the 83 *CIC*, as noted above; the "Ministry of the Word" is a title distinct from "Christian Education." What the parents' role in catechesis involves is clearly stated in the section on catechesis, not in the section on education. There is in the 83 *CIC* no statement this writer was able to find that gives parents the right to choose either the content or the means of catechesis beyond the "formation for Christian life" (content) and by word and example (means) (cc. 774, 776).

It might be argued that according to the rule of canon 18, in questions of doubt, a broad interpretation must be given to the parents' right to education and education choice, since laws regarding rights must be interpreted broadly. But there is another right in play here – the right of the bishop to "moderate" (this word is all over the 83 *CIC*) the work of catechesis in his diocese, a right which he explicitly has. Since this right is not at all in doubt, "interpretation" is not needed to argue for it.

Yet there are other rights involved in this matter, above all the rights of the child. A properly prepared child who has reached the age of reason cannot be denied the sacraments of penance and Eucharist. And still another right pertains to the child. As a member of Christ's faithful, the child has the right to call upon the bishop's *munus docendi*, especially as regarding catechesis (c. 213). It would seem that the parent may not restrict the child's right to the bishop's pastoral care for him or her. The child has the right to enter and be formed in the life of the local Church under the moderation of the bishop and parish pastor. The child has the right to catechesis from the mouth of the one who has primary responsibility for it (cc. 381 §1, 756 §2). And the parents have a right and duty (c. 914) to see that the child receives this catechesis, in an appropriate way.[28]

---

28 An argument is sometimes made that if the parents, without the (at least tacit) authorization of the bishop, have attempted to catechize their child for the sacraments, that canons 843 and 913 require that the pastor admit the child to these sacraments. However, a very cogent argument can be made that the pastor who refuses to admit to the sacraments a child who has not been prepared in accord with the bishop's explicit norms on the matter is, in fact, exercising an appropriate vigilance in not admitting a child who is

In sum, the teaching of the 1983 *Code of Canon Law* on the matter seems clear: While parents have the right and duty to care for the ongoing *education* of their children, and to choose the means of that education (even homeschooling), they do not have absolute rights in the matter of *catechesis*. The majority of rights in the matter of catechesis belong to the bishop and to the child and in some sense to the pastor. The parents have a right and duty to catechize by "word and example," and a right to provisions for appropriate catechesis from their bishop and pastor, but they do not enjoy the exclusive right[29] to determine the means and especially the content of that catechesis.

Obviously, the code allows the bishop, taking into account the conditions and situation of his diocese, may issue norms which "commission" parents to be the sacramental catechists of their children. He may chose textbooks and other aids which parents are bound in conscience to use if he so requires, or he may allow parents to choose appropriate resources. But the decision regarding whether this is a legitimate option in a particular diocese belongs to the bishop. The bishop can, at least as his authority is delineated in the 83 *CIC,* quite legitimately mandate attendance at parish catechetical preparation programs, an appropriate exercise of his duty to moderate the Ministry of the Word in his diocese. In a word, there is no right described in the 1983 *Code of Canon Law* by which a parent may, legitimately, deny the directive of the bishop regarding sacramental catechesis for a child. If the parent does so, it seems to me that the responsibility for the denial of the right to the sacraments rests with parents.[30]

IV. Documents following the 1983 Code of Canon Law

As might be expected, in the documents which follow the promulgation of the 1983 *Code of Canon Law*, there is again found a key to understanding the mind of the legislator, especially in those documents promulgated by the Holy Father himself or by the dicasteries which have competence in the matter under question.

a) *Gratissimam Sane*

In 1994 Pope John Paul II sent a letter to the families of the world entitled *Gratissimam sane*.[31] This letter, which starts out in a very "folksy" sort of tone,

---

not appropriately formed (cc. 843 §2, 914). For certainly a child who has been formed in defiance of the bishop's directives in this matter (directives which he legitimately issues) has not received an appropriate formation, especially in that way proper and peculiar to parents, i.e., by "word and example."

29 Or possibly even the primary right.

30 Obviously, a bishop will be well-advised to enter into dialogue with parents who feel strongly about this issue, to see if a *modus vivendi* can be worked out which at least partially satisfies all parties, since the persons who will ultimate "lose" if the parties become locked in confrontation are the children.

31 John Paul II, *Gratissimam sane*, February 2, 1994: *AAS 86* (1994) 868-925 [Hereaf-

seems to be the Holy Father's response to the United Nations declaration of the year 1994 as the *International Year of the Family* (*GSa* 3). The Holy Father welcomes this proclamation with joy, but does not hesitate to state again certain principles that have been noted in previous documents of the Church and in his own papacy. There are no footnotes (at least, not in the edition contained on the official Vatican website) in *Gratissimam sane*, but there are familiar echoes:[32]

> *Parents* are *the first and most important educators* of their own children, and they also possess a *fundamental competence* in this area: they are *educators because they are parents.* They share their educational mission with other individuals or institutions, such as the Church and the State. But the mission of education must always be carried out in accordance with a proper application of the *principle of subsidiarity.* This implies the legitimacy and indeed the need of giving assistance to the parents, but finds its intrinsic and absolute limit in their prevailing right and their actual capabilities. The principle of subsidiarity is thus at the service of parental love, meeting the good of the family unit *(GSa* 16).

But there is something different in this document, in this section, even in this same paragraph:

> For parents by themselves are not capable of satisfying every requirement of the whole process of raising children, especially in matters concerning their schooling and the entire gamut of socialization (*GSa* 16).

Yet, the document continues the discussion on the parents' role:

> Subsidiarity thus complements paternal and maternal love and confirms its fundamental nature, inasmuch as all other participants in the process of education are only able to carry out their responsibilities *in the name of the parents, with their consent* and, to a certain degree, *with their authorization (GSa* 16).
>
> In the sphere of education *the Church* has a specific role to play. In the light of Tradition and the teaching of the Council, it can be said that it is not only a matter of *entrusting the Church* with the person's religious and moral education, but of promoting the entire process of the person's education *"together with" the Church.* The family is called to carry out its task of education *in the Church,* thus sharing in

---

ter *GSa*].

32   All of the emphases in this discussion of *GSa* are found in the English text of *Gratissimam sane* on the Vatican Website [www.va.vatican/holy_father/john_paul_ii/letter/documents/hf_jp-ii_let_02021994_en.html], n.25.

> her life and mission. The Church wishes to carry out her educational mission above all *through families* who are made capable of undertaking this task by the Sacrament of Matrimony.
>
> Certainly one area in which the family has an irreplaceable role is that of *religious education,* which enables the family to grow as a "domestic church." Religious education and the catechesis of children make the family a true *subject of evangelization and the apostolate* within the Church. We are speaking of a right intrinsically linked to the *principle of religious liberty.* Families, and more specifically parents, are free to choose for their children a particular kind of religious and moral education consonant with their own convictions. Even when they entrust these responsibilities to ecclesiastical institutions or to schools administered by religious personnel, their educational presence ought to continue to be *constant and active* (*GSa* 16).

It might appear that the Holy Father is indeed upholding an exclusive right on the part of the family with regards to the actual delivery of religious education of children. But the text does not say this, nor does it say that it is proposing something new, nor indicate that this is something that the Holy Father is trying to clarify. The point of this document is to clarify for families (and others) their responsibilities. Parents have duty regarding the religious education of their children. They have a right to choose religious education consonant with their own convictions, but their convictions are presumed to be those of the Church, in which the bishops, as has been made quite clear in the constant teaching of the Church, have a pre-eminent role in moderating that kind of instruction which is catechesis.

b) *The Truth and Meaning of Human Sexuality*

On December 8, 1995, the Pontifical Council on the Family issued a document entitled *The Truth and Meaning of Human Sexuality: Guidelines for Education Within the Family.*[33] While this document does reiterate many of the statements already found in Church teaching, the context is a specific one: "(I)t is extremely important for parents to be aware of their *rights and duties,* particularly in the face of a State or a school that tends to take up the initiative in the area of sex education" (n. 41). The document quotes Pope John Paul II, "Sex education, which is a basic right and duty of parents, must always be carried out under their attentive guidance, whether at home or in educational centres chosen and controlled by them" (n. 43). The document goes on to note that this was a right often not exercised by Christian parents in the past, and that the Church, by means of this document, intends to "give parents back confidence in their own capabilities and help them to carry out their task" (n. 47). For our purposes here, it is enough

---

33 Pontifical Council for the Family, *The Truth and Meaning of Human Sexuality: Guidelines for Education With the Family* (Washington, DC: United States Conference of Catholic Bishops, 1996).

to note that this document has a specific focus – parental rights vis-à-vis education in human sexuality – which is not at issue in this presentation.

c) *General Directory for Catechesis*

The *General Directory for Catechesis*,[34] issued by the Congregation for Clergy in 1997 (whose competence in matters touching catechesis was confirmed in 1988 by *Pastor bonus*[35]) revises and updates the *General Catechetical Directory*, issued by the same dicastery in 1971. This new document has for its object that same goal as pursued by the 1971 document – "to provide those fundamental theological-pastoral principles drawn from the Church's Magisterium, particularly those inspired by the Second Vatican Council, which are capable of better orienting and coordinating the pastoral activity of the ministry of the Word and, concretely, catechesis" (*GDC* 9). But its "immediate end… is to help in the composition of catechetical directories and catechisms" (*GDC* 11). The experience of the pastoral life of the Church following the council, with its many successful and not-so-successful adventures in catechetics, makes this new document particularly necessary and timely, to say nothing of the re-focus in catechesis which would be motivated by the promulgation of the Latin *editio typica* of the *Catechism of the Catholic Church* in 1997.[36] This new *General Directory for Catechesis* reflects the solicitude of both Pope Paul VI and Pope John Paul II for catechesis, as well as that of the General Assemblies for the Synods of Bishops (*GDC* 6).

What does the *General Directory for Catechesis* have to say about catechesis and catechetics?

It is absolutely clear that the *GDC* considers catechesis to be a fundamentally ecclesial task, rooted in the Church's mission to evangelize. As such, it cannot but be under the direction of the successor of the apostles in the local Church, the diocesan bishop. One finds in the *GDC* such statements as "The Bishops are 'beyond all others the ones primarily responsible for catechesis'" (*GDC* 222). Furthermore, the parish is the privileged locus of catechesis: "The parish is, without doubt, the most important locus in which the Christian community is formed and expressed" (*GDC* 257), and "the parish…is the educational community to which reference must be made by catechesis" (*GDC* 262, c). The catechist is not one who appoints himself or herself as such, but is "sent" (*GDC* 247, a) and "transmits the Gospel in the name of the Church" (*GDC* 236, a).

The *General Directory for Catechesis* in no way considers catechesis a pri-

---

34   Congregation for Clergy, *General Directory for Catechesis*, August 15, 1997 (Washington, DC: United States Conference of Catholic Bishops, 1998) [hereafter *GDC*].

35   John Paul II, Apostolic Constitution *Pastor bonus*, June 28, 1998; *AAS* 80 (1998); *CLD* 6 (1969).

36   Found at www.vatican.va/latin/latin_catechism.html

vate endeavor, which cannot be exercised outside of communion with the local church (and therefore with the diocesan bishop): "In the Diocese catechesis is a unique service performed jointly by priests, deacons religious and laity, *in communion with the Bishop*"(emphasis added, *GDC* 219, a). Each member of the Church has a distinctive role to play with regard to catechesis, but "On the other hand it is a fundamental ecclesial service, indispensable for the growth of the Church. It is not an action which can be realized in the community *on a private basis or by purely personal initiative* (emphasis added). The ministry of catechesis acts in the name of the Church by its participating in mission" (*GDC* 219, b). "While the entire Christian community is responsible for Christian catechesis… only some receive the ecclesial mandate to be catechists" (*GDC* 222). But even in schools, "*there is an absolute necessity to distinguish clearly between religious instruction and catechesis*" (*GDC* 73, emphasis added).

To be certain, the *General Directory for Catechesis* recognizes, and one might say celebrates, the "primordial" mission parents have in relation to their children (*GDC* 222). Theirs is a type of catechesis that is irreplaceable; they provide the groundwork and strengthen the impact of a "more methodical catechesis" which the *GDC* envisions taking place in the larger Christian community. This fundamental familial catechesis is not the same as this "more methodical catechesis," but it precedes, accompanies, and enriches it (*GDC* 226). The co-ordination of catechesis is an important responsibility of the local Church, hence of the bishop, "because it touches on the *unity of faith* (emphasis in original), which sustains all the Church's actions" (*GDC* 272). What the *GDC* does *not* envision, it would appear, is that the parent, *on his or her own initiative*, would assume the role of the catechist sent by the Church, at the direction of the bishop.

And lest it be forgotten, the *GDC* reminds its readers that it is the Congregation for the Clergy, and by inference, not any other dicastery, that has competence in matters of catechesis: "The Pope, in what regards catechesis, acts in an immediate and particular way through the Congregation for the Clergy, which 'assists the Roman Pontiff in the exercise of his supreme pastoral office'"(*GDC* 270). The document closes with the notation that the Holy Father "*approved this General Directory for Catechesis and ordered its publication*" (emphasis in original).

The *General Directory for Catechesis,* then, continues and expands on what the 1983 *Code of Canon Law* has spoken of somewhat briefly – the distinction between religious education and catechesis. While it might be argued that the former belongs in some sort of primary and exclusive way to parents, the latter most certainly belongs in a primary and directive way to the diocesan bishop.

d) *The Family and Human Rights*
In December 1998, at the invitation of the Pontifical Council on the Family, a group of experts met for three days to reflect on the topic of human rights and

the rights of the family, in light of the celebration of the fiftieth anniversary of the *Universal Declaration of Human Rights*,[37] issued by the United Nations. On November 15, 2000, the Pontifical Council on the Family issued the document which was the fruit of that reflection: *The Family and Human Rights*.[38] A chief concern of those who carried out this reflection seems to have been that there had arisen, even in the ambit of the United Nations, several directions and tendencies which seemed to negate certain truths that had been declared in the original *Declaration,* especially as regards the dignity of all human life and the nature and rights of the family. This, then, is the context in which the document must be read and understood.

And what is found in this document is, in fact, consonant with all that has gone before it regarding the rights of the family. *The Family and Human Rights* recalls that the *Declaration* itself emphasizes that parents have the right to choose and guide their children's *education* (*FHR* 67, italics in original). Parents "share their educational mission with other individuals or carried out in accordance with a proper application of the *principle of Subsidiarity*." It should not be forgotten that "all other participants in the process of education are only able to carry out their responsibilities *in the name of the parents, with their consent* and, to a certain degree, *with their authorization*" (*FHR* 68, italics in original). This right is highlighted over and against a tendency in "developed" nations for the State to deprive parents of educational choice, in the name of giving all children equal rights to education. The purpose of this document is to remind the State that it cannot usurp parent's rights with regard to their children's education. The point of this document is not to legislate, nay, not to even mention, anything with regard to the role of legitimate Church authority in the matter of catechesis.

V. Summary

There does not appear to be any assertion, on the part of the Second Vatican Council, the recent papal magisterium, the 1983 *Code of Canon Law,* or the dicastery whose competence is catechetics (The Congregation for the Clergy) of an *exclusive* right on the part of parents to determine the means or content of the formal catechesis of their children, *except* in what pertains to catechesis regarding human sexuality. However, since what concerns catechesis in his diocese pertains to the diocesan bishop, he may "permit," "commission" parents to formally catechize their children.[39] Prudence and the salvation of souls may indicate that he do so. What parents do enjoy is the right to choose the means and content by which their children will receive a *general* education.

---

37   UN General Assembly, *Universal Declaration of Human Rights*, December 10, 1948. Found at www.un.org/en/documents/udhr.

38   Pontifical Council for the Family, *The Family and Human Rights,* November 15, 2000 (Vatican City State: Libreria Editrice Vaticana, 2000) [Hereafter *FHR*].

39   The bishops of the United States have indicated a strong preference that this be carried out in the context of the parish catechetical program, see *Addendum* below.

Some contemporary issues regarding home-based catechesis

As noted above, the question of home-based catechesis comes to the fore with a certain insistence when the times of children's reception of first penance, first Eucharist, and confirmation approach.

A casual glance at the list of websites listed when one does a Google search on "Catholic home schooling" or "Catholic homeschoolers" indicates how many parents are choosing to educate their children at home, and how many different positions are taken by such home-schooling parents with regard to the question of home-based catechesis for the sacraments.

I cannot claim to have investigated every website which deals with "Catholic home schooling," but there does seem to be a trend in certain of the ones I have visited.

a) There is sometimes a tendency to equate "catechesis" with "education."[40] This results in an attempt to argue from what can be deduced legitimately from the Church's teaching about parental freedom regarding education to a corresponding position regarding parental freedom with regard to catechesis. But, as noted above, catechesis cannot be equated with education. As this article has argued, what legitimately applies to the latter cannot be inferred without nuance or argumentation to apply to the former.

b) In some quarters there is a pronounced lack of understanding of the Church's teaching regarding the valid Magisterium of the diocesan bishop. Parents are urged to choose catechetical texts that are "truly Catholic," by which is meant that said texts agree "with the Pope" and the "Magisterium."[41] But those sorts of decisions – what conforms to the Magisterium – are not the competence of private individuals, but rather the Holy See (through the dicasteries appointed to these sorts of tasks, which would seem to be the Congregation for the Doctrine of the Faith and the Congregation for the Clergy) and the local bishop in communion with the Holy See. Private individuals, no matter how pious, may not decide on his or her own what conforms to the magisterial teaching of the Church. I would argue, further, that deciding what constitutes an appropriate catechetical resource for *a particular time and place* precisely belongs to the diocesan bishop, in virtue of his charism as the successor of the apostles in unity

---

40 Cf. the website of one of the prominent home-schooling organizations in the country, Seton Home Study School, at www.setonhome.org. This confusion is especially prominent in the sections www.setonhome.org/mission-statement (in which texts from Pope Leo XII and St. Thomas Aquinas are quoted without citation, and a text from Pope Pius XI is mentioned without full citation) and www.setonhome.org/home-schooling-based-on-catholic-church-teaching.

41 Cf. the website entitled www.keepingitcatholic.org, especially under the tab "Sacraments/Issues" and articles on sacramental preparation under the tab "Articles."

with the successor of Peter.[42]

A Particular Issue

However, it is important here to discuss two letters that came from the Pontifical Council for the Family, under the presidency of Edouard Cardinal Gagnon, because they are quoted or referenced by some home-schooling websites and articles as if they were a kind of "proof text."[43] (These letters were not included in the discussion *supra* of magisterial teaching regarding the matter, for reasons that will become clear below.) The letters can be found in the twelfth volume of *Canon Law Digest*,[44] and in *Roman Replies and CLSA Advisory Opinions*.[45] Unfortunately, no context for these letters is supplied, but they apparently are both replies, in English originals, to parents who took issue with some sort of required catechetical program. The first letter, dated April 12, 1988, is brief and seems to reference textbooks used for education in human sexuality in a Catholic setting. The letter reprises what has been said in *Familiaris consortio* and other places about parents' pre-eminent rights regarding such education, a right not at issue here. But the second letter, which is not dated, does not seem to confine itself to questions regarding education in, or catechesis regarding, human sexuality. It reads in part:

> It should be clear, therefore, that the Code's particular norms concerning catechetical instruction and Catholic education follow the general norm of canon 226, §2. Thus, specifically regarding catechetical instruction, the code stipulates in canon 774, §2 that it is the primary obligation of parents "to form their children in the faith and practice of the Christian life by word (i.e. teaching) and example." This norm, with regard to Catholic education, is paralleled by canon 793, §1. It is in the light of these canons that the rights and duties of ecclesiastical person are to be interpreted. These persons are to *assist* (emphasis in original) the parents in fulfilling their sacred obligation and in executing their sacred right, not to take them over. Thus,

---

42 From my own experience as a parish Director of Religious Education I can say that what some parents seem to want to vindicate is not the right to catechize their children, but a right to *exclusively* catechize their children, i.e., the right not to attend parish catechetical programs. Various reasons are given for this, but in some cases there is a disturbing, to my mind, fear that an hour a week spent with other children will somehow expose one's children to the evil influences these other children may bring, and to situations perceived to be morally or spiritually dangerous. This may be a valid fear with regard to pre-adolescents and adolescents preparing for confirmation, but it seems a bit misplaced in the case of a supervised hour a week spent in a class by a seven-year-old preparing for first Communion.

43 For example, see www.keepingitcatholic/doctrine.html#gagnon.

44 *CLD* 12:119-120.

45 Schumacher, William A. and Lynn Jarrell, ed. *Roman Replies and CLSA Advisory Opinions 1989* (Washington, DC: Canon Law Society of America, 1989) 1-3.

canons 776, 777, when speaking about the pastor and catechetical instruction, direct him *to provide for* the catechetical formation of young people and children. In fact, canon 776 commands the pastor "*to promote and foster the role of the parents* (emphasis in original) in the family catechesis."

The role of the pastor, therefore, is to give a service of assistance by providing the parents with the means to form their child. The parents, however are not obliged to accept this assistance if they prefer to exercise exclusively their obligation and right to educate their own children. (This is a natural right, and is not altered by the right of the Church. e.g., canons 793 and 794, 914.) In times past, parents were only too happy to be assisted by the Catholic school system in the formation of their children. Now, however, this is no longer the case in many a diocese where Catholic schools are permitted to use certain catechetical texts which, though bearing an *imprimatur,* are gravely deficient in following the Magisterium.

However, while the parents may legitimately exercise their right exclusively to give catechetical formation to their children, they must follow the norms which have been made regarding this by competent authority (cf. canon 843, §2). Parents should keep in mind that though they have a natural right to teach their children, they must follow the teaching which is handed on by the Church and the particular norms published by competent authority for a suitable catechetical formation. But, while the code states that the pastor should judge about the fitness of a child's preparation for the reception of confirmation and the Eucharist (canons 890, 914), it also requires that the pastor's judgment be made together with the parents…Thus, so long as you are teaching the children the doctrine handed on by the church and observe the norms published by competent authority, I do not see how you can be denounced any more than the parents themselves.[46]

At first read, it would seem that these letters are invested with the sort of authority that would bring about a resolution of the issue, and the end of discussion. However, a few comments can be made which should be taken into account.

a) The most striking thing about these letters is that they are *private* replies. As such, if they are to be considered legal texts, they are the sort of thing that would bind only the persons and in the matter for which they were given (c. 16 §3). Hence, if basing itself on these two letters, the claim were made that "Rome has spoken" regarding the matter, as if this were a definitive answer to the entire question of exclusive parental rights vis-à-vis catechesis, such a claim would be without foundation.

---

46   The letter goes on to endorse two particular catechetical resources.

b) Even before the promulgation of *Pastor bonus,* the Congregation for the Clergy had competence in matters regarding catechetics. The Pontifical Council for the Family did not.

c) The authentic interpretation of the *Code of Canon Law* is not a competence of a dicastery other than the Pontifical Council for the Interpretation of Legislative Texts, and its predecessors.

d) In any case, the first letter (not quoted here) explicitly refers to a matter regarding education in human sexuality. As noted above, there is no question that in matters regarding this delicate topic, the Holy Father has, indeed, indicated an exclusive right on the part of parents to impart this formation. Its provisions cannot be extended to all catechesis without some sort of argumentation to that effect.[47]

VI. Conclusion

In conclusion, it seems to me that the person whose rights must be kept front and center in any debate about catechesis is the child. It is the child who has a right to the sacraments, the child who has a right to the authentic ministry of catechesis, and the child who has a right, as it were, not to have the disagreements between the adults in charge be so exacerbated as to deny his or her other rights! The bishop does have rights and duties to make certain appropriate catechetical formation is available for *all* persons in his diocese, and parents similarly have the right and duty to preserve ecclesial communion not only with the pope, but with the local successor to the apostles appointed by the pope. In charity and justice, it behooves all the parties concerned to exert themselves to come to a workable solution that respects the rights of all concerned.[48]

---

47 Some other comments can be made regarding this second letter. For example, the letter talks about a right of the parents "exclusively" to catechize their children. However, when the English text of *Familiaris Consortio* is consulted, the only place where "exclusive" (or its cognates) is used in reference to parental rights is in no. 40, which states that "The family is the primary *but not the only* (emphasis added) and exclusive educating community" (the footnote reference in *Familiaris Consortio* is to *GE* 3). There is no statement in the *Code of Canon Law* which talks about an exclusive right of parents to catechize. Nor is there any support in the papal magisterium for such claims as "…(If) the diocese is obedient to the Magisterium, then it will know the rights, duties and obligations inherent in the Sacrament of Matrimony which includes the *total* (emphasis added) education of children." as is found on the "Keeping it Catholic" website at www.keepingitcatholic.org/certify. In short, I do not think it is legitimate to build a justification for a presumed parental "right" exclusively to home-catechize upon these statements from the Pontifical Council for the Family.

48 For example, in many parishes, those who wish to catechize their children at home are made to feel welcome to do so, with the exception that during the year prior to the reception of first penance and first Communion, all children are required to attend a parish-based, "classroom" program. For those catechizing at home, this can be seen as the complement to, rather than a replacement for, the preparation done at home.

Seminar

The Sexual Abuse Crisis: Care For The Canonists
Brother Loughlan Sofield, ST

The sexual abuse crisis has taken a major toll on the Catholic Church in the last decade. Canonists, because of their involvement with bishops in dealing with both the abused and abusers, have been among those most affected by the crisis. As a result, canonists may be experiencing burnout, discouragement, emotional, physical, and psychological exhaustion. These reactions may be accompanied by feelings of frustration, anger, impotence, helplessness, sadness and guilt. (When asked during the workshop at the Canon Law Society Convention what reactions those present experienced, anger surfaced most frequently, and the anger was directed toward a variety of people.) Dealing with the sexual abuse crisis may also have raised questions of integrity as well as spiritual doubts. Perhaps one of the most powerful reactions may have been a sense of profound loss.

A twenty-year longitudinal study on priests discovered that priests were different than other men in only two ways. First, they died younger, because men who live alone have a tendency to eschew self-care. Second, they were more tender-minded than men in general. Tender-minded individuals are more sensitive and compassionate, but they also have a greater need to be accepted and loved. This can be a deadly combination. It is my belief that not only priests but canonists in general are tender-minded. Therefore, they are more likely than others to experience strong emotions and reactions, creating greater stress.

I would like to focus our attention on three areas: avoiding burnout, understanding and dealing with anger, and approaching loss in a way that can be life giving.

Avoiding Burnout
Canonists have been prime candidates for burnout during this last decade. Not only have they been dealing with the sexual abuse issue, but in addition they have been the major resource and support for congregations of women religious being faced with the evaluation by Rome.

Burnout is not the result of the amount of work you do, but rather of having unrealistic expectations of oneself. Canonists have had major external expectations placed upon them during these recent years and have probably internalized some, if not many, of these expectations. Individuals are not filled with life one moment and then suddenly burned out. Burnout progresses through four predictable stages.

Stage I – Obsession with work/ministry

In the first stage of burnout, one becomes involved with ministry to the exclusion of everything else, including the living of a balanced life. The person becomes one-dimensional, completely absorbed with this singular issue of ministry. If one's self-esteem is excessively dependent on one's ministry there is a greater tendency toward burnout. There are two characteristics which are evident in individuals who are in the first stage of burnout: boredom and sadness.

Stage II - Exhaustion and questioning

Unless something is done to interrupt this downward spiral, the person will descend into the second stage of burnout. During this stage the person is usually consumed with a state of physical and emotional exhaustion. In addition she/he begins to question basic values and commitment. This stage is characterized by the absence of joy.

Stage III - Withdrawal and disappointment

The third stage is the critical stage in burnout. The person at this stage begins to both physically and emotionally withdraw from others, including his/her potential support systems. A person in this stage will frequently spend inordinate periods of time alone, in their office, with the door closed, often completely absorbed in the computer. In addition to the withdrawal, this stage is characterized by a disappointment and demeaning of others.

The reason that this stage is critical is because burnout is actually depression and becomes apparent at the third stage. All the classic symptoms of depression become apparent: the absence of hope; sleeping and eating patterns change dramatically; and, there is a stricture of tightening of the muscles, affecting many bodily functions, such as bowl movement and menstrual periods. I am not implying that the only cause of depression is burnout. There are many things which can cause depression: illnesses, especially cancers; chemical imbalance in the body; loss; and, there are even people diagnosed with an endogenous depression, where there is no apparent, precipitating cause.

Stage IV - Terminal cynicism

This stage is the result of a complete erosion of self-esteem and characterized by a free floating hostility. The person at this stage is critical of everyone and everything.

Recommendations for Avoiding Burnout

1. *It is imperative to have people in your life who know and care for you and to whom you have given permission to confront and challenge you when they see you assuming unrealistic expectations.* They are people whom you

trust and with whom you share honestly and openly. These listening friends, though, must realize that when they offer you honest feedback, it will not always be graciously received. Frequently when people are experiencing burnout, they respond with hostility even to those who are their closest friends and allies.

2. *Allow others to see your pain, hurt and vulnerability.* Many leaders in ministry find it difficult to let others see their humanness. Those who are unable or unwilling to share their vulnerability live extremely lonely lives. Those individuals who are able to share their humanity usually find compassionate responses from the people they encounter in their ministry.

3. *Be as compassionate, loving, and gentle with yourself as you are with those to whom you minister.* Most ministers, including canonists, by their very nature, are compassionate, loving, and gentle. People with these qualities are attracted to ministry. The problem is that while ministers tend to extend these qualities to others, they are often not very compassionate, loving, gentle, tender, and forgiving toward themselves. Again, it may have been something in the formation of the past that militates against applying these Christian attitudes toward oneself.

4. *Be like Jesus.* In an article in *Sisters Today* George Wilson described the number of times that Jesus said no and set limits.[1] When we are unable to say no or set realistic limits we are not being Christ-like.

In addition to reflecting on the recommendations for avoiding burnout in your own life, I would like to propose one additional recommendation. Have the concern and love to confront your peers whom you perceive as burning out. When people are experiencing burnout they are usually unable to take the remedial steps reverse this process. They need individuals who care enough about them to challenge them and confront them at these times. I believe that canonists need to be concerned about each other. However, again I must advise you that when someone is burning out they are not usually receptive to such challenges. They are very likely to become hostile toward the challenger.

Dealing Positively with Anger

As mentioned above, the major effect identified by the workshop participants to the sexual abuse crisis was anger, an almost undifferentiated anger directed toward a variety of people and institutions. The canonists were both angry toward others, as well as being the recipients of other's anger.

Research has shown that anger is a very difficult emotion for many people in ministry. There are generally five triggers of anger: frustration, blows to self-esteem, injustice, loss, and physical harm. Many of the canonists whom I have encountered can clearly identify the first four of these triggers, especially in dealing with the sexual abuse issue. Therefore, I can say with a great deal of certainty

---

[1] George Wilson, "The Noes of Love," *Sisters Today* 45 (1973) 625-32.

that canonists will experience much anger. This should not be a source of anxiety, since anger is energy and that energy can be used in very positive ways.

Remember, though, that it is not the situation that produces the emotion: it is our beliefs or perceptions that produce our emotions. Two people experiencing the exact same situation will not experience the same emotion. Each may perceive it differently. If one sees the situation as unjust, she/he will experience anger. Another looking at the same situation does not perceive any injustice and, therefore, will not experience anger. Emotions are subjective, not objective.

The way in which one deals with the anger experienced will depend on that person's belief systems about anger. If the person believes that anger is wrong, bad and sinful they will be prone to store the anger. Stored anger has a number of debilitating effects.

Stored Anger
- Will affect you physically. Strong emotions, and anger is a strong emotion, will produce too much cortisol, metacortisol, acth, and adrenalin. Continually, producing too much of those elements in your body can cause ulcers, strokes, heart attacks, and even death.
- Can affect you emotionally. One of the major causes of depression among highly religious people is anger turned inward.
- Will often result in individuals who become "pressure cookers," constantly exploding, often at the wrong person and with the wrong intensity.
- Passive aggressive behavior is an expression of stored anger. These are individuals who are so fearful of their anger that they can never admit it and, therefore, they are unable to express it. Through their passive behavior, not doing certain things, they frustrate others, who in turn become angry, and unconsciously express the anger of the passive aggressive. Usually, passive aggressive individuals are unaware of what they are doing.
- Boredom is masked anger. My psychiatric supervisor made me aware of this dynamic. Individuals who are incapable of acknowledging their anger convert it into a more acceptable emotion and that emotion is often boredom. Adolescents seem prone to this dynamic.
- When anger is stored it will often come out as abuse. Sometimes it will be abuse of substances, but it can just as easily be self abuse or abuse of others. I'm sure you can verify this from your experience of dealing with battered spouses in the Tribunal.

Expressed anger
When a person's belief system about anger is that anger is okay, is not wrong, and is not sinful, they will express their anger. Anger can be expressed destructively or constructively. The most destructive expression of anger is when the energy generated by the anger is converted into hostility and is directed toward another. Anger is an emotion. Hostility is a behavior. Anger is not a sin. Hostility

is. The list of the seven capital sins in the new *Catechism of the Catholic Church* no longer lists anger. There are a number of different expressions of hostility, such as direct hostility, displaced hostility, and free-floating hostility.

Anger can also be expressed positively. There are at least three positive ways of expressing anger. First, utilize the model of feel – think – talk – act. Individuals who are incapable of even feeling their anger will never be able to express it positively. Once you are in touch with your anger, the enclosed chart helps you to think about it. What triggered my anger? What belief or perception produced the emotion? Who can I talk with about constructive ways to deal with my anger? Finally, how would I like to express my anger in a more positive way? There are very positive ways of dealing with the energy generated by our anger. Effective social justice ministers, for instance, utilize the energy that evolves from the injustices they experience and perceive to marshal that energy to overcome injustices.

Second, pity and compassion are the antidotes for hostility. The emotions come from the pictures we run in the theatre of our own mind. Those who constantly choose to focus on their personal hurts, put downs and injustices remain perpetually angry, with all the resultant physical reactions. Instead, if one can conjure up pity or compassion for the other, there will be a complete dissipation of the anger.

Third, in the current psychological literature the treatment of choice for anger is forgiveness. The most positive and effective way to deal with anger is to choose to forgive. Forgiveness is a choice to let go of the desire to get even with someone who has hurt us. No one can ever prevent you from forgiving. You have complete control over forgiveness. However, you do not have control over reconciliation. The best you can do is attempt reconciliation. However, if the other person does not want to become reconciled, then that resolution is completely out of your control.

There are two major reasons why people do not forgive. The second reason is because they have never forgiven themselves for some of their past actions. The major reason why people don't forgive is that they do not have any models of forgiveness.

Ultimately, forgiveness is a gift to oneself. It gives you back the fullness of life and extracts you from someone else's nightmare. As Mr. Mandela said in his presidential address, "If I did not forgive I would still be in prison. Forgiveness is a slow process that begins with the acknowledging of the hurt and the desire to begin that process. The process includes such steps as: praying for the gift of forgiveness; reflecting on the implications of not forgiving; identifying models of forgiveness; and, considering some of the positive attributes of the person to be forgiven. You might be interested in comparing your own beliefs about forgiveness with the beliefs included in the attached chart.

Addressing Loss

One of the most devastating aspects of the sexual abuse crisis in the Church has been the profound loss it has engendered. At the present time there are extreme degrees of loss being experienced both in people's personal and ecclesial life. We observe rampant losses in the personal lives of many of the people we encounter. In addition, there are increasing varied and profound losses experienced by many in their dioceses and parishes. Parishes and schools are being closed. Parishioners that have always had a pastor, "their priest," find that they must now often share that priest with one or more parishes. The economic situation is causing the elimination of valuable, committed church workers. The losses experienced have not only been the tangible ones such as these, but also the more ethereal ones, for example, the loss of a dream. Many of the more traditional members of congregations are still grieving the loss of a Church that was the foundation of their lives. They have been unable to cope with the many changes ushered in by the Second Vatican Council. More recently, the sexual abuse scandal has left Catholics grieving the trust that they always believed they could have in their priests and religious.

All losses are stressors. One of the dynamics that makes loss especially painful and that exerts such power in the lives of people is the fact that grieving is never completed. Whenever there is an experience of a loss in the present, it resurrects the unfinished grieving from the losses of the past.

There are a number of concrete steps that can reduce the amount of stress generated by loss. Here are a few.

1. *Take time to embrace the loss.* Allow yourself to experience the conflicting emotions that are rampant during loss. Failure to take this first step will dramatically increase the stress.
2. *Accept all the myriad feelings that accompany the experience of loss.* The *Catechism of the Catholic Church* states that emotions are neither positive nor negative and they are certainly not sinful.[2] Jesus was a man who experienced the complete range of human emotions and Jesus was incapable of sinning. One of the major emotions experienced at times of loss is anger. The formation of the past, which sometimes labeled anger as bad and sinful, makes it very difficult for some Christians to accept feelings of anger.
3. *Talk about the feelings.* This is often the most difficult step. Talking about feelings and emotions resurrects that unfinished business of the past. While there may be a desire to talk about the feelings, there is often a corresponding fear. This is why the feelings are often verbalized indirectly through symbols of loss. This can explain the phenomenon observed in parishes,

---

2 *Catechism of the Catholic Church*, 1767.

for example, the removal of an altar railing or statue can result in powerful reactions by the parishioners.

4. *Consciously enter into the grieving process.* The more losses that have been repressed in the past, the greater the amount of grieving that must be addressed. Sometimes religion has tended to overly spiritualize the loss and avoid the grieving. The amount of grieving that is required differs from person to person and is influenced by how loss has been embraced in the past.

5. *Ritualize the loss.* The Church is rich in ritual. Some families, communities and cultures have developed powerful rituals to deal with loss. Consult some of the spiritual literature which offers a variety of suggestions for ritualizing loss.

6. *Allow new people into your life and embrace the new experiences of life.* Christians claim to be death and resurrection people. The challenge is to rise above the dying and grieving and to adopt the new life that is being offered by the Lord.

By following these steps, or similar ones, you assume control over the losses and prevent them from causing undue stress. You can help to transform the losses into opportunities for growth and transformation.

Conclusion

Canonists have been subject to much stress in the last decade. Their intimate involvement with those involved with the sexual abuse scandal has had negative effects on some. It is important for canonists to take personal responsibility for their own emotional health. I have tried to address three particular areas of concern. First, take the necessary steps to maintain zeal and avoid burnout. Second, explore the ways you deal with anger in your life and determine if you are dealing with it in positive or negative ways. Third, the dynamic of loss is very potent and must be personally attended to.

Appendices:
- Anger Diagram
- Beliefs about Forgiveness

Appendix A
Anger Diagram

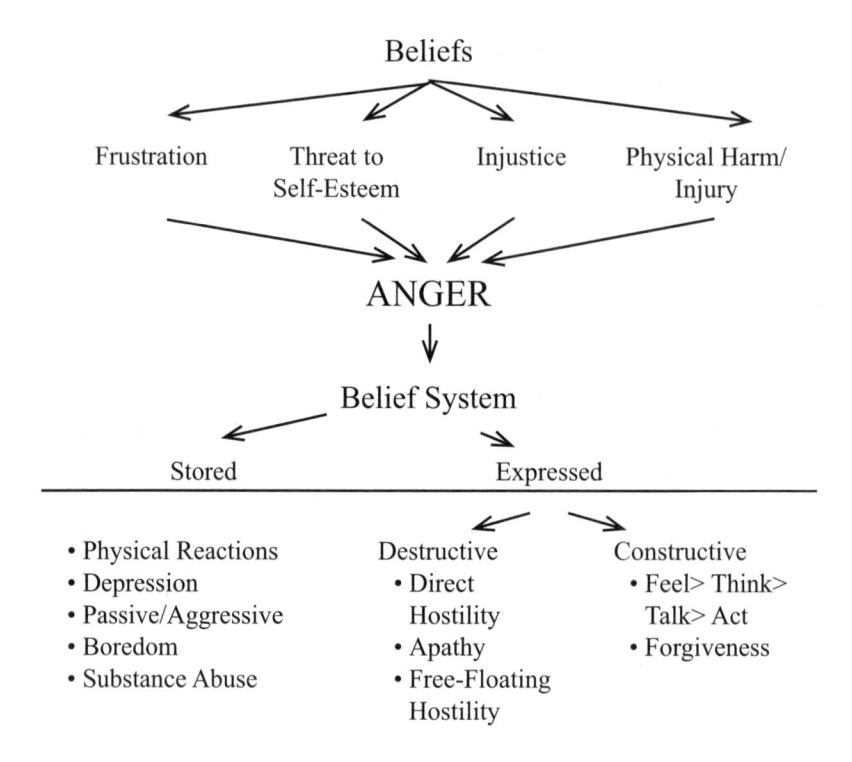

```
                        Beliefs
          ←——————————↙    ↓    ↘——————————→
   Frustration    Threat to    Injustice    Physical Harm/
                 Self-Esteem                    Injury
          ↘—————————→  ↓  ←—————————↙
                      ANGER
                        ↓
                   Belief System
                  ↙           ↘
              Stored         Expressed
```
_____

                                  ↙   ↘
- Physical Reactions   Destructive   Constructive
- Depression   • Direct   • Feel> Think>
- Passive/Aggressive   Hostility   Talk> Act
- Boredom   • Apathy   • Forgiveness
- Substance Abuse   • Free-Floating
                          Hostility

230

Appendix B
Beliefs about Forgiveness

It is important to clarify your own beliefs about forgiveness.

Below are some beliefs intended to serve as a catalyst to stimulate your own thinking.

Do not evaluate these, but rather clarify your own beliefs about forgiveness.

- Forgiveness is a gift from God.
- Forgiveness is a gift to oneself.
- Forgiveness is an act of the will, a decision to let go of the desire to get even with someone who has hurt you.
- Jesus preached forgiveness, the loving of one's enemies.
- Forgiveness is at the essence of the Judeo-Christian tradition.
- There is a difference between forgiveness, reconciliation and justice.
- We forgive because we need to be healed.
- The person who chooses not to forgive is devoid of the power to love.
- Forgiveness is a slow process.
- Research indicates that forgiveness is the trait most strongly linked to happiness.
- It takes courage to forgive.
- Forgiveness is the only solution for the violence in our world today.
- Forgiveness does not have to be communicated to the other.
- Forgiveness does not approve the behavior of the other.
- Forgiveness is not easy and is not the normal human reaction.
- The major reason why people do not forgive is that they do not have any models of forgiveness in their lives.
- Not to forgive is to be a perennial victim of those who have hurt us.
- Forgiveness will not result in forgetting.
- Forgiveness is the treatment of choice for anger.
- God sometimes gives people the grace to forgive immediately

Seminar

Issues for Latin Tribunals by the Presence of Eastern Catholic Cases
Reverend Monsignor Michael A. Souckar

I. Introduction: Immigrants' Story

The headline read "Illegal immigrants caught coming ashore on Miami Beach." The news article continued by saying that a small boat filled with approximately thirty immigrants, mostly women and children, had been intercepted in the pre-dawn hours of the morning. Speaking in their native language, the immigrants indicated to immigration officials that they had spent more than a day sailing from the Bahamas to Florida but that their journey had actually begun five days prior in Cuba. Federal officials took the wet and confused immigrants into custody and said that they will soon be repatriated to their native country. As most often happens in such cases, the smugglers who had put their human cargo in such jeopardy – after collecting their usually exorbitantly high fees – escaped into the night, abandoning the wet, hungry and worried women and children.

To those of us living in Florida, and perhaps many others here today, this news report may seem less than surprising; in fact, it is rather ordinary. There are regular reports of immigrants attempting to come to the United States through such entry points as Miami, Los Angeles, New York, Juarez and elsewhere. What may surprise you about this news article is that it is not dated 2011 or 2000 or even 1980. Rather, the dateline was 1925. In addition, the immigrants cast ashore on Miami Beach were not Cubans or Haitians, Dominicans or Colombians. Rather, they were all Syrians and most of them were Catholics. Among their number should have been my maternal grandmother and her five-year old daughter, Mary. But for a last-minute qualm of conscience, my grandmother, who had already traveled from Homs, Syria to Cuba three years prior, was intending to join her fellow Syrian immigrants in the risky and illegal plan to enter the United States. Her husband, my maternal grandfather, had left Syria four years earlier and entered the United States through Ellis Island in New York. Like so many others from all parts of the world, he was seeking better economic opportunities for himself and his family and was lured to the USA by anecdotes of those others who had left their homeland where jobs were scarce and opportunities were few. Somehow – no one really knows even to this day – my grandfather made his way from New York to Miami where he worked as a charter fisherman. Once he had established himself he sent word to his wife in Cuba that she and their young daughter should join him in Miami. Hence, when my grandmother heard that a there was a chance to sneak into the United States she was willing to give it a try. The plan was for the group to leave Cuba, stopover in the Bahamas and then proceed on to Florida. The day before they were to depart Cuba, my grandmother had second thoughts and backed out of the deal. Only later did she learn that the group had been intercepted. They were not sent back to the Bahamas or to Cuba but to "the old country," i.e. Syria. My grandmother always said that it was the providential hand of God that led her to have second thoughts and to abandon the ill-fated clandestine move to the USA

The story of my family's immigration to the USA – both that of my grandfather via Ellis Island and my grandmother and aunt via the third-country of Cuba – continues to be the story of so many of today's immigrants. Various news reports speak of the emigration of Christians from the Holy Land. Due to the political and social unrest there and the very real threat of violence against Catholic communities, many are choosing to leave these traditionally Eastern Christian lands. Like previous waves of immigrants these Eastern Christians are moving to non-Eastern lands like the United States, Australia, Brazil and parts of Europe. During the 2010 Extraordinary Synod of Bishops of the Middle East, the bishops expressed their solidarity with the Catholic faithful who are under such difficulties in their native lands, even as they acknowledged the unfortunate reality of some many Eastern faithful fleeing their homeland. The annual statistical year book of the Holy See does not yet reflect the exodus of Catholics leaving the Middle East, due to continuing political unrest, prejudice and lack of economic opportunities. This may simply be a lag in reporting numbers or something of a denial of the reality. Nonetheless, the latest wave of Eastern Catholic immigrants presents its own pastoral and canonical challenges; challenges which pastors and diocesan officials in the United States will face with increasing regularity.

2. Arabic and Eastern Catholic Populations
2.1 US Census and Arab Populations

The US Census Bureau no longer reports on the religious identification of Americans. It does, however, track how people identify their ethnicity. One significant group of Eastern Catholics which has experienced several waves of immigration is those who have an Arabic ancestry. Some statistical information on the self identifying Arab population in the US provides a snapshot of this portion of the Eastern Catholic population.

In 2000, the US Census Bureau reported that 1.19 million people in the United States identified themselves as being of at "least one Arab ancestry." Of these, 850,025 (0.3 % of US population) identified themselves as of "Arab ancestry alone"; while 1,189,731 (.42% of the US population) identified themselves as being of "Arab ancestry alone or in combination with another ancestry." In 1990, the Arab population accounted for .2% of the total US population. The specific national groups identified by the 2000 US Census in order of population were the following:

- Lebanese: 440,300 (28%)
- Egyptian: 142,800 (14.5%)
- Syrian: 142,800 (9%)
- Palestinian: 72,100 (7%)
- Jordanian: 39,700 (4%)
- Moroccan: 38,900 (4%)
- Iraqi: 37,700 (3%)
- "Arab" or "Arabic": 205,800 (9.6%)

In 2000, the US Census Bureau published a special report entitled "We the People of Arab Ancestry in the United States."[1] This report provides several interesting characteristics of the Arab population.

- The largest percentage of the Arabic foreign-born population (46%) entered the US between 1990 and 2000. The smallest number (9.6%) had entered before 1970.
- One out of four Arabs in the United States had Lebanese ancestry.
- More than half of the Arab population was married.
- The Arab population was more likely to be married (61%) than the total population and less likely to be separated, widowed or divorced (13%).
- Almost half of residents of Arab ancestry (46%) were born in the USA
- Around three out of four people with Arab ancestry spoke only English at home or spoke English "very well."
- More than 40% of Arabs had a bachelor's degree or more education.
- Men of Arab ancestry were more likely, and women of Arab ancestry less likely, to be in the labor force than their counterparts in the total population.
- Arab men and women earned more than men and women in the general population.

2.2 Eastern Catholics in the United States of America

According to the *Annuario Pontificio* 2011 there are twenty-one Eastern Catholic Churches *sui iuris*. Ten of these Eastern Catholic Churches *sui iuris*– the Maronite, Melkite, Ruthenian, Ukrainian, Romanian, Chaldean, Armenian, Syriac, Syro-Malabar and Syro-Malankara Churches *sui iuris*–have established seventeen jurisdictions in the United States (sixteen eparchies/archeparchies and one exarchate). This leaves eleven Catholic Churches *sui iuris* who have not established jurisdictions in the USA but many of them do have faithful living here. These include the Russian, Belarussian, Coptic and Slovak Churches *sui iuris*.

The handout provided lists all the Eastern Catholic Churches *sui iuris* and those which have established hierarchies in the United States. You will also find there some statistical information on the Eastern Catholic population in the United States as well as the instances of marriage, as reported in the 2011 edition of

---

[1] A. Brittingham and G. P. de al Cruz, *We the People of Arab Ancestry in the United States: Census 2000 Special Reports* (Washington, DC: US Census Bureau, 2000). Available online at http://www.census.gov/prod/2005pubs/censr-21.pdf.

the *Official Catholic Directory*. It is important for tribunal officials to be familiar with the presence of these Eastern Catholic jurisdictions, when they were established, and whether or not they have functioning tribunals.

3. Eastern Catholics and Latin Canonists
3.1 Rights of Eastern Catholics and the Obligations of Latin Canonists
　The theme of this seventy-third annual convention of the Canon Law Society of America is "Safeguarding the Rights of the Christian Faithful in the Church Today." The title of this seminar is "Issues for Latin Tribunals by the Presence of Eastern Catholic Cases." It is the objective of this seminar to discuss those canonical matters with which canonists working in Latin tribunals and chanceries should be especially familiar so as to help safeguard the rights of the Eastern Catholic faithful in the Church today. One may ask how or why Latin canonists should be obliged to safeguard the rights of the Eastern Catholic faithful. Is this yet another obligation placed on tribunals and chanceries to serve yet another special-interest group? Is it merely the politically correct thing for Latin canonists to concern themselves with Eastern Catholics and the exercise of their rights?

　In fact, this obligation comes from the Church's teachings and her laws as found in the *CIC*/83 and the *CCEO*. The Eastern Catholic Churches *sui iuris* and their rites are part and parcel of the one Roman Catholic Church, its heritage and living practice of the faith as handed on to us by the Apostles and preserved and promoted over the centuries in the deposit of faith. *CCEO* canon 39, quoting Vatican Council II's decree on the Eastern Churches, *Orientalium Ecclesiarum*, states: "The rites of the Eastern Churches, as the patrimony of the entire Church of Christ, in which there is clearly evident the tradition which has come from the Apostles through the Fathers and which affirm the divine unity in diversity of the Catholic faith, are to be religiously preserved and fostered." *CCEO* canon 41 states: "The Christian faithful of any Church *sui iuris*, even the Latin Church, who have frequent relations with the Christian faithful of another Church *sui iuris* by reason of their office, ministry, or function, are to be accurately instructed in the knowledge and practice of the rite of that Church in keeping with the seriousness of the office, ministry or function which they fulfill."

　What, then, are the rights of the Eastern Catholic faithful for which Latin canonists in tribunals or chanceries should be accurately instructed? How are Latin canonists to know about the Eastern Catholic Churches *sui iuris* and the practice of their distinct rites? *CCEO* canon 16 says that "the Christian faithful have the right to receive assistance from the pastors of the Church from the spiritual goods of the Church, especially the word of God and the sacraments." Similarly, *CCEO* canon 17 says that "the Christian faithful have the right to worship God according to the prescriptions of their own Church *sui iuris*, and to follow their own form of spiritual life consonant with the teaching of the Church." In effect, the *CCEO* is saying that Eastern Catholics have the right to observe their proper rite which is defined as "a liturgical, theological, spiritual and disciplinary heritage, differentiated by the culture and the circumstances of the history of peoples, which is expressed by each church *sui iuris* in its own manner of living the faith" (cf. c. 28 §1).

As we all know, with rights most often come corresponding or related obligations. The *CCEO* clearly states that all Eastern Catholics, regardless of their state of life, have an obligation to know, observe, preserve and promote their proper rite and to do so with an awareness of and positive engagement with the other Churches *sui iuris*, including the Latin Church. *CCEO* canon 40 obliges Eastern Catholic hierarchs, clergy, members of religious institutes and all the lay faithful to know, appreciate and foster their own rite and to follow it everywhere. Hierarchs have a special obligation to see that the rite of their church *sui iuris* is properly protected and observed and that any changes admitted to the rite are part of its organic development.

3.2 Who is Responsible for Eastern Catholics?

In 1982, the Sacred Congregation for the Oriental Churches, in response to a petition presented by the Eastern Catholic bishops of the United States, clarified several issues relative to the Eastern Catholic faithful in the United States. First of all, it was the decision of the Congregation to confirm the position of the Eastern bishops that they enjoyed exclusive jurisdiction over the Catholic faithful of their Church *sui iuris* and that this jurisdiction was not cumulative; that is to say, it is not shared with other bishops, especially Latin diocesan bishops. In addition, the Congregation stipulated that where an Eastern Catholic parish had not been established, it was the exclusive prerogative of the Eastern Catholic bishops to designate a priest of another Church *sui iuris* to provide for the pastoral care of the faithful. This priest could be of the Latin Church or another Eastern Catholic Church. It was merely required that the designating Eastern bishop consult with the proper bishop of the priest who was to be so designated. Even in these instances, however, the proper Eastern bishop continued to hold exclusive jurisdiction over those faithful. In other words, their proper bishop remained the bishop of their Church *sui iuris*, not the bishop or the priest designated to provide for their pastoral and sacramental needs. Finally, in the accompanying letter to the president of the episcopal conference in the United States, it was mentioned that those Eastern Catholics for whom no Eastern jurisdiction (an exarchate or eparchy) had yet been established were subject to the local territorial Latin bishop.

The *CCEO* took up some but not all of these matters and in so doing abrogated the special law of 1982. Even though some eleven Eastern Catholic Churches *sui iuris* have established jurisdictions in the United States, there still remain a significant number of the Eastern Catholic faithful who lack a proper pastor because no parish has been established for their domicile. *CCEO* canon 916 §§4-5 provide that in such situations, the eparchial bishop of those faithful is to appoint a pastor to provide for their spiritual needs, even if that priest should be of another Eastern Catholic Church *sui iuris*. Thus, for example, a Romanian Catholic living in Fort Lauderdale, Florida where no Romanian parish exists is to be entrusted to the spiritual care of a priest chosen by the bishop of the Romanian Eparchy of Our Lady of Deliverance. This priest could belong to the Latin Church, the Maronite Church, the Melkite Church, etc. It should be noted, however, that these Eastern Catholics entrusted to the care of a hierarch or pastor of another Church *sui iuris* do not change their ecclesial ascription; they remain ascribed to their proper Eastern Catholic Church *sui iuris* (cf. *CCEO* c. 38).

3.3 Sources of Eastern Canon Law

The sources of Eastern canon law include the *CCEO*, other universal law, and the particular law of the various Eastern Catholic Churches *sui iuris*. Because the one *CCEO* is the common law for all twenty-one Eastern Catholic Churches *sui iuris*, there are many matters which the legislator has left to the particular law of the individual churches. The norms of these various particular laws have an impact on the work of canonists, both Latin and Eastern.

The Maronite Patriarchal Church promulgated its particular law on 4 June 1996 and it became effective the same date. It consists of 105 articles which identify the corresponding canons of the *CCEO*.[2] It is now under consideration for a revision. The Byzantine Ruthenian Metropolia of Pittsburgh promulgated its particular law on 29 June 1999 with an effective date of 1 October 1999. It consists of 38 canons which are numbered equally to the corresponding canons of the *CCEO*. It is available via the Metropolia's website. The English translation of the Ukrainian Major Archepiscopal Church's particular law is dated 2006 and consists of 146 canons.

4. Eastern Catholics and their Ascription to a Church Sui iuris
4.1 How to Identify Eastern Catholics: What's in a Name?

Some people can identify from what county in Ireland a person comes just by listening to that person's Irish brogue. Most Americans can distinguish a Midwestern accent from a southern drawl. This is to say that where we come from–our heritage–is often more apparent than we like to think. One helpful tool in identifying Eastern Catholics is to look at surnames. Most would not think that "Souckar" is Mexican or that "Smilanic" is Italian. Some familiarity with family names of Arabic and Eastern European background can be an easy first-indicator that you may be dealing with an Eastern Catholic (or an Eastern Orthodox). Of course, one difficulty with this method is the reality of inter-marriage. My Melkite Catholic sisters now carry the English and Irish surnames of their husbands. So, keeping an ear open for Eastern European or Arabic surnames is helpful, but one is still bound to miss many Eastern Catholics.

4.2 Baptism and Ascription to a Church Sui Iuris

A far more reliable method for identifying Eastern Catholics is the baptismal certificate. The *CIC*/83 and the *CCEO* state that it is by baptism that the faithful

---

2   The text is available via the Metropolia's website, http://www.byzcath.org.

are ascribed to a Church *sui iuris* and thus follow a particular rite. While baptism is the means of ecclesial ascription, it is the law which determines to which Church *sui iuris* a person is ascribed. It is often mistakenly thought–by laity and clergy alike–that the parish church of baptism, the ritual used for baptism or even the ecclesial ascription of the one who baptizes determines the ecclesial ascription of the one baptized. For example, a child baptized at St. Rose of Lima Latin parish in Miami by Msgr. Seamus Doyle of Ireland using the Latin ritual must surely be a Latin Catholic. The law of the Church, however, does not work that way.

4.2.1 Children

CCEO canons 29-30 address the ascription of children who are to be baptized. A child who has not yet to complete his fourteenth year is by the reception of the sacrament of baptism *ipso iure* ascribed to the Catholic Church *sui iuris* of his Catholic father. This is the case regardless of who baptizes the child or where the baptism takes place. If only the mother of this child is Catholic, the child is *ipso iure* ascribed to the mother's Church *sui iuris*.

CIC/83 canon 111 §2 and *CCEO* canon 29 §1 have added a new provision regarding the ascription of those to be baptized who are under the age of fifteen. If the parents are of different Catholic Churches *sui iuris*, for example a Maronite father and Latin mother, and "if both parents by agreement freely request it," the child can be ascribed to the mother's church *sui iuris*. This is an exception to the law and, in all honesty, runs contrary to the socio-cultural practices of most Eastern Catholic lands and peoples. It is the general Eastern norm that the wife and children follow the religious practices of the husband/father. This may seem somewhat foreign to our American mentality but that is no excuse to disregard the law or to pretend that it does not exist.

4.2.1 Recording of Baptism

CCEO canon 689 §1 states that among the things to be noted by the pastor of the place where baptism is celebrated is "the church *sui iuris* in which the baptized persons are to be enrolled." Unfortunately, no similar requirement is found in the *CIC*/83. This is especially problematic in the instances where the parents are of differing Churches *sui iuris* and they have decided to have the child ascribed to the mother's Church *sui iuris*. Although *CCEO* canon 683 clearly states that "baptism must be celebrated according the liturgical prescriptions of the church *sui iuris* in which according to the norm of law the person to be baptized is to be enrolled," this does not resolve the problem. One cannot simply presume that because the child was baptized in a parish of the mother's Church *sui iuris* or according to that Church's ritual, that it was the explicit decision of the parents that the child be ascribed to that Church *sui iuris*. It seems to me that *CIC*/83 canon 111 §1 should be amended to correct this oversight.

Until that is done, it is my recommendation to officials of Latin dioceses that they establish particular norms to resolve this problem. One option is to require what the *CCEO* states; namely, that the pastor note in the baptismal register that the child is ascribed to the "X Catholic Church *sui iris* in accord with the norms of *CIC* canon 111 §1; i.e., the Church *sui iuris* of the mother." Ideally, the pastor would give written indication that the parents clearly stated before him that this was their intention for their child. Another option is to have the parents sign a statement indicating their choice that the child be ascribed to the mother's Church *sui iuris*. The pastor or the one who baptizes the child should attest this declaration which would then be kept in the permanent files of the parish. Even if this written declaration is used, the pastor should still note in the baptismal register the exact ecclesial ascription of the child. In addition, it would be wise for any such diocesan norms to remind pastors that the baptismal certificate for this child should clearly indicate the Church *sui iuris* to which the child ascribed at baptism. It is not sufficient to rely on the phrase "according to the Latin Rite" or "according to the Maronite Rite of the Catholic Church" as often appears on pre-printed baptismal certificates. Despite *CCEO* canon 683's demand that the baptismal ritual be that of the Church *sui iuris* to which the baptized is to be ascribed, this does not determine ascription nor does it override the canonical norms regulating ascription. The child could be baptized according to whatever Catholic ritual, but that does not determine the child's ecclesial ascription.

4.3 Transfer of Ascription

Both the *CIC* and the *CCEO* provide for the change of ecclesial ascription, namely a transfer of membership from one Church *sui iuris* to another. There are, however, important differences between the two codes.

Most often a change of ascription is associated with marriage, when one spouse chooses to join the Church *sui iuris* of his/her spouse. It is exactly here, however, that the most important difference between the two codes is found. *CIC* canon 112 §1, 2° allows the husband or wife to transfer to the Church *sui iuris* of his/her spouse at the time of marriage or during the marriage. Once the marriage ends, the one who transferred has the right by the law itself to return to his/her original Church *sui iuris*. For example, a Latin man marrying a Melkite woman may choose to change his ascription and join the Melkite Church *sui iuris*, either at the time of the marriage or during the marriage. Likewise, the Melkite woman is permitted by the law itself to become a Latin Catholic at the time of the marriage or during the marriage.

However, *CCEO* canon 33, reflecting Eastern cultural values and traditions, only affords this privilege to the wife and not the husband. Therefore, an Eastern Catholic woman may join the Church *sui iuris* of her husband–be that another Eastern Catholic Church *sui iuris* or the Latin Church *sui iuris*–at the time of the marriage or anytime during the marriage. However, the Eastern Catholic man is not free to change his ecclesial membership and join the Church *sui iuris* of his wife. During the redaction of the Eastern law, it was proposed that the Eastern code mirror the *CIC*/83 and afford to both the husband and the wife the freedom to join the Church *sui iuris* of the spouse. This proposal, however, was rejected. As the reports in *Nuntia* indicate, it was agreed that the Eastern law should follow the Eastern social custom that the wife follows the religious practices of her husband and, if necessary, adapts her religious practice to his at the time of marriage and throughout the marriage. It would be unheard of for a man to adapt his religious practice to that of his wife.[3]

The other way by which those aged fifteen and older can change their ecclesial ascription is by a formal transfer from one Church *sui iuris* to another. This should be an exceptional thing and only occur for the most serious reasons. Again, experience indicates that marriage is most often–although by no means exclusively–the occasion for such requests for a transfer of ascription.

All transfers of churches must have the approval of the Holy See. This approval is provided by the law itself, explicitly granted through the Congregation for the Oriental Churches or, on occasion, can be presumed. In 1992, the Secretariat of State published a decree indicating that the approval of the Holy See can be presumed when a Catholic requests to change ecclesial ascription and the two bishops/eparchs involved have an established jurisdiction in the same territory and they both agree to the transfer.[4] Therefore, in the United States, a Melkite can transfer to the Maronite Church, provided the two bishops agree. In this instance, the required approval of the Holy See is presumed.

Does this include the possibility of an Eastern Catholic transferring to the Latin Church? Basically, the answer to this question is found in the more fundamental question whether or not the Latin Church is to be understood as a Church *sui iuris*. It is clear from both codes as well as the *praxis* of the Holy See that, at least in matters of transfer of ecclesial ascription, the Latin Church is to be considered a Church *sui iuris*. Therefore, it is legitimate for Eastern Catholics to transfer to the Latin Church by taking advantage of this presumed approval of the Holy See. It would be helpful for the Holy See to clarify this.

The recording of these transfers can be problematic. Whenever there is a transfer, the pastor/hierarch who witnesses this transfer is to ensure that the necessary notation is made in the person's baptismal register. Often enough this is overseen by eparchial and/or diocesan officials. However, it is my opinion, that the transfers otherwise permitted by the law–principally those happening via marriage–are not suitably monitored by eparchial/diocesan officials. My research has not found any diocese or eparchy that requires pastors to report the number of transfers realized at the parish level. In addition, the Holy See does not inquire about any transfers in its annual statistical reports by dioceses and

---

3   See *Nuntia* 29 (1989) 36-74.

4   See Pope John Paul II, Secretariat of State rescript *ex audientia*, 26 November 1992: *AAS* 85 (1993) 85.

eparchies, nor is it included in the quinquenial reports. This is a serious gap in records and leaves the Holy See, the Churches *sui iuris*, diocesan bishops, and eparchial bishops ignorant of the actual numbers of transfer either from or to any given Church *sui iuris*. The Holy See is said to be the arbiter of inter-ecclesial matters. One must ask how it can fulfill this important duty, if it does not know of the transfers that are occurring. Furthermore, how does anyone know the impact transfers of ecclesial ascription are having on the Eastern Catholic Churches *sui iuris*–either to their advantage or disadvantage? Therefore, it is my recommendation that diocesan bishops and eparchial bishops require pastors to report annually the number of transfers from and to their Church *sui iuris*, as well as the specific Churches *ad quem* and *ab quo* involved.

5. Sacrament of Matrimony
5.1 Canonical Form of Marriage.

According to the Eastern tradition, theology, and law, a valid marriage requires a sacred rite (*sacer ritus*) which must include the blessing of a bishop or priest. *CCEO* canon 828 §1 states that "only those marriages are valid that are celebrated with a sacred rite, in the presence of the local hierarch, local pastor or a priest who has been given the faculty of blessing the marriage by either of them, and at least two witnesses." On the other hand, *CIC*/83 canon 1108 §1 states that "only those marriages are valid which are contracted before the local ordinary, pastor , or a priest or deacon delegated by either of them, who assist, and before two witnesses." *CIC*/83 canon 1112 goes on to allow for the "extraordinary form" of marriage: "where there is a lack of priests and deacons, the diocesan bishop can delegate lay persons to assist at marriages." Because of the required sacred rite, the *CCEO* has no equivalent canon. Hence, there is no possibility of marriage by the "extraordinary form" when one or both parties is an Eastern Catholic. It is clear from these canons that the role of the cleric at marriage is radically different. The blessing given by the bishop or priest is essential for a valid celebration of the sacrament of matrimony. Therefore, for marriages involving at least one Eastern Catholic, three elements are required: 1) the priestly blessing (sacred rite); 2) delegation of the priest by the proper pastor or local hierarch; and, 3) two witnesses. Unlike the Latin Church, dispensation from canonical form for Eastern Catholics is reserved to the Holy See or the Patriarch within the patriarchal territory (cf. *CCEO* c. 835).

5.2 Ritual Used for Marriage

The canonical norm is that priests are to celebrate the sacraments according to the rituals of the Church *sui iuris* to which they are ascribed. To celebrate the sacraments in another ritual requires the faculty of bi-ritualism which is granted by the Apostolic See, through the Congregation for the Oriental Churches.

For a licit celebration of marriage, however, the ritual used is to be that of the Church *sui iuris* of the parties, or of one of them in an inter-ecclesial marriage (*CCEO* c. 40 §3). The law itself establishes an exception in the celebration of matrimony, allowing a properly delegated priest to marry a couple according to ritual of their Church *sui iuris*, even if he is not himself ascribed to that Church (*CCEO* c. 674 §2; *CIC* c. 846 §2). However, for a priest to celebrate the rite of marriage according to the ritual of the Church *sui iuris* to which neither party belongs, he is required to obtain a special faculty from the Holy See. Hence, according to Salachas and Nitkiewicz, "a duly delegated Eastern priest may celebrate the marriage of Latin faithful according to the Latin rite; to officiate at their wedding according to an Eastern rite requires the specific faculty from the Holy See. A duly delegated Latin priest may celebrate the marriage of Eastern faithful according to the Eastern rite; to officiate at their wedding according to the Latin rite requires the specific faculty from the Holy See. One exception to this is a Latin priest who serves as the proper pastor of Eastern faithful, who can licitly celebrate the marriage of such a couple in the Latin rite (*CCEO* c. 916 §4)."[5]

5.3 Place of Marriage

Ordinarily, the marriages of Eastern Catholics are celebrated before the pastor of the groom. This is the opposite of the *CIC*/83 which calls for marriage ordinarily to be celebrated by the pastor of the bride. Permission, however, can be granted for the marriage to be celebrated in the parish of the bride, with the pastor obtaining the necessary delegation (cf. *CCEO* cc. 829 §1 and 831 §2). Maronite particular law addresses this situation when it states: "Normally, the pastor of the groom blesses the Crowning [Marriage] in his parish; but he can also give permission for the marriage to be sealed outside his parish. If the marriage is to be celebrated in another eparchy, the permission of both Eparchial Bishops is required for the liceity of the marriage" (art. 83).

5.4 Specific Diriment Impediments and Marriage Consent

Most of the canonical norms regulating diriment impediments for the sacrament of matrimony as well as the necessary elements for marital consent are the substantively the same for Eastern and Latin Catholics. There are, however, a few differences between the *CIC*/83 and the *CCEO*. Pastors preparing couples for marriage or tribunal officials involved in claims of nullity should be familiar with these differences.

5.4.1 Age (CCEO canon 800)

CCEO canon 800 §1 stipulates that to enter marriage validly a man must have completed his sixteenth year and a woman her fourteenth year of age. According to §2 "it is within the power of the particular law of any Church *sui iuris* to establish an older age for the licit celebration of marriage."

Several Eastern Catholic Churches *sui iuris* with jurisdictions in the United

---

[5] Salachas, Dimitri and Krzysztof Nitkiewicz, *Inter-Ecclesial Relations between Eastern and Latin Catholics*, English ed. George Dmitry Gallaro (Washington, DC: Canon Law Society of America, 2009) 29-30.

States have issued particular law on the question of the minimum age for valid marriage. The particular law of the Ruthenian Metropolia of Pittsburgh states: "For the licit celebration of a marriage, a person must be at least the minimum age required by the secular law of the place where the marriage is to be celebrated." The particular law of the Maronite Church establishes a higher age for valid marriage. A man "must have completed his eighteenth year" and "women must have completed their fourteenth year" to contract marriage validly (cf. art. 81). Because *CCEO* canon 800 clearly states that the particular law of a church *sui iuris* can establish a higher age for marriage only for liceity, the marriage of seventeen year old Maronites is not invalid but it is illicit. Marini argues that, if this particular law was approved by the Holy See and thereby becomes special law (*ius speciale*) for Maronite Catholics, it would then derogate from the canonical age of sixteen found as found in the *CCEO* and the particular norm of the Maronite Church would be an invalidating law.[6]

5.4.2 Prior Bond (CCEO canon 802)

The Eastern Catholic norm on prior bond is the same as that found in the *CIC*/83. Since it is not uncommon, especially in the United States, for Eastern Catholics to marry an Eastern Orthodox, care must be taken by pastors and tribunal officials relative to the freedom of Eastern Orthodox who were previously married and seek to marry a Catholic, Eastern or Latin. Orthodox divorce by *okionomia* is not sufficient to render a marriage null or declare it dissolved. In addition, Orthodox divorce is often a civil act dissolving the marriage and as such does not meet the Catholic Church's requirements. Therefore, in these cases a formal case is required.[7]

5.4.3 Affinity (CCEO canon 809)

According to *CIC*/83 (c. 1092) and the *CCEO* (c. 809 §1) "affinity invalidates a marriage in the direct line in any degree whatsoever." However, the *CCEO* extends this diriment impediment "in the collateral line in the second degree." Therefore, an Eastern Catholic man is not free to marry a woman who once was his sister-in-law, nor is an Eastern Catholic woman free to marry a man who once was her brother-in-law. For validity, the Eastern Catholic party needs a dispensation from this impediment.

5.4.4 Public Propriety (CCEO canon 810)

The notion of public propriety and its invalidating effect on marital consent is broader in the *CCEO* than what is found in the *CIC*/83. *CCEO* canon 810

---

6   See Marini, Francis J., "The Adjudication of Interritual Marriage Cases in the Tribunal," *CLSA Proceedings* 61 (1999) 240-241.

7   For a further analysis of this question see Salachas and Nitkiewicz, 28, 32-33, 39-41. See also G. Montini, "La procedura di investigazione prematrimoniale è idonea alla comprovazione dello stato libero di fedeli ortodossi che hanno attentato il matrimonio civile," *Periodica* 97 (2008) 47-98.

§1 states that "the impediment of public propriety arises: 1° from an invalid marriage after common life has been established; 2° from notorious or public concubinage; 3° from the establishment of common life of those who although bound to a required form for the celebration of marriage, attempted it before a civil official or non-Catholic minister." The canon goes on to stipulate that "this impediment invalidates marriage in the first degree of the direct line between a man and the blood relatives of the woman and between a woman and the blood relatives of the man." Therefore, Eastern Catholics who have attempted civil marriage, a marriage before a non-Catholic minister or who have cohabitated in a manner which is public or notorious have incurred this impediment and require a dispensation to marry validly.

5.4.5 Spiritual Relationship (CCEO canon 811)

The impediment of spiritual relationship found in the *CIC*/17 was omitted in the *CIC*/83. It remains, however, in *CCEO* canon 811 §1 which states that "from baptism there arises a spiritual relationship between a sponsor and the baptized person and the parents of the same that invalidates marriage." In cases of a conditional baptism, the diriment impediment is only present if "the same sponsor was employed for the second ceremony" (cf. *CCEO* c. 811 §2). This impediment binds the sponsor regardless of his or her own ecclesial ascription. That is to say that a Latin Catholic serving as a sponsor for an Eastern Catholic is impeded from marrying the baptized or his/her parents. This should especially be kept in mind when the one being baptized is an adult and the fiancée is proposed as the baptismal sponsor.

5.4.6 Condition (CCEO canon 826)

CCEO canon 826 states: "Marriage based on a condition cannot be validly celebrated." *CIC*/83 differs significantly in that it limits an invalidating condition to that which concerns the future (cf. *CIC*/83 c. 1102). For the Eastern Catholic, a marriage entered with any condition–past, present or future–by either party would be invalid. Therefore, a marriage involving an Eastern and Latin Catholic where the Latin Catholic gives consent based on a past or present condition is invalid.

5.4.7 Proxy (CCEO canon 837 §2)

While the *CIC*/83 permits Latin Catholics to exchange marital consent by proxy, this is not possible for Eastern Catholics. *CCEO* canon 837 §2 states: "Marriage cannot be validly celebrated by proxy unless the particular law of one's own Church *sui iuris* establishes otherwise, in which case it must provide the conditions under which such a marriage may be celebrated."

In addition, several Eastern Catholic Churches *sui iuris* have issued particular law on this matter. The Maronite particular law in article 84 states: "Marriage by proxy cannot be contracted validly without the written permission of the Eparchial Bishop or Vicar [General] where the marriage takes place, for serious reasons and under the following conditions: 1° The presence of a priest with legitimate faculties, at least two (2) witnesses, and the presence of the procurator with a current mandate signed before the Eparchial Bishop or Vicar [General] of the place where the mandator [principal] resides, provided that the mandatory does not revoke the mandate before sealing the contract; 2° Persons residing in the same city, locality or eparchy cannot contract a marriage by proxy except for some reason known to the Eparchial Bishop and to which he has agreed." The Ukrainian particular law reiterates the common law and states that marriage cannot be validly celebrated by proxy (c. 109). The Ruthenian Metropolia of Pittsburgh's particular law does not address the question of marriage by proxy. Hence, the universal law also applies for them.

In all instances, it is important to remember that the Eastern Catholic is bound to these norms on proxy even when he/she is marrying a Catholic of the Latin Church *sui iuris*.

6. Judicial Matters
6.1 Determining the Proper Competence for Marriage Cases

Both codes fundamentally agree on the determination of the competent tribunal for marriage cases, even in the instances of inter-ecclesial marriages (cf. *CIC*/83 c. 1673 and *CCEO* c. 1359). The 2005 Instruction from the Pontifical Council for Legislative Texts, *Dignitas connubii,* also addressed the question of competence. Article 16 states: "A tribunal of the Latin Church, ... can hear the cause of nullity of the marriage of Catholics of another Church sui iuris: 1° *ispo iure*, in a territory where, besides the local ordinary of the Latin Church, there is no other local hierarch of any other Church *sui iuris*, or where the pastoral care of the faithful of the Church *sui iuris* in question has been entrusted to the local ordinary of the Latin Church by designation of the Holy See or at least with its assent (c. 916 §2); 2° in other cases by reason of an extension of competence granted by the Apostolic Signatura whether stably or *ad casum*."

6.1.1 Forum of the Place of Marriage

As to the tribunal of the place where the marriage was celebrated, Marini reasonably argues that, although the codes are silent on the matter, the tribunal of the parish of marriage should be understood as competent.[8] Hence, a marriage between a Maronite and Melkite celebrated in the Maronite parish of the bride would leave the Maronite tribunal (either St. Maron or Our Lady of Lebanon) competent. Similarly, a Latin man marrying a Ruthenian woman in his Latin parish would make the Latin tribunal of that parish competent according to *CIC*/83 canon 1673, 1°.

6.1.2 Forum of the Respondent or Petitioner

As to the tribunal of the petitioner or respondent, both codes are substantively the same in their requirements but with one very important difference. When

---

8   See Marini, 214.

seeking to determine if the tribunal of the petitioner is competent, *CIC*/83 canon 1673, 3° requires that both parties reside in the territory of the same episcopal conference, while *CCEO* canon 1359, 3° says they must reside in the territory of the same nation. This means that the Eastern tribunal of the petitioner living in Miami is competent even if the respondent lives in Puerto Rico. If a Latin tribunal attempted to claim competence in such a case it could not because Puerto Rico is not part of the United States Conference of Catholic Bishops. At the same time, the provision of *CCEO* canon 1359, 3° often enough cannot be used because it is not uncommon for an Eastern spouse who is not a US citizen to return to his or her native land after a marriage has ended. Of course, if the spouse now living in the foreign country (or outside the territory of the USCCB) is willing to become the petitioner, the tribunal can declare itself competent as the forum of the respondent (*CIC*/83 c. 1673, 2°; *CCEO* c. 1359, 2°).

6.1.3 Forum of Most Proofs

Finally, there is the establishment of competence by the tribunal which in fact is the place of most proofs (*CIC*/83 c. 1673, 4°; *CCEO* c. 1359, 4°). Marini poses an interesting scenario in an inter-ecclesial marriage wherein he concludes that a tribunal of neither party could be competent as the place of most proofs.[9] In this scenario, a Ruthenian woman marries a Latin man in her Ruthenian parish in Pennsylvania before her proper Ruthenian pastor and according to the Byzantine Ruthenian marriage ritual. The couple immediately moves to Chicago and begin to attend a local Ukrainian Catholic parish. Seven years later the couple separate and divorce civilly. The Latin husband moves to the West Coast while the Ruthenian wife remains in Illinois. Because "her expert witness and most of her other witnesses live in Illinois, and most of her witnesses are members of the Ukrainian parish," she asks the Ukrainian Eparchy of Chicago to accept her petition to declare her marriage null. Marini concludes that, "under these facts, the case can be adjudicated in the tribunal of the Ukrainian Eparchy of Chicago, which is arguably the tribunal where most of the evidence will be collected even though neither party is Ukrainian and the marriage did not take place in a Ukrainian parish or according to the Ukrainian ritual." He supports his argument by citing James Provost to say that "it is the location of the proofs which is the determining factor, and that church *sui iuris* membership of the parties is not relevant to this basis of competence."[10] While I do not disagree with the conclusions of Marini or Provost–namely that the Ukrainian Eparchy can claim competence as the forum of most proofs–I do not see why their same argument would not conclude that the Melkite Eparchy of Newton which also has jurisdiction in Chicago also could be competent; or, for that matter, the Romanian Eparchy or the Maronite Eparchy of Our Lady of Lebanon in St Louis, all of which have jurisdictions covering Chicago. If, in the words attributed to Provost, "church *sui iuris* membership of

---

9   See Marini, 219-220.

10   Provost, James H., "Competence of Tribunals of Latin and Eastern Church," *Roman Replies and CLSA Advisory Opinions 1997*, 91-97.

the parties is not relevant to this basis of competence," all the less is the Church *sui iuris* membership of the witnesses relevant. Given the overlapping Latin and Eastern jurisdictions in the USA, following Marini's argument, any of the ecclesiastical jurisdictions in Illinois could claim to be the forum of most proofs.

On a practical level and for the promotion of good relations between Catholic Churches *sui iuris*, it is my suggestion that whenever a third Church *sui iuris* is seeking to claim competence–be it because of most proofs or otherwise–the judicial vicar of both parties should be contacted and asked if there is any objection to the case proceeding. The validity of the claim of competence would not depend on the absence of any objection, but it would avoid any inter-ecclesial uneasiness when it discovered *post factum* that the marriage was declared null.

Finally, trials involving Eastern Catholics heard in a Latin tribunal proceed according to the procedural law of the Latin code, but the case is decided according to the substantive law of the Eastern code and the particular law of the specific Church *sui iuris*.

7. Conclusion

It has been the aim of this presentation to review those more pertinent canons of the *CIC*/83 and the *CCEO* with which canonists working Latin tribunals should be familiar. The Eastern Catholic population in the United States is not limited to any particular part of our country and it can be reasonably presumed that the unfortunate socio-political events currently unfolding in the Arab world will lead to an increase of Eastern Catholic immigrants in many parts of the United States of America. Latin bishops, pastors, and canonists have a serious obligation to be familiar with the canonical norms found in the *CCEO* so that they can be of service to the Eastern Catholics present in Latin dioceses and parishes. Our presentation has limited itself to the questions of ascription to a Catholic Church *sui iuris* and matters related to the sacrament of matrimony. There are many other administrative and judicial matters that could have been included in this presentation but must be left to another opportunity.

Allow me to conclude this presentation by expressing my gratitude to those Latin canonists who took the time to better acquaint themselves with *CCEO* so as to be able to respond to the issues faced by Latin tribunals raised by the presence of Easter Catholics. It is sincerely hoped that this presentation has been informative and useful as we work together for the safeguarding of the rights of the Christian faithful in the Church today.

Appendices:
- Eastern Catholic Churches *Sui Iuris* and Eastern Catholic Jurisdictions
- Eastern Catholic Statistics in the USA for 2011

Appendix A
Eastern Catholic Churches Sui Iuris *and Eastern Catholic Jurisdictions in the USA*

Alexandrian Tradition
- Coptic Patriarchal Church of Alexandria
- Ethiopian Church

Antiochiene Tradition
- Syro-Malankara Church*
  - Syro-Malankara Catholic Church Apostolic Exarchate in USA (14 July 2010)
- Maronite Patriarchal Church of Antioch*
  - Eparchy of Saint Maron of Brooklyn (19 January 1966)
  - Eparchy of Our Lady of Lebanon [formerly of Los Angeles] (1 March 1994)
- Syriac Patriarchal Church of Antioch*
  - Our Lady of Deliverance Syriac Catholic Diocese [USA and Canada] (18 November 1995)

Constantinopolitan (Byzantine) Tradition
- Albanian Church
- Belorussian Church
- Bulgarian Church
- Georgian Church
- Greek Church
- Greek-Melkite Patriarchal Church of Antioch*
  - Eparchy of Newton (10 January 1966)
- Hungarian Church
- Italo-Albanian Church
- Macedonian Church
- Romanian Church*
  - Romanian Catholic Diocese of Saint George in Canton (4 December 1982)
- Ruthenian Church*
  - Metropolitan Archeparchy of Pittsburgh, Byzantine† (25 February 1924)
  - Byzantine Catholic Eparchy of Passaic (31 July 1963)
  - Byzantine Eparchy of Parma (21 February 1969)
  - Holy Protection of Mary Byzantine Catholic Eparchy of Phoenix [formerly of Van Nuys] (3 December 1981)
- Slovak Church
- Ukrainian Major Archiepiscopal Church*
  - Metropolitan Archdiocese of Philadelphia Ukrainian (28 May 1913)
  - Ukrainian Catholic Diocese of Stamford (8 August 1956)
  - Diocese of Saint Nicholas in Chicago for Ukrainians (1961)
  - Ukrainian Catholic Diocese of Saint Josaphat in Parma (3 December 1983)

Chaldean (East Syrian) Tradition
- Patriarchal Chaldean Church*
  - Eparchy of Saint Thomas the Apostle (26 January 1982)
  - Eparchy of Saint Peter the Apostle (25 July 2002)
- Syro-Malabar Church*
  - Saint Thomas Syro-Malabar Catholic Diocese of Chicago (13 March 2001)

Armenian Tradition
- Armenian Patriarchal Church of Cilicia*
  - Armenian Catholic Eparchy of Our Lady of Nareg [USA and Canada] (7 May 1995)

* = Established hierarchy in USA
† = Metropolitan Church *sui iuris* (cf. *CCEO* cc. 155-173)

APPENDIX B
Eastern Catholic Statistics in the USA for 2011

Eparchy	Catholic Population	Catholic Marriages	Inter-Faith Marriages
Eparchy of St. Maron in Brooklyn	31,752	77	14
Eparchy of Our Lady of Lebanon	45,842	75	43
Maronite total	*77,594*	*152*	*57*
Metropolitan Archeparchy of Pittsburgh	58,492	44	24
Byzantine Eparchy of Parma	8,752	19	3
Holy Protection Eparchy	2,451	15	5
Byzantine Eparchy of Passaic	15,965	34	14
Byzantine (Ruthenian) total	*85,660*	*112*	*46*
Metropolitan Archeparchy of Philadelphia	14,826	55	22
Ukrainian Catholic Diocese of Stamford	13,173	23	15
Ukrainian Diocese of St. Josaphat in Parma	8,500	6	1
Diocese of St. Nicholas in Chicago for Ukrainians ‡	10,500	50	35
Ukrainian total	*46,999*	*134*	*73*
Eparchy of St. Thomas the Apostle (Chaldean)	125,000	323	5
Eparchy of St. Peter the Apostle (Chaldean) +	60,000	154	0
Chaldean total	*185,000*	*477*	*5*
Eparchy of Newton (Melkite)	24,540	50	12
Our Lady of Deliverance (Syriac) +	22,500	28	12
Armenian Eparchy of Our Lady of Nareg +	25,000	35	24
Romanian Diocese of St George ++	5,978	17	7
St. Thomas Syro-Malabar Diocese +	87,000	85	12
Syro-Malankara Apostolic Exarchate	N/A	N/A	N/A
Grand total	*560,271*	*1,090*	*248*

+ = No established tribunal
++ = Uses the tribunal of the Eparchy of St Maron in Brooklyn
‡ = "Through special permission of the Holy See, local Latin rite tribunals handle the cases within the diocese."

Officer's Report

Report of the President
Reverend Michael P. Joyce, CM

It is my privilege to present the 2010-2011 annual report of the President of the Canon Law of Society to its membership. This report read in conjunction with the reports of the Executive Coordinator, the Treasurer, and the various committees present the activity of the Society during the past year. However, there is much that is not reported here. What is not included is the actual canonical ministry exercised through the year by the members of the Society.

Convention Follow-Up

The membership passed a resolution at the seventy-second convention of the Society to have "the Board of Governors direct the Publications Advisory Board to expedite its investigation of providing the *Canon Law Digest* on-line, and, if the project seems feasible and affordable, proceed with all deliberate speed to set in motion the process of on-line conversion, indexing documents by canons, chronology, source, and subject matter, maintaining permanent access, constant updating, and easy downloadability. The Publications Advisory Board shall report its find[ing]s to the Board of Governors and membership within a year."

The Publications Advisory Board reported in January to the Board of Governors that it began researching the publication of the *Canon Law Digest* electronically according to the directives of the resolution. You may refer to the report of the Publications Advisory Board included in the Committee Reports for the current status of work on the resolution.

The second resolution passed at the convention by the membership was "that the CLSA compile and maintain a list of canonists willing to assist the delegate from the Congregation for the Doctrine of the Faith to the United States, the Ordinary, and the Ordinariate and individual Ordinariate parishes, clergy, and other juridic persons to help the with their creation and their ongoing canonical needs." The Office of the Executive Coordinator assembled a list of canonists who are willing to assist the above-named parties. I then wrote to Cardinal Donald Wuerl who is the delegate of the Congregation for the Doctrine of the Faith informing him of the resolution. I included the list of canonists assembled by the Office of the Executive Coordinator with the letter. I also referred him to Sister Sharon Euart for further assistance in contacting any of the canonists whose services he sought.

Cardinal Wuerl responded to the letter and asked that his appreciation be extended to the canonists who offered their services. He is awaiting a response from the Congregation relative to the establishment of the Ordinariate before he enters into a discussion on how those who offered their services can be engaged in the effort.

Committees

Several appointments have been made during the year. You can find these appointments in the specific committee reports. As past Presidents have noted in their reports, the availability of members to serve on committees has become increasingly difficult due chiefly to increasing responsibilities of canonists in their positions and the increasing call for assistance in other areas of canonical practice such as advocacy.

I thank committee members who are currently serving. Your willingness to work on a committee exhibits clearly a sacrifice on your part of time and energy as you take on the responsibility of serving on the committee. I also thank those of you who have expressed a willingness to serve on a committee of the Society. Please do not be discouraged if you have not yet been asked to serve. The Board of Governors has kept your offer so that as openings in committees arise you may be asked to serve at that time.

It is a truism that the Society is both resolution and committee driven. Resolutions present the Society with directions of action to pursue. The committees are the vehicles that are used to research and recommend directions. The *Futures Initiative Project* redesigned the committee structure of the Society in light of changes that have occurred over the years. It has taken several years for some committees to organize and stabilize. I now look forward to the works that will be forthcoming from them.

Meetings and Visits

Ordinarily, the President attends the annual meeting of the Canadian Canon Law Society. Since our convention for 2010 was simultaneous with that of the CCLS, there was no separate visit for the President to make.

Dr. Anne Asselin, J.C.D., the Dean of the Faculty of Canon Law at St. Paul's University in Ottawa, invited me to deliver a lecture to the students and faculty of the department as well as to other members of the University. I gladly accepted her invitation and visited the university from February 9th to the 11th. This was my first visit to the university. I enjoyed becoming acquainted with the university that so many members of the Society have attended. It was a delight to meet informally with colleagues as well as to meet with the students to inform them about the CLSA and possible membership. The topic of my lecture was about the employment status of priests and remuneration.

In May, I attended the annual conference of the Canon Law Society of Great Britain and Ireland in Harrogate, England. The site is a Victorian spa town and it shows some of the elements that were used during that period. I was warmly welcomed by Monsignor David Hogan and his colleagues. It was good to meet members of our Society present at the conference as members of the CLSGBI.

Several years ago, the Board of Governors instituted a policy that in the intervening year between visits to Rome, the President can attend the annual meeting of the Canon Law Society of Australia and New Zealand. That Society is meeting September 12-15 in Melbourne, Australia. I am writing this report prior to my visit there. I am looking forward to it and meeting again with Father Anthony Kerin, the President of the Society.

I was unable to attend any of the meetings of the regional organizations. I thank each of the groups for the invitation to participate in their annual gatherings. Members of the Board of Governors graciously offered to represent me and the Society at those meetings. I thank them for taking on this additional charge and I thank the organizations for welcoming them and hosting them.

Varia

At its post-convention meeting, the members of the Board of Governors discussed concerns that were raised during the annual business meeting about the opening prayer service. The members agreed that the BOG would ask the Convention Liturgy Planning Committee to be sensitive to the appropriate of rituals used during the course of the convention.

Concluding Reflections

I take this opportunity to thank again the membership of the Canon Law Society for entrusting to me the responsibility of President of the Society. It is a humbling experience in the Christian sense of the word. The opportunities that serving as Vice-President and President have presented in working more closely with you has demonstrated to me in more detail the competencies that you have and use for the service of promoting the communion of the Church. I thank each member of the Society for the work that you do in promoting the mission of the Society.

I thank Father Larry Jurcak for the service he has given to the Society over these past three years as Vice-President, President, and Past President. He has faced significant challenges and resolved them with thoughtfulness, thoroughness, and grace. He fulfilled the responsibilities of leadership of the Society without shirking his ministry as Vicar for Clergy for the Diocese of Cleveland and then assuming the office of pastor. I personally am grateful to Father Jurcak for providing a model of leadership for the Society for me to follow.

I also thank Mrs. Rita Joyce as she prepares to assume the office of President of the Canon Law Society of America. She often took on tasks voluntarily and willingly to help relieve others on the leadership team. I now offer her my assistance as she assumes her new responsibilities.

My thanks also go to Sister Sharon Euart, RSM who serves as Executive Coordinator. Her competence, experience, and vision have served the Society well, not only in her current position but also in other roles that she has had in the past. I personally am grateful to Sister Sharon for the assistance she has given to me over this past year. She has helped keep me informed and in focus. I also thank Ms. Katie Richards as executive assistant in the Office of the Executive Coordinator. She is always ready to help with any request that I make.

Thanks also to the members of the Board of Governors whose responsibility is to govern the Society. The richness of the diversity of the Board has been a help to me in keeping in mind the same richness of diversity that exists in the membership of the Society and the Board. In particular I thank Monsignor Michael Padazinski and Father Manuel Viera, OFM as they complete their service as senior consultors. I have been able to turn to them for wisdom at various times and they have generously shared their perspectives with me. They have also taken initiative in bringing various matters to my attention. I also extend thanks to Siobhan Verbeek as she completes her service as Secretary. This position is quite demanding and Siobhan has fulfilled it well and gracefully.

I thank Bishop J. Terry Steib, S.V.D., Bishop of the Diocese of Memphis, and the Reverend James Swift, then Visitor of the Midwest Province of the Congregation of Mission, who both gave permission for me to stand for election. They both have been understanding as I worked to fulfill my responsibilities to both the Diocese of Memphis and to the Society.

I also thank those who have served as my mentors in the canonical ministry both formally and informally, those in the seminary and the Catholic University of America and those with whom I have ministered over the years and in various locations. All of them have provided me with outstanding examples of justice, charity, and peace.

Words of thanks seem inadequate as I think of you, my colleagues in canonical ministry. Rather the words of Isaiah come to mind: "Those who hope in the Lord will renew their strength. They will soar as with eagle's wings; they will run and not grow weary; they will walk and never tire. (Is 40:31) I am in fact grateful for the work that you do in protecting and promoting the rights of the Christian faithful as you exercise your canonical ministry which so often goes unappreciated. Thank you also for the support that you have extended to me. I thus conclude this report by praying for you, "May the Lord bless you and protect you. May the Lord make his face shine upon you and give you peace."

Officer's Report

Report of the Treasurer
Reverend Gregory T. Bittner

Since my election to the position of Treasurer, I have spent the last year becoming familiar with the budgets and financial operation of the four business units which comprise the CLSA. It is not lost on me that you have placed your trust in me to oversee the financial operations of the society. I accept this fiduciary responsibility humbly and with God's grace intend to protect your hard earned and placed assets.

This report begins with last fiscal year's (2010-2011) results. If you look at the Part II: 2011-2012 Budget and its accompanying schedules which follow this report and concentrate on fiscal year 2010-2011 Budget and Actual's columns you will be able to understand where the following summary and highlights originate. The General Operations unit appears to be on budget and expenses have been trimmed to the bone. While the General Operations unit budgeted a deficit for the fiscal year 2010-2011; nevertheless, as in past years, it has actually made a profit. Income exceeded expenses by more than $36,000. Included in that gain, was more than $4,500 made on the Special Faculties Seminar held in Tampa, FL in February, 2011. The unaudited Balance sheet appears very favorable.[1]

The Publications unit was basically financially stagnant as there were no new publications during the past fiscal year resulting in no new income or expenses for new publications. Income received was from sale of inventory of prior publications and royalties. We continue to pay Bright Key Inc. expenses for their services covering inventory, maintenance and storage. The Publications unit posted a gain of $20,000 over expenses. The unaudited Balance sheet appears very favorable.

The Conventions unit also had a very successful year as the Buffalo Convention netted a substantial profit which allowed the unit to pay off a prior loan from the General Operations unit. Income exceeded expenses by almost $8,000 which included the repayment of almost $25,000 to the General Operations unit from a loan for losses on the 2008 convention. The unaudited Balance sheet appears very favorable.

The Scholarship unit took most of my time to try to understand how scholar-

---

1 The audited financial statements of Linton Shafer Warfield & Garrett, P.A. were completed following the 2011 convention and can be found beginning on page 260.

ships are accounted for and what number of scholarships we can financially budget. During fiscal year 2010-2011 three students received scholarships of $7000 each. The Resource and Asset Management (RAM), which I chair, recommended some changes in the accounting operations for scholarships to the Board of Governors (BOG) which I hope will set the Scholarship unit on a sound financial course now and for the future. A positive highlight for the Scholarship unit was a generous bequest in the amount of $40,000 received in June 2011. The unaudited Balance sheet appears favorable.

In addition to the everyday business operations, I have reviewed the Investments of the Society. The former Treasurer Tom Anslow and the RAM moved the Society's Investments to Christian Brothers Investment Services (CBIS) in 2008. CBIS provides a number of investment vehicles. The Society maintains two separate investment accounts, one for the General Operations unit and one for the Scholarship unit. Both investment accounts are with Catholic United Investment Trust (CUIT) Balanced Fund and have the same investment mix and objectives. The investment mix is generally 60% stocks and 40% fixed income. The return on our investments has mirrored the general market returns for similar balanced funds over the last fiscal year, July 1, 2010 to June 30, 2011. The Balances for both funds are shown below.

CLSA Business unit	Balance as of June 30, 2011	Balance as of June 30, 2010
General Operation unit	$553,793.99	$426,381.80
Scholarship unit	$400,470.62	$334,334.22

Our investments have done very well, and provide the Society with a solid financial cushion for the future.

The Executive Coordinator, at the request of the BOG, contracted with a new Accountant/Auditor, Mr. Joseph McCathran, a principal of Linton, Shafer, Warfield and Garrett, PA, CPA. The engagement began in April 2011. It was suggested that our former Accountant/Auditor, Mr. Joseph Godbout, continue for the next fiscal year to provide a smooth transition. Mr. Godbout has been engaged by the Society for more than 15 years. The BOG believed it was time to engage a new Accountant/Auditor.

Since the new Accountant/Auditor has just been contracted with by the Society, the Executive Coordinator's Office has postponed the three year Formal Audit until the fall of 2011. The formal audit will be included in the CLSA Proceedings for 2011 when it is published. I expect to be in contact with the new Accountant/Auditor in the fall of 2011 during the audit. Because a new Accountant/Auditor has been engaged the Financial Reports in this Booklet consist of unaudited reports. The reports are generated from the Executive Coordinator's office by our financial software.

Regarding the future of the Society, it has been my recommendation to the BOG that it seriously consider a dues increase to the membership. The current dues are $200 per member. The last dues increase was in 2003. My recommendation is based upon the fact that we have for the past few years budgeted a deficit in the General Operations unit which relies principally on membership dues for its income. While we have actually succeeded in making a profit and have not realized an actual deficit in the past years; nevertheless, at some point we are going to spend the money budgeted and then we will see a deficit. The financial guidelines for the Society found in the BOG Handbook suggest that the General Operations unit CUIT Balanced Investment Fund could be utilized to offset General Operations Expenses. The RAM will be exploring this option and attempt to come up with a way to tap the CUIT Balanced Investment Fund for a portion of the yearly gain to help offset expenses in the General Operations unit and still maintain the solid foundation and growth potential of the investment fund.

I believe we should also look at how we are marketing the scholarship that we are able to offer to canon law students. In the recent past the scholarship has not been awarded because there were no applicants and in the past fiscal year 2010-2011 only one application was received. I would expect that in the present economic climate and with the present high cost for canonical studies that we would have more applicants from which to choose.

The 2011-2012 Budget along with prior year's budget and actual income and expenses follow this report.

I will provide a report highlighting the 2011-2012 fiscal year Budget in the RAM Committee report.

Independent Auditor Report
Linton Shafer Warfield & Garret, P.A.
Certified Public Accountants

Board of Governors
Canon Law Society of America

We have audited the accompanying statement of financial position of Canon Law Society of America (a nonprofit organization) as of June 30, 2011 and the related statements of activities and changes in net assets, and cash flows for the year then ended. These financial statements are the responsibility of the Society's management. Our responsibility is to express an opinion on these financial statements based on our audit.

We conducted our audit in accordance with auditing standards generally accepted in the United States of America. Those standards require that we plan and perform the andit to obtain reasonable assurance about whether the financial statements are free of material misstatement. An audit includes examining, on a test basis, evidence supporting the amounts and disclosures in the financial statements. An audit also includes assessing the accounting principles used and significant estimates made by management, as well as evaluating the overall financial statement presentation. We believe that our audit provides a reasonable basis for our opinion.

In our opinion, the financial statements referred to above present fairly, in all material respects, the financial position of Canon Law Society of America as of June 30, 2011, and the changes in its net assets and its cash flows for the year then ended in conformity with accounting principles generally accepted in the United States of America.

The year 2010 financial statements were reviewed by other accountants, and their report thereon dated August 26, 2010 stated they were not aware of any material modifications that should be made to those statements for them to be in conformity with accounting principles generally accepted in the United States of America. However, a review is substantially less in scope than an audit and does not provide a basis for the expression of an opinion on the financial statements as a whole.

Our audit was conducted for the purpose of forming an opinion on the financial statements as a whole. The Schedules of Program Services and Supporting Services are presented for purposes of additional analysis and are not a required part of the financial statements. Such information is the responsibility of management and was derived from and relates directly to the underlying accounting and other records used to prepare the financial statements. The information has been subjected to the auditing procedures applied in the audit of the financial statements and certain additional procedures, including comparing and reconciling such information directly to the underlying accounting and other records used to prepare the financial statements or to the financial statements themselves, and other additional procedures in accordance with auditing standards generally accepted in the United States of America. In our opinion, the information is fairly stated in all material respects in relation to the financial statements taken as a whole.

Linton Shafer Warfield & Garret, P.A.
November 21, 2011

Statement of Financial Position
June 30, 2011 and 2010

	2011	2010
Assets		
Current Assets		
Cash	215,129	170,567
Cash - scholarship fund	52,210	25,647
Accounts receivable	2,084	2,600
Inventory	88,082	99,778
Prepaid expenses	21,816	15,761
Total Current Assets	379,321	314,353
Furniture and Equipment - at cost		
Furniture and equipment	15,383	13,968
Less: accumulated depreciation	(7,973)	(6,217)
Furniture and Equipment, Net	7,410	7,751
Other Assets		
Investments	553,794	426,382
Investment - scholarship fund	400,471	334,334
Total Other Assets	954,265	760,716
Total Assets	**$ 1,340,996**	**$ 1,082,820**
Liabilities and Net Assets		
Current Liabilities		
Accounts payable	$ 1,598	$ 6,030
Royalties payable	256	158
Deferred revenue	23,775	20,825
Total Current Liabilities	25,629	27,013
Total Liabilities	25,629	27,013
Net Assets		
Unrestricted		
Undesignated	746,217	598,358
Board designated - reserve fund	55,412	55,412
Board designated - special projects/ publications	56,102	48,086
Total Unrestricted	857,731	701,856
Temporarily restricted	457,636	353,951
Total Net Assets	1,315,367	1,055,807
Total Liabilities and Net Assets	**$ 1,340,996**	**$ 1,082,820**

The accompanying notes are an integral part of this statement.

STATEMENT OF ACTIVITIES AND CHANGES IN NET ASSETS
For the Year Ended June 30, 2011
(With comparative totals for year 2010)

	\multicolumn{4}{c	}{Unrestricted}	Temp- orarily Restricted	2011 Total	2010 Total
	Undesig- nated	Special Projects	Reserve Fund	Total			
Revenue							
Membership dues	$245,300	$ -	$ -	$245,300	$ -	$245,300	$252,500
Convention, workshops	132,737	-	-	132,737	-	132,737	112,929
Sale of publications	-	69,302	-	69,302	-	69,302	77,995
Contributions	-	-	-	-	56,540	56,540	9,815
Interest and dividends	7,816	-	-	7,816	5,831	13,647	14,354
Royalties	-	7,067	-	7,067	-	7,067	9,782
Reprint permissions	-	700	-	700	-	700	700
Appreciation on fair value of investments	79,603	-	-	79,603	60,350	139,953	84,030
Net assets released from restrictions	19,036	-	-	19,036	(19,036)	-	-
Total Revenue	484,492	77,069	-	561,561	103,685	665,246	562,105
Expenses							
Program Services							
Publications	-	69,053	-	69,053	-	69,053	76,454
Convention, workshops	95,267	-	-	95,267	-	95,267	93,079
Membership services	13,222	-	-	13,222	-	13,222	19,647
Committees	8,266	-	-	8,266	-	8,266	8,045
Holy See and Austrialia	1,974	-	-	1,974	-	1,974	8,288
Scholarship fund	19,036	-	-	19,036	-	19,036	14,752
Total Program Services	137,765	69,053	-	206,818	-	206,818	220,265
Supporting Services	198,868	-	-	198,868	-	198,868	196,449
Total Expenses	336,633	69,053	-	405,686	-	405,686	416,714
Changes in Net Assets	147,859	8,016	-	155,875	103,685	259,560	145,391
Net Assets - Beginning of Year	598,358	48,086	55,412	701,856	353,951	1,055,807	910,416
Net Assets - End of Year	$746,217	$56,102	$55,412	$857,731	$457,636	$1,315,367	$1,055,807

The accompanying notes are an integral part of this statement

STATEMENTS OF CASH FLOWS
For the Year Ended June 30, 2011

	2011	2010
Increase (Decrease) in Cash		
Cash Flows From Operating Activities		
Changes in Net Assets	$ 259,560	$ 145,391
Adjustments to reconcile changes in net assets to net cash provided by operating activities:		
Depreciation	1,756	2,262
Unrealized (gain) loss on investments	(139,953)	(84,030)
Change in assets and liabilities:		
(Increase) Decrease in accounts receivable	516	(1,231)
(Increase) Decrease in prepaid expenses	(6,055)	1,139
(Increase) Decrease in inventory	11,696	16,335
Increase (Decrease) in accounts payable	(4,432)	5,900
Increase (Decrease) in royalties payable	98	(30)
Increase (Decrease) in deferred revenue	2,950	13,100
Net Cash Provided by Operating Activities	126,136	98,836
Cash Flows From Investing Activities		
Purchase of investments	(53,596)	(14,251)
Purchases of fixed assets	(1,415)	(781)
Net Cash Used in Investing Activities	(55,011)	(15,032)
Increase in Cash and Cash Equivalents	71,125	83,804
Cash Balance - Beginning of Year	196,214	112,410
Cash Balance - End of Year	$ 267,339	$ 196,214
Supplemental Disclosures		
Income taxes paid	$ -	$ -
Interest paid	$ -	$ -

The accompanying notes are an integral part of this statement.

Notes to Financial Statements
For the Year Ended June 30, 2011 and 2010

1. Nature of Activities

The Canon Law Society of America (CLSA) is a national, not-for-profit corporation, established in November 1939 in Washington DC to promote canonical and pastoral approaches to significant issues within the Roman Catholic Church. In addition to a publication service, CLSA conducts an annual convention and other symposia to promote a better understanding of church law and its pastoral applications. Major sources of gross income are from membership dues, sales of publications and books and annual convention.

2. Basis of Financial Statement Presentation

According to Financial Accounting Standards Board (FASB) Codification Standards, CLSA is required to report information regarding its financial position and activities according to three classes of net assets:

> (1) *Unrestricted Net Assets* - represents resources that are currently available for support of CLSA's operations.
>
> (2) *Temporarily Restricted Net Assets* - represents resources that may be utilized only in accordance with the restricted purposes established by CLSA's bylaws. When a restriction expires, temporarily restricted net assets are reclassified to unrestricted net assets and reported in the statement of activities and net assets as funds are released from temporary restrictions.
>
> (3) *Permanently Restricted Net Assets* - represents resources for which the principal is to be maintained intact and the income, may only be spent in accordance with the intent of the donor. CLSA currently does not have any permanently restricted net assets.

The financial statements are prepared on the accrual basis of accounting, whereby, revenue is recognized when earned and expenses are recognized when incurred.

3. Summary of Significant Accounting Policies

Cash and cash equivalents - For purposes of the statement of cash flows, CLSA considers all cash accounts and all highly liquid debt instruments purchased with an initial maturity of three months or less to be cash equivalents.

Investments - Investments in marketable securities with readily determinable fair values are reported at their fair values in the statement of financial position. Investment income or loss (including gains and losses on investments, interest and dividends) is included in the statement of activities as an increase or decrease in unrestricted net assets unless the income or loss is restricted by donor or law.

Investments consist principally of two mutual funds. Fair value of investments in securities is based on the latest reported sales price at June 30, 2011.

Accounts receivable - Accounts receivable are stated at the amount management expects to collect from outstanding balances. The provision for uncollectible accounts is based on management's evaluation of the collectability of accounts receivable. CLSA considers accounts receivable to be fully collectible; accordingly, no provision for doubtful accounts is required. Books and publication receivables are considered uncollectible if not collected within 90 days after the sale.

Inventory - The inventory of books and publications is valued at cost, on the first-in, first-out method.

Property and Equipment - Purchases of furniture and equipment are recorded at cost. CLSA's policy is to capitalize expenditures for equipment purchased in the amount of $300 or more. Depreciation is calculated over an estimated useful life of five to ten years using the straight-line method. Depreciation and amortization for the years ended June 30, 2011 and 2010 totaled $1,756 and $2,262.

Fair Value - Financial Accounting Standards Board (FASB) Codification Standards defines fair value, establishes a framework for measuring fair value, and expands disclosures about fair value measurements and establishes a hierarchy for valuation inputs.

Fair value is the price that would be received to sell an asset or paid to transfer a liability in an orderly transaction between market participants at the measurement date. A fair value measurement assumes that the transaction to sell the asset or transfer the liability occurs in the principal market for the asset or liability or, in the absence of a principal market, the most advantageous market. Valuation techniques that are consistent with the market, income or cost approach are used to measure fair value.

The fair value hierarchy prioritizes the inputs to valuation techniques used to measure fair value into three broad levels:

- Level 1 - inputs are based upon unadjusted quoted prices for identical instruments traded in active markets.
- Level 2 - inputs are based upon quoted prices for similar instruments in active markets, quoted prices for identical or similar instruments in markets that are not active, and model-based valuation techniques for which all significant assumptions are observable in the market or can be corroborated by observable market data for substantially the full term of the assets or liabilities.

- Level 3 - inputs are generally unobservable and typically reflect management's estimates of assumptions that market participants would use in pricing the asset or liability. The fair values are therefore determined using model-based techniques that include option pricing models, discounted cash flow models, and similar techniques.

Revenue Recognition - CLSA bills membership dues annually on a basis which conforms to CLSA's fiscal year-end. Dues, workshop and convention registrations received in advance of the next fiscal year are deferred and recognized as revenue in the subsequent year.

Contributions are recognized when the donor makes a promise to give to the Society that is, in substance, unconditional. Contributions received are recorded as unrestricted, temporarily restricted, or permanently restricted support depending on the absence or existence and nature of any donor restrictions. Contributions restricted by the donor are reported as increases in unrestricted net assets if the restrictions are met or expire in the fiscal year in which the contributions are recognized. When a restriction expires, temporarily restricted net assets are reclassified as unrestricted net assets. Revenue from convention and workshop registration fees are recognized when the events take place.

Tax Status - CLSA is exempt from federal income tax under Section 501(c)(3) of the Internal Revenue Code. CLSA has not been classified by the Internal Revenue Service as a private foundation. Income which is not related to the exempt purpose, less applicable deductions, is subject to Federal and state corporate income tax. For tax purposes the organizations open audit years are 2008 to 2011.

Expense Allocations - Directly identifiable expenses are charged to programs and supporting services. Overhead and expenses related to more than one function are not allocated but are included in supporting services.

Estimates - In preparing financial statements in conformity with generally accepted accounting principles, management is required to make estimates and assumptions that affect the reported amounts of assets and liabilities, the disclosure of contingent assets and liabilities at the date of the financial statements, and the reported amounts of revenues and expenses during the reporting period. Actual results could differ from those estimates.

Financial Instruments - CLSA's financial instruments consist of investments, accounts receivable, accounts payable and accrued expenses. It is management's opinion the CLSA is not exposed to significant interest rate or credit risk arising from these instruments. Unless otherwise noted, the fair values of these financial instruments are market values of these financial instruments, and approximate their carrying values.

4. Investments

Investments at June 30, 2011 and 2010, which are all considered level 1, consist of the following:

	Cost	Market
Balanced funds	$909,418	$954,265
Total Investments 6/30/2011	$909,418	$954,265
Total Investments 6/30/2010	$855,823	$760,716

By fund type at June 30, 2011 and 2010:

	2011		2010	
	Cost	Market	Cost	Market
Unrestricted	$519,439	$553,794	$471,630	$426,382
Restricted	389,979	400,471	384,193	334,334
Total Investments	**$909,418**	**$954,265**	**$855,823**	**$760,716**

CLSA invests in a professionally managed portfolio that contains balanced funds. Such investments are exposed to various risks such as interest rates, market and credit. Due to the level of risk associated with such investments and the level of uncertainty related to changes in the value of such investments, it is at least reasonably possible that changes in risks in the near term would materially affect investment balances and the amounts reported in the financial statements.

Investment income, which is included in the Statement of Activities for the years ended June 30, 2011 and 2010 is comprised of the following:

	2011		2010	
	Unrestricted	Temporarily Restricted	Unrestricted	Temporarily Restricted
Net Unrealized gains (losses)	$79,603	$60,350	$48,305	$35,725
Interest and dividends	7,816	5,831	8,007	6,347
Net Investment Income	**$87,419**	**$66,181**	**$56,312**	**$42,072**

5. Concentration of Credit Risk

CLSA maintains its cash in bank deposit accounts, which at times, may exceed federally insured limits. CLSA has not experienced any losses in such accounts and believes it is not exposed to any significant financial risk on cash.

6. Commitments

Office Lease - CLSA leased office space in Washington DC for a 10 year period ending December 31, 2017. Monthly rent payments for the first through the fifth year of the lease are $1,564. Monthly rent payments for the sixth through the tenth year will be increase by the CPI each July 1st. Rent expense for the years ended June 30, 2011 and 2010 was $18,768. Minimum future rental obligations are: 2012 - $18,766; 2013 - $18,766; 2014 - $18,766; 2015 - $18,766; 2016 – 18,766; 2017 - $18,766.

Copier Lease - CLSA entered into a four year lease for a copier beginning August 2008. The lease payment is $230 per month. Minimum future lease obligations are as follows: 2012 - $2,760; 2013 - $460.

Postage Lease - CLSA entered into a fifty-four month lease for a postage machine ending November 1, 2010. The lease payment is $127 per quarter.

7. Board Designated Funds

The Board has designated that net income from the sales of publications and books be set aside for special purposes known as the special projects fund.

Balance - Beginning of Year		$48,086
Add	Publication income	69,302
	Royalty income	7,067
	Reprint permissions	700
Less	Publication expenses	(69,053)
Balance - End of Year		$56,102

The Board has designated $55,412 as a reserve account to be set aside for future purposes. The income from the reserve account is to be used for operations.

8. Temporarily Restricted Net Assets

The activity in the temporarily restricted net assets at June 30, 2011 is as follows:

	6/30/10	Income	Expenses	6/30/11
Scholarship Fund	$353,951	$122,721	$(19,036)	$457,636
Total	$353,951	$122,721	$(19,036)	$457,636

9. Annual Meeting Site Reservation Agreements

CLSA has reserved hotel space for future annual meetings. The terms of these reservation agreements provide that a few will be assessed to CSLA if the reservation is canceled due to site change, within a specified period prior to the meeting dates.

10. Executive Coordinator's Contract

CLSA has contracted with Sisters of Mercy of the Americas South Central Community and Sister Sharon Euart to serve as their Executive Coordinator beginning August 1, 2008 and ending July 31, 2011. The agreement has been renewed extending the contract date to December 31, 2012.

11. Subsequent Events

Management has evaluated subsequent events through November 21, 2011, the date that the financial statements were available to be issued. There were no significant events to report.

12. Reclassifications

Certain reclassifications have been made to prior year amounts to conform to the current year presentation. Those reclassifications consist primarily of cash and liabilities in the Scholarship fund that were included as investments in the prior year but have been separately reported in the current year.

Supplementary Information
Schedule of Program Services
For the Year Ended June 30, 2011

	2011	2010
Publications		
Cost of publications sold	$ 14,641	$ 22,741
Executive coordinator office	10,615	9,844
Royalty expense	1,786	1,927
Advertising	-	13
BrightKey	42,011	41,929
Total Publication Expenses	69,053	76,454
Convention and Pre-convention Workshop		
Coordination	49,494	67,763
Translation services	14,072	-
Pre-convention expenses	-	3,614
Food service	1,050	1,859
Honoraria	6,560	4,700
Speakers' travel	4,307	1,041
Printing	2,610	4,140
Freight	334	203
Other	3,269	816
Postage	1,133	2,021
Convention chair	1,002	1,649
Liturgy	1,797	950
Supplies	6,682	2,198
Convention planning	2,067	1,443
Convention company	330	145
Liturgy chair	560	537
Total Convention and Pre-Convention Workshop	95,267	93,079
Membership Services		
Postage	5,050	4,574
Printing	3,082	3,963
Newsletter	5,090	11,110
Total Membership Services	13,222	19,647

Schedule of Program Services continued

	2011	2010
Visit to Holy See and Australia Trip	1,974	8,288
Committees		
Church governance	$ 67	$ 2,965
Resource & asset management	198	1,620
Publications advisory board	3,930	1,088
Nominations	2,050	1,071
Clergy	703	-
Laity	959	739
Other	295	281
Advocacy registration	-	250
Sacramental law	64	31
Total Committees	8,266	8,045
Scholarship Fund		
Scholarships paid	18,250	14,000
Scholarships expenses	786	752
Total Scholarship Fund	19,036	14,752
Total Program Services	$ 206,818	$ 220,265

The accompanying notes are an integral part of this schedule.

Annual Budget
Fiscal Year 2011-2012

GENERAL OPERATIONS		
Income	$	230,000
Expenses	$	254,490
Excess/(Deficit)	**$**	**(24,490)**
PUBLICATIONS		
Income	$	150,600
Expenses	$	113,337
Excess/(Deficit)	**$**	**37,263**
CONVENTIONS		
Income	$	114,250
Expenses	$	113,300
Excess/(Deficit)	**$**	**950**
Subtotal Gen. Ops., Pub. & Conv.*	**$**	**13,723**
SCHOLARSHIP FUND		
Income	$	63,712
Expenses	$	63,500
Excess/(Deficit)	**$**	**212**
Grand Total*	**$**	**13,935**

*Note: Since the income in the Scholarship Fund by definition belongs to the Scholarship Fund, it cannot be used to balance the overall budget. Hence, the first three "companies" as a while need to achieve a balance independently, and the number labeled as "Grand Total" is not a simple "operational" profit. An excess in the Scholarhsip Fund represents an increase in the fund, which is needed for the fund to grow.

GENERAL OPERATIONS

	Budget FY 11-12	Actual FY 10-11	Budget FY 10-11	Actual FY 09-10	Budget FY 09-10
INCOME					
Investment Income/ CBIS	$ 5,000	$ 7,809	$ 6,000	$ 7,983	$ 6,000
Interest Income/RCT	$ -	$ 7	$ 50	$ 23	$ 3,000
Dues Income (Note 1)	$ 225,000	$ 245,300	$ 240,000	$ 252,500	$ 246,000
TOTAL INCOME	**$ 230,000**	**$ 253,116**	**$ 246,050**	**$ 260,506**	**$ 255,000**
EXPENSES					
Staff Compensations and Benefits (Note 2)	$ 131,772	$ 118,559	$ 117,430	$ 114,023	$ 115,680
Service Charges					
Bank Service Charges/Wachovia	$ 50	$ 93	$ 50	$ 1	
Flex Fund/RCT	$ 100	$ 90	$ 100	$ 38	
Credit Card Fees	$ 6,000	$ 2,867	$ 6,500	$ 2,983	$ 7,500
Sub-total	$ 6,150	$ 3,050	$ 6,650	$ 3,021	$ 7,500
OEC Expenses (by account number)					
Postage Meter Lease and Supplies	$ 1,100	$ 1,110	$ 900	$ 568	$ 900
Insurance & Workers Compensation	$ 2,500	$ 1,984	$ 2,500	$ 2,103	$ 2,000
Hospitality	$ 500	$ 526	$ 500	$ 359	$ 500
Postage/UPS/FedEx	$ 800	$ 766	$ 1,000	$ 713	$ 750
Office Supplies	$ 2,500	$ 2,784	$ 2,800	$ 2,956	$ 3,500
Telephone/ISP/DSL	$ 3,000	$ 3,191	$ 3,500	$ 2,778	$ 3,800
Travel	$ 2,500	$ 1,680	$ 3,000	$ 1,554	$ 3,000
Taxes	$ 100	$ -	$ 100	$ 135	$ 200
Furniture & Equipment	$ 1,000	$ 933	$ 1,000	$ 1,006	$ 1,200
Books and Periodicals	$ 400	$ 206	$ 400	$ 273	$ 500
Prof. Collaboration w/ National Orgs.	$ 500	$ 2,345	$ 500	$ 1,278	
Rent	$ 18,768	$ 18,768	$ 18,768	$ 18,768	$ 18,768
Copier Lease & Maintenance	$ 4,300	$ 3,508	$ 3,700	$ 3,577	$ 3,750
Sub-total	$ 37,968	$ 37,800	$ 38,668	$ 36,069	$ 38,868

GENERAL OPERATIONS continutued

	Budget FY 11-12	Actual FY 10-11	Budget FY 10-11	Actual FY 09-10	Budget FY 09-10
Professional Services					
Accountant/Auditor (Note 4)	$ 6,000	$ 6,000	$ 6,000	$ 6,000	$ 6,000
Web Design & Maintenance	$ 5,500	$ 5,940	$ 6,500	$ 8,925	$ 11,300
Legal Services	$ 500	$ -	$ 500	$ -	$ 1,000
Sub-total	$ 12,000	$ 11,940	$ 13,000	$ 14,925	$ 18,300
Member Services					
General Printing	$ -	$ -	$ 100	$ -	$ 100
General Postage	$ 1,000	$ 1,038	$ 1,500	$ 350	$ 1,800
Newsletter Printing (Note 5)	$ 500	$ 2,463	$ 5,500	$ 6,778	$ 8,000
Newsletter Postage (Note 5)	$ 500	$ 2,627	$ 4,000	$ 4,332	$ 3,000
Proceedings Printing	$ 5,000	$ 4,574	$ 6,500	$ 3,963	$ 8,500
Proceedings Postage	$ 4,000	$ 4,012	$ 5,500	$ 4,225	$ 4,500
Sub-total	$ 11,000	$ 14,714	$ 23,100	$ 19,647	$ 25,900
Board of Governors, Meetings					
Food	$ 5,400	$ 4,305	$ 5,500	$ 3,410	$ 5,600
Lodging	$ 12,000	$ 11,311	$ 11,000	$ 9,412	$ 9,000
Meeting Space	$ 500	$ 664	$ 500	$ 500	$ 500
Postage/UPS	$ 100	$ 11	$ 100	$ 38	$ 250
Supplies	$ 50	$ 125	$ 100	$ 30	$ 100
Telephone	$ 100	$ 96			
Travel	$ 9,500	$ 6,029	$ 8,500	$ 6,206	$ 9,000
Rome or Australia Trip	$ 10,000	$ 1,974	$ 10,000	$ 8,288	$ 10,000
Sub-total	$ 37,650	$ 24,515	$ 35,700	$ 27,884	$ 34,450
Board of Governors, Officers					
President	$ 6,000	$ 3,164	$ 7,000	$ 3,862	$ 7,000
Vice President/Past President	$ 700	$ 853	$ 1,000	$ 568	$ 1,500
Treasurer/Secretary (Note 6)	$ 500	$ -	$ 600	$ 242	$ 600
Sub-total	$ 7,200	$ 4,017	$ 8,600	$ 6,672	$ 9,100
Seminars & Meetings					
Special Faculties Seminar (Note 7)		$ (4,567)			
Sub-total		$ (4,567)			

GENERAL OPERATIONS continutued

	Budget FY 11-12	Actual FY 10-11	Budget FY 10-11	Actual FY 09-10	Budget FY 09-10
Committees					
Constitutional Committees *(order of Const.)*					
Nominations Committee	$ 1,800	$ 2,050	$ 1,500	$ 1,071	$ 3,000
Resolutions Committee	$ 100	$ -	$ 100	$ -	$ 100
Resource & Asset Management	$ 1,500	$ 198	$ 1,500	$ 1,620	$ 2,000
Professional Responsibilities Committee	$ -	$ -	$ 200	$ -	$ 100
Standing Committees *(alphabetical)*					
Church Governance Committee	$ 250	$ 67	$ 2,000	$ 2,965	
Clergy Committee	$ 1,500	$ 703	$ 500	$ -	$ 200
Institutes of Consecrated Life Cmte.	$ 150	$ -	$ 400	$ -	$ 100
Laity Committee	$ 2,500	$ 959	$ 2,500	$ 739	
Research & Development	$ 250	$ -	$ 100	$ -	$ 750
Sacramental Law Committee	$ 1,200	$ 64	$ 1,200	$ 31	$ 1,200
Approved Cmte. Work Contingency	$ 1,000	$ 296	$ 1,000	$ 281	$ 1,000
Sub-total	$ 10,250	$ 4,337	$ 11,000	$ 6,707	$ 8,450
Miscellaneous					
General Operations Contingencies	$ 500	$ -	$ 500		$ 1,000
Sub-total	$ 500	$ -	$ 500	$ -	$ 1,000
Additional Transactions - Previous FY					
Secretary (Note 6)		$ -	$ 100	$ -	$ 100
Publications Advisory Board (Note 8)		$ 2,362	$ 2,400	$ 1,088	$ 2,500
Canon Law Digest Committee (Note 8)		$ -	$ 500	$ -	$ 2,000

GENERAL OPERATIONS continuted

	Budget FY 11-12	Actual FY 10-11	Budget FY 10-11	Actual FY 09-10	Budget FY 09-10
Former Committees					
Advisory Opinions Committee		$ -	$ 100	$ -	$ 100
Diocesan Synods Task Force				$ -	$ 100
Professional Responsibility Rev. Task Force				$ -	$ 2,100
Reg. Workshops for Adv. In Penal Cases				$ 250	$ 100
Roman Replies Committee				$ -	$ 100
Sub-total		$ 2,362	$ 3,100	$ 1,338	$ 7,100
TOTAL EXPENSES	**$ 254,490**	**$ 216,726**	**$ 257,748**	**$ 230,286**	**$ 266,348**
EXCESS/DEFICIT	**$ (24,490)**	**$ 36,389**	**$ (11,698)**	**$ 30,220**	**$ (11,348)**

Note 1: This line includes all income from dues (past dues, current dues and new member dues).

Note 2: This line includes the Executive Coordinator & Executive Assistant salaries, compensation for one Temporary Assistant, all medical benefits, payroll taxes and a minimal cost for outsourcing the payroll for one employee.

Note 3: An additional line is provided for an optional temporary assistant to be used as needed.

Note 4. This item is apportioned between General Ops and Publications, at a distribution rate of 75% and 25% respectively.

Note 5: These line items are based on four Newsletters distributed electronically.

Note 6: The Secretary and Treasurer now share one budget line, whereas in the past they each had a separate budget.

Note 7: This negative number represents a profit of $4,567 from the seminar.

Note 8: These committees' expenses are now included in the Publications Budget.

PUBLICATIONS

	Budget FY 11-12	Actual FY 10-11	Budget FY 10-11	Actual FY 09-10	Budget FY 09-10
INCOME					
Publication Sales	$ 100,000	$ 56,621	$ 90,000	$ 62,915	$ 65,000
Reprint Permissions	$ 600	$ 700	$ 400	$ 700	$ 300
Royalty Income	$ 5,000	$ 7,382	$ 5,000	$ 9,782	$ 9,000
Shipping/Restocking - BrightKey	$ 40,000	$ 11,983	$ 20,000	$ 15,080	$ 20,000
Resolution Implementation (Note 1)	$ 5,000				
TOTAL INCOME	**$ 150,600**	**$ 76,686**	**$ 115,400**	**$ 88,477**	**$ 94,300**
EXPENSES					
Staff & Professional Services					
Staff Salary (Note 2)	$ 4,237	$ 3,509	$ 3,509	$ 3,342	$ 3,342
Accountant	$ 2,000	$ 2,000	$ 2,000	$ 2,000	$ 2,000
Publications Advisory Board (Note 3)	$ 2,150				
Canon Law Digest Committee (Note 3)	$ 500				
Sub-total	$ 8,887	$ 5,509	$ 5,509	$ 5,342	$ 5,342
Royalties Paid					
Royalties/*CCEO*	$ 250	$ 181	$ 400	$ 192	$ 450
Royalties/*CIC*	$ 1,500	$ 1,106	$ 1,200	$ 1,229	$ 1,400
Royalties/*Dignitas Connubii*	$ 450	$ 423	$ 500	$ 339	$ 600
Royalties/*Selected Issues*	$ 100	$ 58	$ 100	$ 119	$ 200
Royalties/*Reception and Communion*	$ 50	$ 18	$ 100	$ 48	$ 50
Sub-total	$ 2,350	$ 1,786	$ 2,300	$ 1,927	$ 2,700
Publication Expenses					
Advertising - Printing	$ 500	$ -	$ 1,500	$ 13	$ 1,000
Advertising - Electronic	$ 500	$ -	$ 500	$ -	$ 1,000
Book Production	$ 40,000	$ 4,067	$ 40,000	$ 1,005	$ 25,000
Storage of Negatives	$ 100	$ 88	$ 100	$ 78	$ 100
Copyright Applications	$ 150	$ 70	$ 150	$ 175	$ 150
Outsourcing - BrightKey	$ 50,000	$ 42,011	$ 47,000	$ 41,929	$ 47,000
Sub-total	$ 91,250	$ 46,236	$ 89,250	$ 43,201	$ 74,250

PUBLICATIONS continued

	Budget FY 11-12	Actual FY 10-11	Budget FY 10-11	Actual FY 09-10	Budget FY 09-10
Office of the Executive Coordinator					
Postage	$ 200	$ 80	$ 200	$ 104	$ 400
Supplies	$ 100	$ 154	$ 100	$ 39	
Sub-total	$ 300	$ 234	$ 300	$ 142	$ 400
Special Projects Resolution Implementation (Note 1)	$ 5,000				
Sub-total	$ 5,000				
Service Charges Bank Service Charges - Wachovia	$ 50	$ -	$ 50	$ -	$ 50
Credit Card Fees	$ 5,000	$ 2,099	$ 5,000	$ 3,101	$ 4,500
Sub-total	$ 5,050	$ 2,099	$ 5,050	$ 3,101	$ 4,550
Miscellaneous Publications Contingencies	$ 500	$ -	$ 500	$ -	$ 500
Sub-total	$ 500	$ -	$ 500	$ -	$ 500
TOTAL EXPENSES	**$ 113,337**	**$ 55,865**	**$ 106,309**	**$ 54,801**	**$ 92,242**
EXCESS/DEFICIT	**$ 37,263**	**$ 20,822**	**$ 9,091**	**$ 33,676**	**$ 2,058**

Note 1: These lines are for the Resolution approved by the membership at the 2010 convention.

Note 2: Publications is currently responsible for 10% of staff salary only.

Note 3: The Committees associated with Publications were previously in the General Operations budget.

CONVENTIONS

	Budget FY 11-12	Actual FY 10-11	Budget FY 10-11	Actual FY 09-10	Budget FY 09-10
INCOME					
Convention Fees (Note 1)	$ 97,500	$ 103,750	$ 105,625	$ 94,300	$ 99,125
Pre-Conv. Fees (Note 2)	$ 13,750	$ 19,800	$ 15,000	$ 15,875	$ 18,750
Exhibitors' Fees	$ 2,700	$ 3,470	$ 3,600	$ 2,700	$ 4,500
Sponsors' Donations	$ -	$ 300	$ -	$ -	$ 1,000
Additional Banquet Fees	$ 100	$ 300	$ -	$ 54	
Guest Registrations	$ 200	$ 550	$ -		
Contribution from Gen Ops (Note 3)	$ -	$ (24,950)			
TOTAL INCOME	**$ 114,250**	**$ 103,220**	**$ 124,225**	**$ 112,929**	**$ 123,375**
EXPENSES (Note 4)					
Professional Services					
General Conv. Chair	$ 1,800	$ 1,022	$ 1,800	$ 1,649	$ 1,800
Conv. Liturgy Chair	$ 600	$ 560	$ 600	$ 537	$ 500
Conv. Planning Cmte	$ 2,000	$ 2,067	$ 2,000	$ 1,443	$ 2,000
Office of the Executive Coordinator	$ 1,000	$ 998			
Convention Company	$ 500	$ 330	$ 700	$ 145	$ 700
Sub-total	$ 5,900	$ 4,957	$ 5,100	$ 3,773	$ 5,000
Pre-Convention					
Honoraria	$ 3,000	$ 3,000	$ 3,000	$ 3,000	$ 3,000
Liturgy	$ 400	$ 400	$ 400	$ 400	$ 400
Printing	$ 200	$ -	$ 500	$ 45	$ 1,000
Shipping	$ 50	$ -	$ 50	$ 27	$ 100
Speaker's Travel	$ 1,500	$ 1,256	$ 300		
Supplies	$ 200	$ 13	$ 200	$ 142	
Sub-total	$ 5,350	$ 4,669	$ 4,450	$ 3,614	$ 4,500
Convention					
Convention Company/ Nix (Note 5)	$ 39,000	$ 32,296	$ 76,000	$ 35,100	$ 80,000
Convention Hotel/ Hyatt (Note 5)	$ 27,000	$ 11,237		$ 32,663	
Audio Visual (Note 5)	$ 8,000	$ 5,960			
Food	$ 2,000	$ 1,050	$ 1,200	$ 1,859	$ 1,500
Honoraria (Note 6)	$ 5,500	$ 3,560	$ 3,900	$ 4,700	$ 4,800
Liturgy	$ 2,000	$ 1,397	$ 1,500	$ 950	$ 2,500
Postage	$ 2,200	$ 1,133	$ 2,200	$ 2,022	$ 1,500
Printing	$ 4,000	$ 2,610	$ 6,000	$ 4,140	$ 9,000
Shipping	$ 500	$ 334	$ 500	$ 203	$ 600
Speaker's Travel	$ 1,200	$ 3,050	$ 2,500	$ 1,041	$ 2,000
Supplies	$ 7,000	$ 6,669	$ 4,000	$ 2,198	$ 5,500
Telephone/Internet	$ 100	$ -	$ 150	$ 60	
Sub-total	$ 98,500	$ 69,296	$ 97,950	$ 84,935	$ 107,400

CONVENTIONS continued

	Budget FY 11-12	Actual FY 10-11	Budget FY 10-11	Actual FY 09-10	Budget FY 09-10
Service Charges					
Bank Service Charges/ Wachovia	$ 50	$ -	$ 50	$ 35	$ 50
Credit Card Fees	$ 3,000	$ 2,271	$ 1,000	$ 642	
Sub-total	$ 3,050	$ 2,271	$ 1,050	$ 677	$ 50
Miscellaneous					
Conventions Contingencies	$ 500	$ -	$ 500		
Sub-total	$ 500		$ 500	$ -	$ -
Additional Transactions - Previous FY					
Pre-Convention Postage		$ -	$ 50		
Translation Services (Note 7)		$ 14,072	$ 10,400		
Sub-total	$ -	$ 14,072	$ 10,400	$ -	$ -
TOTAL EXPENSES	**$ 113,300**	**$ 95,265**	**$ 119,450**	**$ 92,999**	**$ 116,950**
EXCESS/DEFICIT	**$ 950**	**$ 7,955**	**$ 4,775**	**$ 19,930**	**$ 6,425**

Note 1: Assume 300 attendees @ $325 each.

Note 2: Assume 55 attendees @ $250 each.

Note 3: This contribution from General Operations was made to cover the hotel bill in 2008.

Note 4: The expenses for Fiscal Year 2010-2011 include all reimbursements received from the Canadian Canon Law Society for joint expenses incurred during the 2010 simultaneous conventions.

Note 5: This used to incompass all hotel fees, the Nix bill (coordination fees) and Audio Visual fees; we are now splitting up these expenses into three separate accounts.

Note 6: This line reflects an increase in honoraria payments to speakers, the last increase was in 1992.

Note 7: The CLSA did not pay the Translation Service Company for the translation of the Keynote Speaker (Bishop Arrieta) during the 2010 convention; however, we were obligated to pay the equipment rental fees (a separate company).

SCHOLARSHIP FUND

	Budget FY 11-12	Actual FY 10-11	Budget FY 10-11	Actual FY 09-10	Budget FY 09-10
INCOME					
Investment Income					
Interest Income/Wachovia	$ 100	$ 44	$ 150	$ 79	$ 300
Sub-Total	$ 100	$ 44	$ 150	$ 79	$ 300
Transferred Funds Income					
Board Des. Res. Reserve Fund (Note 1)	$ 55,412				
Sub-Total	$ 55,412				
Scholarship Donations Income					
Donations Accompanying Dues	$ 1,200	$ 1,475	$ 1,500	$ 2,085	$ -
Donations from Appeal	$ 6,000	$ 7,295	$ 6,000	$ 7,330	$ 7,000
Donations from Convention	$ -	$ 200	$ -	$ 400	
Donations from Regional Meetings (Note 2)	$ 1,000	$ 1,570	$ 1,000		
Donation from Bequest		$ 40,000			
Sub-Total	$ 8,200	$ 50,540	$ 8,500	$ 9,815	$ 7,000
TOTAL INCOME	**$ 63,712**	**$ 50,584**	**$ 8,650**	**$ 9,894**	**$ 7,300**
EXPENSES					
Service Charges					
Money Market Fees/ Wachovia	$ 50	$ 20	$ 50	$ -	$ 50
Sub-total	$ 50	$ 20	$ 50	$ -	$ 50
Postage					
General Postage	$ 50	$ 7	$ 50	$ 2	$ 150
Appeal Postage	$ 800	$ 615	$ 800	$ 641	$ 700
Sub-total	$ 850	$ 622	$ 850	$ 643	$ 850
Printing					
General Printing	$ 200	$ -	$ 200	$ -	$ 600
Appeal Printing	$ 200	$ 144	$ 200	$ 108	$ 50
Sub-total	$ 400	$ 144	$ 400	$ 108	$ 650
Scholarships					
Current Awards (Note 3)	$ 28,000	$ 18,250	$ 21,000	$ 14,000	$ 14,000
Approved Future Awards (Note 4)	$ 21,000				
Sub-total	$ 49,000	$ 18,250	$ 21,000	$ 14,000	$ 14,000

SCHOLARSHIP FUND continued

	Budget FY 11-12	Actual FY 10-11	Budget FY 10-11	Actual FY 09-10	Budget FY 09-10
Transfers to Scholarship CUIT Fund (Note 5)					
Residue from Board Des. Res. Reserve Fund	$ 5,000				
Transfer of Scholarship Donation Income	$ 8,200				
Sub-Total	$ 13,200				
TOTAL EXPENSES	**$ 63,500**	**$ 19,036**	**$ 22,300**	**$ 14,751**	**$ 15,550**
EXCESS/DEFICIT	**$ 212**	**$ 31,549**	**$ (13,650)**	**$ (4,857)**	**$ (8,250)**

Note 1: This transfer is to close, as recommended by the auditor during the FY 2009-2010 audit, the 'Board Designated Restricted Reserve Fund'. This transfer was approved by resolution of the Board in June 2011.

Note 2: FY 2010-11 was the first year to designate these donations as a separate line item.

Note 3: Assumes 4 awards at $7,000 each.

Note 4: This line is to represent the awards approved to current scholarship recipients - to be given out in future fiscal years.

Note 5: These lines represent transfers from the operating Scholarship Wachovia Money Market account to the Scholarship Investment Account. An indication that the Society is dedicated in building up the Scholarship Investment Fund.

Officer's Report

Report of the Executive Coordinator
Sister Sharon A. Euart, RSM

August 2011 marked the completion of the three year term of the Executive Coordinator. It seems an appropriate time to review the work of Office of the Executive Coordinator for that period as we look forward to the coming years. I remain grateful to the members of the Society and to the Board of Governors for your assistance and support in addressing the needs of the Society and how best to carry out its mission. In this three-year review I will offer observations on the accomplishments, activities, challenges and future initiatives in the four areas of service: general operations, conventions, publications, and scholarship. I will also offer a few personal reflections on future trends for the Society.

GENERAL OPERATIONS
OEC Staffing
We are pleased to announce that on August 17 Katie Richards, Executive Assistant, gave birth to Brigid Elizabeth, a beautiful baby girl. During Katie's maternity leave we were fortunate to have Amy Tadlock, a CUA JCL candidate completing her thesis, assist us in the office on a part-time basis. In addition, Carlos Sacasa, also a CUA JCL student, provided staff assistance when needed. This was most helpful since the months of August and September are generally busy times for the OEC with end of the fiscal year activities and preparation for the annual convention. At the end of July we congratulated Susan Mulheron on completing her JCL and thanked her for her two years of excellent service to the Society as our student administrative assistant. Susan is returning to the Archdioceses of St. Paul/Minneapolis to serve as a judge in the Archdiocesan Tribunal. The Archdiocese is fortunate to be getting an excellent canonist and a wonderful person to serve the Tribunal. We will miss her presence in Suite 111. We are grateful for the excellent staff we have and are most appreciative of their service to the Society and its members.

Website Management
In July 2009, we launched the new CLSA website with YourMembership.com as the host. Since that time, we have made numerous improvements in the site including, for example, online payment of dues and event registration and evaluation, download availability of resources to members and non-members, online opportunities for BOG and committee interaction, surveys, and web-conferencing. With the technical knowledge of Katie and Susan, we continue to identify and develop new features that will enhance the site and provide increased op-

portunities and services to members and non-members.

The number of online publications available on the website has increased since the 2010 convention. We have added *Marriage Studies V* and the 1983-2000 *Roman Replies & CLSA Advisory Opinions* to our electronic publications catalogue. The out-of-print 1983-1995 volumes of *RRAO* are free to members and available for a modest fee to others. These publications are available in our Online Bookstore under Publication Downloads. At its recent meeting the Publications Advisory Board discussed making available additional volumes of *AO* as downloads from the website. The PAB's plan is to upload all volumes of *AO* except the most recent two years thereby eliminating the need for the compilation volumes of *AO*. Please see the report of the PAB in this Booklet for more detailed information

With the electronic publication of all four 2011-2012 *CLSA Newsletters*, we envision providing more visuals, sharper photos and links for our readers thereby increasing not only the use of the CLSA website but also other websites containing relevant and up-to-date information for our members. It is worth noting that since the 2009 launching of the new website, the number of members paying dues online and registering for the annual convention and workshops has increased significantly. For the current fiscal year, the vast majority of members who have paid dues have done so online; the same is true for the 2011 convention. Registration for the February Special Faculties Seminar was conducted only online as was the evaluation of the workshop. This is a trend we anticipate will continue to increase in the future.

We are pleased to announce the availability of the second printing of the *New English Translation of the Code of Canon Law: Latin English Translation* as an e-book and a physical book. Both editions contain the changes introduced in *Omnium in mentem* as well as editorial corrections. The e-book and the physical book will be available on the CLSA website in the Online Bookstore. Please see the flyer in your convention bags for details regarding cost and dates of availability for each version.

In my 2010 annual report, I noted that an implication of the increased use of electronic technology is the need for staff skilled and knowledgeable about website management, new upgrades, IT networks, and advances in electronic publication. This requires a review of the position descriptions and shift in the key competencies needed in the OEC to serve the members and the mission of the Society. It also will require planning in order to provide adequate compensation for such competencies. It is worth noting that in utilizing the IT skills and knowledge of our current OEC staff, the CLSA has saved significant dollars that would otherwise have been paid to technology consultants. We are most grateful for this contribution!

Membership

A positive outcome of the new website has been the increase in CLSA membership over the past three years, with the largest increase occurring during 2009-2010. For the three fiscal years we experienced a growth in total membership of 202 members – 99 active, 46 associate and 57 students. Of this group, one half are diocesan priests and just over one quarter are lay persons; the remaining percentage is comprised of religious men and women and permanent deacons. It would seem that the increase in the number of new lay members will continue to increase while the number of new religious continues to decline. Another factor in the profile of new members is the international characteristic. Almost one quarter of the new members for this period are from outside the United States with the larger numbers coming from Canada, United Kingdom, Italy, Ireland, Kenya and Scotland. Many of the new members find the CLSA through the website and apply for membership online. We continue to be encouraged by the increasing number of students who join the Society as members. It is important that we encourage such membership and participation in the activities of the Society; many of them will be our future leaders. They come to us with a knowledge and experience of electronic technology that will influence the range services that the CLSA will develop and provide in the near future.

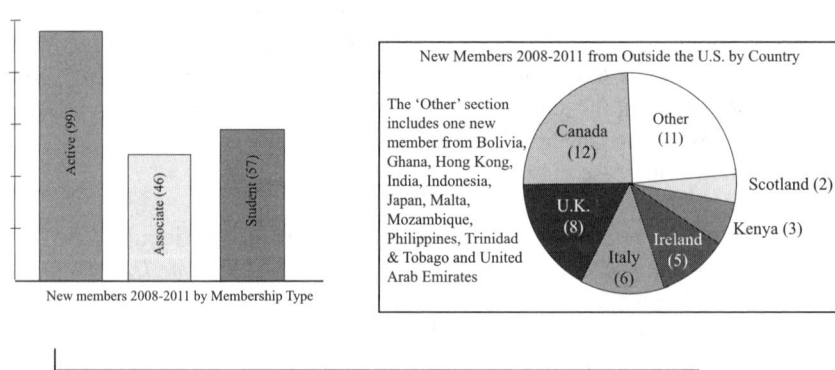

New members 2008-2011 by Membership Type

New Members 2008-2011 from Outside the U.S. by Country

The 'Other' section includes one new member from Bolivia, Ghana, Hong Kong, India, Indonesia, Japan, Malta, Mozambique, Philippines, Trinidad & Tobago and United Arab Emirates

Canada (12), Other (11), Scotland (2), Kenya (3), Ireland (5), Italy (6), U.K. (8)

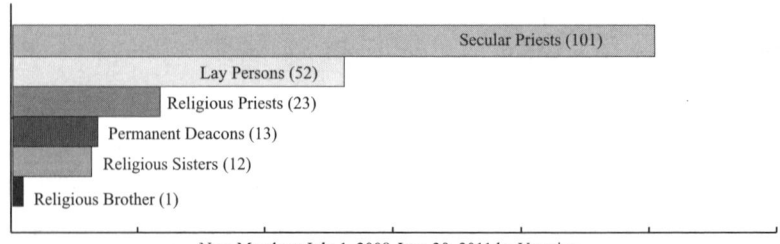

Secular Priests (101)
Lay Persons (52)
Religious Priests (23)
Permanent Deacons (13)
Religious Sisters (12)
Religious Brother (1)

New Members July 1, 2008-June 30, 2011 by Vocation

Operational Costs

We are pleased to report that again this year General Operations ended the fiscal year in the black despite a projected shortfall. This is due to several factors:

• An increase in the number of members paying dues this year enabled us to

attain 101.55% of the 2010-2011 budgeted amounts. In January of this year we contacted those who had not yet paid dues for the current year and this resulted in a significant increase in those paying for the current year.
- CLSA new membership continues to increase thereby exceeding the budgeted amount for 2010-2011.
- Success of the February Seminar on Special Faculties from the Congregation for the Clergy.
- Savings on the printing and postage for the CLSA *Newsletter* as a result of publishing two issues electronically was considerable. For the coming year all four issues will be made available electronically to members.
- Expenses for the President's bi-annual trip to the meeting of the Canon Law Society of Australia and New Zealand were less than budgeted due to cost-savings in travel.
- Expenses for CLSA committees were significantly lower than projected. This was due to the use of web-conferencing and conference calls in some instances and to less activity this year for other committees.

While we believe we have been responsible in reducing General Operations expenses, it will be important in the future to maintain minimally the current level of income for General Operations in order to maintain or increase the level of service to members.

Collaboration with Other Groups

In response to the Future Initiatives Report 2008 recommendations, we have initiated or responded to opportunities to collaborate with the United States Conference of Catholic Bishops, other Catholic organizations in the Washington, DC areas and elsewhere in the United States and in Rome. For the past three years we have participated in annual gatherings of the executive directors and staff of the national Catholic organizations located in the Washington metropolitan area. In addition we continue to have on-going relationships with CARA, the USCCB, RCRI and other national organizations. This past August the Symposium on Lay Ecclesial Ministry, for which the CLSA is a co-sponsor, held the second symposium at St. John's in Collegeville, MN. The CLSA had four participants: Rev. James Donlon, Mrs. Rita Joyce, Mrs. Siobhan Verbeck and Ms. Zabrina Decker. Prior to the symposium the participants reviewed papers that were presented, participated in webinars that provided up-to-date information on various aspects of lay ecclesial ministry. Following the symposium, the participants reported on the four day event in an article which was published in the September CLSA *Newsletter*. The CLSA delegates described the symposium as "an awe-inspiring experience" during which the presence of the CLSA participants was affirmed. They contributed to the discussions and often added clarity regarding the use of canonical language and the particularity of church structures. All considered the meeting a cause for hope, an opportunity for the Society to make a contribution at the national level, and expressed gratitude for the opportunity to be a part of the conversation.

Seminar On the Special Faculties from the Congregation for the Clergy

The February workshop on the Special Faculties from the Congregation for the Clergy which was held at the Bethany Center in Tampa, FL was well attended and well received. Msgr. Anthony McDaid from the Congregation for the Clergy was the presenter. The participants highly recommended that the CLSA sponsor more such workshops highlighting the smaller size, speaker-group interaction, prayer and social opportunities, and current topic as most beneficial and desirable. The OEC provides the staff back up for any committee wishing to sponsor or co-sponsor such opportunities. From all perspectives, the February seminar was a successful endeavor.

CLSA Committees

The formation of the new structure of CLSA committee recommended by the Future Initiative Project has evolved over the past three years. All the committees have been established; two have been re-constituted over the past two years. The updated mandates for the committees have helped focus the work of the committees and identify areas for new initiatives. Some of the committees had ongoing projects resulting for the 2008 consolidation; new committees continue to explore new directions. With fewer ongoing committees it is critical that the committees actively engage the membership through publications, workshops, seminars, web-conferences, surveys, think tanks, online discussions or other means to promote the educational mission of the Society. Such projects can bring energy and enthusiasm to the members and revenue to the Society, both of which are increasingly important today.

CLSA Handbooks

One of the goals of the Executive Coordinator and the OEC has been to develop several handbooks or manuals to assist those responsible for various aspects of leadership in the Society. During the past three years, we have completed the following handbooks/manuals: Board of Governors Handbook (2009), Committee Handbook (2009) and Convention Manual (2011). These resources contain the various policies and procedures, roles and responsibilities that pertain to the proper functioning of the respective groups. Each handbook/manual is updated annually following the annual convention.

Auditor

The CLSA has engaged the services of Linton, Shafer, Warfield & Garrett, PA, Certified Public Accountants as our new auditor beginning with the 2010-2011 audit. The company is a regional firm, operating in the Washington area for over 45 years. The firm has approximately 40 non-profit clients in the area all served by the Rockville, MD office. The firm conducts the audit for the Catholic national organizations that share offices in the Silver Spring area: CMSM, LCWR, RCRI, and RFC. We are most grateful to Mr. Joseph Godbout for his dedication to the CLSA and for his service as auditor and accountant for twenty years. His assistance over the years is most appreciated.

CONVENTIONS

The 72nd convention in Buffalo was, by all accounts, a very successful convention. It was well received by the attendees and the evaluations are overwhelmingly positive especially with regard to the program and speakers. While we cannot anticipate the same level of attendance for future conventions, it is clear that an attractive program, even more than the city or hotel, generates more attendees. The in-kind contributions of the Diocese of Buffalo, Diocese of Youngstown and others helped significantly to defray cost for the 2010 convention – a factor that we cannot budget for each year but for which we are most grateful.

We continue to work closely with the Convention Planning Committee and the Convention Chairperson for the 2011 convention in Jacksonville. We completed preparation of the new Convention Manual which provides detailed information regarding roles and responsibilities, convention program and policies. It was distributed to those involved in the planning and execution of CLSA conventions. Once again, the staff of the OEC prepared the materials for distribution during the 2011 convention. This enables us to keep the expenses for printing and mailing at a minimum.

PUBLICATIONS

The full report on CLSA publications can be found in the report of the Publications Advisory Board. The PAB continues to be a valuable resource for the Executive Coordinator and the OEC. Its expertise, research and advice with the preparation and publication of CLSA publications is greatly appreciated. Its service in coordinating the publication efforts of the CLSA have enabled the Society to move forward in an organized and responsible way, including the CLSA's entry into electronic publishing. During this fiscal year there were no new CLSA publications with the exception of *CLSA Proceedings* and *Roman Replies and CLSA Advisory Opinions,* which are annual membership services. PAB is working with CLSA committees in the preparation of pastoral resources that might be made available to a broad audience of pastoral ministers as well as canon lawyers.

We continue to make four CLSA publications available on Amazon.com and hope to expand the number of publications in the future. This move, however, depends on the availability of OEC staff to fill the orders within two days as required by Amazon.

SCHOLARSHIPS

As we reported in the recent CLSA *Newsletter* we are pleased to have offered one scholarship this year to Ms. Annette Wellman who will begin studies in canon law at St. Paul's in Ottawa. The appeal was held this year during Lent of 2011 and generated not only an increase over the budgeted amount but also a very generous bequest from the estate of Eleanor Fazzalaro and Msgr. Francis Fazzalaro. Msgr. Fazzalaro graduated with his JCD from Catholic University in

1949 and was a long time CLSA member until his death in 2007. We are also grateful for the contribution made by Regional Meetings. This year we received over $1500 from the regional conferences.

As in the recent past, we received contributions memory of members who have served the Society and are now deceased. We made want to acknowledge these memorials in a meaningful way on the website, in the CLSA *Newsletter*, and in our annual report.

Scholarship contributions were made in memory of the following:

> *Rev. Dennis Burns*
> *Rev. Ricardo Garcia*
> *Rev. Joseph Morrell*
> *Rev. Cecil Parres, C.M.*
> *Rev. Fred Sackett, O.M.I.*
>
> **May they rest in peace**

GOALS FOR THE OFFICE OF THE EXECUTIVE COORDINATOR

Three years ago, I identified the following goals for my term as Executive Coordinator:

1. To hire the staff necessary to carry out administrative and financial responsibilities, including, but not limited to, computer proficiency, data entry/management, means of communication such as website and *Newsletter* development, and bookkeeping procedures;
2. To initiate contact with Catholic organizations and groups whose mission and agendas include canonical matters or issues having canonical implications;
3. To seek opportunities to collaborate and cooperate with other groups whose educational goals might benefit from the CLSA's canonical input and expertise;
4. To be present to groups and/or activities with and in which the CLSA might have an interest and through which the Society's service to the broader Church might be enhanced;
5. To assist in implementation of the recommendations of the Futures Initiative Project as approved by the Board of Governors.

Having completed my initial term as Executive Coordinator on August 1, 2011, with the assistance of dedicated and competent staff, I believe we have accomplished a great deal; yet there is more to do to make the Society a vibrant and valuable resource for the canonical community and the Church. I will continue to focus on how the OEC can better serve the membership while, at the same time, introducing procedures and services that will help move the Society forward for the years to come.

I am grateful for your support and welcome your suggestions or comments on how the Office of the Executive Coordinator might better serve you and the canonical needs of our Church.

Committee Reports

Constitutional Committees

Committee: Nominations
Constituted: Constitution, Article X
Charge: The mandate of the Committee is:
1. To submit to the active members, at least one month prior to the date of election, the names of nominees as provided for in Article IX of the Constitution; (and)
2. To formulate and recommend to the Board of Governors plans for maintaining and increasing the membership of the Society.

Members: Rev. Msgr. Ricardo E. Bass, *Chair*
Dr. Diane L. Barr
Dr. Patricia M. Dugan
Rev. Lawrence Jurcak, *ex officio*

Annual Report

The Nominations Committee met in Washington, DC on March 1-3. All members of the committee were present for the meeting.

During the afternoon of March 1st, lists of possible candidates for various offices were compiled from recommendations to the committee from the membership at large, those identified by members of the committee and those suggested by the Board of Governors. Attention was paid to selecting candidates who would offer sound leadership to the Board of Governors while representing diverse constituencies and regions.

The following day committee members began contacting prospective candidates. After securing candidates for each of the required offices, the following slate of candidates was forwarded to the Board of Governors for presentation to the members gathered at the 2011 convention in Jacksonville, Florida.

Vice-President/President Elect:
Rev. John R. Vaughan
Rev. Manuel Viera, OFM

Secretary:
Mr. Jay M. Conzemius
Ms. Zabrina Decker

Consultor:
Ms. Catherine Gilligan
Rev. Mr. Gerald T. Jorgensen
Rev. John E. List
Rev. Bruce Miller

The Nominees' *Curricula Vitae* and Photographs were compiled by the Executive Coordinator's office. That office published the booklet regarding the 73rd Annual Convention and included the information pertaining to the candidates.

The Committee wishes to thank those who have been willing to consider serving the Society as an elected officer.

Rev. Msgr. Ricardo E. Bass

****

Committee:	Resolutions
Constituted:	Constitution, Article X
Charge:	The mandate of the Committee is:

1. *To solicit, develop and draft proposed resolutions which will express the concerns of the Canon Law Society of America;*
2. *To consult with the membership at large and, in particular with the Board of Governors, the standing and ad hoc committees of the Society, and the organizers of the convention;*
3. *To formulate resolutions on given points in response to requests of the members of the Society;*
4. *To compose differences in the formulation of similar proposals and to revise all proposals so that the meaning of each is clear; (and)*
5. *To encourage resolutions which authentically express in a positive way the activities and concerns of the Society.*

Members: Br. Patrick T. Shea, OFM, *Chair*
Rev. Gregory T. Luyet
Rev. J. Michael Clark

Annual Report

The bulk of the Committee's work occurs immediately prior to and during the annual convention. At the last convention, the committee assisted in the formulation of two resolutions, both of which were subsequently adopted; one dealt with the possibility of using electronic publication of the Canon Law Digest, while the second involved offering the assistance of CLSA members in the development of an Anglican Ordinariate in the United States. The Committee will probably be involved in the solicitation of resolutions. We hope to remind members that the two resolutions adopted at the last convention were sent to the committee well in advance of the convention and this gave the committee and others time to consider the resolutions and offer advice to the proponents.

Members of the committee have been in occasional e-mail contact and plan to schedule a meeting by means of conference call on a date, yet to be determined but probably in August, when a determination can be made as to what role each committee member plays at the Convention.

Br. Patrick T. Shea, OFM

****

Committee:	Resource and Asset Management
Constituted:	Constitution, Article X, as last amended in 2008
Charge:	The mandate of the Committee is:

        1. To develop a comprehensive budget for all the activities of the Society and report on the funding available for projects;

        2. To submit the proposed budget for the coming fiscal year to the Board of Governors for approval at its spring meeting;

        3. To conserve, invest and disburse the monies of the Scholarship Fund in accord with the criteria established by the Society;

        4. To select recipients for the CLSA scholarships based on criteria approved by the Board of Governors; (and)

        5. To advise the Treasurer on all matters pertaining to the Society's investments.

Members: Rev. Gregory T. Bittner, *Chair*
                  Rev. Phillip J. Brown, SS
                  Mrs. Rita F. Joyce, *ex officio*
                  Rev. Joseph R. Binzer, *Investment Consultant*
                  Sr. Margaret A. Stallmeyer, CDP, *Investment Consultant*
                  Rev. Thomas E. Cronkleton, *Advisor*

Annual Report

    The RAM Budget Committee met by web-conference on Tuesday, February 22, 2011. Members included the Treasurer, Rev. Gregory T. Bittner, Ms. Rita Joyce, V.P. and Rev. Phillip Brown, SS. The Executive Coordinator, Sr. Sharon Euart, RSM, and her Executive Assistant, Katie Richards, were present. Rev. Tom Cronkleton was also present as an Advisor to the Committee. The web-conference seemed to work well for this kind of meeting and was very inexpensive. The committee arrived at a budget to present to the BOG.

The Investment Advisors to the RAM were asked to continue in their capacity until December 31, 2013, and consented to providing consul to the RAM committee.

The RAM committee presented its budget to the BOG at the April 2011 meeting. The BOG received the budget and after much discussion decided to postpone a final vote on the budget until a few items were finalized and the RAM had an opportunity to rework the Scholarship unit budget. The budgets of the General Operations unit, the Publications unit and the Convention unit were preliminarily approved.

At that same time, a subcommittee of the BOG consisting of Manual Viera and Meg Romano-Hogan, was requested to review an application for a scholarship that had been received just after the BOG meeting had concluded and adjourned. The subcommittee enthusiastically endorsed the candidate and the BOG was polled through the CLSA web site and consented to the granting of a scholarship. This brings to four, the number of recipients who will be on a scholarship of $7000 each, for the 2011-2012 fiscal year.

RAM committee members, Rita Joyce, Gregory Bittner, Philip Brown and advisor Tom Cronkleton communicated by conference call on June 20, 2011 to review preliminary materials and a proposed resolution that had been mailed to each RAM member concerning the Scholarship Fund and its operations and accounting. The substance of the resolution was to discontinue a Balance Sheet line item in the General Operations unit called the Board Designated Restricted Reserve Account Fund in the amount of $55,415 and transfer the total fund amount to the Scholarship Fund unit. The $55,415 represented a portion of the balance of the General Operations CUIT Balanced Fund Investment. Our Accountant/Auditor, Mr. Joseph E. Godbout, CPA, had recommended in the past that this line item be removed. Based on discussions at that meeting, the RAM presented a resolution concerning funding of the Scholarship fund and the Scholarship budget to the BOG for their approval. The BOG was polled through the CLSA web site on the resolution, the Scholarship Budget, and the Budgets for the other three units. The resolution passed unanimously and the budgets were passed by an overwhelming majority of the BOG (9-1, with one member not voting). Results of the voting were reported on July 1, 2011.

The Investment advisors to the RAM were also consulted with respect to the resolution and its effect on investments and gave their consent to its immediate implementation.

Highlights of the fiscal 2011-2012 Budget include the following. The budget is balanced and projects an overall profit for the Society. The Publications unit is expected to cover the projected deficit in the General Operations unit. The

Convention and Scholarship budgets are forecast in the black.

In the General Operations unit we again budget a deficit. As can be seen from the prior year's schedules a deficit was budgeted for the last few years. The deficits have not been realized because expenses have been less than budgeted. This will not last forever. Dues income continues to decrease. The expenses of the Executive Coordinator's office with respect to salaries continue to rise and this year we had to budget additional money for a temporary worker to cover Katie's maternity leave. In coming years we will have a small increase for our rent of CLSA office space.

The Publications unit expects to make a significant profit this year as new publications should be in the pipeline. Income from new publications should cover any expenses.

The Convention unit is running a very tight budget. Honoraria have been increased modestly for speakers; the last such increase being almost 20 years ago.

The Scholarship unit has budgeted for four $7000 scholarships for fiscal year 2011-2012. Significant changes to scholarship accounting and funding will take place during the new fiscal year. A onetime transfer of a Board Designated Restricted Reserve Fund Account, listed on the Balance Sheet of the General Operations unit, will provide income to cover current and future scholarship obligations. Donations and bequests will be added to principal and future income will be generated from a percentage (not greater than 5%) of Total Scholarship Fund CUIT Balanced Fund Investments. The RAM continues to work on Scholarship accounting policies.

I want to thank the members of the RAM and the Executive Coordinator's Office for their assistance and input into the financial affairs of the Society. All of us recognize the significant responsibilities we have toward the BOG and the Society. It is our objective and purpose to do our best to utilize the resources you have entrusted us with. This report was generated as of August 1, 2011.

Rev. Gregory T. Bittner

****

Committee: Professional Responsibility

Constituted: Constitution, Article X, as last amended in 1995, and the Code of Professional Responsibilities, canon 9c(1), d(1)

Charge: The mandate of the Committee is:

1. Regarding complaints:

a) To receive complaints of any party aggrieved with respect to provisions of the Code of Professional Responsibility originally adopted by the CLSA in October 1983, and its can. 9d(1)

b) To make an initial finding that the complaint is not frivolous but is serious in character; (and)

c) By majority vote to refer the matter to the hearing officers.

2. To issue advisory opinions and decisions on the application of the Code of Professional Responsibility; (and)

3. To advise on all other questions concerning the professional responsibility of canonists.

Members:
Rev. Msgr. C. Michael Padazinski, *Chair*
Rev. Manuel Viera, OFM, *ex officio*
Mrs. Meg Romano-Hogan, *ex officio*
Rev. Msgr. Michael A. Souckar, *Hearing Officer*
Sr. Lynn M. McKenzie, OSB, *Hearing Officer*

Annual Report

The Committee on Professional Responsibility has received no formal complaints or requests for inquiry into an allegation of any of the rules or standards of professional responsibility of the Society during the past year. The committee stands ready and willing to respond to any inquiry or complaint which is brought to its attention.

Rev. Msgr. C. Michael Padazinski

****

COMMITTEE REPORTS

ON-GOING COMMITTEES

Committee: Church Governance
Constituted: 2009
Charge: The mandate of the Committee is:
1. *To initiate as needed any projects pertinent to the study of canon law pertaining to Church structures and governance or the implementation thereof, including but not limited to the following:*
   - *a) diocesan and parish temporalities;*
   - *b) consultative bodies;*
   - *c) diocesan and parish structures;*
   - *d) power of governance;*
   - *e) comparative law issues;*
   - *f) inter-ritual matters;*
   - *g) Eastern canon law and institutions*
2. *To oversee projects referred to the committee by the Board of Governors;*
3. *To oversee its subcommittees working on projects concerning Church governance; (and)*
4. *To collaborate with national organizations and other groups dealing with issues of Church governance.*

Members: Rev. Msgr. Daniel F. Hoye, *Chair*
Sr. Ann F. Rehrauer, OSF
Rev. Msgr. Steven J. Raica
Dr. Patricia M. Dugan
Chorbishop John D. Faris

Annual Report

The Committee has received the agreement of PAB to translate "Latin Pastor and Oriental Faithful" by Lorenzo Larusso, OP. Chorbishop John Faris anticipates the project being completed in the Fall of 2011. It will then be sent to the PAB for final review The Office of the Executive Coordinator has obtained the necessary copyrights.

The Committee will meet during the 2011 Convention. Included on our agenda will be the following items:

• Possible publication on merging and closing of Parishes

- Possible publication on consultative bodies
- Possible publication on what an administrator can do during a vacancy of a diocese

Rev. Msgr. Daniel F. Hoye

****

Committee:	Clergy
Constituted:	2008
Charge:	The mandate of the Committee is:

1. *To initiate as needed any projects pertinent to the study of canon law pertaining to the life and ministry of bishops, priests and deacons or the implementation thereof, including, but not limited to, the following:*

   a) canonical issues related to the sexual abuse of minors,

   b) clergy personnel issues and resources,

   c) advocacy for clergy in penal cases,

2. *To oversee projects referred to the committee by the Board of Governors;*

3. *To oversee its subcommittees working on projects concerning clergy; (and)*

4. *To collaborate with national organizations and other groups dealing with clergy issues.*

Members:
Rev. Msgr. Ricardo E. Bass, *Chair*
Rev. Gregory T. Bittner
Rev. Gary D. Yanus
Rev. Daniel J. Ward, OSB
Rev. James I. Donlon

Annual Report

The members of the Committee met at the annual Canon Law Society meeting in Buffalo, New York in October 2010. The members had three conference calls from Fall 2010-Spring 2011 and also met in Lutz, Florida, on 31 January/1 February 2011.

Rick Bass met with the Publications Advisory Board at the time of the Canon Law Society convention in October 2010. It was decided at that time that the Clergy Committee would begin its part of the Series of Pastoral Resources as soon as it had decided upon topics and authors.

With approval of the PAB Committee, the following topics and authors were selected during a conference call on 4 April 2011:

1. Revs. Mark O'Connell and Bob Oliver: issues concerning Foreign/International priests/seminarians. Rev. Otto Garcia has agreed to be a resource for this topic;
2. Rev. Daniel Ward, OSB and Ms. Amy Strickland: issues concerning Departure and Sustenance from a Diocese or Religious Institute. Rev. James Donlon has agreed to be a resource for this topic;
3. Rev. Patrick Cooney, OSB: has agreed to be one of the individual authors for issues concerning the canonical training of priests; and,
4. Rev. Thomas Cronkleton and Rev. Mr. Jerry Quinn: issues concerning permanent deacons.

All members of the Clergy Committee attended the *Special Faculties* seminar sponsored by the Canon Law Society of America in Lutz, Florida in January 2011.

Rev. Gary Yanus has been in conversation with Bishop A.J. Quinn (retired auxiliary of Cleveland), Tom Hoban and Louis Erste (Laity in Support of Retired Priests) and CARA regarding issues concerning the rights and obligations of retired/senior priests.

Rev. Msgr. Ricardo E. Bass

****

Committee:	Convention Planning
Constituted:	2008
Charge:	The mandate of the Committee is:

    1. To receive from the Board of Governors the approved general theme of the next convention as well as any suggestions from the Committee on Research & Development for the development of the theme;

    2. To recommend to the Board of Governors, in accord with the general theme, topics for major addresses, seminars or other presentations at a future convention, as well as a list of potential speakers and the honoraria for such speakers;

    3. Following the Board of Governors' approval, to arrange for the speakers, addresses and seminars for the annual convention;

    4. To plan all convention liturgies and prayer services; (and)

    5. To review the evaluations of the most recent Convention and assist the Convention Chairperson in planning future arrangements, as needed.

Members: Rev. Patrick J. Cogan, SA, *Chair*
    Very Rev. Paul J. Hachey, SM
    Rev. John J.M. Foster

Sr. Sharon A. Euart, RSM, *ex officio*
Rev. Lawrence Jurcak, *ex officio*
Rev. Michael A. Boccaccio, *Convention Chairperson*
Rev. Msgr. Peter M. Polando, *Convention Liturgies*

Annual Report

The Convention Planning Committee convened at the Executive Coordinator's office in January 2011. The feedback from the 2010 was briefly reviewed and a program for the 2012 convention was prepared for consideration by the BOG. The annual convention theme is now determined by the Research & Development Committee and this greatly facilitates the work of the Committee. The 2012 theme is "The Parish, Parish Life, and Leadership." The following is the 2012 program approved by the BOG:

Keynote Address
- Topic: *Vatican II and the Parish 50 Years Later. A Bishop's Perspective* – Archbishop Gregory Aymond (New Orleans)

Major Addresses
1. *The Parish: 50 Years into the Future* – Msgr. Roch Pagé (Ottawa)
2. *Models of Parish Leadership: Role of Lay Ecclesial Ministers* – Sr. Katarina Schuth, OSF

Seminars
1. *Tribunal Advocacy on the Parish Level* – Sr. Marilyn Vassallo, CSJ
2. *Jurisprudence I* – Ms. Lynda Robitaille
3. *Jurisprudence II* – Rev. Msgr. John Johnson
4. *Use of Experts and Dignitas Connubii* – Deacon Gerald Jorgensen
5. *Inter-ritual Issues and the Parish* – Chorbishop John Faris
6. *Closure of Parishes: Learning from the Diocesan Experience* – Rev. Mark O'Connell and Msgr. Ricardo Bass
7. *New Models of Parish Schools* – Rev. Patrick Lagges and Sister Mary Paul McCaughey, OP
8. *Emerging Models of Parish Leadership Research Project* – Mr. Mark Grey
9. *Revitalizing Parish Consultative Structures* – Ms. Barbara Anne Cusack
10. *Sacramental Life of the Parish: Selected Issues* – Rev. Bruce Miller
11. *Parishes and Religious* – Rev. Daniel Ward, OSB
12. *Update on the Revision of Penal Law* – Rev. Patrick Cogan, SA

Rev. Patrick J. Cogan, SA

Convention Chairperson Report

THE PRESENT

Welcome to our 73rd convention, here in Jacksonville, FL. I wish to thank the volunteers from the local Tribunal and Chancery offices for their valuable help and care. I single out Fr. Tim Lindenfelser, JV; along with his staff he has been outstanding in helping prepare for this convention. As ever, I am eager to do what I can to facilitate a smooth running of this 2011 convention. May your participation in this convention and your delighting in this corner of the Sunshine State be exhilarating. CLSA has gathered in FL 4 times: Miami - '61; Orlando - '80 & '98 and Tampa - '05. 2011 brings J'ville and CLSA together for the first time.

2012:

As I stated in last year's Report Book, our 74th [pre] convention, October [7] 8 - 11 is at the 'Chicago's' Rosemont Hyatt, which indeed has a 'big city' feel about it, www.rosemont.hyatt.com! With 1100 rooms and 2 different designs of 10 floors each, there is a 'metropolitan' ambiance, along with a typical Hyatt open air atrium. Across the street is an Expoteria Cafeteria [& that is what it is]. Within a mile radius are the following: two strip malls; entrance to "L" [Chicago's 'subway' - a 35 minute to downtown center]; Stephens' waterfall park leading into a large forest preserve; a feast of fast to fine eateries [e.g., pizza slices, gourmet crab burgers, tossed salads]; etc. Also, in this 1 mile compound one will find a post office, Kinko's/Fed-Ed [one in hotel too], '7/11' convenience, liquor & bakery stores. An eighteen screen 'Muvico' with its 'Bogart' restaurant and a legit Rosemont Theatre are directly across the street.

A trend developing in the area is free van rides to/from local restaurants. Beyond the mile are drug, gift, book, grocery & department stores [read: taxi or hotel van]. Best 'future' projection for the immediate RH area is a Fashion Outlet Mall, 2012 is earliest opening. Convention attendees would be able to locate it from hotel windows. More info: www.rosemont.com . A casino is expected to be opened in the neighboring Des Plaines about 1.5 miles away. Finally, there are pre-Chicago stops on the "L" where one will find more eateries, malls, entertainment, etc.

The local [and only] Church is 1.5 miles away, Our Lady of Hope – hence transportation is necessitated, if convention Mass is celebrated there. It is a unique and lovely modern designed 'Romanesque' building, www.ourladyofhopechurch.com .

Room rate is $158 for single, double, triple, quadruple. Pricey? Yes, but this is a BIG city; also, review some concessions: [1] 10% discount for hotel restaurants, not in-room service; [2] tax exempt policy applicable to payment made by a Diocese/Institution; [3] O'Hare, perhaps USA's busiest airport, means inexpensive and frequent flights; [4] free to/from airport shuttle service – hardly a 10 minute ride; [5] free shuttle van service to/from any mall within 1 mile;

[6] Visitors' Convention Bureau is arranging for a discount voucher program. Considering, then, being in the outer circle of a major city, we have a bargain! FYI: We have held conventions in Chicago itself: '51, '65 & '81. Rosemont is our 4th visit to IL.

2013:
CLSA holds its 75th convention in Sacramento, CA; [Pre] Convention is October [12] 13 - 16. Once more we shall be at a Hyatt Regency www.sacramento.hyatt.com. Room rate: $149/night single or double; $174, triple; $194 quadruple ... and as always, taxes. The hotel, built in 1988, has 15 floors and 503 rooms, so CLSA could be the major occupant. This will be our 7th visit to California [Los Angeles '59, San Francisco '64 & '83, San Diego '75, La Jolla '97 and Orange County '07].

The Hyatt, recently renovated, is located directly across the street from the State Capital, which has a very picturesque park. Blessed Sacrament Cathedral is a 3-5 minute diagonal walk from the hotel [www.cathedralsacramento.org] – a fine building. Within a 2 block walk are many eateries. "K" street, adjacent to the hotel, is now a pedestrian mall going East to West. It travels through a Westfield Shopping Mall [www.westfield.com/downtownplaza] and directly into Old Sacramento – a tourist's 'must,' www.oldsacramento.com. Paralleling Old S'mento and going beyond – endlessly it seemed – is a promenade walkway along the river. I have never been to S'mento before; I was pleasantly surprised. It is a lovely and appealing city in its own right, with so much within a 5 minute walk. The very clean Capital park, directly across the street from the hotel, provides very attractive and restful settings and sittings! The park claims to have trees representing all 50 of the US States! I believe our convention attendees will enjoy this city.

2014:
CLSA convention #76 will be in St. Louis, MO at the Millennium Hotel [www.millenniumhotels.com/stlouis]. Room rate is $135 plus taxes, for both single and double. Our rooms will be in the North Tower, recently redone and referred to as the 'superior' tower! This tower with its 28 floors is the taller of the two, the other is 10 floors. The 28th floor of the North Tower is a restaurant with spectacular views. In total, the hotel has about 780 rooms. The first and higher tower was built about 1969; the South one about 1974. The hotel will provide free internet for all attendees; as well as a 10% discount for in-hotel dining [not in-room service]. Naturally, the hotel is eager to welcome us. The Millennium was one of 3 sites considered and selected as the best 'offer.'

We have been to St. Louis before in '57, '78 and '96. Our 4th visit to the "Show Me State" or more recently the "Gateway State" was in 2008, Kansas City. 2014 will mark our 5th visit to the state, 4th in St. Louis. A mere 4-5 minute walk is the 18th century "Old Cathedral," Basilica of St. Louis, King, a visit to which I highly recommend, in addition to our convention Mass most likely being celebrated there [www.psichurch.com/churches/140stlouis]. Speaking of sacred places, a church that I would list as a MUST is the Cathedral Basilica of Saint Louis, begun in 1907; its mosaics alone are breath taking [cathedralstl.com].

Along side of the cathedral is the [as in THE] Arch of St. Louis in Jefferson National Memorial park [www.stlouisarch.com]. I'm sure those who have had the opportunity to visit the park, let alone ride to the top, would agree with me that this too is a "MUST"! Eateries, from fast to fine, surround the hotel, all within a 10 minute walk. There is even an upscale grocery store about 7 minutes away [www.culinariaschnucks.com]. Additionally, from the hotel going toward the river is "the Landing" with its old town look. Restoration of its streets and buildings is rather impressive [www.lacledestanding.com]. On both sides of the river are casinos, the larger and more popular of which is across the river [casinoqueen.com]. There will be more than enough to do, visit, site, enjoy during convention free time. For more ideas, go to www.explorestlouis.com .

CONCLUSION

These next 4 CLSA convention sites provide very exciting and different environments. Ranging from the Atlantic Ocean shore of Florida to the banks of the California's Sacramento River, stopping along the way in 'the windy city, Chicago' and 'returning' via the mid-west ARCH way of St. Louis, variety and vibrancy await us. As ever, please know how eagerly I welcome your input and involvement; let alone being able to assist and serve you as General Convention Chair.

Rev. Michael A. Boccaccio

Convention Liturgies

This past spring, Barbara Bettwy, co-chair of the Convention Liturgies section of the Convention Planning Committee asked to be relieved of her responsibilities to the Committee because of work-related and family issues. All of us thank Barbara for the kind and generous work she had performed in the past Conventions.

During the week of 5-8 July 2011, I visited the Convention hotel and the Offices of the Diocese of Saint Augustine. The following details were addressed:

- Reverend Thomas S. Willis, the pastor of the Cathedral Basilica of Saint Augustine, will be our contact for the persons who will be responsible for the leading and playing of music at the opening prayer service of the Convention; the morning liturgies on Sunday through Tuesday; the Thursday morning liturgy; and, the Wednesday afternoon liturgy.
- Ms. Jennifer Sandler, Convention Services Manager at the Hyatt Hotel in

Jacksonville is our contact for the setup of the liturgical space that will be used for our morning liturgies. She has been most cooperative in being able to transform the space as attractively possible for the celebrations of the Mass.
- The Wednesday afternoon liturgy will be celebrated at Immaculate Conception Church that was founded in 1854. The church is located about seven blocks from the Hyatt Hotel.
- Mrs. Fran Amer, Director of Worship for the Diocese of Youngstown, is assisting me in the planning of the liturgies and the composition of the liturgical booklets.

I am grateful to for the cooperation of the people who are mentioned above and to the personnel of my Tribunal

Rev. Msgr. Peter M. Polando

****

Committee:	Institutes of Consecrated and Apostolic Life
Constituted:	2009
Charge:	The mandate of the Committee is:

1. *To initiate as needed any projects pertinent to the study of canon law pertaining to the life and ministry of Institutes of Consecrated and Apostolic Life of the implementation thereof, including, but not limited to, the following:*
    a) sponsorship;
    b) mergers and restructuring of institutes;
    c) governance;
    d) membership;
    e) new forms of consecrated life.
2. *To oversee projects referred to the committee by the Board of Governors;*
3. *To oversee its subcommittees working on projects concerning Consecrated and Apostolic Life; (and)*
4. *To collaborate with national organizations and other groups dealing with issues of Consecrated and Apostolic Life.*

Members: Sr. Mary Catherine Wenstrup, OSB, *Chair*
Sr. M. Dominica Brennan, OP
Br. Patrick T. Shea, OFM
Sr. Sharon L. Holland, IHM
Rev. Kevin W. Niehoff, OP

Annual Report

Since the last convention the committee conducted an online survey of the CLSA membership regarding the five topics named in our mandate. Recently the committee met by conference call to review the survey results, our mandate and propose follow-up possibilities. We discussed three areas of information from the survey.

1. Four topics, mergers, sponsorship, governance and membership are related issues for major superiors and their communities. Several organizations assist communities in these areas, such as TRCRI, NRRO, Vicars, etc. These may or may not meet the needs of canonists are who called on for help.
2. Establishing new communities frequently means an active role of a diocesan bishop and/or a vicar of religious. This is a growing reality with multiple and diverse expressions and questions.
3. Several CLSA members offered assistance to the committee. The committee is interested in pursuing collaboration with these, as well as other organizations.

Committee members suggested possible way to move forward. Those with strong interest are:

1. Revive the Bulletin on Issues in Canon Law.
2. Hold a think-tank or caucus at a future convention so that participants can share experiences and best practices.
3. Generate and present a topic for a seminar at each future convention.
4. Develop strategies for collaborating with groups such as, TRCRI, NRRO, CMSM, LCWR, CMSWR, Vicars, etc.

Committee members who are attending this year's convention will meet in person to further discuss our next move.

Sr. Mary Catherine Wenstrup, OSB

****

Committee:	Laity
Constituted:	2009
Charge:	The mandate of the Committee is:

1. To initiate as needed any projects pertinent to the study of canon law pertaining to the life and ministry of lay persons or the implementation thereof, including, but not limited to, the following:
   a) lay ecclesial ministry,
   b) collaboration with clergy,
   c) rights of the lay faithful;
2. To oversee projects referred to the committee by the Board of Governors;
3. To oversee its subcommittees working on projects concern-

	ing the laity; (and)
	4. To collaborate with national organizations and other groups dealing with the role of the laity in the Church
Members:	Ms. Zabrina R. Decker, *Chair*
	Mrs. Mary C. Edlund
	Rev. Msgr. James M. Sheehan
	Mr. Jay M. Conzemius
	Dr. Lynda A. Robitaille

Annual Report

The committee has been asked to focus on the question of authorization in regards to lay ministry. We are happy to do so. To that end, the Chair of the committee and Lynda Robitaille will be attending the 2011 Collegeville National Symposium on Lay Ecclesial Ministry scheduled for August 2-5 in Minnesota. Siobhan Verbeek, Rita Joyce and Jim Donlan will also be attending as representatives from the Society. This collaboration, with over 30 other groups examining the role of laity in the Church, addresses both goal number one and four in our mandate.

Jay Conzemius is working with a subcommittee from the Committee on Sacramental Law to examine Sacramental record keeping.

The Committee would also be happy to participate in any way the BOG sees fit in the 2011 or 2012 Convention as part of our mandate is to study and pay particular attention to the rights of the lay faithful.

Msgr. Jim Sheehan, who died in August at the age of 39, brought good ideas and a wonderful sense of humor to the committee. He will be missed. His soul now finds peace with the God he served so well.

Thank you for your support.

Ms. Zabrina R. Decker

****

Committee:	Publications Advisory Board
Constituted:	2007
Charge:	The mandate of the Committee is:
	1. To advise the Board of Governors about all aspects of current, periodic and proposed Canon Law Society of America publication projects, including financial, literary, educational and marketing issues;
	2. To monitor the progress of all Society publication projects;

>   3. To implement the procedures for peer review of Society publications;
>   4. To review the coordination and management of the Society's publications activity on the part of the Office of the Executive Coordinator; (and)
>   5. To provide a written report to the Society's membership at the annual convention.

Members: Rev. Msgr. John A. Alesandro, *Chair*
Rev. Msgr. Kevin E. McKenna
Very Rev. Lawrence A. DiNardo
Rev. Patrick M. Cooney, OSB
Rev. Thomas J. Green
Chorbishop John D. Faris, *ex officio*
Rev. Patrick J. Cogan, SA, *Canon Law Digest*

Annual Report

Meetings

During the past year, the members met in person at the October 2010 Convention in Buffalo, New York, at the CLSA office in Washington, D.C., on February 14-15, 2011, and again on June 27-28, 2011. The chair also participated by conference call in the BOG meeting in January and attended the April, 2010, BOG meeting to offer progress reports on publications.

Electronic Publishing

One of the principal topics of PAB this past year has been the challenge of moving into electronic publishing in various forms. One aspect of this goal was supported by a convention resolution last year in Buffalo, sponsored by Jim Coriden, that directed PAB "to expedite its investigation of providing the *Canon Law Digest* on-line, and, if the project seems feasible and affordable, proceed with all deliberate speed to set in motion the process of on-line conversion, indexing documents by canons, chronology, source, and subject matter, maintaining permanent access, constant updating, and easy download-ability." PAB was directed to report its findings to the BOG within a year.

This topic has been on PAB's agenda for some time, in particular, the desire to convert *CLD* to an electronic database, in effect transforming future volumes into a subscription service. PAB has also been seeking to make more and more publications accessible on the CLSA website, particularly when they had gone or were soon going out of print (e.g., copies of the *Proceedings, Roman Replies and Advisory Opinions*). These are accessible through the "Online Bookstore" tab on the website.

A significant step forward in this effort was made by Bill Woestman when he single-handedly scanned the first twelve volumes of *CLD* onto a CD in PDF format that permitted the documents to be searched. The CD itself is a good start for a major conversion to an ongoing database. To intensify its efforts in this area PAB had a special meeting in Washington in February (in addition to its annual summer meeting) to discuss with Jim Coriden his proposal and to share ideas on the best method for achieving this much desired goal.

The following are some questions and possibilities that emerged out of the discussion:

1. The CLSA should not stay with the practice of publishing successive volumes of *CLD* but, rather, convert the entire project to an ongoing electronic database to which subscribers would have access. The database would not be "issued" at periodic intervals, but would be maintained piece-by-piece as documents became available. This would still require an editor or committee to collect the documents as they became available and to put them into the appropriate format for inclusion in the database.
2. It is likely that access would be arranged as a subscription service with an annual fee, probably with two rates: one for non-members and a reduced rate for dues-paying members.
3. Setting up a database with user-friendly electronic research capabilities may be quite costly and will certainly take some time. PAB agreed that we should proceed with a study of how to do set up and maintain such a database and the approximate cost of doing so.
4. Not only will such a database be more valuable for research, but conversion to a web-based instrument will be more in tune with the experience of newer canonists, who are constantly using electronic media rather than books off their personal bookshelves.
5. One possibility for information about how to set up such a database might be to consult with those in charge of similar accessing in libraries. Further research in this area, however, suggested that library systems are too complex and far beyond what is needed by the CLSA, at least at this point in its history.
6. The CLSA can probably achieve its goal of converting *CLD* into a research database by setting up a standard "Wiki" system (e.g., like *Wikipedia*), one in which, however, no one can directly influence the database. Instead, there could be communication portals that permit readers to send improvements and questions to the managers of the database. This will allow the constant correction, expansion and improvement of the research tool.
7. With conversion to an ongoing database, how will the documents be collected? Should a *CLD* committee be set up? Should a compiler be hired? One thing to keep in mind is the fact that, with this approach, the editing need not be as complete and time –constrained as it is now. Up to and including Volume 14, the editor has had the task of completing as full a search of the period in question as possible lest some document be accidentally omitted. Conversely, with a database, documents can be listed as found and, if some

are found at a later time or are even explicitly sought by subscribers who note that they are missing, they can then be added. The database is regularly maintained, it is not divided into sectors of years.
8. Also, the documents would not require major formatting; they would be compiled and pasted into the database in a standard Wiki format. Translating or summarizing, however, would still be required in many cases to make the entry valuable for research.
9. It would seem that the project could be handled by a chief compiler who would also have a point person to liaise with the CLSA committees and the canon law schools. Those involved in the project could communicate by e-mail and telephone. Such a figure might be termed "*Documents Research Coordinator.*" Whoever is appointed to such a role should be under the authority of the Executive Coordinator and also closely associated with PAB.
10. PAB unanimously voted that volume 14 of *CLD* should be published in the style of the first 13 volumes but with a more modest initial printing (perhaps 500 copies rather than 1,000), which would be more in line with the rate of sales of volume 13. It also recommended that no subsequent volumes of *CLD* be planned. Instead, the CLSA should study and implement a way of providing documents in an accessible electronic database.
11. PAB and the Executive Coordinaor's office are continuing to collaborate on this project. Finding the right company or consultant to guide the CLSA in this endeavor is the next step in the process. This will permit the CLSA to describe the steps to be taken and to draw up at least an initial budget for the creation of the database and its ongoing maintenance.

Canon Law Digest, Volume 14

CLD 14 is progressing nicely under the editorship of Pat Cogan. He has noted the improvement in obtaining texts thanks to the availability of many of the documents on-line. The CD put together by Bill Woestman of volumes 1-12 has been selling well. In the future, the effort to maintain chronological volumes of *CLD* will be absorbed into a major shift into the production and maintenance of an electronic database of all submitted documents and translations.

Rotal Jurisprudence

The project to translate sixteen Rotal decisions continued through the past year. Further details on the project can be found in the separate report by the editor of this work. The volume will contain sixteen Rotal decisions whose translations have been approved by the prelate auditors. The work replicates, alongside the English translation, the Latin wording of the *in iure* sections.

Latin Pastor and Oriental Faithful

John Faris, chair of the Research & Development Committee, is in the process of translating and updating this work, which should prove helpful as a practical guide for inter-ecclesial pastoral questions.

Pastoral Resources

PAB continues to urge the publication of a series of "pastoral resources" that would bring canonical expertise into the wider audience of the Church: particularly, parish priests, lay ecclesial ministers, pastoral staffs, and parish volunteers. These publications should offer concise summations of the law with good interpretations that apply the norms to everyday life in the church. Various committees of the CLSA have been pursuing such projects; in particular, the Governance Committee and the Clergy Committee (*see* the individual committee reports). The idea is to develop brief publications, perhaps fifty pages or less, that could be printed in paperback and could be widely marketed, to CLSA members and many others. As a supplement to committee work, the members of PAB dedicated an hour or so at their July meeting to surface topics that may be suitable for *Pastoral Resources*, including the following:

- Granting marriage dispensations
- The duties of tribunal personnel: judge, advocate, defender of the bond, promoter of justice
- The process for a priest's request for a dispensation from celibacy and the other obligations of priesthood in the *via gratiosa*.
- The Clergy Congregation's Special Faculties.
- A guide to penal trials: judge, PJ, advocate.
- Merging religious institutes
- Reconfiguring parishes
- Canonical issues in staffing multiple parishes
- Teaching canon law: the essentials that should be addressed.
- Re-publishing out-of-print monographs and booklets
- Norms for consultative bodies at the parish level.
- Marriage policies.

Inventory
1. Consolidation of Inventory

   PAB continues to monitor and manage the inventory, reducing it where there is little likelihood of additional sales of any significance, in order to consolidate the volumes into fewer pallets and thereby reducing the monthly storage expenses. This past year did not require as much reduction in inventory insofar as signification reduction were executed the previous year. The inventory of the English translation of the Code of Canons of the Eastern Churches was cut back to approximately 1,400 volumes in order to reduce warehousing expenses.

2. Selected Individual Texts in Inventory
   a. *Translation of the Latin Code*
      1. *An Interim Version*: At PAB's recommendation the CLSA will be publishing an interim printing of the current Code of Canon Law: Latin-English translation. The inventory report shows that

there will be a complete depletion of the stock by spring 2012 To cover the need until a new version of the Latin Code is published and a second English edition can be prepared, the CLSA will produce a soft-cover version of the current translation as a "second printing" rather than a "revision." At the same time, this second printing will be made available as an e-book.

2. *Timing*: The interim project will be accomplished during the beginning of 2012. The number of volumes printed will last about two years. The e-book version will be made available immediately upon completion.

3. *Specific improvements*: The second printing will have some corrections in it, including changes found in the 2009 apostolic letter *Omnium in mentem,* corrections of punctuation, spelling, and capitalization in the English as well as typos and misspellings in the Latin. The members of PAB also reviewed changes proposed by the faculty at the School of Canon Law, St. Paul's University, Ottawa. Of the forty-two (42) suggested changes: twenty-seven (27) were accepted; thirteen (13) were deferred to the next full revision of the translation; two (2) were rejected.

b. *Eastern Code*: The inventory has been reduced to approximately 1,400 volumes.

c. *Advisory Opinions Collections*: Volume 2 is depleted. PAB recommended that Volume 2 not be reprinted and that additional volumes not be published. Rather, all advisory opinions, two years after their publication, should be accessible electronically on the CLSA website.

d. *RR&AO*: PAB has recommended that we continue to publish *RR&AO* annually. This year, sufficient documents issued by the Apostolic See were received along with a good number of advisory opinions by canonists to form an interesting volume for distribution at the October 2011 Convention. Approximately 13 Roman documents were received. Twenty-four advisory opinions were submitted, of which six were rejected or deferred and eighteen were edited for publication.

e. *Original CLSA Commentary*: Paulist Press intends to issue the original *Commentary* (which is now out of print) as an e-book. If CLSA were willing to issue a third general commentary, Paulist Press would be interested in publishing it.

Publication Protocol

The publication protocol that was reviewed at last year's annual convention (Buffalo, 2010) was finalized and implemented. A copy can be found on the CLSA website under the "Online Bookstore" tab. Key elements of the protocol that PAB has been following:

1. PAB will review all proposed publications at an early stage to make a recommendation to the BOG about the proposed concept as appropriate for the CLSA to publish.
2. The author/editor must submit the manuscript to the EC and PAB in *Word for Windows* (a format that will permit the EC to build up an electronic database of all publications).
3. PAB will arrange for peer review of the manuscript during its development or, at the latest, at the point of receiving the entire manuscript.
4. PAB will interact with the EC and make recommendations to the EC about the usual elements of publication such as formatting, size of the book, design of the cover. All such technical decisions will be made by the EC in consultation with PAB.

CLSA Budget

PAB developed assumptions for the publications portion of the FY 2012 budget (7/1/11-6/30/12), presenting them to the CLSA Resource and Asset Management Committee in February and to the BOG in April.

1. *Timetable for the budget process*: The RAM committee meets in Washington in February. Prior to that, after the first six months of experience, PAB examines the following to develop a projection for the next fiscal year:
   - the six-month report of sales and inventory
   - a discussion with the Executive Coordinator about the status of all pending publications
   - information from the BOG meeting and the chair of Research & Development (an *ex officio* member of PAB) about the activity of the committees and what publications we can anticipate from them for the next fiscal year.
2. This past year most of the revenue came again from existing publications, in particular, the steady sale of the English translation of the Latin Code. The anticipated completion of *Rotal Jurisprudence* and *Canon Law Digest 14* did not materialize but will certainly be issued during the 2011-2012 fiscal year, one of the factors that led PAB to recommend an increase in the book sales and book production budget items.
3. *Assumptions*: In April PAB recommended to the Executive Coordinator to use the following assumptions for the Publications Portion of the FY2011 budget: revenue of $100,000, expenses of $40,000

Shipping and Handling

The new rates for S&H have been put into effect and seem to be working well. The CLSA has also been utilizing *Amazon* for some marketing and sales. This approach will continue to be expanded to assist in marketing CLSA publications worldwide.

EBSCO Publishing

PAB recommended that the CLSA authorize EBSCO Publishing to include the annual CLSA *Proceedings* in its electronic catalog, which will increase access to the major addresses and seminar publications emerging at the annual conventions.

Future Meetings

PAB accomplishes its mandate by monitoring all publications, working closely with the CLSA office on all aspects of publication, making recommendations, when needed, to the Executive Coordinator and the BOG and interacting with the R&D committee and other committees about activities that may result in publications. PAB's schedule during the current year will be as follows

1. Chair's Report at the BOG meetings in January and April.
2. Conference Call in February to discuss budget assumptions for the next fiscal year.
3. Summer meeting to review all activities: date and place to be determined

If members of the CLSA have comments or suggestions about the Society's publication activity, please feel free to communicate with any of the members of PAB, all of whose contact information can be found on the CLSA website.

Rev. Msgr. John A. Alesandro

Canon Law Digest

There is no further update at this time.

Rev. Patrick J. Cogan, SA

****

Committee: Research and Development
Constituted: 2008
Charge: The mandate of the Committee is:
  1. To initiate or cooperate in all Canon Law Society of America research projects such as seminars, symposia and special studies;
  2. To design and implement Think Tanks that will allow for diverse views on issues of ecclesial life having canonical implications;
  3. To develop and recommend themes for the annual Conventions for submission to the Board of Governors for approval and subsequent referral to the Convention Planning Committee for implementation;
  4. To maintain close communication with all the committees of

the Society in order to facilitate needed research and discussion; (and)

5. To interact with the Publications Advisory Board in order to assess the current and contemplated publications of the Society and offer suggestions and guidance for publication planning.

Members: Chorbishop John D. Faris, *Chair*
Rev. John P. Beal
Very Rev. Patrick R. Lagges
Rev. Robert W. Oliver
Mrs. Rita F. Joyce, *ex officio*

Annual Report

On 2 May 2011, CLSA president, Rev. Michael P. Joyce, CM, reconstituted the Research and Development Committee. Chorbishop John D. Faris was appointed as Chair with a term expiring in October 2014; Rev. John P. Beal and Rev. Patrick Lagges were appointed with terms expiring in October 2012; Rev. Robert Oliver was appointed with a term expiring October 2013.

In the capacity of an *ex officio* member, the Chair attended a meeting of the Publications Advisory Board. In the context of that meeting, there were discussions regarding future initiatives that could be taken by various committees.

Subsequent to that meeting, the Chair was in contact with Msgr. Ricardo Bass, chair of the Clergy Committee, regarding the CLSA workshop of the Special Faculties of the Congregation for the Clergy that might produce a publication.

The R & D Committee will meet during the 2011 CLSA convention to chart directions for future research, workshops, symposia and publications in collaboration with the various CLSA committees.

Chorbishop John D. Faris

****

Committee: Sacramental Law
Constituted: 2008
Charge: The mandate of the Committee is:
1. To initiate as needed any projects pertinent to the study of canon law pertaining to the sacramental life of the Church of the implementation thereof;
2. To oversee projects referred to the committee by the Board of Governors;
3. To oversee its subcommittees working on projects concern-

ing the sacramental life of the Church;
4. To offer suggestions to the Board of Governors for marriage topics for pre-convention workshops; (and)
5. To collaborate with national organizations and other groups dealing with the sacramental life of the Church.

Members: Sr. Victoria Vondenberger, RSM, *Chair*
Rev. John J.M. Foster
Ms. M. Margaret Gillett
Rev. Bruce Miller
Rev. Mark A. Plewka
Rev. Michael A. Vigil

Annual Report

Bookmark reference guide

As 2010 drew to a close, the Chair of the Sacramental Law Committee (SLC), made contact with Tim Ferguson JCL of Detroit who mentioned on the canon law listserve that he wanted to design a quick reference guide about canonical form for marriages of Catholics with Orthodox persons in Orthodox ceremonies indicating when those marriages are presumed to be valid. SLC requested before the January Board of Governors (BOG) meeting permission to pursue this. Tim designed the information so that it can be folded as a bookmark to be kept in the Code. SLC worked with Tim to revise the bookmark which was also sent for review to several CLSA members who are experts in Eastern law. The approved text was sent to the Executive Coordinator (EC) for publication. SLC hoped that a hard copy of the bookmark would be given to CLSA members at the next convention or included in a newsletter. Instead, a link to the bookmark was put on the CLSA website. SLC requested that a notice about link that be included in a CLSA Newsletter for those who do not regularly check the website for such information. Here is the link to the bookmark: http://www.clsa.org/resource/resmgr/docs/2011sacramentallawbookmark.pdf

Exclusion of the *bonum coniugum*

SLC noted the discrepancy between the Research and Development Committee (R&D) 2010 convention report and ours. SLC did not receive from R&D any *bonum coniugum* research suggestion until after the 2010 convention. R&D dated their proposal Sept. 2009 but it was sent to SLC Oct. 2010: Prepare a publication, listing articles that would illustrate various aspects of the use of *bonum coniugum* as a ground of nullity. The project should include translations of existing articles on this topic that are not accessible to all canon law practitioners because they are not published in English.

SLC considered the idea. Members read the suggested articles listed when this topic was first proposed before 2006 by the previous Marriage Research Committee. SLC decided that since that time there have been many regional and some national presentations about exclusion of the *bonum coniugum* which presentations move beyond those articles. We think the best current reference on the topic is the article/presentation by Gus Mendonça which is linked to the CLSA website. [Bruce Miller of SLC reported that Cardinal Raymond Burke addressed the issue in a recent convention saying that this ground for nullity "is only now being studied by the Rota" and the only possible substantial thing that could be excluded that would be invalidating is "*mutuum adiutorium.*"] SLC thinks it is wise for now not to pursue further research on this topic.

Sacramental Records

When the Sept 2010 *CLSA Newsletter* arrived, SLC members immediately discussed our concerns about the statement that the Laity Committee planned to develop: "a publication regarding the 'what, how and whys' of sacramental record keeping for those responsible in the parish... assisting those who may not be canonists to understand this very important task from a canonical and practical perspective..." Our dismay came from previously being told by the BOG that our committee whose title is "Sacramental Law" was not to include anything related to liturgical law for reasons not made clear to us. The committee decided that the SLC Chair would talk with Zabrina Decker, Chair of the Laity Committee, at the convention.

At the convention SLC meeting the Chair reported that during the 2010 convention the Laity Committee was told by Jack Alesandro, chair of the Publications Advisory Board (PAB) that the sacramental records project belonged under the Sacramental Law Committee. SLC decided to ask the BOG for approval that our committee and the Laity Committee work together to research and create this needed reference. Margaret Gillett offered to be our point person who would meet with someone from the Laity Committee to work on this project. The working group will send the results of their efforts to all the members of both committees for review and suggestions. [After the SLC convention meeting, the Chair of the Laity Committee reported that the members of the Laity Committee very much wanted to work with SLC on this project.]

SLC discussed that the sacramental records guidelines should include the following:

- Adoption information and whether baptismal records should be updated to reflect adoption
- The problems involved with computer notations about sacramental records
- The need to keep hard copies even if some records are put on computers
- CLSA (through the BOG) might make a suggestion to USCCB that the conference consider suggesting or offering (we know they cannot mandate usage) a uniform document for baptismal records

Before the 2011 January meeting of the BOG, SLC asked for permission to work with the Laity Committee to begin research and formulation of a handbook or guidelines for sacramental records keeping. After there was no response from the BOG, for the April 2011 meeting SLC again submitted this request and received immediate permission to proceed. The BOG said that due to many diocesan policies being available on line, it was recommended that the committee review resources already on diocesan websites and provide network access to the most helpful of those policies on the committee pages and the CLSA website. It would benefit the entire Society for the group to select the best of the policies and link them as suggested.

After receiving permission from the BOG on 30 March 11, a three person subcommittee was formed. Jay Conzemius from the Laity Committee is Chair with Margaret Gillett and Mark Plewka from SLC.

Sub-commitee on Sacramental Records

Chair Jay Conzemius reports the sub-committee was constituted in May 2011. By conference call the sub-committee decided that they would initially ask members of the canon law listserve and members of CLSA to voluntarily provide their arch/diocesan policies regarding sacramental recordkeeping. As of June 2011 there were only fifteen responses.

After a time for such reports to be received, the committee will divide the non-responding arch/dioceses among them and each will personally contact chancery offices to request the name of a contact person who may provide any arch/diocesan policies on sacramental record keeping. Each contact person will be asked for a link to the policy and a short description of what the policy includes. It will also be noted in a final spreadsheet if there is no policy in place for a particular arch/diocese.

The sub-committee hopes to have the final spreadsheet available and an executive summary of the information gathered by August 2011 so it can be provided to the 2011 CLSA convention participants.

Rotal Jurisprudence: Sentences and Decrees of the Rota in Approved English Translations

This publication will provide approved English translations of rotal decisions so canonists may quote not only from the original Latin text but also from these approved English translations. Thus this publication will be distinguished from other published translations of rotal sentences and decrees in various journals.

Before the meeting of the Sacramental Law Committee at the 2010 convention all of the Sentences/ Decrees from the Rota were translated, sanitized to remove identifying names of people and places, reviewed by a second translator and put into approved format. Most of the translations had been approved by an official in Rome. As of March 2011, twelve of the sixteen translations were in final form ready for publication along with the introduction, brief biographies of the contributors, and the table of contents (waiting for page numbers).

After many delays in Rome, and at the suggestion of Msgr. Kenneth Boccafola at the Rota, reviewers for the Rota were given a deadline after which the Sentences would proceed to publication if no changes were received.

In the future, the delays in Rome could be avoided if the editor is permitted to obtain and work with a few translations at a time so the delays caused by the need to review so many at once will be avoided. The process should move forward more smoothly in the future because the protocol, the format and various other details already have been approved by PAB.

As I complete this report, Rev. Alec Wolff, is doing the final formatting and will send the final text to the EC the first week in August. Using pdf format assures that the translations approved by Rome will be exactly what will be in print. The text in Word format will also be sent to CLSA as requested.

Pre-convention Suggestion
It is part of the mandate of SLC to present to the BOG suggestions for a pre-convention workshop related to tribunal ministry. After discussion of various ideas, we decided to propose the following:

Sentence Writing
- How to craft a sentence that is ready to be sent to the parties
- Perhaps offer sanitized real cases written on grave lack of due discretion making sure the sentence includes lots of quotes from the parties and witnesses (to avoid needing the full acts of the cases for this workshop).
- Groups at tables could be asked to review the evidence and see what other ground(s) of nullity might fit the facts and evidence
- Presenter(s) would then go through at least one such ground for nullity perhaps providing an in iure section for that ground which would be other than one based on canon 1095.

SLC also offered suggested presenters. Because the BOG had the opportunity for the pre-convention workshop on rotal jurisprudence with Gus Mendonça, SLC suggestions were submitted by the BOG to the Convention Planning Committee. It seems our ideas gave rise to two convention seminars by members of SLC, John Foster and Mark Plewka.

Collaboration
From our report in the 2010 convention booklet: "Regarding #5 of the committee mandate, the SLC identified the following organizations for collaboration: Federation of Diocesan Liturgical Commissions, National Association of Pastoral Musicians, North American Forum on the Catechumenate, National Catholic Cemetery Conference, Association for Consultants of Liturgical Space, Form/

Reform, and the USCCB Committee on Divine Worship We were advised by the BOG that the committee may make informal contact in our own name but any formal collaboration must be approved by the BOG."

The Committee adds the following groups to that listing: National Association of Catholic Family Life Ministers; Southwest Liturgical Conference; National Conference for Catechetical Leaders

Future projects

In April 2011 Vice-President Rita Joyce sent SLC a suggestion from the BOG that we consider the topic of Christian Anthropology. "From a Tribunal perspective, how do we look at this and how do we address this subject when dealing with our experts since DC requires that our experts be grounded in Christian anthropology? Apparently this is a suggestion that has come from the Rota to various Tribunals this year." We were to receive clarification from the members of the BOG who proposed this idea which did not come. None of the SLC members wanted to pursue such research. The Chair contacted Catholic University of America and St. Paul University to see if anyone there might be interested. There was little response except a comment that "Christian anthropology" seems to be an accordion term similar to the word "pastoral" which can cover a multitude of meanings. The Chair found an article about the topic on-line which offers an excellent summary of the history of Blessed John Paul II's intellectual prowess and his influence on Church doctrine before and after he became Pontiff. The article is more historical than theological but could serve as an introduction to the concepts John Paul II intended in using the term "Christian anthropology." The article has footnote references so a link is included here to The Christian Anthropology of John Paul II: An Overview by Rev. Thomas McGovern: http://www.christendom-awake.org/pages/mcgovern/chrisanthro.htm

The BOG may want to consider inviting a theologian, perhaps one who teaches a course in Christian Anthropology, to address the possibility of an in depth article reflecting research about Christian Anthropology which research canonists could then use to inform their work involving marriage preparation and tribunal cases. Perhaps the CLSA might want to collaborate with the American Theological Society in this endeavor.

After review during the convention meeting of our many suggestions for research and possible publication which were listed in the 2010 convention booklet report, SLC decided that we will pursue guidelines for sacramental records in collaboration with the Laity Committee That project plus bringing the Rotal Jurisprudence to publication is sufficient focus for now.

For a future project, there seem to be many questions surrounding RCIA which could be pursued for research and possible publication.

Sr. Victoria Vondenberger, RSM

VARIA

Seventy-Third Annual Business Meeting
Jacksonville, FL
October 12, 2011

Minutes

Call to Order and Opening Prayer
   Reverend Michael Joyce, C.M., President, called to order the Seventy-Third Annual Business Meeting of the Canon Law Society of America (CLSA), on October 12, 2011 at 11:00 a.m., at the Hyatt Regency Riverfront Hotel in Jacksonville, Florida. He presided over the meeting as Chair.

   The Chair invited Mrs. Rita Joyce, CLSA Vice-President/President-Elect, to lead the assembly in an opening prayer.

   Following the opening prayer, it was announced that Dr. Barbara Anne Cusack would serve as Parliamentarian for the Business Meeting, and that *Robert's Rules of Order* would resolve matters not provided for in the CLSA's *Constitution* or *Bylaws*.

   The Chair then gave instructions on the voting procedures to be observed for the election of Officers and Consultors during the Business Meeting. The procedures were adopted as described by the Chair.

   The Chair then reviewed the procedures for addressing the assembly, and the CLSA's practices for presenting resolutions. The procedures and practices were adopted as presented by the Chair.

   The Chair then entertained a motion that Associate Members present at the meeting have the opportunity to address the assembly, as called for in Article 5.3 of the CLSA's Constitution. The motion was seconded and approved unanimously by the assembly.

   The Chair then called upon the Secretary, Mrs. Siobhan Verbeek, to read the Minutes of the Seventy-Second Business Meeting of the CLSA, unless there was a proposal to accept the Minutes as published in the 2009 CLSA Proceedings. A motion to accept the Minutes was presented. The motion was seconded, and approved unanimously by the assembly.

Election of Officers and Consultors

The Chair called upon Monsignor Ricardo Bass, Chair of the Nominations Committee, to present the slate of nominees for Officers and Consultors. Monsignor Bass announced the candidates for Officers and Consultors. No additional nominations were added to the slate, as is provided for in Article 9.5 of the CLSA's Constitution.

The Chair then read the provisions of the CLSA's Bylaws regarding elections. The active members of the CLSA were instructed to cast their votes. The tellers collected the ballots and retired to a separate room to count them. Later in the meeting Monsignor Bass returned to the Business Meeting and informed the Chair of the election results. The Chair then announced that:

For the Office of Vice-President/President-Elect:
Two hundred and twelve (212) valid ballots were cast, with 107 votes needed for election. There were 3 abstentions. The votes cast were:

Reverend John Vaughan: 116
Reverend Manuel Viera, O.F.M.: 93

The Chair declared an election with Reverend John Vaughan selected as Vice-President/President-Elect. The election was received with applause.

For the Office of Secretary:
Two hundred and twelve (212) valid ballots were cast, with 107 votes needed for election. There was 1 abstention, and 1 invalid vote. The votes cast were:

Mr. Jay Conzemius: 98
Ms. Zabrina Decker: 112

The Chair declared an election with Ms. Zabrina Decker selected as Secretary. The election was received with applause.

For the Office of Consultor:
Two hundred eleven (211) valid ballots were cast, with 107 votes needed for election. There was 1 abstention. The votes cast were:

Ms. Catherine Gilligan: 113
Reverend Mr. Gerald Jorgensen: 124
Reverend John List: 60
Reverend Bruce Miller: 110

The Chair declared an election with Ms. Catherine Gilligan and Reverend Mr. Gerald Jorgensen selected as Consultors. The election was received with applause.

Reports
President's Report
The Chair referred the assembly to the written President's Report, which was found on pages 1-3 of the *2011 Annual Reports Booklet* that was included in the registration packets for the convention. Since the membership had the opportunity to read the Report in advance of the Business Meeting, he called for any questions or observations on the Report. There were none.

Executive Coordinator's Report
The Chair then invited Sister Sharon Euart, R.S.M., CLSA Executive Coordinator, to the podium to present the Executive Coordinator's Report. Sister Euart referred to her written Report, which was found on pages 18-23 of the *2011 Annual Reports Booklet*. She indicated that the Report was intended to provide a summary of her three-year term as Executive Coordinator by highlighting the several accomplishments, activities, and challenges of the Office of the Executive Coordinator (OEC) and future initiatives and trends.

With respect to the CLSA website, she noted that since 2009, the OEC had effectively maintained and updated the website, enhancing it with resources and publications, and providing online opportunities for the Board of Governors (BOG) and CLSA committees to interact and meet via web-conferencing. In the three-year period covered in the Report, she noted that there had been a notable increase in the members' usage of the website, e.g., for paying membership dues, ordering publications, and registering for the annual convention. She expressed a commitment to continue to develop the website, but cited the need to retain staff who are competent and experienced in website management.

With respect to membership, she noted that numbers had continued to increase, including a large number of international canonists who are interested in gaining access to English-language canon law resources.

With respect to operational costs, she noted that the CLSA was able to end the fiscal year in the black, even though the year had begun with a deficit.

With respect to the CLSA's collaboration with other groups, she highlighted the Society's co-sponsorship of the August 2011 Symposium on Lay Ecclesial Ministry held at St. John's University in Collegeville, Minnesota. The CLSA's delegation to the Symposium had made essential contributions to the discussions by drawing attention to the canonical implications of the matters being discussed, and adding greater clarity with regard to the use of canonical terminology. The CLSA will continue to offer its assistance as research initiatives resulting from the Symposium are being implemented.

With respect to the CLSA Scholarship Fund, she reported that a generous bequest had been received in the amount of $40,000. Individual contributions were also made in the past fiscal year in memory of Reverend Dennis Burns, Reverend Ricardo Garcia, Reverend Joseph Morrell, Reverend Cecil Parres, C.M., and Reverend Fred Sackett, O.M.I.

Sister Euart next provided the membership with an update on the hotel site for the 2012 annual convention, the Hyatt Rosemont, Rosemont, Illinois. She stated that in the Fall of 2010, the CLSA was made aware of a labor dispute at the hotel from Unite Here, a union representing hotel workers. The union urged the CLSA to boycott the Hyatt in Rosemont. She stated that the CLSA had consulted several individuals and groups about the matter, including representatives of Unite Here and Hyatt management. With the assistance of Nix & Associates, the Executive Committee also undertook a review of the contract for the convention. Because the contract does not include a clause releasing the CLSA from financial obligations in the event of a cancellation, the BOG determined that the CLSA could not bear the cancellation fee. She stated that all correspondence from the OEC on the matter has reflected Church teaching, and that the CLSA has been assured that the Society's continued efforts to support the rights of workers has been a testament to the CLSA's good faith efforts. She concluded that Nix & Associates would continue to monitor the situation and would report to the OEC about the matter every three months.

Sister Euart then called for any questions or observations on the Executive Coordinator's Report. There were none.

Prior to exiting the dais, Sister Euart noted that several references had been made during the convention to the circulation of a *Schema* of a revised Book VI of the *Code of Canon Law.* She stated that the CLSA had not been contacted with regard to the review process for the *Schema*, but that individual members of the Society were assisting individual bishops in the review process.

Treasurer's Report
The Chair next invited Reverend Gregory Bittner to provide the Treasurer's Report. Reverend Bittner noted that his written Report was found on pages 4-17 of the *2011 Annual Reports Booklet.*

With respect to general operations, he reported that a small profit was realized in the past fiscal year, which was owed in part to the Special Faculties Seminar offered in February 2011 in Tampa, Florida.

With respect to publications, he noted that the unit was "financially stagnant" since there were no new publications during the past fiscal year.

With respect to conventions, he reported that the 2011 convention in Buffalo, New York was extraordinarily successful, netting a substantial profit that allowed for the repayment of a prior loan from the general operations unit for losses incurred from the 2008 convention.

With respect to scholarships, he reported that he had spent a considerable part of the past fiscal year trying to understand the accounting method related to the awarding of scholarships. As a result of this study, the Resource and Asset Management Committee recommended changes to the accounting operations for the scholarship unit, which he hoped would set the unit on a sound financial course. Attention will also be given to marketing the scholarship in an effort to increase yearly applicants.

With respect to investments, he updated the membership on the September 2011 investment figures, in order to illustrate the loss of income and the difficulty of budgeting within a volatile market. He likewise informed the members that the office of the Executive Coordinator had hired a new Accountant/Auditor.

With regard to the CLSA's financial future, he concluded by encouraging the membership to begin reflecting upon a potential dues increase, since the last dues increase occurred in 2003. He reported that another way to increase income was to look at a total return of the CLSA's investments, rather than simply at interest and dividends. Since the BOG Handbook indicated that a percentage of the investments may be used to offset deficits in general operations, he stated that the Resource and Asset Management Committee would be exploring proposals to implement the policy in a manner that will not adversely impact current investments.

Reverend Bittner then reviewed the 2011-2012 budget, which was found on pages 6-15 of the *2011 Annual Reports Booklet*. He thanked the members of the Resource and Asset Management Committee and the staff of the OEC for their assistance over the past year, and invited any questions or observations on the Report.

Chorbishop John Faris of the Eparchy of Saint Maron asked for clarification on the reporting of future scholarship commitments in the annual budget. Reverend Bittner responded that when a scholarship is awarded the funding for the entire award is placed in a designated account. He is working with the Accountant on the proper way to report this practice in the annual budget reports. There were no other questions or observations on the Treasurer's Report.

Resolutions

The Chair read the applicable CLSA Bylaws that governed the proposing of resolutions from the floor and asked if there were any such resolutions to be presented. There being none, he called upon Brother Patrick Shea, O.F.M., Chair of the Resolutions Committee, and Reverend Michael Clark, Time-keeper, to approach the podium and present the resolution previously submitted to the Resolutions Committee.

The full text of the resolution was projected onto screens in the hall. In addition, printed copies of the resolution were distributed to those in attendance.

Brother Shea thanked the presenters for submitting their resolution well in advance of the convention, and the members of the Committee on Resolutions for their service to the CLSA.

Resolution I: An Offer of Assistance to the USCCB

Proposed by: Reverends Patrick Cogan, S.A. and James Coriden

Be it resolved that the Board of Governors offer the services of the Society to the USCCB to assist in formulating appropriate procedures for the conduct of investigation into the work of theologians in the United States.

Implementation by means of: A letter to the president of the USCCB.

Anticipated Cost: $1.00

Cost supplied by: The CLSA from the unrestricted, general operations funds.

Discussion: The Resolutions Committee moved the resolution. Brother Shea then invited the authors to introduce the rationale. Reverend Patrick Cogan, S.A. of St. Paul University, Ottawa, Canada noted that in recent decades the work of various theologians has been investigated on both the diocesan and national levels. He stated that, as recently as July 2011, Most Reverend Timothy M. Dolan, President of the United States Conference of Catholic Bishops (USCCB) said, "...we bishops should always be mindful of improving the manner in which we engage theologians in a necessary discussion of their work." Reverend Cogan stated that the resolution was put forward to alert the USCCB to the talent that exists within the CLSA, and to extend the CLSA's offer to be of service to the episcopal conference, as was done in the past. Reverend James Coriden of the Washington Theological Union, Washington, DC urged the membership to support the resolution. He recalled that the 1989 document of the USCCB, *Doctrinal Responsibilities*, had been a joint effort of the episcopal conference, the Catholic Theological Society of America, and the CLSA. It was hoped that a similar cooperative approach could be undertaken in developing a published procedure for the USCCB Committee on Doctrine.

Msgr. C. Michael Padazinski of the Archdiocese of San Francisco and a member of the Board of Governors (BOG), reported that the BOG had reviewed the resolution and supported the text as it was proposed.

Msgr. John Alesandro of the Diocese of Rockville Centre spoke in favor of the resolution. He questioned, however, the clarity of the resolution's wording, since the introductions from the authors seemed to indicate an intent to assist with the development of procedures on the national level. The Be it resolved clause was then revised by the authors to read,

> *Be it resolved* that the Board of Governors offer the services of the Society to the USCCB to assist in formulating appropriate procedures for the conduct of investigations *by the USCCB or its committees* into the work of theologians in the United States.

The question was then called from the floor. The resolution was approved unanimously.

Old Business
The Chair opened the floor to discuss any Old Business of interest to the assembly. There was none.

New Business
The Chair opened the floor to discuss any New Business of interest to the assembly. There was none.

Varia
Greetings by Officials of Canon Law Societies

The Chair then invited visiting officials of other Canon Law Societies to the podium to address the assembly.

Monsignor David Hogan, President of the Canon Law Society of Great Britain and Ireland (CLSGB&I), brought the greetings and good wishes of the CLSGB&I. He thanked the CLSA for its hospitality, welcome and cordiality. He invited the assembly to the May 2012 convening of the CLSAGB&I in Edinburgh, Scotland, where he promised that the cordiality extended to him in Jacksonville would be returned in kind.

Very Reverend Anthony Kerin, President of the Canon Law Society of Australia and New Zealand (CLSANZ), bestowed the greetings of the CLSANZ. He acknowledged the presence of Reverend Brendan Daily, Vice-President of the CLSANZ, who was also present at the convention. He thanked the CLSA for its conviviality, hospitality, and cordiality. He reported that, due to a decreasing number of bishops who possess a canon law degree in the episcopal conference of Australia, the conference had recently established a Bishops Council for Canon Law to advise the bishops on canonical matters. He noted that the CLSANZ continue to offer courses in canonical formation with Catholic Religions Australia. He informed the assembly that the CLSANZ's publications, including the *Proceedings* of its annual convention and the canonical journal The Canonist, were available for order through its website. He announced that the CLSANZ's

2012 convention would be held September 10-13 in Auckland, New Zealand, and that its 2013 convention would be held September 2-5 in Adelaide, Australia. He concluded his remarks by stating that he had an opportunity to review the proposed Schema of Book VI of the Code of Canon Law from the Pontifical Council of Legislative Texts and found it to be underwhelming and in need of further revision.

Monsignor Wayne Kirkpatrick, President of the Canadian Canon Law Society (CCLS), bestowed the greetings of the CCLS. He invited the assembly to the CCLS's October 2011 convention in Cornwall, Ontario, and reported that the CCLS was in the process of revising its bylaws and updating its website.

Reverend Michael Joyce reported that he was in receipt of an e-mail message from Monsignor Patrick Valdrini, President of the Consociatio Internationalis Studio Iuris Canonici Promovendo, expressing his regret at not being able to attend the CLSA convention. Professor Kurt Martens of the School of Canon Law at The Catholic University of America was then acknowledged as the Consociatio's delegate in attendance at the convention.

Recognition of Outgoing Convention Chairperson
The Chair invited Reverend Michael Boccaccio, CLSA Convention Chairperson, to come forward. On behalf of the entire CLSA, the Chair thanked Reverend Boccaccio for his five-year service to the Society as Convention Chairperson. The recognition was met with resounding applause.

Adjournment
There being no further business, the Chair entertained a motion to adjourn the meeting. The motion was seconded, and passed unanimously.

At 11:50 a.m., Reverend Joyce formally closed the Seventy-Third Business Meeting of the Canon Law Society of America.

Respectfully Submitted,
Ms. Siobhan M. Verbeek
Secretary

VARIA

CONVENTION MASS HOMILY
Reverend Michael P. Joyce, CM

The words of the scriptures which have just been proclaimed frighten me. I hear them both as a "scholar of the law" and as an ecclesiastical judge. There are years when I wonder if the group that prepared the arrangement of readings in the lectionary chose these readings to coincide with the annual convention of the Canon Law Society of America.

In the Gospel Jesus sounds as though he is accusing us scholars of the law of laying burdens on people but not coming to their assistance. Paul sounds like he is warning us who are judges that we are condemning ourselves with the very standards that we use to judge.

My reactions to the accusation and warning can be defensive and rationalizing. After all, Jesus was addressing associates of the Pharisees and not canon lawyers. Paul was writing to Jews who considered themselves superior to Gentiles and not to ecclesiastical judges. I am off the hook. I can prove it to you by pointing to sound exegesis of the scriptures.

In my better moments, however, I can respond to these charges with a sober self-examination. Karl Barth noted that the Word of God is a Word of Judgment (cf. Karl Barth, *Church Dogmatics*, vol. 3, p. 211). The Word judges all human beings about their conformity to it. When we are conformed to the Word of God, then authentic justice takes effect in the world. The Word that has been proclaimed in our midst today invites us to critique ourselves as canonist about our fidelity in our profession of the gospel.

I must candidly admit to you, my sisters and brothers, my colleagues and co-workers, there are too many times when people have looked for an explanation of the law and instead of giving them something they can understand, I have laid burdens on them. I failed to help them with those burdens when I lost sight of either the situation of the one seeking understanding or of the commands of the Judaic and Christian covenants to love the Lord our God with our whole heart and mind and spirit and to love our neighbor as ourselves.

I too often fall prey to the temptation to judge other people. As ecclesiastical judges, we render judgments on questions about truth and justice, not about people. However as a human being, I step aside at times from my professional learning and experience. I hold people accountable to standards that I set of which they likely have no knowledge. Yet Christ admonishes us, "Do not judge so that you will not be judged." (Mt 7:1)

Still, an honest self-assessment must take into consideration that more often than not, I do help people with their burdens. In fact, that is a significant characteristic and contribution of our service in the Church as canon lawyers. As I continue on the Christian journey, I develop in my appreciation of the dignity and giftedness of those different from me.

These deeds are performed by us because "with the Lord there is mercy and fullness of redemption." It is the presence of God's Spirit in us given at baptism and confirmation and renewed through our participation in the Eucharist that redeems us and restores us in his justice. The Lord does not mark our iniquities. He gives himself to us as a generous gift. He hears our supplicant voices. This gift is experienced most concretely in the person of Jesus Christ "who is present among us and whose love gathers us together." (Eucharistic Prayers for Various Needs and Occasions) I thank God for you who are members of the Society. Your work and lives both support and challenge me as I journey with Christ as his disciple and exercise the Church in the field of canon law. I invite you to give thanks to God for the many gifts you have received and glorify God with the service of our lives and our deeds.

VARIA

ROLE OF LAW AWARD CITATION
Reverend Michael P. Joyce, CM

Each year the Canon Law Society of America presents its distinguished Role of Law Award to an individual considered to be outstanding in the field of canonical science. The By-Laws of the Society directs the Board of Governors to select a person who demonstrates in his or her life and legal practice the following characteristics:

> Embodiment of pastoral attitude, commitment to research and study, participation in the development of law, response to needs or practical assistance, facilitation of dialogue and the interchange of ideas within the Society and with other groups.

These qualifications are a concise re-statement of the constitutionally-expressed purposes of the Society.

The person to whom this award is given is viewed by us as one who embodies all that we, as members of the Society hold dear, as one to whom we can look for guidance and inspiration. Such an official statement alone is perhaps the greatest honor that can be bestowed on anyone – to be selected by one's friends and peers as outstanding among them.

This year's recipient of the Role of Law Award was ordained a priest of the Maronite Church in 1976. After being awarded a doctorate in Eastern canon law by the Pontifical Oriental Institute in Rome in 1980, he served in the administration of the Eparchy of Saint Maron for sixteen years in several offices, the last being Protosyncellus (Vicar General). In 1991, he was ordained a chorbishop of the Maronite Church. He worked at the Catholic Near East Welfare Association from 1996 to 2009. In 2009, he was appointed pastor of Saint Louis Gonzaga Church in Utica, New York.

Our honoree this year has served in a wide variety of ministries in the Catholic Church. He has lectured at the Catholic University of America for more than a decade. He has written a commentary on the structures and governance of the Eastern Catholic Churches as well as numerous articles on the Eastern Churches, Eastern canon law, and ecumenism. He has served in the past as consultor of the National Conference of Catholic Bishops Conference Liaison Committee for Latin and Eastern Church Affairs.

In the field of ecumenism, the recipient of this year's Role of Law Award is currently a member of the Catholic delegation of the Joint Working Group, a liaison body of the Holy See and the World Council of Churches. He also serves on the North American Orthodox-Catholic Theological Consultation and the United States Oriental Orthodox-Roman Catholic Consultation. He has been deeply involved for many years with the Equestrian Order of the Holy Sepulcher. For his work on behalf of Christians in the Holy Land, he was recently awarded the Golden Palm, the highest honor given by the Order.

Our honoree has generously served the Canon Law Society of America. He is a past-president of the Society. He currently is the chair of the Research and Development Committee and a member of the Governance Committee and Publications Committee. He has served in the past as chair of the Eastern Law Committee and as Consultor. He was also chair of the *ad hoc* committee responsible for the preparation of the most recent English translation of the *Code of Canons of the Eastern Churches*.

Tonight we honor a friend, a colleague, an educator, a pastor, and a fellow canonist. He is truly a Catholic who breathes with both lungs of the Church. It my privilege to present the 2011 Role of Law Award, on behalf of the Canon Law Society of America and the Board of Governors, to Chorbishop John D. Faris.

VARIA

ROLE OF LAW AWARD RESPONSE
Chorbishop John D. Faris

I must begin by expressing my deep gratitude to the Board of Governors and members of the Canon law Society of America for this award. All of us dedicated to ministry in the Church are subtly imbued with the attitude that we should not demand or even expect a word of appreciation but, after completion of a task, to accept dismissal as a good and faithful servant. This recognition, while not deserved, is appreciated and encouraging.

I realize that I am the second Eastern Catholic canonist who has been given this award by the Society. Ukrainian Catholic Archimandrite Victor Pospishil received the Role of Law award in 1994. I am humbled to follow in the footsteps of this scholar for whom I have so much affection and esteem.

The Canon Law Society of America can take pride in all that it has done on behalf of the Eastern Catholic Churches. It was the first to publish a vernacular translation of the *Codex Canonum Ecclesiarum Orientalium*. For decades the Society had a committee dedicated to the concerns of Eastern Catholic Churches, a function that has now been entrusted to the present Church Governance Committee. It should also be noted that Eastern Catholic topics figure regularly in the convention programs. We Eastern Catholics are grateful for all these initiatives, but most of all for the interest and loving concern that this Society—with its predominantly Latin Catholic membership—has shown for us.

This evening I would like to reflect briefly on concerns that are rather new for us Catholics: ecumenism and the reform of the Church implicit in it. Before Vatican II, Catholic efforts on behalf of Church unity meant prayers for the return of schismatics or apostates to the Catholic Church. The issue of whether the Church stood in need of reform never arose; in fact, the generally-accepted opinion was that the Church *could not be reformed*. And then, on 28 October 1958, Cardinal Angelo Roncalli was elected to the See of Peter. After the nearly two-decade pontificate of his predecessor, Pius XII, one might surmise that the cardinal electors had intended to elect a short-term caretaker; Roncalli was 76 at the time of his election.[1] They did not seem to be looking for a man of action or innovation.

---

1 Perhaps Pope John XXIII himself perhaps realized that he would not be given enough time to complete the task; during his first consistory of 15 December 1958, he appointed Giovanni Battista Montini, then archbishop of Milan, as a cardinal. Montini was to succeed him as Paul VI.

Nevertheless, within 90 days of his election, Pope John XXIII made an announcement that was to change the world. On 25 January 1959, at the Basilica of Saint Paul Outside the Walls—and this is important—at vespers celebrating the conclusion of the Week of Prayer for Christian Unity, the pope announced the revision of the *Code of Canon Law*, a synod for the Diocese of Rome and—most importantly —the convocation of an ecumenical council. As an aside, the press embargo on the announcement expired before the announcement was made because the services ran a little longer than scheduled; the news was broadcast to the world before anyone in the basilica knew anything about it.[2]

I call this event to your attention because it is important to remind ourselves of the primary purpose of the Second Vatican Council. Pope John XXIII convoked the council for the express purpose of the unity of the Christians and human family. This reconciliation was to be accomplished by means a renewal of the Church.[3]

To reiterate: the purpose of the council was the restoration of the unity of Christians and the means to this end was to be the renewal of the Church. I would postulate that somewhere along the line, the means became the end and the end became marginalized. Have we—as individuals and as a professional society—focused on the renewal of the Church and paid insufficient attention to the primary purpose of the Council, Christian unity? An examination of the mandates of the various on-going committees reveal that the word "ecumenism" is nowhere mentioned; presentations treating ecumenical issues in our conventions are rare.

There may be a few reasons for this oversight. Some canonists retain the formerly-held approach to Church unity that the non-Catholics should renounce their errors and return to the unity of the Catholic Church. Others argue that the quest for Church unity is a utopian ideal and characterize ecumenists as seekers of the pot of gold at the end of the rainbow. Still others among us deem ecumenism to be a praiseworthy endeavor, but are just to busy with putting out fires and keeping the operations going to address the issue.

Perhaps institutional fatigue has set in: Lots of conferences and papers, but "apparently" little to show for it. It is not my intention to justify ecumenism, but to encourage the Society and canonists to engage more actively in ecumenical

---

[2] http://thekeysaremightier.com/blog/?p=105 The pope's secretary, Bishop Capovilla said on that Sunday, 25 January 1959, the pope got up and prayed, but after celebrating Mass, "He remained kneeling longer than usual." He then went to the ceremony for the feast of St. Paul at the Basilica of St. Paul Outside the Walls. The ceremony ran longer than scheduled, and before he could announce the convening of Vatican II, the press embargo on the announcement expired. The council was then "broadcast by the media before the Pope could communicate it to the cardinals."

[3] John XXIII, allocution 11 October, 1962, esp. "Unitas in Christiana et humana familia.": *Enchiridion Vaticanum* 1: 48-50.

initiatives. Now that some of the fruits of the ecumenical movement are about to be harvested, we canonists are needed more than ever.[4] There has been astounding progress in the past fifty years to heal a breach that has existed for a millennium.

Forgive my boldness, but I would assert that canon law as a discipline has not fully embraced ecumenism; nor have canonists devoted enough time and effort to promote the unity of Christians. Permit me to illustrate this point.

As one might expect, neither the 1917 *Codex Iuris Canonici,* nor the pre-conciliar, incomplete *Codex Iuris Canonici Orientalis* (issued between 1948 and 1957) for the Eastern Catholic Churches contain a single canon that promotes ecumenism. The sea-change took place when the council addressed the issue in the dogmatic constitution on the Church, *Lumen gentium,* in the specific decree on the topic, *Unitatis redintegratio* and other documents, such as *Orientalium Ecclesiarum* also treat the issue. It was then left to canon law to codify the conciliar insights into the revised codes for the Latin and Eastern Churches.

The commission entrusted with revising the Latin Code was established by Pope John XXIII on 28 March 1963, shortly before his death. In 1967, the Commission elaborated a set of principles to guide the task of revision. These principles were submitted to the Synod of Bishops and were approved in October 1967. One of the main purposes of the ten *Principles for the Revision of the Latin Code*[5] "was to guarantee harmony between the Church's revised law and the conciliar documents.... The ten principles ... are more than a historical curiosity of the process of revision. They are useful ... in understanding the theory behind certain legal changes..."[6] It is noteworthy that the *Principles* are silent with regard to ecumenism. Had the primary purpose of the council already disappeared from the "radar screen" of canon law? This is not to say that the 1983 Latin code is devoid of canons that foster the reconciliation of Christians, but one would have a difficult time in asserting that it is a priority of the Latin Code.

Because of a variety of historical, ecclesial, liturgical and social factors, the situation is different with regard to the *Code of Canons of the Eastern Churches.* After providing for a rationale and possibility for a common (n. 1), genuinely Eastern code for the Eastern Catholic Churches (n. 2), the 1974 *Guidelines for the Revision of the Code of Oriental Canon Law* treats the *ecumenical character* of the future code (n. 3).

---

4   See Walter Kasper, *Harvesting the Fruits: Basic Aspects of Christian Faith in Ecumenical Dialogue* (London: Continuum International Publishing Group, 2009).

5   *Communicationes* 1 (1969) 77-85.

6   John A. Alesandro, "General Introduction," in James A. Coriden, Thomas J. Green, Donal E. Heintschel, *The Code of Canon Law. A Text and Commentary.* (Mahwah, NJ: Paulist Press, 1985) 6-7.

The *Guidelines* assure the Orthodox that the future code will be only for those persons who are members of an Eastern Catholic Church, that is, the Catholic Church is not presuming to legislate on behalf of the Orthodox Churches. The *Guidelines* go on to refer to *Orientalium Ecclesiarum* (nn. 1 and 24) and emphasize that, "It must be a prime concern of the new code to promote the fulfillment of the desire expressed by the Second Vatican Council that the Eastern Catholic Churches "flourish and execute with new apostolic vigor the task entrusted to them ... as regards the special office of promoting the unity of all Christians."

Pope John Paul II, in his presentation of the 1990 Eastern code, was enthusiastic regarding its ecumenical dimensions: "There is no norm in the code that does not promote the path of unity among all Christians."[7] Pope John Paul II went so far as to "present" the new code to the Orthodox Churches.[8] The late pope took a similar optimistic approach regarding the ecumenical effectiveness of the new code in *Sacri canones*,[9] the apostolic constitution that promulgated it. He referred to the possible obsolescence of the code by indicating that it might be abrogated or changed when full communion of all the Eastern Churches with the Catholic Church has been restored.[10]

---

7   "Discorso del Santo Padre alla Presentazione del Codice dei Canoni delle Chiese Orientali alla XXVIII Congregazione Generale del Sinodo dei Vescovi il 25 X 1990." Published in Nuntia 31 (1990) 10-16. Translation from George Nedungatt (ed.), A Guide to the Eastern Code, (Pontificio Istituto Orientale: Rome, Italy, 2002) 29.

8   Ibid., 29. For a brief commentary on Orthodox "reception" of the Eastern Code, see Nedungatt, op. cit., 53-54.

9   John Paul II, apostolic constitution Sacri canones, 18 October 1990. AAS 82 (1990) 1045-1363. English translation of apostolic letter in Canon Law Society of America, *Code of Canons of the Eastern Churches. Latin-English Edition.* (Washington, DC: Canon Law Society of America, 2001) xxi-xxviii.

10 "Thus it happens that the canons of the Code of Canons of the Eastern Churches must have the same firmness as the laws of the Code of Canons of the Latin Church, that is, that they remain in force until abrogated or changed by the supreme authority of the Church for just reasons. The most serious of those reasons is the full communion of all the Eastern Churches with the catholic Church, in addition to being most in accord with the desire of our Savior Jesus Christ himself." Ibid., xxiii.

The reference to the transitory nature of the current legal arrangements resonates the concluding paragraph of Orientalium Ecclesiarum:

> The holy council finds great joy in the earnest and fruitful collaboration of the Eastern and Western Catholic Churches, and at the same time makes the following declaration: All these legal arrangements are made in view of the present conditions, until such time as the Catholic Church and the separated Eastern Churches unite together in the fullness of communion. (n. 30a)

During the revision process, consideration was given to the possibility of including a canon referring to the transitory character of the code until full communion with all the Eastern Churches was established. This approach was rejected because the Legislator wanted the *Codex Canonum Ecclesiarum Orientalium* to have the same juridic firmness

Ironically, we are encouraged to pray and strive for its obsolescence and the abrogation of the Eastern code. When full communion between the Orthodox and Catholic Churches has been achieved, the Eastern code will have fulfilled one of its primary missions; a new legal arrangement will be necessary.

I would call to your attention a canon in the Eastern code:

> CCEO c. 192 §2. The eparchial bishop is to see in a special way that all Christian faithful committed to his care foster unity among Christians according to principles approved by the Church.

It should be noted that this canon does not have a counterpart in the Latin code. The purpose of these comments is not to compare the two codes, but to urge Latin canonists to engage themselves in ecumenism and make a contribution that will be crucial. We must remember that the Eastern Catholics number only 15 million in a Catholic Church of approximately 1.2 billion; the effectiveness is limited. Their efforts will logically focus on the Orthodox Churches. It will be left to the Latin canonists to formulate institutions needed by a Church that will exist when West has re-united with West.

On 2 October 2010, the North American Orthodox-Catholic Theological Consultation issued a statement entitled, "Steps Toward a Reunited Church: A Sketch of an Orthodox-Catholic Vision for the Future."[11] This document marks an unprecedented effort to begin to visualize the shape of a reunited Catholic and Orthodox Church. While it is difficult to predict what a structure of worldwide ecclesial communion, between our Churches, might look like, it must be admitted that re-united Church cannot be achieved

> "...without new, better harmonized structures of leadership on both sides: new conceptions of both synodality and primacy in the universal Church, new approaches to the way primacy and authority are exercised in both our communions."[12]

This document can serve as an impetus for canonists and the Society as a whole to consider new approaches to Catholic governance and to articulate what structures a "reunited Church" will need.

The success of the ecumenical initiatives of the Church is crucial. To draw from the motto of the Crusades: *Deus lo vult*. God wills it.

---

as the *Codex Iuris Canonici*.

11 The North American Orthodox-Catholic Theological Consultation, *Steps towards a Reunited Church: A Sketch of an Orthodox-Catholic Vision for the Future*. Georgetown University, Washington, DC, 2 October 2010.

12 Ibid., nn. 5-6

VARIA

U.S. TRIBUNAL STATISTICS
2010

Since 1975, the CLSA has published Tribunal Statistics annually in *Proceedings*. These statistics are provided voluntarily by participating tribunal offices in the United States. This year's statistical report was compiled differently than in previous years. Tribunals were asked to submit a copy of the report submitted annually to the Apostolic Signatura, as well as some basic financial information, either by sending it to the CLSA office or filling out the information online. This change should result in more accurate comparison of statistics between U.S. tribunals in the future and be simpler for tribunal personnel to complete.

Participation in the survey was down slightly compared to previous years. The CLSA received information from 84% of tribunals, compared to 88% the last two years. This discrepancy should be considered when analyzing this year's data to previous years, particularly in comparing the total number of decisions made. Included in this year's report is the number of decisions found contrary to nullity from each reporting tribunal, with the percentage of negative decisions out of the total calculated. Following the same gradual trend as indicated in the past several years, the number of cases introduced and decisions made in U.S. tribunals continues to decline, while expenses continue to rise. The tribunals of Arlington, Atlanta, Boise, Bridgeport, Brownsville, Crookston, Denver, Fall River, Fort Wayne-South Bend, Galveston-Houston, Gary, Juneau, Kansas City-St. Joseph, Lafayette in Louisiana, Las Vegas, Manchester, Miami, Newark, Orange in California, Phoenix, Rockville Centre, San Francisco, Santa Fe, eparchy of St. Maron of Brooklyn, Stockton, Venice, Victoria in Texas, Ukrainian eparchy of St. Josaphat in Parma, Washington, Wichita and Winona did not participate.

Five Year Comparison

Year	Documentary Cases	Formal Cases (Previous Year)	Formal Cases (This Year)	Cases Abated	Formal Decisions	Fees Received	Diocesan Subsidy	Total Expenses	Percentage of tribunals reporting
2010	4147	15368	16787	1284	14360	$5,193,872	$26,447,648	$31,612,970	83.78%
2009	12239	17457	19039	1846	17106	$4,980,461	$26,104,591	$31,123,946	88.11%
2008	14089	18704	19805	2002	18503	$5,551,648	$26,434,692	$32,465,062	88.11%
2007	12593	19168	19864	2451	18644	$5,411,389	$25,444,135	$30,950,916	86.49%
2006	14246	20466	21850	2603	20117	$6,109,704	$22,381,454	$27,936,716	86.49%

Formal Cases

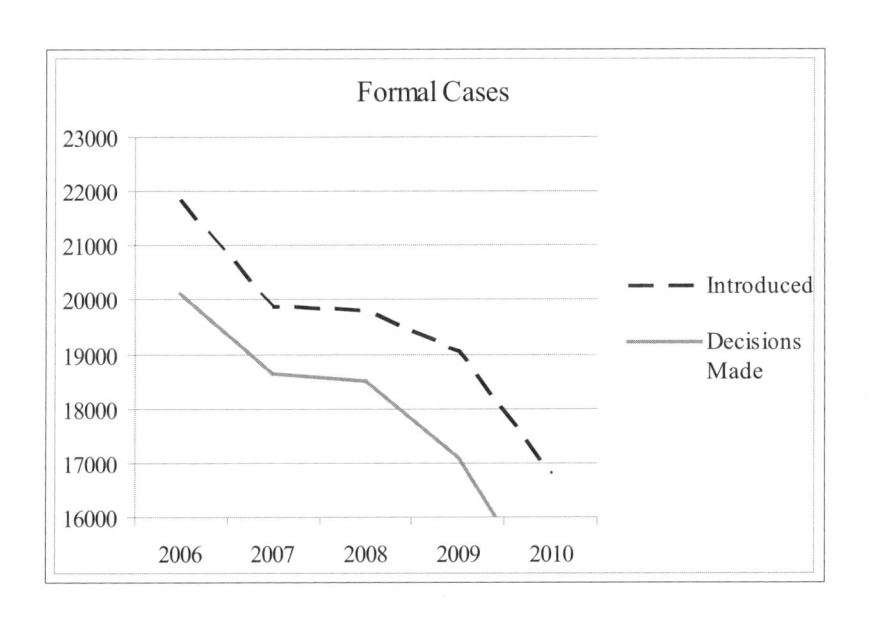

(Graph showing "Introduced" and "Decisions Made" from 2006 to 2010, y-axis from 16000 to 23000)

First Instance Statistics: 2010

(Arch)Diocese	Documentary Cases Closed	Formal Cases Held Over	Formal Cases Introduced	Sentence in Favor of Nullity	Sentence Contrary to Nullity	Total formal decisions (affirmative and negative)	Percentage of Total Decisions Found Contrary to Nullity	Peremption/ Renunciation	Total Fees Received	Amount of Diocesan Subsidy	Total Annual Expenses
Albany		42	83	78	2	80	3%	5			
Alexandria	7	98	40	40	3	43	7%	14	$11,375	$170,960	$182,335
Allentown		141	172	136		136		22	$62,380	$364,500	$426,880
Altoona-Johnstown	2	20	91	69	1	70	1%	4	$300	$71,000	$60,000
Amarillo		22	38	29	4	33	12%	2	$7,360	$31,000	$38,300
Anchorage	5	44	44	27		27		3	$10,343	$60,993	$71,336
Austin	32	148	202	138	4	142	3%	20	$69,619	$253,449	$324,669
Baker		75	27	42	3	45	7%	22	$9,335	$101,648	$110,983
Baltimore	193	165	192						$122,364		
Baton Rouge	15	135	130	107		107		10	$44,942	$193,182	$299,992
Beaumont	9	105	68	54		54		4	$19,100	$170,280	$189,380
Belleville	10	82	60	37	1	38	3%	1	$10,320	$52,547	$62,867
Biloxi		127	38	33	3	36	8%	13	$2,780	$25,604	$129,969
Birmingham	11	70	65	62	2	64	3%	1	$22,610	$159,420	$187,385

(Arch)Diocese	Documentary Cases Closed	Formal Cases Held Over	Formal Cases Introduced	Sentence in Favor of Nullity	Sentence Contrary to Nullity	Total formal decisions (affirmative and negative)	Percentage of Total Decisions Found Contrary to Nullity	Peremption/ Renunciation	Total Fees Received	Amount of Diocesan Subsidy	Total Annual Expenses
Bismarck		34	45	39		39			$12,625	$224,660	$237,285
Boston	2	98	202	152	4	156	3%	16			
Brooklyn	17	197	112	180		180		42	$129,475	$356,717	$497,467
Buffalo	118	38	100	103		103			$58,963	$189,729	$249,727
Burlington	2	54	47	32	3	35	9%	5		$52,570	$49,360
Camden	1	108	54	53	2	55	4%	14	$129,999	$402,434	$532,433
Charleston	12	32	85	61	1	62	2%	7	$96,123	$300,792	$396,915
Charlotte	18	116	119	128	5	133	4%	4	$62,410	$393,247	$532,590
Cheyenne	6	43	52	61	1	62	2%		$33,000	$97,000	$130,000
Chicago	32	346	411	401	3	404	1%	18	$384,300	$1,334,332	$1,718,632
Cincinnati		255	257	254	54	308	18%	18	$89,072	$451,694	$510,021
Cleveland	250	350	373	458	2	460	0%	18	$162,688	$482,177	$658,678
Colorado Springs	56	65	41	36	14	50	28%	9	$19,965	$176,469	$196,434
Columbus	19	179	206	211	2	213	1%	19	$115,767	$343,906	$431,225
Corpus Christi		106	183	73		73		4	$24,447	$87,947	$112,394
Covington	3	31	53	54		54			$3,700	$186,800	$190,500
Dallas		235	238	193	22	215	10%	22		$384,228	$381,482
Davenport	6	92	70	69		69		7	$28,220	$105,680	$133,900
Des Moines	58	60	94						$35,595	$104,010	$139,605
Detroit	7	64	390	382	3	385	1%	34			
Dodge City	3	24	32	50		50		3	$2,855	$68,895	$71,750
Dubuque	16	98	146	129		129		4	$58,949	$161,958	$220,907
Duluth		55	27	34	1	35	3%	5	$6,920		$59,642
El Paso		124	56	86		86		2			
Erie		89	122	139		139			$30,491	$315,901	$346,392
Evansville	8	4	59	58		58		2	$18,700	$194,079	$212,779
Fairbanks		12	15	9		9			$1,500		
Fargo		54	53						$6,843	$184,729	$191,572
Fort Worth	10	649	281	221	3	224	1%	27			
Fresno	203	130	163	148		148		5			
Gallup		22	21	20	1	21	5%	3	$6,575		$22,277
Gary		145	69			44			$26,940	$198,963	$236,292
Gaylord	4	51	38	42	5	47	11%	9		$95,584	
Grand Island	1	53	40	41		41		3	$3,160	$185,527	$188,687

(Arch)Diocese	Documentary Cases Closed	Formal Cases Held Over	Formal Cases Introduced	Sentence in Favor of Nullity	Sentence Contrary to Nullity	Total formal decisions (affirmative and negative)	Percentage of Total Decisions Found Contrary to Nullity	Peremption/ Renunciation	Total Fees Received	Amount of Diocesan Subsidy	Total Annual Expenses
Grand Rapids	131	101	153	113	1	114	1%	12		$169,839	$169,839
Great Falls-Billings	36	17	19	20		20		7	$2,275	$35,166	$37,441
Green Bay		42	148	134	4	138	3%		$53,285	$125,989	$179,274
Greensburg		20	84	67		67		2			
Harrisburg		277	198	176	10	186	5%	18	$110,000	$393,416	$503,416
Hartford		115	126	70	15	85	18%	20			
Helena		84	43	38		38		2		$100,000	$100,000
Honolulu	1	26	58	43	1	44	2%	7	$18,075	$142,102	$160,177
Houma-Thibodaux	1	32	36	38		38		2	$14,960	$42,683	$57,643
Indianapolis	20	130	80	76	2	78	3%	18	$52,629	$314,420	$367,048
Jackson	4	16	57	36	4	40	10%	11		$94,723	$94,723
Jefferson City	22	147	102	107	4	111	4%	8		$149,751	$154,066
Joliet		66	199	185	27	212	13%	1	$32,445	$496,500	$561,500
Kalamazoo	7	62	67	62		62		2	$25,220	$57,963	$83,183
Kansas City in Kansas		231	252	198	4	202	2%	19	$65,831	$171,548	$237,379
La Crosse		79	161	169	1	170	1%	12	$57,485	$101,186	$195,564
Lafayette in Indiana	76	79	98	72	4	76	5%	22			
Lake Charles	64	91	63	82	6	88	7%	3	$32,295	$140,154	$172,449
Lansing	9	122	154	126	3	129	2%	12	$29,785	$365,359	$395,144
Laredo	33	27	17	16	1	17	6%		$9,352	$71,616	$80,968
Las Cruces		111	51	49	3	52	6%	9	$23,425	$81,445	$105,395
Lexington	5	97	54	86	3	89	3%	14		$145,653	$145,653
Lincoln		79	55	36	5	41	12%	15			
Little Rock	28	99	178	188		188		11	$25,515	$148,485	$174,000
Los Angeles		463	465								
Los Angeles, Eparchy of Our Lady of Lebanon of	1	20	36	33		33		1	$21,750	$350	$22,100
Louisville	13	8	140	122	2	124	2%	1	$14,125	$115,545	$129,670
Lubbock	53	62	50	48		48		11	$11,585	$59,500	$71,085
Madison		54	61						$22,382	$103,877	$126,259

(Arch)Diocese	Documentary Cases Closed	Formal Cases Held Over	Formal Cases Introduced	Sentence in Favor of Nullity	Sentence Contrary to Nullity	Total formal decisions (affirmative and negative)	Percentage of Total Decisions Found Contrary to Nullity	Peremption/ Renunciation	Total Fees Received	Amount of Diocesan Subsidy	Total Annual Expenses
Marquette		39	39	43	1	44	2%		$5,270	$30,054	$35,966
Memphis	9	79	102	63	4	67	6%	3	$6,175	$169,407	$175,582
Metuchen		101	53	90	2	92	2%	5	$30,485	$254,962	$285,447
Military Services		214	90	69		69		14	$39,585	$161,398	$215,075
Milwaukee	1	272	226	277	1	278	0%	29	$94,073	$391,929	$486,002
Mobile		88	70	54	3	57	5%	11	$46,132	$298,481	$344,613
Monterey	45	57	44	31	4	35	11%	11	$17,145	$74,842	$91,987
Nashville & Knoxville	30	181	107	56	14	70	20%	7		$365,076	$365,076
New Orleans	5	151	157	73	5	78	6%	2	$51,300	$311,230	$362,530
New Ulm	15	39	25	36		36			$1,650	$210,755	$212,405
New York	4	121	151	101	8	109	7%		$165,067	$1,155,583	$1,320,650
Newton, Eparchy of		14	12	15		15		4	$9,600	$12,744	$21,855
Norwich, Connecticut		39	53	52	2	54	4%		$8,375	$255,419	$263,794
Oakland		221	108	95	1	96	1%	6	$74,570	$427,546	$502,116
Ogdensburg		93	48	55	2	57	4%	10	$19,737	$92,388	$112,125
Oklahoma City	118	74	206	183	14	197	7%			$224,660	$224,660
Omaha	124	120	154	118	9	127	7%	6	$44,720	$225,214	$269,934
Orlando		67	276	224	67	291	23%	2	$157,434	$265,098	$389,536
Owensboro	16	71	84	55	2	57	4%	2	$7,940	$214,148	$222,088
Palm Beach	153	70	78	77	2	79	3%	2			
Parma, Byzantine Catholic Eparchy	2	14	10	12	2	14	14%	2			
Passaic, Byzantine-Ruthenian Eparchy		15		6		6			$2,800	$14,000	$16,800
Paterson		107	58	34	1	35	3%	6	$52,160	$225,998	$278,158
Pensacola-Tallahassee	16	18	80	63	5	68	7%	5	$9,501	$72,922	$82,423
Peoria	95	99	122	136	1	137	1%	4	$61,064	$453,494	$392,395

(Arch)Diocese	Documentary Cases Closed	Formal Cases Held Over	Formal Cases Introduced	Sentence in Favor of Nullity	Sentence Contrary to Nullity	Total formal decisions (affirmative and negative)	Percentage of Total Decisions Found Contrary to Nullity	Peremption/ Renunciation	Total Fees Received	Amount of Diocesan Subsidy	Total Annual Expenses
Philadelphia, Archeparchy for Ukrainians			8	5	1	6	17%	1	$1,525	$2,400	$3,925
Phoenix, Holy Protection of Mary Byzantine Eparchy		2						2	$1,000	$6,800	$7,800
Pittsburgh		151	227						$145,000	$536,000	$681,000
Pittsburgh, Archeparchy for Byzantines	5	3	5	8		8			$1,525	$1,200	$1,460
Portland in Maine	89	76	157	118		118		35	$35,000	$317,106	$352,106
Portland in Oregon	10	401	153	171		171		4	$44,840	$192,383	$237,223
Providence		71	97	95	10	105	10%	2	$65,711	$266,952	$346,841
Pueblo	62	27	34	22		22		10	$3,899	$122,306	$126,205
Raleigh	190	114	135	108	2	110	2%	7	$36,366	$194,400	$211,088
Rapid City	13	42	24	30	1	31	3%	6	$7,955	$62,958	$70,913
Reno		58	31	31	1	32	3%	1	$20,315	$120,400	$140,715
Richmond	23	104	212	185	10	195	5%	7		$476,925	$476,925
Rochester	3	30	56	53	3	56	5%	7	$35,249	$184,859	$220,108
Rockford	150	59	208	194	3	197	2%	10			
Sacramento		277	156								
Saginaw		26	81	61	1	62	2%	1	$2,805	$139,626	$139,044
Salina	27	82	68	54	3	57	5%	13	$14,238	$41,803	$56,041
Salt Lake City	82	22	70	59	1	60	2%	10	$18	$91	$109
San Angelo		68	47	70		70		9	$6,785	$201,596	$208,381
San Antonio	27	64	263	263	12	275	4%	6	$100,598	$186,468	$291,565
San Bernardino	252	133	136	97	17	114	15%	11	$59,375	$290,876	$350,251
San Diego		159	248	161	3	164	2%	11	$62,686	$256,399	$319,085
San Jose		77	119	71		71		2	$20,520	$56,860	$77,380
Santa Rosa	51	23	32	30	3	33	9%	4	$19,050	$120,373	$139,423
Savannah	20	28	61	58	1	59	2%	14	$21,404	$162,211	$183,615

(Arch)Diocese	Documentary Cases Closed	Formal Cases Held Over	Formal Cases Introduced	Sentence in Favor of Nullity	Sentence Contrary to Nullity	Total formal decisions (affirmative and negative)	Percentage of Total Decisions Found Contrary to Nullity	Peremption/ Renunciation	Total Fees Received	Amount of Diocesan Subsidy	Total Annual Expenses
Scranton		79	158	117	1	118	1%	14	$78,553	$216,450	$295,003
Seattle	31	222	181	179		179		12	$77,875	$381,913	$523,331
Shreveport		46	45	33	3	36	8%	2	$30,600	$144,805	$175,405
Sioux City	2	60	83	64	2	66	3%	11	$24,427	$117,245	$141,672
Sioux Falls		41	94	88	3	91	3%	6	$27,938	$119,080	$133,115
Spokane	12	27	59	62		62		3	$10,715	$16,270	$26,985
Springfield, Cape Girardeau	68	167	138	102	30	132	23%	44	$25,785	$188,477	$213,962
Springfield, Illinois	95	162	137	131		131		4	$52,997	$158,942	$211,939
Springfield, Massachusetts	57	97	94	93		93		5	$22,470	$191,582	$214,052
St. Augustine	23	168	100	158		158		7			
St. Cloud		78	65	79	78	157	50%	1	$29,891	$183,875	$185,751
St. Louis	175	296	249	234	5	239	2%	24	$159,245	$320,462	$479,707
St. Paul and Minneapolis		236	242	114	48	162	30%	67	$123,640	$655,107	$778,747
St. Petersburg	284	46	215	209	8	217	4%				
Steubenville	5	27	47	33	1	34	3%	3	$9,550	$49,236	$58,786
Superior		29	56					3	$11,400	$98,904	$110,304
Syracuse		14	151						$77,150	$40,018	$117,168
Toledo	15	83	162	142	1	143	1%	10	$35,924	$188,207	$224,131
Trenton	4	196	113	110	5	115	4%		$72,500	$261,126	$333,626
Tucson	2	163	95	65	1	66	2%	61	$34,134	$59,871	$94,005
Tulsa		52	63	62	2	64	3%	9		$65,000	$65,000
Tyler		50	56	62	4	66	6%	5	$11,320	$83,155	$94,475
Venice		126	150	107	11	118	9%	13			
Wheeling-Charleston	7	163	84	58	1	59	2%	6			
Wilmington	10	103	71	95		95		1	$16,525	$129,676	$146,201
Worcester		2	66	42		42		2	$36,000	$129,879	$165,879
Yakima		44	36						$30,529	$131,972	$153,203
Youngstown	80	86	87	81		81		6	$19,528	$306,179	$301,090

Second Instance Statistics 2010

(Arch)Diocese	Second Instance Pending at beginning of year	Introduced	Closed	Decree Confirmation	Sentence in Favor of Nullity	Sentence Contrary to Nullity
Baltimore	105	623	640			
Baton Rouge		130				
Boston	4	199	191	188		3
Camden	3	36	36	34		2
Charleston				61		
Charlotte				157	157	2
Cleveland	11	346	329		328	1
Columbus	23	75	84	11	8	8
Covington	28	54	77	77		
Davenport	1	45	46	46		
Des Moines		51	51	51	51	
Detroit	56	451	489	485	3	1
Dubuque	16	226	218	214	2	1
Evansville	1	40	40	39		1
Fresno	2	84	69		67	
Grand Rapids		535	535	535		
Green Bay		277	277			
Hartford	3	100	103	98	2	3
Indianapolis	33	53	38	28	28	5
Kansas City in Kansas	5	210		210		
Lafayette in Indiana	21	83	92	92	1	
Lake Charles				82		
Lexington	1	64	32	29		3
Lincoln	5	6	7			
Louisville	17	115	121	121	121	
Memphis	11	46	53	53	53	
Metuchen		1	1	62	62	
Milwaukee	11	417	406	406	406	1
Mobile	25	117	94	85	2	6
Nashville & Knoxville	12	76	84	3	3	

(Arch)Diocese	Second Instance Pending at beginning of year	Introduced	Closed	Decree Confirmation	Sentence in Favor of Nullity	Sentence Contrary to Nullity
New Orleans	69	440	437		427	4
Newton, Eparchy of		24	24	24		
Norwich, Connecticut		49	49	45	2	2
Omaha				201	68	6
Owensboro	9	53	48		49	2
Paterson	9	53	46	46	4	
Philadelphia, Archeparchy for Ukrainians		1	1	1		
Pittsburgh, Archeparchy for Byzantines	1	3	4	8	8	
Portland in Maine	15	172	174	171	3	
Portland in Oregon	129	253	242	242		
San Bernardino	10	98	98		98	
San Jose	10	128	129	129	129	
Seattle	2	292	281	274	4	2
Sioux City	3	35	33	33		
Springfield, Massachusetts	37	203	206	202	206	
St. Cloud	6	40	31	31	31	
St. Paul and Minneapolis	155	436	435	422	7	6
St. Petersburg				209		1
Steubenville	2	47	46		46	
Toledo	28	338	279	279		
Trenton	2	53	52	48	2	2
Youngstown	12	93	105	192	105	

VARIA

Contributors

Doctor Diane L. Barr, JD, JCD, Chancellor, Archdiocese of Baltimore, Maryland

Reverend John P. Beal, JCD, Professor, The Catholic University of America, Washington, District of Columbia

Reverend James A. Coriden, JCD, JD, Professor, Washington Theological Union, Washington, District of Columbia

Very Reverend Lawrence A. DiNardo, VE, JCL, Vicar for Canonical Services, Director, Department of Canon and Civil Law Services, Diocese of Pittsburgh, Pennsylvania

Chorbishop John D. Faris, Pastor, St. Louis Gonzaga Church, Utica, New York, 2011 Role of Law Award Recipient

Reverend John J.M. Foster, JCD, Assistant Professor, The Catholic University, Washington, District of Columbia

Sister Sharon L. Holland, IHM, JCD, Canonical Consultant, Religious Institutes and Sponsored Ministries

Reverend Monsignor Daniel F. Hoye, JCL, Pastor, Christ the King Parish, Diocese of Fall River, Massachusetts

Rita F. Joyce, JD, JCL, General Counsel, Department for Canon and Civil Law Services, Diocese of Pittsburgh, Pennsylvania

Very Reverend Anthony L. Kerin, B.Theol., JCL, Dup. Litt. Lat., President, Canon Law Society of Australia & New Zealand; Assistant Judicial Vicar, Archdiocese of Melbourne, Victoria, Australia

Reverend Kevin E. McKenna, JCD, Pastor, Sacred Heart Cathedral, Diocese of Rochester, New York

Reverend Monsignor Mark A. Plewka, JCL, Judicial Vicar, Diocese of Pueblo, Colorado

Margaret Romano-Hogan, STB, JCL, Tribunal Director, Diocese of Fort Worth, Texas

Brother Loughlan Sofield, ST, Author and Consultant; Senior Editor, *Human Development*

Reverend Monsignor Michael A. Souckar, JCL, Archdiocese of Miami, Florida

VARIA

Participants

Joseph Abraham
  Reno, NV
Peter Akin-Otiko
  Jacksonville, FL
John Alesandro
  Rockville Centre, NY
Krystyna Amborski
  San Fransisco, CA
Thomas Anslow
  Los Angeles, CA
Charles Antonicelli
  Washington, DC
Gary Applegate
  Kansas City, KS
Christopher Armstrong
  Cincinnati, OH
Thomas Arnao
  Rockville Centre, NY
Joseph Arsenault
  Kansas City, KS
Anne Asselin
  Ottawa, ON
Joseph Augustine
  Wheeling, WV
Alberto Avella
  Grants, NM
Renata Babicz-Baratto
  Lexington, KY
Wayne Ball
  Richmond VA
Diane Barr
  Baltimore, MD
Carole B. Barras
  Savannah, GA
Mark Bartchak
  Altoona-Johnstown, PA
Mary Ann Bartolac
  Kansas City, KS

Virginia Bartolac
  Kansas City, KS
James Bartoloma
  Camden, NJ
Carlotta Bartone
  Philadelphia, PA
Ricardo Bass
  Harrison Twp, MI
John Beal
  Erie, PA
John Bell
  Plano, TX
Iden Bello
  Laredo, TX
Vincent Bertrand
  Springfield, MO
Barbara Bettwy
  Erie, PA
Gregory Bittner
  Birmingham, AL
Remek Blaszkowski
  Jacksonville, FL
Mary Gen Blittschau
  Evansville, IN
Michael Boccaccio
  Norwalk, CT
James Bonke
  Indianapolis, IN
Dominic Bottino
  Camden, NJ
Janelle Boyum
  New Ulm, MN
Michael Bradley
  Chicago, IL
Marie Breitenbeck
  Atlanta, GA
Timothy Broglio
  Washington, DC

Steve Brown
  Cincinnati, OH
Thomas Brundage
  Anchorage, AK
Cindy Bryan
  Charleston, SC
Anne Bryant
  Houston, TX
Michael Burchfield
  Fresno, CA
James Burke
  Boston MA
Michael Burke
  Swansea, UK
Jeffrey Cabral
  Fall River, MA
Jesus Cabrera
  Milwaukee, WI
Steven Callahan
  San Diego, CA
Michael Carigilo
  Youngstown, OH
Anthony Celino
  El Paso, TX
Deborah Cerullo
  Providence, RI
Charles Chaffman
  Los Angeles, CA
Anna Marie Chamblee
  Fort Worth, TX
Cherry Clark
  Baltimore, MD
J. Michael Clark
  Owensboro, KY
Brian Clarke
  Scranton, PA
Timothy Cloutier
  St. Paul, MN

John Cody
  Columbus, OH
Patrick Cogan
  Ottawa, ON
Jay Conzemius
  Pittsburgh, PA
Patrick Cooney
  Indianapolis, IN
Joe Corbett
  Atlanta, GA
James Coriden
  Washington, DC
Paul Counce
  Baton Rouge, LA
John Crerand
  Columbus, OH
Thomas Cronkleton
  Cheyenne, WY
Joachim Culotta
  St. Louis, MO
Barbara Anne Cusack
  Milwaukee, WI
Brendan Daly
  New Zealand
Jamin David
  Baton Rouge, LA
Zabrina Decker
  Milwaukee, WI
Robert Deeley
  Boston, MA
David Deibel
  Napa, CA
Jesus Del Angel
  Fresno, CA
Frank Del Prete
  Newark, NJ
Robert DeLand
  Saginaw, MI
Carol DeLois
  Cheyenne, WY
Louis DeNinno
  Pittsburgh, PA
John Dermond
  Trenton, NJ

James DeViese
  Wheeling, WV
Paul DiGirolamo
  Philadelphia, PA
Lawrence DiNardo
  Pittsburgh, PA
John P. Donovan
  Syracuse, NY
Patricia Dugan
  Canon Law Books
Brian Dunn
  Antigonish, Nova Scotia
Frederick Easton
  Bloomington, IN
Mary Edlund
  Dallas, TX
Peter Eke
  Gaylord, MI
Martins Emeh
  Rockford, IL
Arthur Espelage
  Venice, FL
Sharon Euart
  Executive Coordinator
  CLSA
George Fagan
  Limon, CO
John Faris
  Utica, NY
Thomas Feeney
  Corpus Chrisiti, TX
David Fellhauer
  Victoria, TX
Christopher Ferrer
  Austin, TX
Victor Finelli
  Allentown, PA
J. Michael Fitzgerald
  Richmond, VA
Robert Flummerfelt
  Las Vegas, NV
Kenneth Fortener
  New Hope, KY
John J. M. Foster
  Washington, DC

Thomas Fransiscus
  Reno, NV
Matthew H. Frisoni
  Albany, NY
Canuto E. Fuentebella
  Aruba
Timothy Gadziala
  Atlanta, GA
Leonardo Gajardo
  Baltimore, MD
Engelberto Gammad
  San Jose, CA
John Gargan
  Dallas, TX
Anthony Generose
  Scranton, PA
John Giel
  Orlando, FL
J. Fernando Gil
  Orlando, FL
M. Margaret Gillett
  Dallas, TX
Catherine Gilligan
  Little Rock, AR
Garry Giroux
  Brasher Falls, NY
Paul Golden
  Vincentians
James Goodwin
  Fargo, ND
Robert Graffio
  San Francisco, CA
William Graham
  Baltimore, MD
Jason Gray
  Peoria, IL
Thomas Green
  Catholic University
John Griffiths
  Chicago, IL
Edward Grimes
  Dublin, Ireland
Janice Grochowsky
  Dodge City, KS

Ralph Gross
  Milwaukee, WI
Luis Guzman
  Orlando, FL
Paul Hachey
  Atlanta, GA
Kathleen Hahn
  Grand Island, NE
Edward Hankiewicz
  Grand Rapids, MI
Mary Ellen Hauck
  Indianapolis, IN
Leo Hausmann
  Rapid City, SD
Robert Hemberger
  Wichita, KS
Fernando Heria
  Miami, FL
Patrick Hill
  Los Angeles, CA
Charles Hill
  Los Angeles, CA
Marie Hilliard
  Philadelphia, PA
Christina Hip-Flores
  Brentwood, MD
Jordan Hite
  Baltimore, MD
Thuan Hoang
  San Francisco, CA
Michael Hoeppner
  Crookston, MN
Thomas Hofmann
  Charleston, SC
Sharon Holland
  Monroe, MI
Carol Houghton
  Harrisburg, PA
David Hogan
  President CLSGB&I
Daniel Hoye
  Mashpee, MA
Eduardo Huerta
  Canon Law Professionals

James Innocenzi
  Trenton, NJ
Jolene Jasinski
  Beaver Falls, PA
Bernard Johnson
  Vina, CA
Gerald Jorgensen
  Dubuque, IA
Rita Joyce
  Pittsburgh, PA
Michael Joyce
  Memphis, TN
Lawrence Jurcak
  Cleveland, OH
Thomas Kadera
  Cheyenne, WY
Samuel Kalu
  Lafayette, IN
Robert Kaslyn
  Washington, DC
Connie Kassahn
  Cheyenne, WY
James Kee
  Mobile, AL
John Keehner
  Youngstown, OH
Anthony Kerin
  President CLSANZ
Elaine Kerscher
  Joliet, IL
Rita Killackey
  Overland Park, KS
Adela Maria Kim
  Peoria, IL
Wayne Kirkpatrick
  President CCLS
David Klein
  Camden, NJ
Jose Kochuparambil
  Lubbock, TX
Thomas Koons
  Allentown, PA
K.S. Kopacz
  Fargo, ND

Richard Kosisko
  Greensburg, PA
Michael Kotarski
  Flint, MI
Joseph Koury
  Portland, ME
James Kruse
  Peoria, IL
Francis Kub
  Chicago, IL
Rose Mary Kuklok
  Santa Rosa, CA
Patrick Lagges
  Chicago, IL
Bonnie Landry
  Lake Charles, LA
Richard Lelonis
  Pittsburgh, PA
Andres Ligot
  San Jose, CA
Judene Lillie
  New Orleans, LA
Timothy Lindenfelser
  Jacksonville, FL
John List
  Lexington, KY
Douglas Loecke
  Dubuque, Iowa
Daniel Logan
  Jacksonville, FL
Douglas Lucia
  Ogdensburg, NY
William Lum
  Canon Law Professionals
Gregory Luyet
  Fort Smith, AR
Richard Lyons
  Metuchen, NJ
Sandra Makowski
  Charleston, SC
W. Curtis Mallet
  Lafayette, LA
Marc Mancini
  Paterson, NJ

Michele Mangan
  San Jose, CA
Salvatore Manganello
  Buffalo, NY
Peter Mangum
  Shreveport, LA
Tomas Marin
  Miami, FL
Kurt Martens
  Washington, DC
Jose Martinez
  Las Cruces, NM
Joseph Matt
  Kansas City, MO
John McAllister
  Little Rock, AR
Jeremiah McCarthy
  Savannah, GA
Rose McDermott
  Washington, DC
Kevin McKenna
  Rochester, NY
Lynn McKenzie
  Cullman, AL
Timothy McNeil
  Omaha, NE
Mario Medina-Balam
  Mexico City
Gerard Mesure
  Philadelphia, PA
George Michalek
  Lansing, MI
Bruce Miller
  Alexandria, LA
Christopher Moore
  Hagerstown, MD
Francis Morrisey
  Ottwawa, ON
Joseph Mozer
  Boston, MA
R. Francis Muench
  Richmond, VA
Susan Mulheron
  St. Paul, MN

Martin Nelson
  Sour Lake, TX
Glenn Nelson
  Rockford, IL
Joseph Newton
  Indianapolis, IN
Thu Nguyen
  Houston, TX
Steve Nguyen
  Honolulu, HI
Jackeline Niederheitmann
  Charleston, SC
Kevin Niehoff
  Albuquerque, NM
James Nowak
  Naperville, IL
Mary Judith O'Brien
  Saginaw, MI
Kelly O'Donnell
  San Diego, CA
Thomas O'Donnell
  Pittsburgh, PA
James Oliver
  Philadelphia, PA
Kathryn Olsen
  Oklahoma City, OK
Thomas Olson
  St. Cloud, MN
Anthony Omenihu
  New York, NY
George Oonnoonny
  New York, NY
Agustin Opalalic
  San Diego, CA
Sinclair Oubre
  Port Arthur, TX
C. Michael Padazinski
  San Francisco, CA
Rafael Padilla
  Port Charlotte, FL
Roch Page
  Ottawa, ON
William Palladino
  Boston, MA

Duaine Pamment
  Laingsburg, MI
John Payne
  New Orleans, LA
F. Stephen Pedone
  Worcester, MA
John Peiffer
  Irving, CA
Nicholas Pericone
  New Orleans, LA
Phu Phan
  Canyon, TX
Anthony Pileggi
  Kansas City, MO
Robert Pine
  Austin, TX
Mark Plewka
  Pueblo, CO
Stanley Pondo
  Indianapolis, IN
John Porter
  Grand Rapids, MI
Linda Price
  Scranton, PA
George Puthusseril
  Miami Shores, FL
Gerry Quinn
  St. Louis, MO
Angel Quitalig
  San Francisco, CA
Nicholas Rachford
  Lorain, OH
Margaret Ramsden
  Orange, CA
Gloria Regush
  Calgary, AB
Ann Rehrauer
  Green Bay, WI
Richard Reidy
  Worcester, MA
Charles Renati
  San Francisco, CA
John Renken
  Ottawa, ON

John Reynolds
  Palm Coast, FL
Mark Richards
  Sacramento, CA
Thomas Richstatter
  Tell City, IN
Michael Riley
  Des Moines, IA
Kenneth Riley
  Kansas City, MO
J. Michael Ritty
  Feura Bush, NY
Lynda Robitaille
  North Vancouver, BC
Meg Romano-Hogan
  Fort Worth, TX
Eloise Rosenblatt
  San Jose, CA
Charles Rowland
  Charleston, SC
James Ruef
  Columbus, OH
Patricia Ruiz
  Fresno, CA
Caesar Russo
  Jacksonville, FL
Carlos Sacasa
  Washington, DC
Joseph Salvo
  Summerville, SC
Marvin Samiano
  Honolulu, HI
John Santone
  South Bend, IN
Edward Schaefer
  St. Rose, IL
Mary Schaumber
  Tulsa, OK
Joseph Scheib
  Pittsburgh, PA
Jerry Scherkenbach
  St. Paul, MN
J. Gerard Schreck
  Savannah, GA

John Schuster
  Calgary, AB
David Schuyler
  Cupertino, CA
Phillip Schweda
  Lansing, MI
Gilbert Seitz
  Baltimore, MD
John Sekellick
  Jessup, PA
Donetta Shaw
  Kansas City, MO
Patrick Shea
  Cleveland, OH
Sean Sheridan
  Washington DC
Langes Silva
  Salt Lake City
Joseph Sinchak
  Mobile, AL
Harmon Skillin
  Stockton, CA
Jaroslaw Skrzypek
  New Madrid, MO
Kevin Slattery
  Jackson, MS
H. Roberta Small
  Camden, NJ
Daniel Smilanic
  Chicago, IL
Rosemary Smith
  Convent Station, NJ
Patricia Smith
  Aston, PA
Michael Souckar
  Miami, FL
Charles Strebler
  Cleveland, OH
Amy Strickland
  Silver Spring, MD
Karen Sullivan-Kight
  St. Augustine, FL
David Szatkowski
  Hales Corners, WI

Amy Tadlock
  Washington, DC
Linda Tedde
  Youngstown, OH
Allison Townley
  Kansas City, MO
Gregory Trawick
  Owensboro, KY
Francis Tse
  Hong Kong
Ann Tully
  Indianapolis, IN
Sebastian Tumusiime
  Peoria, IL
Silvana Usandivaras
  New York, NY
Irene Valles
  Las Cruces, NM
Marilyn Vassallo
  Shreveport, LA
John Vaughan
  Owensboro, KY
Andrew R. Vaughn
  Milwaukee, WI
Desmond Vella
  New York, NY
Siobhan Verbeek
  Washington DC
Manuel Viera
  Cincinnati, OH
Victoria Vondenberger
  Cincinnati, OH
Jeffrey Waldrep
  Jackson, MS
Meg Walter
  Charleston, SC
John Ward
  Baltimore, MD
Peter Waslo
  Philadelphia, PA
Katharine Weber
  Mobile, AL
Brian Welding
  Pittsburgh, PA

Rick Wells
  St. Petersburg, FL
Daniel Welter
  Chicago, IL
Robert Wendelken
  Cleveland, OH

Mary Catherine Wenstrup
  Covington, KY
Thomas Wisniewski
  Darby, PA
Joseph Wolf
  Davenport, IA

Gary Yanus
  Cleveland, OH
David Zimmer
  Minot, ND
Jonathan Zingales
  Cleveland, OH